T0330855

Manager–Subordinate Trust

This volume in the Routledge Global Human Resource Management Series is dedicated to analyzing the process of trust development between managers and subordinates in different countries of the main cultures of the world.

Behavior and trust are linked in a process that can either reinforce or diminish the trust between the two parties. This book examines that process in an array of countries, contextualizing each setting through a brief historical, institutional, and cultural overview. Addressing the dominant HR practices and main local leadership styles of each country, it draws upon an extensive country-by-country data set of leader–subordinate trust to analyze the universal and culturally-specific elements of this process. With its rigorous research, insightful analysis, and consistent presentation, this book will help readers to systematically compare the behavior–trust process across countries, draw conclusions, and analyze HR implications.

Pablo Cardona is Professor of the Department of Managing People in Organizations at IESE Business School in Barcelona, Spain. He has a Ph.D. in management from the University of California, Los Angeles (UCLA), USA and an MBA from IESE.

Michael J. Morley is Professor of Management at the Kemmy Business School, University of Limerick, Ireland. He has served as Head of the Department of Personnel and Employment Relations, Head of the Department of Management & Marketing, Assistant Dean of Research and Director of the School's Graduate Centre of Business.

Routledge Global Human Resource Management Series

Edited by Randall S. Schuler, Susan E. Jackson, Paul Sparrow and Michael Poole

Routledge Global Human Resource Management is an important new series that examines human resources in its global context. The series is organized into three strands: Content and issues in global human resource management (HRM); Specific HR functions in a global context; and comparative HRM. Authored by some of the world's leading authorities on HRM, each book in the series aims to give readers comprehensive, in-depth and accessible texts that combine essential theory and best practice. Topics covered include cross-border alliances, global leadership, global legal systems, HRM in Asia, Africa and the Americas, industrial relations, and global staffing.

Managing Human Resources in Cross-Border Alliances
Randall S. Schuler, Susan E. Jackson and Yadong Luo

Managing Human Resources in Africa
Edited by Ken N. Kamoche, Yaw A. Debrah, Frank M. Horwitz and Gerry Nkombo Muuka

Globalizing Human Resource Management
Paul Sparrow, Chris Brewster and Hilary Harris

Managing Human Resources in Asia-Pacific
Edited by Pawan S. Budhwar

International Human Resource Management, (second edition)
Policy and practice for the global enterprise
Dennis R. Briscoe and Randall S. Schuler

Managing Human Resources in Latin America
An agenda for international leaders
Edited by Marta M. Elvira and Anabella Davila

Global Staffing
Edited by Hugh Scullion and David G. Collings

Managing Human Resources in Europe
A thematic approach
Edited by Henrik Holt Larsen and Wolfgang Mayrhofer

Managing Human Resources in the Middle-East
Edited by Pawan S. Budhwar and Kamel Mellahi

Managing Global Legal Systems
International employment regulation and competitive advantage
Gary W. Florkowski

Global Industrial Relations
Edited by Michael J. Morley, Patrick Gunnigle and David G. Collings

Managing Human Resources in North America
Current issues and perspectives
Edited by Steve Werner

Global Leadership
Research, Practice, Development
Edited by Mark Mendenhall, Gary Oddou, Allan Bird and Martha Maznevski

Global Compensation
Foundations and Perspectives
Edited by *Luis Gomez-Mejia and Steve Werner*

Global Performance Management
Edited by *Arup Varma, Pawan S. Budhwar and Angelo DeNisi*

Managing Human Resources in Central and Eastern Europe
Edited by *Michael J. Morley, Noreen Heraty and Snejina Michailova*

Forthcoming:

Global Careers
Michael Dickmann and Yehuda Baruch

Global Leadership (2nd edition)
Research, Practice, Development
Mark E. Mendenhall, Joyce S. Osland, Allan Bird, Gary Oddou, Martha L. Maznevski, Michael J. Stevens, Günter K. Stahl

Manager-Subordinate Trust
A Global Perspective
Edited by *Pablo Cardona and Michael J. Morley*

Managing Human Resources in Asia-Pacific (2nd edition)
Edited by *Arup Varma and Pawan S. Budhwar*

Manager–Subordinate Trust

A Global Perspective

Edited by Pablo Cardona and Michael J. Morley

NEW YORK AND LONDON

Please visit the companion website at
www.routledge.com/textbooks/globalhrm

First published 2013
by Routledge
711 Third Avenue, New York, NY 10017

Simultaneously published in the UK
by Routledge
2 Park Square, Milton Park, Abingdon, Oxon OX14 4RN

Routledge is an imprint of the Taylor & Francis Group, an informa business

© 2013 Taylor & Francis

The right of Pablo Cardona and Michael J. Morley to be identified as
editor of this work has been asserted by him/her in accordance with
sections 77 and 78 of the Copyright, Designs and Patents Act 1988.

Library of Congress Cataloging in Publication Data
  Manager-subordinate trust : a global perspective /
  edited by Pablo Cardona, Michael J Morley.
  p. cm.—(Routledge global human resource management series)
  Includes bibliographical references and index.
  1. Industrial relations. 2. Management.
  I. Cardona, Pablo, 1964– II. Morley, Michael.
  HD6971.M3273 2012
  331.2—dc23
  2012021202

ISBN: 978–0–415–89810–2 (hbk)
ISBN: 978–0–415–89811–9 (pbk)
ISBN: 978–0–203–35757–6 (ebk)

Typeset in Times New Roman and Franklin Gothic
by Swales & Willis Ltd, Exeter, Devon

Contents

Foreword

Global Human Resource Management is a series of books edited and authored by some of the best and most well-known researchers in the field of human resource management (HRM). This series is aimed at offering students and practitioners accessible, coordinated, and comprehensive books in global HRM. To be used individually or together, these books cover the main areas in international and comparative HRM. Taking an expert look at an increasingly important and complex area of global business, this is a groundbreaking new series that answers a real need for useful and affordable textbooks on global HRM.

Several books in the series are devoted to HRM policies and practices in multinational enterprises. Some books focus on specific areas of global HRM policies and practices, such as global leadership, global compensation, global talent management, and global labor relations. Other books address special topics that arise in multinational enterprises, such as managing HR in cross-border alliances, managing global legal systems, and the structure of the global HR function. There is also a book of global human resource management cases. Several other books in the series adopt a comparative approach to understanding human resource management. These books on comparative human resource management describe HRM topics found at the country level in selected countries. The comparative books utilize a common framework that makes it easier for the reader to systematically understand the rationale for the similarities and differences in findings across countries.

This book, *Manager–Subordinate Trust: A Global Perspective*, is one that fits into the categories of books addressing special topics and comparative HRM. The book is edited by Pablo Cardona and Michael J. Morley and contains 16 chapters that examine the manager–subordinate trust relationship in 14 different countries, all written by country experts. The editors provide an opening chapter that provides the overall framework used by all the chapter authors. It also provides the background and rationale for the importance of understanding the manager–subordinate relationship in global human resource management. As with all the books in the **Global Human Resource Management** Series, the chapters utilize the most recent and relevant research and reflect the experiences of the specific country being investigated.

The publisher and editor have played a very major role in making this series possible. Routledge has provided its global production, marketing, and reputation to make this series feasible and affordable to academics and practitioners throughout the world. In addition, Routledge has provided its own highly qualified professionals to make this series a reality. In particular, we want to indicate our deep appreciation for the work of our series editor, John Szilagyi. He has been very supportive of the Global Human Resource Management Series and has been invaluable in providing the needed support and encouragement to us and the many authors and editors in the series. He along with Manjula Raman and the entire staff have helped make the process of completing this series an enjoyable one. For everything they have done, we thank them all.

Randall S. Schuler, Rutgers University and the Lorange Institute of Business Zurich
Susan E. Jackson, Rutgers University and the Lorange Institute of Business Zurich
Paul Sparrow, Manchester University Management School
Michael Poole, Cardiff University

This volume in the *Global Human Resource Management Series* is dedicated to analyzing the process of trust development between managers and subordinates in a range of different countries representing the main cultural regions of the world. The process of trust development starts with those behaviors of the manager that may impact the subordinate's trust on him or her and continues with the subordinate's responses that in turn affect the manager's trust on the subordinate and lead to more trusting behaviors from the manager. In this way, behaviors and trust are linked in a process that can reinforce or diminish the trust between the two parties.

As a phenomenon, trust has been viewed as a fundamental building block of effective management. Though largely from a Western perspective, the cumulative evidence on its value and impact demonstrates that employees' trust is key for organizational performance and effectiveness (Barney & Hansen, 1994). More specifically, it has been established that trust facilitates cooperation, assures social interaction, and reduces negotiation costs between organizational members (Blau, 1964; Coleman, 1988; Creed & Miles, 1996). Trust has also been shown to be critical in fostering positive interactions within cross-functional teams, in establishing intra-organizational relations, and in developing more effective workplace coordination among various groups (Williams, 2001).

Within the context of management style, leader–follower trust has been shown to increase subordinates' commitment toward fulfillment of organizational goals, compliance, and extra-role behaviors (Barney & Hansen, 1994; Dirks & Ferrin, 2001). Furthermore, social exchange research demonstrates that subordinates who perceive that they are treated positively feel the need to reciprocate and engage in citizenship behavior (Coyle-Shapiro, 2002). Consequently, the level of trust that managers have in their subordinates affects the nature and the quality of their exchanges.

Research evidence indicates that trustors are assessed in a diverse way across different cultures (Doney *et al.*, 1998). Therefore, it is important to comprehend the peculiarities of manager–subordinate trust relationships in a specific cultural context. However, there have been surprisingly few systematic studies of manager–subordinate trust across cultures. Where they do exist, they have often been confined to advanced economies and dedicated to comparing the underlying dynamics in two or three countries (Tsui *et al.*, 2007).

In the first chapter of this book, we develop and empirically test a general model of manager–subordinate trust based on the quantitative data gathered in 18 countries. In the subsequent country chapters, we further explore and contextualize this model, using local literature as well as country-derived qualitative data. Finally, in the last chapter, we explore the moderating role of culture in the model and draw important conclusions for future research efforts, as well as set out potential implications for HR practice.

Pablo Cardona and Michael J. Morley

References

Barney, J.B. & Hansen, M.H. (1994). Trustworthiness as a source of competitive advantage. *Strategic Management Journal*, 15: 175–190.

Blau, P.M. (1964). *Exchange and Power in Social Life*. New York: Wiley.

Coleman, J.S. (1988). Social capital in the creation of human capital. *American Journal of Sociology*, 94: 95–120.

Coyle-Shapiro, J.A. (2002). A psychological contract perspective on organizational citizenship behavior. *Journal of Organizational Behavior*, 23: 927–946.

Creed, W.E. D. & Miles, R.E. (1996). A conceptual framework linking organizational forms, managerial philosophies, and the opportunity costs of controls. In R.M. Kramer & T.R. Tyler (eds), *Trust in Organizations: Frontiers of Theory and Research*. Thousand Oaks, CA: Sage, pp. 16–38.

Dirks, K.T. & Ferrin, D.L. (2001). The role of trust in organizational settings. *Organization Science*, 12: 450–467.

Doney, P.M., Cannon, J.P. & Mullen, M.R. (1998). Understanding the influence of national culture on the development of trust. *Academy of Management Review*, 23: 601–620.

Tsui, A.S., Nifadkar, S.S. & Ou, A.Y. (2007). Cross-national, cross-cultural organizational behavior research: Advances, gaps, and recommendations. *Journal of Management*, 33: 426–478.

Williams, M. (2001). Are intellectual capital performance and disclosure practices related? *Journal of Intellectual Capital*, 2(3): 192–203.

Acknowledgments

This book is the product of a larger collaboration project called Cross-Cultural Management Network (CCMN). This network was initiated a few years ago by some professors at IESE Business School and, from the beginning, it was supported by the school, which, with research funding, helped organize a meeting of the research collaborators in Barcelona. For the creation of the network, we counted on the tireless and enthusiastic collaboration of Helen Wilkinson, who was the first network coordinator. We also want to thank Professor Steven Poelmans for his help in the design of the qualitative study, and Professors Yih-teen Lee and Miguel Canela for their help in the analysis of the quantitative study and constant support during the project.

1 Manager–Subordinate Trust Relationships across Cultures

PABLO B. CARDONA, MICHAEL J. MORLEY, AND
SEBASTIAN REICHE

Introduction

Trust is one of the key determinants of performance in business organizations and a necessary outcome of true leadership (Kouzes & Posner, 1993). As a result, trust has been an important construct in the social sciences and has also received increasing attention by organizational researchers (Colquitt *et al.*, 2007; Mayer *et al.*, 1995; Whitener *et al.*, 1998), especially in the field of manager–subordinate relationships (Brower *et al.*, 2000; Dirks & Ferrin, 2002). While past research has offered multiple perspectives to advance our understanding about the nature of trust relationships in an organizational context (for a comprehensive review, see Bachmann & Zaheer, 2006), scholars have also singled out some of the rather unanswered questions that deserve further attention.

One area of intense debate concerns the relative status and importance of trust as cause, effect, or interaction (Rousseau *et al.*, 1998). For example, despite convincing conceptual arguments, existing research provides mixed evidence for the influence of trust on work-related behaviors and outcomes (Dirks & Ferrin, 2001). These findings may stem from a limited consideration of asymmetric perceptions of trust between social actors in the literature (Schoorman *et al.*, 2007). Studying the dynamics of trust formation in dyadic hierarchical relationships thus promises to refine our understanding of what drives trust and how trust benefits the individual in organizational settings. In addition, the existing literature on trust has traditionally adopted a largely Western focus, thereby often ignoring how, and to what extent, trust formation may vary in other cultural contexts. However, initial evidence suggests that cultural differences, especially concerning the relationship between the individual and the collectivity that prevails in a society, affect individuals' propensity to trust (Huff & Kelley, 2003) and their evaluation of potential trustees (Doney *et al.*, 1998). Understanding the role of culture in trust formation is thus important to advance our knowledge about trust dynamics and establish the potential significance of contextual influences on its development.

Drawing upon existing evidence that views leader–member exchange relationships and trust building as cyclical, iterative, and mutually reinforcing processes (Blau,

1964; Brower *et al.*, 2000; Graen & Scandura, 1987), we propose that managerial fairness will influence subordinates' trust in managers, which in turn will lead subordinates to engage in organizational citizenship behavior (OCB). Based on this behavior, managers will judge subordinates' trustworthiness and then reciprocate with fairness. Whereas we view trust as an affective state (McAllister, 1995), we consider fairness as a specific managerial trustworthy behavior perceived by subordinates and OCB as a specific behavioral response of subordinates perceived by managers.

Theory and Model

The increased scholarly interest in the concept of trust has led to a wealth of different definitions and conceptualizations of trust (e.g. Bachmann & Zaheer, 2006; Mayer *et al.*, 1995; Rousseau *et al.*, 1998). Although these definitions typically vary in their specific content, most researchers acknowledge that trust comprises an intention to be vulnerable to the actions of a referent based on the expectation that this referent will behave in a certain manner (Colquitt *et al.*, 2007). Trust is also viewed as a multidimensional construct (Dirks & Ferrin, 2002) and a central focus in the literature has been an attempt to differentiate between an affective and cognitive dimension of trust (Lewis & Weigert, 1985; McAllister, 1995). Whereas affective trust is reflected in an emotional bond between actor and referent that may cause the referent to demonstrate concern about the actor's welfare, cognitive trust commonly entails a belief or expectation that the referent is reliable, has integrity, is predictable, and/or will act in a fair manner (Dirks & Ferrin, 2002). In the cross-cultural research program reported in this book, we limit our attention to affective trust for two reasons. First, given our desire to examine the reciprocal nature of trust formation in manager–subordinate dyads, our focus is on the direct, affective relationship between a trustor and a referent rather than more general beliefs or expectations about a referent's competence, ability, etc. Second, implicit to the conceptualization of cognitive trust are certain behaviors, such as fairness, that lead to a conceptual overlap with the behavioral antecedents and outcomes of trust that we explicitly examine in our research. As a result, we define trust as an affective state that entails an expectation about a referent's genuine care, concern, or emotional reciprocation.

Both the development of leader–member exchange relationships and the development of trust have been described as cyclical, mutually reinforcing processes (Blau, 1964; Graen & Scandura, 1987; Zand, 1972). According to these models, the behavior of each player influences the other in an iterative fashion (Brower *et al.*, 2000). In this vein, managerial fairness serves as a key behavior to enable exchanges with subordinates (Konovsky & Pugh, 1994) and has received much research attention as an antecedent of trust (Brockner *et al.*, 1997; Pillai *et al.*, 1999). Based on these initial behaviors on the part of the manager, subordinates are likely to hold a belief about their managers' future intentions or behaviors (Lewis & Weigert, 1985). These expectations will influence subordinates' trust in them and in turn lead subordinates to act accordingly (Mayer *et al.*, 1995; Rousseau *et al.*, 1998). An important behavioral outcome of subordinates' trust that has been discussed in the literature is OCB (Colquitt *et al.*, 2007; Dirks & Ferrin, 2002), defined as a job-related behavior that is discretionary, is not formally or directly recognized by the organizational reward system, and yet promotes organizational functioning (Organ, 1990). As a result of this subordinate behavior, the manager will make judgments about the trustworthiness of the subordinate and will respond with comparable trusting behavior. This will reinforce subordinates' initial expectations and initiate continuous trust building (Zand, 1972). Hence, we contend that subordinates' assessments of managers' trustworthiness are occurring in parallel to managers' evaluations of subordinates' trustworthiness (Brower *et al.*, 2000). To fully understand leader–member exchange relationships, we thus need to study both subordinates' trust in managers and managers' trust in subordinates.

In sum, the model conceptualizes the transition between behaviors and affective states in trust formation. We argue that there is a reciprocal relationship between fairness as a managerial behavior and subordinates' OCB and that these behaviors both initiate and result from affective trust between manager and subordinate, thus leading to manager–subordinate trust building. Conceptually, subordinate trust in manager and manager trust in subordinate therefore act as mediators in the relationship between fairness and OCB. Figure 1.1 illustrates this model.

Testing the Model

To test our model set out in Figure 1.1, we collected quantitative data from manager–subordinate dyads across six different regions, covering a total of 18 countries.[1] Subsequently, we engaged in a second round of qualitative data collection. In this round, we employed semi-structured ethnographic interviews, focus group interviews, and a Delphi panel, the basic purpose of which was to aid interpretation and contextualization of the data.

Table 1.1 provides details on the sample sizes and the key variables' mean scores per country, as well as the corresponding region.

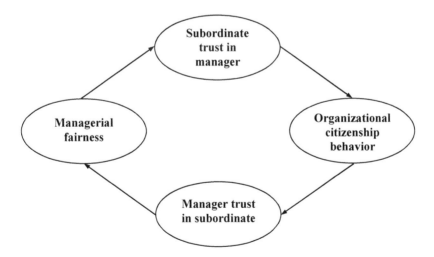

Figure 1.1 The reciprocal model of hierarchical trust

1 The authors of this study are listed at the end of the chapter.

Table 1.1 Sample size and mean scores on the main variables per country

Country	Region	Number of managers	Number of subordinates	Managerial fairness	Subordinate trust in manager	Manager trust in subordinate	Organizational citizenship behavior
Brazil	Latin America	42	126	4.47	4.15	4.29	4.19
China	Asia	51	153	3.81	3.78	3.78	3.76
Colombia	Latin America	35	93	4.38	4.17	4.33	4.30
Germany	Western Europe	37	92	4.16	3.88	4.27	4.20
Greece	Western Europe	46	138	3.81	3.66	3.70	3.66
Ireland	Western Europe	30	76	4.34	4.10	4.28	4.07
Mexico	Latin America	50	135	4.29	4.18	4.20	4.02
Norway	Western Europe	40	111	3.96	3.46	4.02	4.02
Pakistan	Asia	49	141	3.79	3.68	3.52	3.65
Peru	Latin America	41	112	4.31	4.13	3.95	3.63
Philippines	Asia	47	138	4.31	4.15	4.19	4.24
Poland	Eastern Europe	31	83	4.37	3.91	4.04	3.85
Romania	Eastern Europe	51	153	4.20	3.91	4.12	3.92
Russia	Eastern Europe	52	156	4.29	4.22	4.04	4.07
Spain	Western Europe	42	126	4.17	4.09	4.06	3.68
Thailand	Asia	32	89	4.01	3.71	3.58	3.82
United States	North America	38	114	4.16	4.08	3.96	3.79
West Africa[a]	Africa	27	75	4.23	4.05	3.68	3.72
Total		**741**	**2111**	**4.15**	**3.96**	**4.00**	**3.92**

Note
[a] Data collected from Nigeria and Ivory Coast are combined in the analyses under the label of West Africa.

Participants were recruited from different organizations to represent as wide a variety of sectors/organizations as possible, aiming for a maximum of 10 percent of respondents from the same company for each country included in our study. Our sample contains managers and subordinates working both in the public and in the private sector and includes both middle and top managers. Questionnaires were developed in English and then translated into the local language, using a back-translation method (Brislin, 1986). Each country collaborator subsequently verified the quality of the translation before starting the data collection.

We employed two separate sources for data collection—a manager and a subordinate questionnaire—in order to reduce the risk of common-method bias. Managers were contacted directly by the researchers in each respective country and then asked to identify up to three subordinates to whom they would forward the subordinate survey. In the manager survey, managers were asked to rate their subordinates' OCB and their trust in their subordinates. In the subordinate survey, subordinates rated both the perceived fairness of their managers' behavior and their trust in their managers. All data were collected through either study-and-pencil questionnaires or online surveys. Our choice of survey medium was driven by the technical capabilities and preferences of the respondents being surveyed. The layout of the two surveys (study pages and web pages) was identical. Recent research has compared traditional study surveys with online data collection and found no effects of the survey medium on response characteristics (Simsek & Veiga, 2001).

In total, 2140 manager surveys were administered, which yielded 741 manager responses (a 34.6 percent response rate). All 741 managers forwarded the subordinate survey to three of their subordinates each, resulting in 2111 subordinates (a 96.3 percent response rate) completing the questionnaire across all 18 countries. The final sample ranges from 75 to 156 dyads per country (see Table 1.1). The 741 managers in our sample had an average age of 39.8 years and an average organizational tenure of 8.9 years. In addition, 69.5 percent of all managers were male, 44.3 percent were middle managers and 50.1 percent occupied a top-management position. The 2111 subordinates in our sample had an average age of 34.4 years and on average had been with the organization for 6.4 years. In addition, 53.4 percent of subordinates were male. On average, the managers and subordinates in our study had worked together for 3.9 years.

Measures

All variables were measured using multi-item, five-point Likert scales. Items were placed in random order in the questionnaire.

Managerial fairness. Based on the literature on organizational justice (e.g. Folger & Konovsky, 1989), we developed a three-item scale of *managerial fairness* (1 = "totally disagree" to 5 = "totally agree"), including "My supervisor always fulfills his/her promises" and "My supervisor deals with me honestly." Building on the notion that fairness measures should be specific to the setting in which the study is being conducted (Greenberg, 1990), our items were specifically written for the manager–subordinate context that formed the basis of the present study. The three items were averaged to create a scale score (α = .81).

Trust. We used a four-item measure adapted from McAllister's (1995) affective trust scale to operationalize *subordinate trust in manager* (1 = "totally disagree" to 5 = "totally agree"). Two example items are "If I shared my problems with my manager, I know he/she would respond constructively and caringly" and "I can talk freely to this individual about difficulties I am having at work and know that he/she will listen." We averaged all four items to create a score for the subordinate trust in manager scale (α = .83). In order to measure *manager trust in subordinate*, we developed a new scale adapting the items used to measure subordinate trust in manager (1 = "totally disagree" to 5 = "totally agree"). Two example items are "I feel secure about the decisions that this subordinate makes at work" and "We have a sharing relationship. We can freely share our ideas, feelings and hopes." Again, all four items were averaged to create a scale score (α = .81).

OCB. The literature does not agree on the dimensions that best represent *organizational citizenship behavior*. Smith *et al.* (1983) first measured the construct and proposed two dimensions: altruism and general compliance. Later on, research added other dimensions to the OCB construct. Coleman and Borman (2000) suggested that citizenship dimensions can be grouped in three categories: directed toward specific individuals, directed toward the organization as a whole, and task-oriented OCB. In this study, we focus on subordinates' OCB that is directed toward the organization as a whole. Our rationale for examining this dimension of OCB is based on the contention that employees tend to perceive actions by agents of the organization as actions of the organization itself (Levinson, 1965). Since managers are responsible for several duties that affect employees' organizational membership, such as performance evaluations or training, managers serve as organizational representatives and will elicit specific attitudes and attributions toward the organization from their employees (Rich, 1997). Citizenship behavior directed toward the organization can thus be viewed to form an integral part of the manager–subordinate relationship, and recent research has shown manager–subordinate trust to be related to organization-directed rather than individual-directed citizenship behavior (Brower *et al.*, 2000). To measure this dimension of OCB, we used six items from Lee and Allen (2002), including "This subordinate defends the organization when other employees criticize it" and "This subordinate expresses loyalty toward the organization." The six items were averaged to create a scale score (α = .82).

Control variables. We controlled for a number of variables to improve our model estimation. We first controlled for the period of time the manager and subordinate have worked together in a hierarchical relationship. *Relationship duration* was self-reported by the manager and measured in years. We also controlled for the *age difference* between manager and subordinate. Accordingly, we measured manager and subordinate age in years and computed a difference score. Similarly, we controlled for the possibility that trust building may vary depending on whether manager and subordinate have the same gender or not. To account for *gender difference*, we measured gender as a dummy variable (1 = "male"; 2 = "female") and then recoded it as a new dummy variable (0 = "gender difference"; 1 = "gender equality").

Results

Preliminary Analyses

In order to conduct meaningful comparisons in cross-national studies, measurement invariance has to be achieved for the variables across all countries considered

(Schaffer & Riordan, 2003). Using a covariance structure analysis, we performed a separate confirmatory factor analysis for each of our four endogenous variables in the study using MPlus (Muthén & Muthén, 2007) to test whether the same factor model holds across all populations. Accordingly, we constrained the parameters in each of the four measurement models to be equal across all groups (Vandenberg & Lance, 2000).

To find a model that meets this requirement, we had to delete a few items (Cheung & Rensvold, 1999), including one item of our manager trust in subordinate scale (new α = .76) and three items of our OCB scale (new α = .79). With these items excluded, we did not find any evidence of substantial unequal variance, indicating that our constructs have the same meaning in all cultures studied. Specifically, the measurement model of our three-item scale of managerial fairness produced a χ^2 of 189.32 with 68 degrees of freedom. The corresponding RMSEA was .04, the CFI and TLI were .94 and .95, respectively. Our four-item factor structure of subordinate trust in manager resulted in a χ^2 of 424.40 (df = 138), RMSEA of .04, CFI of .92, and TLI of .94. In addition, the three-item factor structure of manager trust in subordinate produced a χ^2 of 215.47 (df = 68), RMSEA of .04, CFI of .91, and TLI of .93. There was slightly less evidence of measurement equivalence for our three-item scale of OCB (χ^2 = 381.81, df = 68, RMSEA = .05, CFI = .86, TLI = .89), suggesting that this variable is less etic in nature than our other variables. However, given that our study entails data from a wide variety of cultures, perfect measurement invariance is unlikely to be achieved. Thus, we consider the fit of the constrained measurement model acceptable. In addition, we did not find any significant differences in the confirmatory factor analyses of our four endogenous constructs at the subordinate and manager levels.

Table 1.2 presents descriptive statistics and correlations for the variables at the dyad level. Given that our control of gender difference was not significantly correlated with any of our endogenous variables, we decided to exclude it from all subsequent analyses (Becker, 2005).

To test for potential higher-level (i.e. manager and country) effects in our data structure, we computed the variance components and intraclass correlation coefficients (ICCs) for each of our four study variables across both the manager and the country level. Table 1.3 shows that only 42 to 54 percent of the variance in each variable consists of within-manager, between-subordinate variance, with about two-thirds of the remaining variance being within-country, between-manager variance and one-third between-country variance. Whereas the ICCs for between-manager variance were substantially higher than for between-country variance, all scores are above the recommended value of .05 (see Bliese & Hanges, 2004), pointing to the need to explicitly account for subordinate-level, manager-level, and country-level effects in our analysis.

Test of the Model

To simultaneously test our hypothesized relationships, we used multi-level structural equation modeling techniques with MPlus. We included manager as a random effect and country as a fixed effect in our model. All variables were entered at the subordinate level (Level 1) with only the intercept set to operate at the manager level (Level 2). The model with our hypothesized relationships has a satisfactory fit

Table 1.2 Descriptive statistics and correlations among the study variables at the individual level[a]

Variable		Mean	SD	1	2	3	4	5	6	7
1	Managerial fairness	4.15	0.76	**0.81**	0.76**	0.41**	0.33**	0.01	0.02	0.01
2	Subordinate trust in manager	3.96	0.84	0.74**	**0.83**	0.41**	0.30**	0.05	-0.03	-0.03
3	Manager trust in subordinate	4.00	0.77	0.32***	0.33***	**0.76**	0.64***	0.10*	-0.00	-0.02
4	Organizational citizenship behavior	3.92	0.79	0.28**	0.26**	0.57**	**0.79**	0.13*	0.10*	-0.03
5	Relationship duration	3.87	4.56	0.02	0.05*	0.12**	0.12**	—	-0.01	-0.03
6	Age difference	5.23	9.85	0.01	-0.02	-0.01	0.03	-0.07*	—	-0.07*
7	Gender difference	0.63	0.48	0.00	-0.02	-0.01	-0.01	0.01	-0.06*	—

Notes

[a] Bold values = alpha coefficients; means, standard deviations, alpha coefficients and correlations below the diagonal are at subordinate level (n = 2111); correlations above the diagonal are at manager level (n = 741).

* $p < 0.05$

** $p < 0.01$

Table 1.3 Variance components and intraclass correlations (ICCs) for study variables[a]

	Managerial fairness	Subordinate trust in manager	Manager trust in subordinate	Organizational citizenship behavior
Between-subordinate variance	53.17%	53.84%	48.91%	42.59%
Between-manager variance	31.33%	31.10%	32.65%	42.51%
Between-country variance	15.50%	15.06%	18.44%	14.90%
Total	**100%**	**100%**	**100%**	**100%**
ICC(1) country	0.073	0.070	0.096	0.064
ICC(1) manager	0.311	0.535	0.373	0.290

Note
a Likelihood ratio tests show that each variance component explains a significant ($p < 0.01$) amount of variance in each of the four study variables.

with the data (χ^2 = 866.49, df = 161, p < .01; RMSEA = .05; CFI = .91; TLI = .90). Applying sequential chi-square difference tests, we next compared this model with a series of two nested models (Anderson & Gerbing, 1988). First, we tested the possibility that the relationship between managerial fairness and OCB is only partially mediated by subordinate trust in manager. Accordingly, we added a direct path from managerial fairness to OCB. This unconstrained model (χ^2 = 865.71, df = 160, p < .01; RMSEA = .05; CFI = .91; TLI = .90) generated an insignificant chi-square decrease of .78 (Δdf = 1, p > .05), indicating that the added path does not significantly improve the original model. Second, we also tested the possibility that the relationship between subordinate trust in manager and manager trust in subordinate is only partially mediated by OCB. Therefore, we added a direct path from subordinate trust in manager to manager trust in subordinate. Again, this unconstrained model (χ^2 = 866.18, df = 160, p < .01; RMSEA = .05; CFI = .91; TLI = .90) generated an insignificant chi-square decrease of .31 (Δdf = 1, p > .05), indicating that the original model cannot be significantly improved by adding the additional path. Our original model was therefore retained as the model that best explains our data (see Figure 1.2).

Using bootstrapping techniques (Shrout & Bolger, 2002), we performed significance tests for all indirect effects in our model. The results show that managerial fairness has a significant indirect effect on OCB (β = .09, p < .05), subordinate trust in manager has a significant indirect effect on manager trust in subordinate (β = .07, p < .05), OCB has a significant indirect effect on managerial fairness (β = .27, p < .01), and manager trust in subordinate has a significant indirect effect on subordinate trust in manager (β = .34, p < .01). Finally, the control variable relationship duration was significantly positively related with OCB (β = .16, p < .01) and manager trust in subordinate (β = .09, p < .05). Overall, these findings support our trust

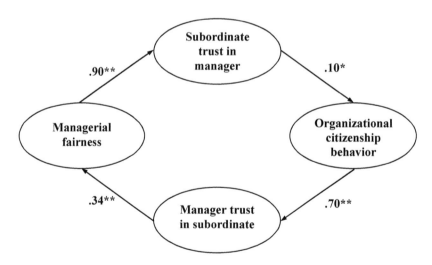

Figure 1.2 Results of two-level structural equation model for manager–subordinate dyads[a]

Notes

[a]   Fit: χ^2 = 866.49, df = 161, p < .01; RMSEA = .05, CFI = .91, TLI = .90, n = 2111.
    Parameter estimates are standardized regression weights.

*   p < .05

**   p < .01

    Control variables and their paths are not shown for the sake of clarity.

model. In the next chapters, we aim to explore these results at the country level, using local literature as well as qualitative research to understand the data.

The Qualitative Research

In each country, we conducted a qualitative study in order to understand and go beyond the quantitative findings. The first objective of the qualitative study was to provide more detailed and contextualized descriptions of trustworthy behaviors, and generate instances of such behaviors in order to illustrate the results found in the quantitative study. Second, we wanted to contrast managers' and subordinates' perceptions of trust to find some explanation for the potentially differential processes of developing trust in hierarchical relationships. Finally, we intend to get a better idea of how culture influences trust. In this study, we use the term managerial trustworthy behaviors (MTB) to denote the manager's behaviors that increase the trust of their subordinates in the manager. To facilitate the comparison between the quantitative and qualitative results, we keep the name of OCB (organizational citizenship behaviors) for the subordinates' behaviors that increase the manager's trust in them.

The qualitative data were collected from three different sources: semi-structured ethnographic interviews, focus group interviews, and a Delphi panel.

Semi-structured interviews. In each country, 7–10 middle managers belonging to different organizations were selected, with at least 30 percent of them being female. During the interviews, participants were first asked to think about a person they trust in the organizational context and then answer a few open-ended questions about trust, such as: "Why did you choose this person?", "Why do you trust him or her?", and "How would you describe trust in this particular example?". They were also asked to rank a list of words related to trust (ranking scale ranged from more to less related). This list contained words such as: consistency, reliability, credibility, commitment, integrity, loyalty, and reciprocity. Different country interviewers could add other words that might be related to trust in their specific culture.

Focus group interviews. In each country, we designed three focus groups, using three pairs of managers and their collaborators. The first group included the three managers, the second one included the three collaborators, and the third one included the three manager–collaborator dyads together (i.e. six participants in total). The goal was to gather information about trust from the different points of view of managers and collaborators, and contrast their perceptions about trust by sharing that information. The selection of pairs had to meet the following criteria: at least 30 percent female participants overall, at least one female and one male manager, age differences between manager and subordinate of below ten years, and a minimum experience of working together of one year. The focus groups lasted for one hour each and the discussion included the following questions: "How do you think trust is formed in the manager–subordinate relationships?", "Did you trust your manager (subordinate) from the beginning? Why or why not?", and "How do you notice that your boss (subordinate) trusts you?".

Delphi panel. In each country, 4 experts were selected and invited to participate in the study. Two of them were academics (including sociologists and professors of management or organizational behavior) and the other two were business practitioners. This group was asked to comment on the reciprocal model of trust in manager–subordinate relationships, explaining why this model may or may not work in their countries. They were then asked to use examples to interpret and illustrate the results of our study. Panelists were also asked about broader questions on the manager–subordinate relationship, such as: "Can you say that people in your country generally trust their bosses?""And vice-versa, do people trust their collaborators? Why or why not?". Finally, participants in the Delphi panel were asked to comment on the role of trust in their countries. The panel followed a two-round interactive process in an online platform. In the first round, panelists answered several questions about trust in general and about the model in particular. In the second round, they read other experts' opinions and were able to make further comments.

The Country Chapters

Out of the 18 countries that participated in the quantitative study, 14 were able to finalize the qualitative study and write a country chapter. In addition to the specific qualitative research on manager–subordinate relationships, in each country we studied the role of trust toward the institutions of the country, and conducted a local literature review on prevailing human resource practices, leadership styles, and forms of trust. In each chapter, the qualitative results are structured along four sections: a) contextual factors in hierarchical trusting relationships, b) personal factors in hierarchical trusting relationships, c) antecedents and outcomes of hierarchical trusting relationships, and d) dynamics of manager–subordinate trust. In order to facilitate the reading of the book, we have followed the same structure in each chapter. We also start each chapter with an introduction that provides bullet points with the main findings of the chapter.

Authors of the Quantitative Study

Pablo Cardona (IESE, Spain), Sebastian Reiche (IESE, Spain), Yih-teen Lee (IESE, Spain), Miguel Angel Canela (IESE, Spain), Marisa Aguirre (Universidad de Piura, Peru), Esther Akinnukawe (Lagos Business School, Nigeria), Jon P. Briscoe (Northern Illinois University), César Bullara (ISE, Brazil), Maria Victoria Caparas (University of Asia & the Pacific, Philippines), Dan V. Caprar (University of New South Wales, Australia), Dallied Charlemagne (Afrique Business School, Ivory Coast), Tor Grenness (Norwegian School of Management, Norway), Wei He (Chinese University of Hong Kong), Konrad Jamro (University of California, Irvine), Astrid Kainzbauer (Mahidol University, Thailand), Kathrin Koester (University of Heilbronn, Germany), Alma Lazo (IPADE, Mexico), Alejandro Moreno (INALDE, Universidad de la Sabana, Colombia), Michael Morley (University of Limerick, Ireland), Vivian Myloni (Athens University of Economics and Business, Greece), Sadia Nadeem (National University of Computer and Emerging Sciences, Pakistan), Alexey Svishchev (MGIMO, Russia), Scott N. Taylor (University of New Mexico, USA), Helen Wilkinson (IESE, Spain).

References

Anderson, J.C. & Gerbing, D.W. (1988). Structural equation modeling in practice: A review and recommended two-step approach. *Psychological Bulletin*, 103: 411–423.

Bachmann, R. & Zaheer, A. (eds). (2006). *Handbook of Trust Research.* Cheltenham: Edward Elgar.

Becker, T.E. (2005). Potential problems in the statistical control of variables in organizational research: A qualitative analysis with recommendations. *Organizational Research Methods*, 8: 274–289.

Blau, P.M. (1964). *Exchange and Power in Social Life*. New York: Wiley.

Bliese, P.D. & Hanges, P.J. (2004). Being both too liberal and too conservative: The perils of treating grouped data as though they were independent. *Organizational Research Methods*, 7: 400–417.

Brislin, R.W. (1986). The wording and translation of research instruments. In W.J. Looner & J.W. Berry (eds), *Field Methods in Cross-Cultural Research*. Beverly Hills, CA: Sage, pp. 137–164.

Brockner, J., Siegel, P.A., Daly, J.P., Tyler, T. & Martin, C. (1997). When trust matters: The moderating effect of outcome favorability. *Administrative Science Quarterly*, 42(3): 558–583.

Brower, H.H., Schoorman, F.D. & Tan, H.H. (2000). A model of relational leadership: The integration of trust and leader-member exchange. *Leadership Quarterly*, 11: 227–250.

Cheung, G.W. & Rensvold, R.B. (1999). Testing factorial invariance across groups: A reconceptualization and proposed new method. *Journal of Management*, 25, 1: 1–27.

Coleman, V.I. & Borman, W.C. (2000). Investigating the underlying structure of the citizenship performance domain. *Human Resource Management Review*, 10: 25–44.

Colquitt, J.A., Scott, B.A. & LePine, J.A. (2007). Trust, trustworthiness, and trust propensity: A meta-analytic test of their unique relationships with risk-taking and job performance. *Journal of Applied Psychology*, 92: 909–927.

Dirks, K.T. & Ferrin, D.L. (2001). The role of trust in organizational settings. *Organization Science*, 12: 450–467.

Dirks, K.T. & Ferrin, D.L. (2002). Trust in leadership: Meta-analytic findings and implications for research and practice. *Journal of Applied Psychology*, 87: 611–628.

Doney, P.M., Cannon, J.P. & Mullen, M.R. (1998). Understanding the influence of national culture on the development of trust. *Academy of Management Review*, 23: 601–620.

Folger, R. & Konovsky, M.A. (1989). Effects of procedural and distributive justice on reactions to pay raise decisions. *Academy of Management Journal*, 32: 115–130.

Graen, G.B. & Scandura, T.A. (1987). Toward a psychology of dyadic organizing. In B.M. Staw & L.L. Cummings (eds), *Research in Organizational Behavior*, vol. 9. Greenwich, CT: JAI Press, pp. 175–208.

Greenberg, J. (1990). Organizational justice: Yesterday, today, and tomorrow. *Journal of Management*, 16: 399–432.

Huff, L. & Kelley, L. (2003). Levels of organizational trust in individualist versus collectivist societies: A seven-nation study. *Organization Science*, 14: 81–90.

Konovsky, M.A. & Pugh, S.D. (1994). Citizenship behavior and social exchange. *Academy of Management Journal*, 37: 656–669.

Kouzes, J.M. & Posner, B.Z. (1993). *Transformational Leadership. The Credibility Factor.* Palo Alto, CA: TPG/Learning Systems.

Lee, K. & Allen, N.J. (2002). Organizational citizenship behavior and workplace deviance: The role of affect and cognitions. *Journal of Applied Psychology*, 87: 131–142.

Levinson, H. (1965). Reciprocation: The relationship between man and organization. *Administrative Science Quarterly*, 9: 370–390.

Lewis, J.D. & Weigert, A. (1985). Trust as a social reality. *Social Forces*, 63: 967–985.

McAllister, D.J. (1995). Affect- and cognition-based trust as foundations for interpersonal cooperation in organizations. *Academy of Management Journal*, 38: 24–59.

Mayer, R.C., Davis, J.H. & Schoorman, F.D. (1995). An integrative model of organizational trust. *Academy of Management Review*, 20: 709–734.

Muthén, L.K. & Muthén, B.O. (2007). *MPlus User's Guide* (5th ed.). Los Angeles, CA: Muthén & Muthén.

Organ, D.W. (1990). The motivational basis of organizational citizenship behavior. *Research in Organizational Behavior*, 12: 43–72.

Pillai, R., Schriesheim, C.A. & Williams, E.S. (1999). Fairness perceptions and trust as mediators for transformational and transactional leadership: A two sample study. *Journal of Management*, 25: 897–933.

Rich, G. (1997). The sales manager as a role model: Effects of trust, job satisfaction and performance of salespeople. *Journal of the Academy of Marketing Science*, 25: 319–328.

Rousseau, D.M., Sitkin, S.B., Burt, R.S. & Camerer, C. (1998). Not so different after all: A cross-discipline view of trust. *Academy of Management Review*, 23: 393–404.

Schaffer, B.S. & Riordan, C.M. (2003). A review of cross-cultural methodologies for organizational research: A best-practices approach. *Organizational Research Methods*, 6: 169–215.

Schoorman, F.D., Mayer, R.C. & Davis, J.H. (2007). An integrative model of organizational trust: Past, present, and future. *Academy of Management Review*, 32: 344–354.

Shrout, P.E. & Bolger, N. (2002). Mediation in experimental and nonexperimental studies: New procedures and recommendations. *Psychological Methods*, 7: 422–445.

Simsek, Z. & Veiga, J.F. (2001). A primer on internet organizational surveys. *Organizational Research Methods*, 4: 218–235.

Smith, C.A., Organ, D.W. & Near, J.P. (1983). Organizational citizenship behavior: Its nature and antecedents. *Journal of Applied Psychology*, 68: 655–663.

Vandenberg, R.J. & Lance, C.E. (2000). A review and synthesis of the measurement invariance literature: Suggestions, practices, and recommendations for organizational research. *Organizational Research Methods*, 3: 4–69.

Whitener, E.M., Brodt, S.E., Korsgaard M.A. & Werner, J.M. (1998). Managers as initiators of trust: An exchange relationship framework for understanding managerial trustworthy behavior. *Academy of Management Review*, 23: 513–530.

Zand, D.E. (1972). Trust and managerial problem solving. *Administrative Science Quarterly*, 17: 229–239.

2 Manager–Subordinate Trust Relationships in the United States

CARLOS RODRÍGUEZ-LLUESMA, YOSEM E. COMPANYS, AND PABLO GARCÍA RUIZ

Introduction

The United States of America (henceforth, the US) borders both the North Atlantic Ocean and the North Pacific Ocean, between Canada and Mexico. As the third country in the world in terms of area (9,826,675 square kilometers), the US is rich in fossil fuels (gas and coal especially, holding around 27 percent of the world's total reserves of the latter) and ores. At 313 million people, the population of the US is the third largest in the world after China and India and is moderately evenly distributed, although the four biggest states (California, Texas, New York, and Florida) amount to almost a third of the total. An estimated 82 percent of the population lives in urban areas. In its little more than two centuries of history, population growth has been explosive, especially during the late nineteenth and early twentieth centuries, when the US was seen as a land of opportunity that attracted thousands of immigrants to its coasts. Today, the US is one of the most ethnically diverse countries in the world, though according to the 2000 US Census only 2.4 percent of all Americans identify themselves as members of more than one race.

The US was established on the premise that sovereignty rested on the people, not the government. As a former British colony whose territories were at one time or another colonized by other countries, such as Spain, France, and Russia, the US was a nation in effervescence during its first century and a half of development, during which a growing national sense coexisted with strong cultural divides, such as the North–South division as demarcated by the Mason-Dixon Line. During the twentieth century, the US has witnessed its economic, cultural, and military power rise, reaching its apogee after the Second World War on to this day. According to the World Economic Forum's 2010–2011 Global Competitiveness Report, the US economy is ranked first in the world. The US economy is market-oriented, such that individuals and firms are free to make their own economic decisions. Federal and state governments make purchases of goods and services in the open market instead of producing them. US firms sit at or near the top in most industries worldwide, ranging from agricultural products to auto making, pharmacy, media, military equipment, aerospace, and consumer electronics, to name just a few. US *per capita* GDP income stands at seventh in the world at approximately $47,200. But the

US is also characterized by a high level of income inequality, with the labor force fragmented into two tiers, with those at the bottom lacking access to opportunities for educational and professional/technical advancement. As such, they are unable to secure the comparable pay raises, health insurance coverage, and other benefits accrued to those at the top.

Given the country's relatively short existence, the US exhibits a higher degree of labor mobility than its Western European counterparts, but it is quite homogeneous in terms of its economic and political decision-making structures. Despite this homogeneity, important differences exist across regions, especially between the North and South regions that contested the US Civil War. During the twentieth century, newer regional differences have developed as economic prosperity has attracted legions of diverse immigrant groups to different regions, such as Southern California, Florida, and the Southwest. These different cultural crucibles are generally of European origin, with their differences owing to the different sets of social and political conditions during the periods of first settlement and, second, to the physical and economic environments to which they adapted. Despite these interregional differences, the US continues to share a very strong national identity.

This chapter will report on the results of an empirical research study of trust in US manager–subordinate dyads and the cultural and organizational values that underpin them. It will also explore how a variety of institutional factors provide a context for trust within organizations. The insights from this chapter will be of interest not only to those firms intending to do business in the US, but also to those firms with even a moderately international reach, as the US is a primary exporter of human resource practices through the global operations of US academic institutions, and manufacturing and service firms.

Highlights of Manager–Subordinate Trust in the United States

- Social trust (the degree to which an individual is willing to trust a stranger) has declined precipitously in the past 50 years. Presumably a more contextual factor, trust in public institutions has also declined since the eruption of the financial crisis in 2008. Despite this negative tendency, social trust in the US remains above average as compared with most OECD countries.
- Unionization has also declined steeply in the US, falling from 20.1 percent in 1983 to 11.9 percent in 2010. Labor relations tend to be less cooperative than in other Western economies. Although with notable exceptions, conflict resolution practices between employers and employees tend to happen at the dyadic level, very rarely going beyond the firm level.
- Managers in the US are expected to act as leaders, inspiring subordinates, acting decisively, and "getting the job done." Subordinates are expected to perform according to set goals.
- Our respondents stated that subordinates tended to trust their managers (and vice-versa). Individuals in both groups tend to trust those similar to them (homophily) and those with whom they have interacted for a longer period

of time. Participants saw gender as a neutral factor in trust creation, but our quantitative data, which suggested otherwise, revealed the possibility that this result might be an artifact of social desirability.

- Aggregate data from different sources enabled us to characterize a "good working relationship." From the subordinates' viewpoint, it includes attributes such as clarity of goals, perceived support, justice, and feedback. For managers, subordinates contribute to a good working relationship by getting things done, being "ahead of the curve," and showing loyalty.

- Respondents referred to an "incubating period" in which both parties monitored each other closely. Only after a threshold had been attained did trustful behavior arise. Respondents reported that closing this incubating period beforehand constituted a clear pitfall. The process of going through, and closing, this initial phase of the relationship proved especially difficult in virtual teams.

Historical Perspective

The first people in the USA were believed to have come from Asia through a land bridge known as Beringia around 30,000 years ago. Hunting artifacts have been found at sites throughout North and South America, indicating that life was probably already well established in much of the Western Hemisphere by some time prior to 10,000BC. Most tribes of Native Americans, particularly in the wooded eastern region and the Midwest, combined hunting, gathering, and the cultivation of maize and other products for their food supplies.

Spaniards came to America in 1492, led by Christopher Columbus and sponsored by the Queen and King of Spain, Isabel and Ferdinand. While Columbus never set foot on the land that would become the US, the first explorations were launched from the Spanish possessions that he helped establish. The first of these took place in 1513, when a group of men under Juan Ponce de León landed on the Florida coast and founded San Agustín (the present city of St. Augustine) in 1565, the first settlement and still inhabited today. Spanish possessions would encompass about half of current US territories. Over the next 100 years, further Spaniard, Portuguese, Dutch, French, and British explorers set sail to conquer "The New World."

In the early 1600s, successive waves of British colonizers settled in the Northeastern region of the US Puritan British citizens fleeing religious persecution in England founded Jameston, Virginia, in 1607, which constituted the first claim of British possession of the New Land, which would last for a century and a half. The independence process from England started in the early 1770s. Events like the Boston "Massacre" of 1770, when British troops fired on a mob that had attacked a British sentry outside Boston's State House, and the Boston "tea-party" of 1773, when British-taxed tea was thrown into the harbor, marked the escalating steps toward the American Revolutionary War (1775–1783). Before the end of the conflict, on the 4th of July, 1776, the 13 American colonies declared themselves as an independent state. In the course of roughly a century, the US reached its current territorial configuration through the conquest or purchase of Native American, Spanish, Mexican, French, Dutch, and Russian territories.

The nineteenth century, together with an explosive expansion to the West, North and South, also brought another war with the British Empire in 1812 and, above all, the Civil War, which pitted seceded states from the South favoring slavery against the North, composed of the abolitionist states loyal to President Abraham Lincoln. The war, in which more than 630,000 people died on both sides, put an end to slavery, but also made evident a cultural divide between North and South that would enter well into the twentieth century in the form of segregation of African Americans from social life, and the Civil Rights movement inspired, among others, by Martin Luther King.

In economic terms, the second half of the nineteenth century lay the foundations for US economic, military, and cultural predominance in the twentieth century. The emergence of a huge internal market afforded by the construction of a reliable railway system and fueled by the country's wealth of natural resources, spurred a plethora of big corporations with a growing global reach that drew from a pool of cheap immigrant labor and abundant financing. Beyond commerce, the USA also expanded geographically, conquering Cuba, the Philippines, Puerto Rico, Guam, and the Hawaii Islands before the end of the nineteenth century. During the twentieth century, the US affirmed its predominance through its decisive military and financial assistance to the European nations battling Germany and its allies during both world wars, and also as the forefront of the Western countries opposed to the Soviet Union and its Communist satellites. The US has gained a huge cultural influence through its dominance of media and business corporations, so much so that some authors have likened the globalization process to a McDonaldization (Ritzer, 1983), in reference to the fact that it was mostly American beliefs and practices that were being spread.

Currently, the USA faces tremendous economic, cultural, and geopolitical challenges due, among other factors, to the emergence of China as a world superpower, the demise of friendly regimes in North Africa and subsequent rise of Islamist parties, general instability in the Mesopotamian area, and also to a bulging and increasingly ungovernable deficit.

Institutional Context

Economic Context

According to the World Bank, the US is the world's largest economy and the seventh in terms of GDP per capita. One of the few really global players in world commerce, American exports amount to 10 percent of the world total. Businesses in the US encounter fewer bureaucratic obstacles compared to other OECD nations, as the role of the government remains relatively small, and only a few companies are government-owned, such as the Postal Service, the Nuclear Regulatory Commission, and the National Railroad Passenger Corporation. The biggest consumer of energy in the world, the American economy is a leading player in the manufacture of transportation equipment (including cars, aircraft, and space equipment), computer and communications, pharmaceuticals and biotechnology, health services, food products, chemicals, machinery, energy, and financial and professional services.

Despite its resilience, recent years have seen the US economy under growing strain due to both long-term trends and more episodic reasons. The former include inadequate investment in deteriorating infrastructures, soaring medical and pension costs, high trade and budget deficits, and wage stagnation. These factors impinge particularly on lower-income families. Besides these long-term trends, other, more circumscribed causes have contributed to a stalling American economy. First, the war in Iraq, launched in coalition with other Western countries in March–April 2003, which required major shifts in national resources to the military and a sizeable increase in public spending. Higher oil prices between 2005 and the first half of 2008 also put a dent on disposable income and, therefore, on private consumption. Due in part to this factor, the merchandise trade deficit reached a record $840 billion in 2008 before shrinking to $507 billion in 2009, and skyrocketing back to $647 billion in 2010. By the second quarter of 2008, added trouble from the global economic downturn, the sub-prime mortgage crisis, investment bank failures, falling home prices, and tight credit had thrust the US into its longest recession since the Great Depression, as GDP contracted for five consecutive quarters. By 2010, the account balance amounted to approximately −$470.2 billion.

Social Context

Life expectancy at birth is 80.5 years for women and 75.5 years for men (US Census Bureau, 2010). The total fertility rate is high by OECD standards, at 2.1 children per woman as of 2007. Despite its wealth, poverty remains a reality in the US, with over 10 percent of the population living below the poverty line, though programs such as Social Security and Medicare have helped relieve part of the burden among senior citizens. The states provide assistance to the poor to different degrees, and the Department of Agriculture subsidizes the provision of low-cost food and food stamps through state and local governments. Unemployment assistance is funded through worker and employer contributions. Employment grants the right to a retirement pension under the Social Security program, spouses and dependent children being eligible for survivor benefits. Many Americans also enjoy private pension schemes funded by themselves as well as by their employers. These individual retirement accounts, such as the 401(k) plan, allow employees to contribute part of their earnings, deferring the attending taxes. Healthcare coverage remains partial (approximately 18 percent of the population is not covered by any kind of insurance). Around two thirds of the population receives employer-funded healthcare coverage, while one sixth has their coverage paid for or subsidized by the federal or state government. Prescription drugs and healthcare costs in general add up to over $1 trillion per year and keep rising steadily, thus posing a huge challenge for an already deficit-ridden country.

Political and Legal Systems

The US is a federal republic of 50 states. The Founding Fathers who drafted the Constitution in 1787 wanted to avoid the tyrannous governing they associated with Europe, so they established a government of separate institutions that shared powers. Authority is divided into three tiers of national, state, and local government, with the American people electing officials to serve in each of them. At the national level, the government is split into three autonomous branches—legislative, executive, and judicial. Each has its own distinct responsibilities, but they can also partially limit the authority of the others through a complex system of checks and balances. The Legislative Branch consists of the Congress, which is responsible for making the federal laws. Congress consists of two houses: the Senate and the House of Representatives. The Executive power lies with the President of the US, entrusted with executing, enforcing, and administering the laws and government. The Bureaucracy is part of the Executive Branch. The judicial power of the US is vested in the Supreme Court and the federal courts. Their job is to interpret and apply US laws through cases brought before them. Another important power of the Supreme Court is that of Judicial Review, whereby they can rule laws unconstitutional. In practice, the US alternates between the Republican and the Democrat parties. While generally dissenting on the level of taxation and moral issues, such as abortion, both parties would be considered right-wing by European standards.

Educational System

Education spending amounts to 5.7 percent of total public spending in the US (United Nations Development Programme, 2011). Education in the US is provided mainly by the public sector, with control and funding coming from the federal, state, and local levels. The literacy rate is 99 percent (UNESCO, 2011). Formal education has the 6-4-4 structure (i.e. six years of primary or elementary education, four years of secondary or high school education, and another four years to gain a bachelor's degree). Child education is compulsory. There is no national curriculum overseen by the federal government. Instead, each state is responsible for governance of their specific school system. Education is required for students until age 16 or 18, depending on the state in which they reside. While compulsory education is widely available for free, tuition fees for undergraduate and graduate degrees are very high and rapidly growing, especially at first-tier universities.

Human Resource Practices

The US has a labor force population of 153.9 million, a labor force participation rate of 64.3 percent and an unemployment rate of 8.6 percent. About 78 percent of the labor force is employed in the services sector, a little under 2 percent in agriculture, and 20 percent in industry (US Bureau of Labor Statistics, 2011). The unionization of the workforce has steadily declined in recent decades. In 2010, the union membership rate was 11.9 percent, down from 12.3 percent a year earlier (US Bureau of Labor Statistics, 2011). The number of wage and salary workers belonging to unions declined by 612,000 to 14.7 million. In 1983, the first year for which comparable union data are available, the union membership rate was 20.1 percent.

Industrial relations in the US have traditionally been seen as considerably more conflictual and manager-driven than in other Western economies (see Kochan *et al.*, 1986). Perhaps the most prominent value in American culture is individualism, as embodied in the archetype of those pioneers who conquered the American West. Organizations embody individualistic patterns, especially in subordinates' capacity to question the orders of their superiors, with dispute resolution procedures relying heavily on manager–subordinate interaction. Industrial relations for the most part also incorporate the idea of meritocracy—that is, the idea that personal achievement, regardless of other factors such as age or tenure in the organization, should be met by rewards and promotion. Agents normally resort to collective action only when individual action has proven unsuccessful. Though public opinion viewed positively the increased involvement of the government in labor relations resulting from the need to respond to the Great Depression, the preference for decentralized institutions, self-governance, and a free economy has kept both a low level of unionization and a lack of organization among employers. As a consequence of these factors, industrial relations mostly develop at the firm level. Union representatives and management interact mainly through the negotiation of an agreement which dictates the terms and conditions for the next two or three years. During that interim, interaction takes the form of deciding, through grievance procedures, whether the employer remains faithful to the contract. Related to these factors are also a higher level of turnover among employees and enhanced difficulty in manager–employee cooperation, compared with other Western economies.

Most current practices and innovations in human resource management come from American firms and academic institutions, with American multinational companies acting as their carriers (Springer & Springer, 1990). Originally—and in contrast to the North European model, which tends to regard employees not as autonomous agents but as a class—the American human resource management (HRM) model conceives the employee as an individual who has an economic relationship with the firm (Hyman, 1995). Human resource management in the US has changed noticeably in the past three decades, due mostly to two reasons. First, it has become increasingly clear—especially among knowledge-intensive firms—that competitive advantage can only be sustained through the skilful development and management of people. Second, it has become imperative to adopt a more international focus on issues such as productivity, managing international alliances, managing expatriates, and developing an adequate talent pool.

From a different perspective, the past 30 years have also witnessed a shift from administrative/technical people management toward a more strategic partnership, with top management relying on measures of organizational effectiveness as guiding principles for measuring HR contribution to the firm (Becker & Huselid, 2006). This new orientation in HR practices has dramatically increased workers' performance levels. While labor productivity grew 1.5 percent per year between 1973 and 1994, it has grown 2.5 percent per year since then (Shaw, 2006).

Leadership Style

The belief that American society is individualistic remains partial at best. Unlike other European societies that present a bipolar distribution between strong states and families, American society has brimmed with voluntary organizations. Alongside a strong private business sector in which economic gain features as the paramount motivator, a series of other voluntary organizations, such as churches, professional societies, charitable institutions, private schools, etc., serve as vehicles for promoting collective goods. In the past couple of generations, social relations have become increasingly atomized due to the erosion of marriage, the breakdown of communities such as neighborhoods and churches, and an increased wariness due to higher crime levels (Fukuyama, 1996). Traces of this tension between self-interest and altruism can be identified in models of leadership that juggle entrepreneurship, passion, and drive, on the one hand, and a sense of communal responsibility, on the other hand (Chhokar *et al.*, 2007: 480; but see Hofstede *et al.*, 2010, for a characterization of American culture as highly individualistic).

Culturally, American society does not easily accept marked power differentials, underscoring the premise of "liberty and justice for all" (Hofstede *et al.*, 2010) and, in general, a democratic and meritocratic approach to work. This habit translates into the workplace as a tendency to value open communication, a flat organization chart, and accessibility on the part of managers. Reciprocally, employees expect participation and a relatively democratic approach to power relations. A high degree of geographical and social mobility inclines Americans to easily interact with strangers, furthering trust radiuses beyond family and kin. As individuals who value competition and self-transcendence, Americans tend to approve of a winner-takes-all society in which each one strives to better their condition in terms of status and monetary rewards. This factor is compounded by a high degree of tolerance for new ideas and a short-term view of performance, creating a pragmatist conception of social and workplace relations.

In line with these fundamental cultural values, leaders are expected to motivate and inspire, but mostly to solve problems, "to get the job done." Grand discourses without clear reference to short-time interventions seem suspect, as an experientialist approach to gaining knowledge is favored over more analytic approaches. Leaders are expected to take action quickly, forcefully and decisively, as time is seen as a scarce resource that needs to be used rationally. Short-term objectives feature centrally in organizational action. In summary, some leader characteristics valued in American culture include: the desire to succeed and make an impact through hard work, a focus on results, and risk-taking (Chhokar *et al.*, 2007).

Content analysis of media, focus groups, and several interviews conducted as part of this study offered additional insights into the perceptions of leadership in the US. The media analysis showed that the term "leader" carries with it some sort of mystical aura of inspiration and charisma that allows leaders to be in control in difficult situations, as well as to provide a sense of direction to their followers. For example, Fortune (2004) dubbed Carlos Gutiérrez, then CEO at Kellogg's Cereals, "The man who fixed Kellogg." Similarly, Anne Mulcahy, then CEO at Xerox, was represented as controlling the firm all by herself: "Anne Mulcahy has Xerox by the horns" (Businessweek, 2003). While newspaper headlines have their own hyperbolic logic, it nonetheless remains evident that only by investing leaders with extraordinary capacities do these two headlines avoid being ludicrous. The discussion of leadership in a focus group showed that leaders differ from managers in that they radiate charisma, optimism, and hope. They also blaze new trails, creating novel possibilities of action for others. They also communicate in a particular way, by providing a vision and sense of purpose. In doing so, they may help their followers articulate their own aspirations. Converging with our analysis of media content, participants both in our focus groups and in our interviews provided an implicit conceptualization of leaders as extraordinary people whom followers should admire. Most tellingly, one participant in one of our focus groups showed her puzzlement at the interviewer's statement that, in some cultures, leaders are viewed with suspicion. Other characteristics relevant to this study included a concordance between words and deeds (to which some referred with the term "authenticity"), a focus on results, and the capacity to rally followers around a common cause.

Literature Review on Trust

Strong tendencies toward atomization and association have traditionally coexisted in the US The figure of the rugged pioneer blazing trails and facing an inhospitable environment has exerted a strong influence on the American collective unconscious and way of life. But it is also true that the extraordinary vibrancy of their voluntary associations (or "civil society") has surprised those who have studied the country, starting with Tocqueville and Max Weber (Fukuyama, 1996). In the last 60 years, though, sociability has declined steadily. Marriage has deteriorated, as marked by a skyrocketing divorce rate, and membership of voluntary associations such as organized religion, unions, parent–teacher associations, and fraternal organizations have all plummeted between 15 and over 50 percent (Putnam, 2001). As Fukuyama (1996: 309) puts it, some organizations still boast large numbers of associates, but they constitute mostly communities of interest, whose members interact with the organization by paying their dues and staying informed through regular newsletters. Those that provided a goal superordinate to those of individuals and which, consequently, could provide reasons for trust that went beyond self-interest have become rarer. To illustrate, one longitudinal survey cited by Fukuyama (2000: 310) reported that the percentage of American people who believe that "most people" can be trusted fell from 58 percent in 1960 to only 37 percent in 1993. Crime and litigation rates—both related to the absence of social trust—have soared during the same period (Fukuyama, 2000: 311).

Despite this decline, the US population ranks in the upper-middle range of trust, below Northern European countries, with the bottom tier being populated by South American, Asian, and African countries (Delhey &Newton, 2005; Rothstein & Uslaner, 2005). In terms of demographics, whites are more trusting than blacks or Hispanics. People with higher family incomes are more trusting than those with lower family incomes. The married are more trusting than the unmarried. The middle-aged and the elderly are more trusting than the young. People who live in rural areas are more trusting than those who live in cities (Pew Research Center, 2007t).

A recent study on trust in 23 countries (Edelman Trust Barometer, 2011) showed that trust in companies has decreased. Only 46 percent of people between the ages of 25 and 64 trusted companies, with media being trusted by just 27 percent of the sample. Out of the four institutions (NGOs, companies, media, and government), NGOs were the most trusted (55 percent). These levels marked a decline with respect to 2010, but showed a recovery compared to 2009 levels, which most likely reflected the full swing of the financial crisis that started in 2009. From a global point of view, and based on a composite score synthesizing trust in all four institutions, trust in the US has dropped from 53 to 42, well below the average of 55.

According to the World Value Survey (2005–2008), the US is placed above the middle point of trust. Likewise, an international study (Cummings *et al.*, 1971) of attitudinal differences among managers conducted in five regional clusters (Greece, Spain, Central Europe, Scandinavia, and USA) showed that US managers were, on average, the most trusting in all five clusters, though also the most belligerent and most risk-taking.

Contextual Factors in Hierarchical Trusting Relationships

This section reports the results obtained through interviews, focus groups, and experts participating in Delphi panels.

Most of our participants drew a distinction, at the macro level, between rural and urban areas. Urban residents would exhibit less trusting and helpful behaviors than non-urban residents, holding organizational affiliations constant. Asked about possible causes explaining this phenomenon, participants pointed to an increased sense of threat in urban America due mostly to a sense of higher crime rates as compared to other areas. Other related factors mentioned with regard to the higher occurrence of trusting behaviors in non-urban America included less demographic homogeneity and a sense of community.

As compared with other countries, our experts rated the US as more individualistic than countries outside the cultural English-speaking cluster. To illustrate, Mexico and, in general, Latin America are very group-oriented cultures where belonging to a collectivity means sharing responsibility for joint outcomes, a belief inculcated through the educational and institutional systems. In the US, on the other hand, individualism has been fostered through such collective archetypes as the pioneer and the myth of the "American dream," the hope for both natives and immigrants to this "Land of opportunity" to better their condition, regardless of the social or economic status from which they might have started out. On the other hand, the experts in our Delphi panels also referred to the existence of "enclaves of trust" located in strong communities (the Amish being an extreme example), which would moderate the general tendency.

Again, our experts presented a mixed diagnosis of power distance in the US, and on its influence on trusting relationships. Generally speaking, and in consonance with Hofstede *et al.*'s (2010) studies, power distance in the US would be relatively low compared with, for example, other OECD countries such as Germany. One expert pointed again to the difference between the US and other American countries. She held that the high power distance in Latin American countries could be due to Spanish and Portuguese colonization and their Hacienda and patronage systems, as well as to the patriarchalism encapsulated in native traditions. In stark contrast to these developments, early colonists of the US almost eradicated native cultures and brought with them autonomy from authority as their founding value, which would become central to the American institutional system as a whole. On the other hand, a non-American expert with long years of residence in the US provided the counterpoint of stronger feeling rules than in other Western countries. Specifically, she mentioned a pressure to conform to the prevailing rule of "being nice," which prescribed only upbeat responses to the question, "How are you doing?" and, in general, proscribed sharing experiences relative to one's personal life that did not hit a happy note.

Another of our experts pointed to a strong cultural ambivalence because "people tend to value 'equality' (and dread 'elitism'), which would imply a low power distance. However, they also tend to value 'excellence,' which would imply a high power distance." Again, explanations would lie in organizational or regional factors. For example, in an organization with a strong "excellence" culture, such as elite technology or consulting companies, power distance would be high. In organizations in which meritocracy was less of a reality due to lower competitive pressures, power distance would be low. As a final, more contextual factor, our experts mentioned a decrease in trust in all institutions due to the view that managers, particularly those in top positions, have failed most working people, retirees, and constituents, resolving their own situation first, rather than that of their employees (and the country). The full effect and duration of this factor remain to be determined.

At the organizational level, focus group participants believed that any factor affording increased interaction, especially of the informal kind, facilitated trust creation and maintenance. Participants mentioned physical propinquity as a key aspect, moderated by such circumstances as the availability and desirability of places to "hang out," whether the physical layout of the locale induced or discouraged the confluence of managers and subordinates (compatibility of schedules was also mentioned in this regard). In general, any factor that fostered a close working relationship was deemed as conducive to trust.

Several organizational factors play into the level of trust between managers and subordinates. According to our experts, the intensity of required knowledge seemed crucial for manager–subordinate trust. In general, knowledge-intensive industries placed a premium on retaining high-value employees because of the high start-up costs of replacing them. These industries would score even lower in power distance than the general American workforce because of the specialization of the knowledge involved: managers often depended on even very young recruits who may bring fresh knowledge from college. This circumstance induced a more egalitarian treatment between managers and subordinates, which facilitated trust. Two participants in focus groups who had worked in technology companies emphasized that this particularity does not hold so much in times of strong economic growth, as the scarcity of these workers provides them with better-paying alternatives, reducing their tenures across all companies, and also decreasing the level of trust they may have with their managers (and vice-versa). Many high-tech companies have developed HR practices aimed at pampering their employees, which tend to increase trust.

A second factor, company size, exerted strong effects on the development of trust. According to our respondents, executives in larger firms tended to hinder trust in their subordinates because they felt more powerful because of their visibility and status. Conversely, executives in smaller firms might feel more vulnerable and try harder to gain their subordinates' trust. On the other hand, larger firms tended to have more reporting systems, which enhanced accountability on the part of both managers and subordinates. Experts did not agree on whether the existence of these mechanisms enhanced trust (via the enhancement of a sense of safety) or diminished it (via an enhancement of calculative rationality). As pointed out above, work organization strongly moderated the effect of company size. Working in production cells, for example, fostered a good emotional climate, which enhanced trust not only in one's peers, but indirectly in supervisors.

Company age also influenced manager–subordinate trust. Over time, organizations develop procedures, routines, and values that strongly structure both work and interaction among participants. Executives in older organizations are likely to have been socialized into very definite schemata of how work should be done and how employees and managers should interact. This circumstance works against the development of trust in the case of newcomers, especially under conditions of high turnover and cultural or demographic heterogeneity between manager and subordinate.

Personal Factors in Hierarchical Trusting Relationships

Our respondents, regardless of their hierarchical position, believed that several personal factors could exert a causal influence on the degree of trust in their relationships. Both managers and subordinates reported that they tended to trust people who are similar to them in a dimension central to their jobs or social identity. One subordinate opined that:

> So, insofar as bosses or subordinates have something in common with the focal person, the person will tend to trust them. But someone's status (boss or subordinate) will not necessarily cause someone to trust him or her more or less. My guess as to why trust in others is common is that there is a strong cultural pressure [in the US] to conform to the norm [in organizational contexts]. And because, by and large, people do conform, it follows that it is usually safe to trust a person. Conformity implies similarity.

An important *caveat* in this regard concerns the need for a professional demeanor at all times, as other factors bear on the degree of trust in the relationship, *conditional on* the manager's or (particularly) the subordinate's professionalism. In fact, one respondent emphasized that a lack of professionalism may actually revert the beneficial influence of similarity and turn it into a liability.

Again, both managers and subordinates converged on "length of relationship" as the most critical factor for a trusting relationship, as trust could be "faked" over short spans of time. Caring relationships take time to establish and cannot be regulated or manufactured. Without the necessary time to build a deeper caring relationship, it is hard to gain trust. Managers often referred to the communication between them and the people they trust as one where the other person was unbiased, objective, and expressed care or concern. Factors other than the length of the relationship seemed more ambivalent to most of our respondents. Take age, for example. A young person may trust an older manager because he may see her as a caring, protecting parental figure. But a young person may also be suspicious of older people precisely because of that very same reason, and hence may not trust them. The same applies to "tenure." An experienced person may inspire trust, but he or she may also inspire distrust, as tenure may mean allegiance to the organization and not to the focal person. And so on. The length of the relationship may also have both effects.

However, one of our experts warned of the possibility of a selection bias in this perception of length of tenure as the most critical factor: "I would say that a long-term relationship is likely to suggest that the people in the relationship will trust one another (otherwise they would have severed the relationship)."

Both participants in focus groups and interviewees saw gender for the most part as a neutral factor, which had a bearing outside of "regular" conditions (i.e. when a romantic liaison might be developing). More specifically, while respondents expressed the desirability of a mixed workforce, they downplayed the importance of gender as compared to managerial abilities, such as being inspirational and providing clear feedback and goals, and capabilities such as diligence and proactivity.

One of our experts gave a more nuanced insight into the relative importance of the personal factors under consideration, stating that homophily (the tendency to like those most similar to you) operated as a meta-factor which worked across situations. In her own words:

> The relative weight of each causal factor will vary depending on whether it becomes a basis for a similarity judgment or not. For example, age might have an effect on its own, as people in similar age cohorts tend to have gone through similar experiences, hold similar cognitive schemata and are more likely, ceteris paribus, to share a relatively common value system. But it is also true that age similarity might have an effect of itself, just by the fact that you and I are of similar age: we feel closer because of this very fact. The question is when age becomes the focal basis of comparison between you and me. For example, if I am a relatively senior person and physical activity is involved, age will likely become a salient basis of comparison. The same will happen with all other personal factors: they will become more or less powerful depending on the context.

Focus group participants were prompted to comment on the correlations between each of several personal factors and each of the constructs in our model (see Table 2.1).

Among other suggestions, our data seem to indicate that the older the subordinate, the less the manager shows trusting behaviors. Participants explained this inverse relationship in terms of both social networks and a high-pressure environment. First, subordinates with longer tenures in the company—not necessarily under their current manager—might feel more confident because of perceived support by key players in the company. This confidence might induce some kind of moral hazard—that is, the proclivity on the subordinate's part to favor personal goals over organizational (the manager's) goals—a behavior which would engender distrust. A second explanation, related to the previous one, would explain this inverse relationship between age and trust in terms of the perceived threat that longer-tenured subordinates would pose for their managers.

Our study also showed that, contrary to our respondents' first opinion, gender does matter for manager–subordinate trust. While we lack data on this factor's effect on subordinates' trust in managers, our data imply that a gender disparity makes trusting difficult for managers. When asked to comment on this contradiction, managers stated that trusting a person of a different gender sometimes felt like a juggling act between showing care for that person and making oneself liable to being perceived as too encroaching, especially in the case of male managers and female subordinates. Panel experts, on the other hand, commented that our respondents' first responses might have been subject to the "social desirability" bias, which consists of the tendency to respond to questions in a manner coherent with values held by society in general or with the researcher in particular. More research on this topic is warranted.

Antecedents and Outcomes of Manager–subordinate Trust

Managers and subordinates in our focus groups defined a "good professional relationship" in different but complementary terms, with trust featuring as a central factor in both sets of accounts. For managers, a good professional relationship included, unsurprisingly, the subordinate's getting the work done, but also being "ahead of the curve." As one manager put it:

Table 2.1 The United States: significant controls (correlations)

	Gender manager (1–> man, 2–> woman)	Age manager	Academic level manager	Academic level subordinate	Gender subordinate	Organizational tenure subordinate
MTB	0.200*		−0.259**			−0.309**
OCB		0.224*		0.264**	−0.266**	
MTS					−0.301**	
STM			−0.230*			−0.269**

Notes
** Correlation significant at 0.01 level.
* Correlation significant at 0.05 level.
MTB = managerial trustworthy behavior, STM = subordinates' trust in managers, MTS = managers' trust in subordinates, OCB = organizational citizenship behavior.

I find it very frustrating when subordinates come to you often to get directions and cannot foresee where the next bottleneck is. I did not get my MBA to run a kindergarten. I need them to be ahead of the curve, to use their brains.

Beyond task completion, managers also included loyalty on the part of subordinates as a key element in a good professional relationship with them. One of the managers held that:

Loyal employees make your life so much easier. Monitoring performance is part of my job, but (…) it prevents me from doing other things. On top of that, it really hurts to put your soul into your work and find out that they [subordinates] are waiting for any reason to stab you in the back. It's a professional relationship and I'm not their father, but even so …

Subordinates placed clarity in goal setting as the first ingredient of a good professional relationship. Failure to provide a clear orientation engendered anxiety.

I can't see how possibly she [his manager] would want me to do my job, as I don't know what my priorities should be. They change from month to month, and sometimes from week to week. I have tried hard to see through the changes, but I still haven't gotten how the [priorities-changing] mechanism works.

Related to clarity in goal-setting, subordinates also mentioned periodic feedback on their own performance. Other managerial factors conducive to a good relationship from the subordinates' point of view included coherence between words and actions, procedural justice, and periodic feedback. On the negative side, some subordinates mentioned managers' high compensation as a demotivating factor.

Participants in our focus groups also reported on the antecedents and outcomes of managers' trust in their subordinates. Going the extra mile featured as a central characteristic of a trustworthy subordinate. One manager wondered:

How can I trust the guy if he is not willing to chip in when things are tough? I know they are supposed to work 9 to 5, but I don't work 9 to 5. It won't break their backs to stay longer from time to time. Trust goes beyond the economics of the job. We are people, and we should be willing to help out to a reasonable degree when the other is in a dire strait. A little of tit for tat is good for everyone.

Managers also appreciated their subordinates' periodic reporting without their having been required to do so. More generally, managers valued proactivity on the part of their subordinates in such matters as anticipating resource needs and suggesting ways to deal with "diplomatic" issues with other departments. Finally, subordinates generated trust in their managers when they showed respect in ways that affirmed their status. Disproportionate attempts at ingratiation, though, were viewed by managers as decreasing trust. As regards outcomes, managers reported that trusting their subordinates lowered their cognitive load and increased their peace of mind. One manager reported that "it [having trustworthy subordinates] allows me to focus on what I need to do instead of always having to perk up my ears in case I hear something is going wrong." This peace of mind and confidence in the job being done within the deadline and according to the required specifications decreased the manager's risk aversion and, as a consequence, increased his willingness to delegate further tasks to his subordinate. Some managers reported delegation and risk aversion entering a virtuous circle: the subordinate's success in completing the newly assigned tasks led to a decrease in the manager's risk aversion, which in turn allowed for further responsibility transfer. On another note, the trustworthy subordinate's focus on the task also had the effect of increasing the manager's confidence level, with the consequence of an increased capacity to accept mistakes. One manager held that:

> It's easier to be candid with someone who minds his business. And I mean it in the sense that the trustworthy subordinate not only gets his job done, but he isn't interested in office politics that much. He gets on with people but he doesn't spend his time poisoning the office.

Our data also address the antecedents and outcomes of subordinates' trust in their managers. Subordinates saw care as central to their definition of a trustworthy manager. Collectively, subordinates viewed trust as a relational construct based on reason, emotions, and conation. In all the examples subordinates offered, those they trusted were able to convince the subordinate that they cared about him or her (in addition to being consistent and predictable in their behavior). One subordinate stated that:

> Your manager can say all the right things and do all the right things but you still do not trust him because something simply "did not feel right." You trust your manager when he shows you that he's not out to squeeze the very last drop out of you. At some point, he or she will have to make a decision—even if a little one—about whether to make one more buck or support you in something you need. That's when you know whether you can trust him or not.

Managers also induced their subordinates' trust when they showed tolerance for "honest mistakes" and listened with genuine interest, as these practices reinforced the subordinates' self-esteem and sense of reciprocity not only to the manager, but also to the organization. Further antecedents of a subordinate's trust in the manager included the latter's consistency and transparency. These two behavioral qualities not only enhanced trustworthiness, but, to some respondents, constituted trustworthiness. In the words of one subordinate, "I don't want the manager to be my papa. I just ask him to be honest to me, to call them as he sees them [...]. Trust is about knowing what the game is about and playing by the rules." Finally, other subordinates pointed to competence—especially the capacity to follow through—as a necessary ingredient to a manager's trustworthiness. One of our respondents held that:

> It's hard to be left on your own. My previous boss took a lot of pride in "delegating." He would give you goals and then, literally holler at you if he thought you sought too much advice. He just wanted results, and didn't understand that sometimes you need resources to get those results. I felt so bad entering his office. Managers should make it easy for subordinates to ask for reasonable help. You sometimes have to walk around and ask, "Hey, how's it going? Anything you need?"

Figure 2.1 below provides a visual summary of the major antecedents and consequences of trust in manager–subordinate relationships, based on qualitative data from our focus groups and expert panels in the US

The Dynamics of Trust in Hierarchical Relationships

All participants in our qualitative study believed that trust takes time to develop. Several factors seemed to play into this development. First of all, some respondents pointed to individual differences in the inclination to trust, based on the indi-

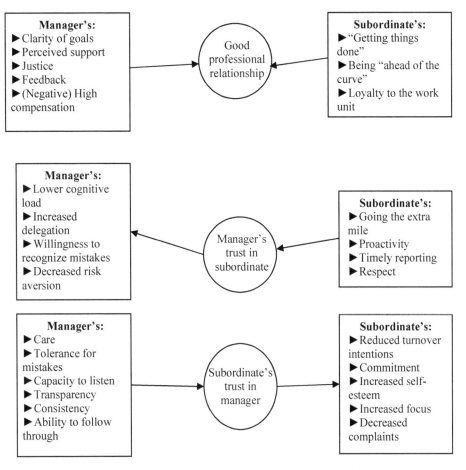

Figure 2.1 Antecedents and outcomes of trust in hierarchical relationships

viduals' personal and professional backgrounds. Other factors aside, participants pointed to two broad paths leading, respectively, to mistrust and to trust. The former would arise out of the interaction between a manager and a subordinate with little inclination to trust due to whatever initial factors. In this case, and similar to Kreps' (1990) trust game, the choice of not trusting the other person would seem warranted because making oneself vulnerable to the other person might bring a hefty downside, which neither the manager nor the subordinate would be willing to endure. Alternatively, if the manager and subordinate are willing to trust even in the absence of a good knowledge of the other person, a good professional relationship becomes possible. One of our respondents proposed the idea of the "trust P&L."

> If you want trust to happen, you need to take a leap. You need to trust from the beginning and hope for the other guy to respond. It's like making an investment because at the beginning you will have to bite the bullet of being in the red, hoping that the other person will not take advantage of you and will be up to par. Otherwise, you are in for a miserable time at the office.

Also, regarding time, other respondents referred to an "incubating" period in which trust did not develop significantly. In other words, trust develops with time, but it takes some time for that process to begin.

Referring to this initial "incubating" period, respondents talked about conscious strategies for managing trust creation. At the beginning of any hierarchical relationship, the basic rules of the game must be established—for example, how much guidance the subordinate may expect, what degree of informality should characterize the interaction, how the department should deal with higher management, and the like. Respondents referred to this first phase of the relationship as "tricky" due to its ambiguity. One of the potential pitfalls was a unilateral resolution of this tentative phase. Characteristically, the manager may close this tentative phase without sufficiently exploring his or her subordinate's expectations and potential contributions to their collaboration. Alternatively, the manager might want to "hit the ground running" and fail to allow time for an implicit agreement on their future collaboration to emerge. Both conditions would seriously limit the development of trust.

Managers and subordinates also pointed to cases in which trust had been betrayed. Characteristically, while trust may take a long time to build up, it can be destroyed almost instantaneously. Several respondents referred to the difficulty in repairing such breaks, which some characterized as inversely proportional to the intensity of the preexisting trust.

Beyond initial dispositions to trust, other factors had a bearing on the dynamics of trust. One of them referred to the alternatives open to the manager in dealing with his/her subordinate. This distinction was portrayed in the following way by a subordinate participating in one of our focus groups:

> The rubber meets the road when your boss has to make decisions about how he lets you take up a new responsibility, has the power to put you on an exciting project, whatever. But you can't always say that because he put you in that project, that he trusted you. It depends on what he could have done. In my office, for example, there are not many people who can do the variety of tasks I do. It's a matter of technical ability. So, does my boss trust me when he gives me all this responsibility? Maybe yes, maybe no. I guess that he should have an easy alternative for me to say that he trusts me.

Interestingly, this respondent argued that behaviors did not suffice as identifying criteria for trust, and asked for the inclusion of other elements (i.e. the availability of assignment options not containing the focal subordinate), a point which warrants further research.

Some respondents pointed to the fact that manager and subordinate often find themselves operating at a distance. Managers in particular quipped about the difficulties in developing trust in these circumstances. Some pointed to the lack of bodily, nonverbal cues for others to pick up regarding the sender's cognitive and emotional state, which created misunderstanding, conflict, and ultimately undermined trust in the relationship. In connection with this issue, some respondents proposed an increase in communication and feedback as a partial solution, and argued for a more structured and conscientious approach to trust building.

Some of our respondents talked about trust development tactics in a more general way, referring not only to the virtual, but also the offline, domain. These tactics, aimed at managing interdependence and its associated risk, varied for managers and subordinates. Most subordinates concurred in caution being the best advisor at the beginning of a work relationship. Especially when not only their managers but also their peers were new to them, subordinates held that diligence, keeping a low profile, and showing signs of amicability were the best credentials to hedge your risk. After this initial period, subordinates could raise their profile. To ensure smooth sailing, subordinates need to know their managers' preferences. One subordinate held that:

> I find it crucial to understand what my manager is about. When I started working with [name] I observed him a lot. I mean that I tried to learn whether he preferred frequent updates or to be left alone until the job was done. It's also very important to know where he's headed, whether he wants to promote, lead the good life, be the center of attention, or a mixture of them all. It's a learning process.

Some other subordinates went further and referred to a process of probing as a critical ingredient of every trust-building program.

> I try to test the waters with very gentle probes, to see whether I can take my trust to the next level. I do things like ask whether he watched the weekend game, to see if that's "kosher" conversation stuff. It's mostly preventative, because I know that we will loosen up in time, and don't want to step on any red line.

Managers in our sample related several different risk management strategies. Several of them expressed the need to mark the hierarchical difference within culturally acceptable boundaries. For example, one of our respondents stated that:

> […] it's often necessary to mark your turf at the beginning, especially with younger subordinates, who may bring different values to the workplace. I agree with all of us being equal, etc., but that does not mean I'm not boss. I've had less than pleasant experiences in the past with subordinates thinking that smiles and accessibility mean we are at the same level. You need to show a little severity at the beginning and then, if he's a producer, let go a little.

Other managers, though, advocated a more egalitarian approach on the basis of some kind of imprinting effect. As first impressions count the most:

> you need to make it easier for the new kid to approach you. I don't want to be Jekyll and Hyde. I tend to loosen a bit more in time, but I think I kind of stand on the loose end from the beginning.

After the initial period of trust development, several managers pointed to high expectations as a powerful tool for increasing their subordinates' trust and efficiency, a phenomenon known in social psychology as the Pygmalion effect (Eden, 1988). One manager put it this way:

> I always demand a lot from people. The business world is a jungle. It's the survival of the fittest. You need to be constantly on your toes. I tell people what I expect of them, and that's a lot. A trusting professional relationship is built on performance. Trust is the icing on the cake. If there is no cake, there is no icing either. If you want the icing, you need the cake.

Table 2.2 Standardized regression weights for the trust model in the United States and the overall sample

	OCB–>MTS	MTS–>MTB	MTB–>STM	STM–>OCB
US only	0.43**	0.34**	0.75**	0.21
Complete model	0.68**	0.34**	0.89**	0.08*

Notes
** Regression weight significant at 0.01 level.
* Regression weight significant at 0.05 level.
No asterisk– Regression weight significant at 0.06 level.

Our quantitative data offer interesting insights into the dynamics of trust (see Table 2.2). Compared to the other countries in the sample taken as a whole, the US shows a very similar pattern. The only divergent regression weight is the one linking the subordinate's trust in his manager and organizational citizenship. In the case of the US, the value converges more closely, though, to extant research, which holds that both constructs are related in the way depicted in the US data. One caveat concerns the fact that the mentioned regression weight was not significant at the 0.05 level.

Our Delphi panel experts agreed that the model seemed applicable both in the US and globally. But, as in the case of the experts in the other countries studied in this book, they pointed out that other factors could be taken into account. Some of them pointed to structural factors at different levels, which might be confounded with cultural factors. Examples included the distribution of small and medium-sized versus large enterprises, the demographic composition of the workforce, the richness of environmental resources, and the prevalence of different modes of production. Other experts pointed to the interaction between organizational and other levels of analysis. Familial structures featured prominently in this regard. On the other hand, our experts agreed that these factors were provided as avenues for further research, as their sufficient consideration would overwhelmingly exceed the length and scope of the present work.

Discussion and Conclusions

Not surprisingly, given that most of the research on trust has been carried out in the US, our results converge with existing research. First of all, trust develops over time (Peterson & Behfar, 2003) and grows out of repeated interactions (Coyle-Shapiro, 2002), especially when the existence of future interactions can be anticipated at the beginning of those interactions (Zand, 1997). All respondents in our study believed that trust is a critical dimension of social relationships in general, and of hierarchical relationships in particular, especially in uncertain and ambiguous contexts (Nahapiet & Ghoshal, 1998; Rousseau *et al.*, 1998). Several participants also held that trust promoted self-esteem and reduced the manager's mental load (McAllister, 1995). Some pointed to trust as increasing efficiency because it dispenses with the effort to hedge risks (Fukuyama, 1996; Williamson, 1981), facilitating coordination and governance of joint efforts (Bradach & Eccles, 1989), and because it enhances cooperation and decreases conflict (Ross & LaCroix, 1996). The absence of trust, on the other hand, takes toll of both manager and subordinate, increasing transaction costs in terms of cognitive load and time spent in hedging the risks incurred in the relationship. As a consequence of an increased risk aversion, boundaries between professional and personal relationships remain rigid.

Our results also confirm and extend other cross-cultural studies in management. In line with Hofstede *et al.*'s (2010) findings, our data point to the US as an individualistic country, as expressed in the archetype of the pioneer and the myth of the American dream. Further, a high-pressure organizational environment contributed to this general feature of American culture, rewarding merit—both substantially and symbolically—over such factors as seniority or tenure in the company. But our data also pointed to a more ambivalent vision of culture, as shown in general conformity to the strong feeling rule of "being nice," which included shunning those who shared cheerless experiences.

Another ambivalence referred to the power distance dimension introduced by Hofstede *et al.* (2010). It stemmed precisely from that very emphasis on goals and rewards mentioned above, and referred to the high valuation of "excellence," in organizational contexts which expressed a high power distance, contrary to Hofstede *et al.*'s findings at the national level.

The quantitative results of our study showed moderate support for the model used in this book. In particular, we found that the subordinate's trust in his or her manager was more strongly correlated with organizational citizenship behavior than in the overall sample. This finding tallies well with extant literature, which posits that trust enhances commitment and commitment leads to organizational citizenship. This result in accordance with our hypothesis encourages further study in the countries in which it has not been obtained.

As noted above, human resource management in the US has changed noticeably in the past three decades, becoming more aware of cross-cultural issues and the centrality of developing people to gain and maintain competitive advantage. During these years, the HRM function has become more strategic and top management teams have increasingly sought the HRM officer's advice. Sets of "high-performance" HRM practices have sprung up, with remarkable effects on productivity (Shaw, 2006). Participants in our study praised the empowerment encapsulated in these practices and supported their diffusion. They also encouraged trying to take advantage of these practices to foster a more collaborative approach to labor relations, closer in this respect to the model prevailing in Germany and the Scandinavian countries. According to several Delphi panel experts, the American emphasis on goals and rewards, while powerful, may sometimes lead to a corrosion of trust and, consequently, of collaboration. In this regard, they advised placing a stronger emphasis on more symbolic ways of managing people—for example, through enhanced work content and increased choice on the part of subordinates.

Commenting on this tension between trust and a sometimes over hyped conception of the individual—of which a heroic conception of leadership is but one expression—our experts held that both managers and subordinates had to forego some ideological remnants of years past. Specifically, they stated that more collective conflict resolution approaches should be considered and not be dubbed as "communistic."

While we have triangulated our data and have made use of both qualitative and quantitative methods of analysis, our study remains partial. In particular, highly educated subjects were over represented in our sample. While we find it safe to claim that their education, international experience, and reflective capacity made them ideal respondents, it is also fair to say that both their familial and work experiences do not reflect the average working American. In addition, we lacked subjects from rural areas. Beyond education and geographical extraction, our data did not tally proportionately with the demographic composition of the US, containing fewer African and Asian Americans than was to be expected. We see this aspect as relevant because some communities have their own cultural codes, which may well play into how subjects interpret and experience trust and how they act according to those ideas. In summary, while we are aware that an enormous research effort remains to be done on the topic of trust, we are confident that this chapter will offer students in this area interesting materials with which to pursue their work.

References

Becker, B.E. & Huselid, M.A. (2006). Strategic human resources management: Where do we go from here?, *Journal of Management*, 32(6): 898–925.

Bradach, J.L. & Eccles, R.G. (1989). Price, authority, and trust: From ideal types to plural forms, *Annual Review of Sociology*, 15:97–118.

Chhokar, J.S., Brodbeck, F.C. & House, R.J. (eds). (2007). *Culture and Leadership across the World: The GLOBE Book of in-Depth Studies of 25 Societies.* Mahwah: Lawrence Erlbaum Associates.

Coyle-Shapiro, J.A. (2002). A psychological contract perspective on organizational citizenship behavior, *Journal of Organizational Behavior*, 23: 927–946.

Cummings, L.L., Harnett, D.L. & Stevens, O.L. (1971). Risk, fate, conciliation, and trust: An international study of attitudinal differences among executives. *Academy of Management Journal*, 14: 285–304.

Delhey, J. & Newton, K. (2005). Predicting cross-national levels of social trust: Global pattern or Nordic exceptionalism?, *European Sociological Review*, 21(4): 311–327.

Edelman Trust Barometer (2011). Retrieved on 12.2.2011 from www.edelman.com/trust2011/.

Eden, D. (1988). Pygmalion, goal setting, and expectancy: Compatible ways to boost productivity, *Academy of Management Review*, 13(4):639–652.

Fukuyama, F. (1996). *Trust: The Social Virtues and the Creation of Prosperity.* Free Press, New York.

Fukuyama, F. (2000). *Trust: The Social Virtues and the Creation of Prosperity.* New York: Free Press.

Hofstede, G.H., Hofstede, G.J. & Minkov, M. (2010). *Cultures and Organizations: Software of the Mind: Intercultural Cooperation and its Importance for Survival.* London: McGraw-Hill Professional.

Hyman, R. (1995). Industrial relations in Europe: Theory and practice, *European Journal of Industrial Relations*, 1(1): 17–46.

Kochan, T.A., Katz, H.C. & McKersie, R.B. (1986). *The Transformation of American Industrial Relations.* Ithaca, NY: ILR Press.

Kreps, D. (1990). Corporate culture and economic theory. In J. Alt & K. Shepsle (eds), *Perspectives on Positive Political Economy.* Cambridge: Cambridge University Press.

McAllister, D.J. (1995). Affect- and cognition-based trust as foundations for interpersonal cooperation in organizations, *Academy of Management Journal*, 38(1):24–59.

Nahapiet, J. & Ghoshal, S. (1998). Social capital, intellectual capital, and the organizational advantage, *Academy of Management Review*, 23(2):242–266.

Peterson, R. & Behfar, K.J. (2003). The dynamic relationship between performance feedback, trust and conflict in groups: A longitudinal study, *Organizational Behavior and Human Decision Processes*, 92: 102–112.

Pew Research Center (2007). *Americans and Social Trust: Who, Where and Why*, February 22.

Putnam, R.D. (2001). *Bowling Alone: The Collapse and Revival of American Community*, New York: Simon and Schuster.

Ritzer, G. (1983). The "McDonaldization" of society, *Journal of American Culture*, 6(1): 100–107.

Ross, W. & LaCroix, J. (1996). Multiple meanings of trust in negotiation theory and research: A literature review and integrative model, *International Journal of Conflict Management*, 7(4): 314–360.

Rothstein, B. & Uslaner, E.M. (2005). All for all: Equality, corruption, and social trust, *World Politics*, 58: 41–47.

Rousseau, D.M., Sitkin, S.B., Burt, R.S. & Camerer C. (1998). Not so different after all: A cross-discipline view of trust, *Academy of Management Review*, 23(3): 393–404.

Shaw, K. (2006). The value of innovative human resource management practices. In E. Lawler & J.O'Toole (eds), *America at Work: Choices and Challenges.* New York: Palgrave McMillan, pp. 227–240.

Springer, B. & Springer, S. (1990). Human resource management in the US. In R. Pieper (ed.), *Human Resource Management: An International Comparison*. Berlin: Walter de Gruyter, pp. 41–60.

UNESCO (2011). *Global Education Digest 2011*. Montreal: UNESCO Institute for Statistics. Retrieved on 5.8.2012 from www.uis.unesco.org/Education/Pages/ged-2011.aspx.

United Nations Development Programme (2011). *Human Development Report 2011. Sustainability and Equity: A Better Future For All*. New York: UNDP and Palgrave Macmillan.

US Bureau of Labor Statistics (2011). *The Employment Situation – November 2011*, news release. Retrieved on 5.8.2012 from www.bls.gov/news.release/archives/empsit_12022011.pdf.

US Census Bureau (2010). *2010 Census Data*. Washington: US Census Bureau. Retrieved on 5.8.2012fromhttp://2010.census.gov/2010census/data/.

Williamson, O.E. (1981). The economics of organization: The transaction cost approach. *American Journal of Sociology*, 87(3):548–577.

Zand, D.E. (1997). *The Leadership Triad: Knowledge, Trust, and Power.* New York: Oxford University Press.

3 Manager–Subordinate Trust Relationships in Greece

BARBARA MYLONI

Introduction

Historical events have profoundly influenced Greece and its culture. Naturally, these events have affected trust levels, making Greeks skeptical of foreign nations and their political leaders. The difficulties in which the country is currently immersed have resulted in a loss of faith in institutions and organizations at the political, economic, and social level.

Recent studies on generalized trust rank Greece in a low position compared with other countries. Variables that negatively influence trust levels, such as corruption and income inequality, seem to hold for Greece as well. On the other hand, it has been found that Greeks are characterized by the social dimension of individualism, rather than collectivism, and this may counteract the negative influence from previous variables and boost trust levels.

Development of trust between workers and, specifically, between managers and subordinates can increase their effectiveness. Our research has shown that effective communication, increased efficiency, and smooth cooperation are some of the outcomes of trust relationships. Trust between people is difficult to build and its development is not due to random events or similarity of characters. It is rather a mutually reinforcing process. Moreover, our Greek respondents believed that the length of the relationship between managers and subordinates and the length of tenure facilitate the development of trust. This work highlights the consequences of trust relationships between managers and subordinates and identifies the development of trust as a necessary factor for increased performance on both sides.

In this chapter, we start by presenting historical events that have affected trust levels in Greece, along with a description of Greeks' trust at the economic, political, and social level. This is followed by a section on "Leadership and Management" and a summary of recent studies related to generalized trust in Greece. We then turn to an extensive discussion of manager–subordinate trust relationships, presenting the contextual and personal factors that affect them, their antecedents and outcomes, and their dynamics.

Highlights of Manager–Subordinate Trust in Greece

- Greek focus group participants are divided as to whether managers are trusted, with the scales leaning slightly on the negative side. This could be due to historical reasons that have shaped Greeks' tendency to low trust levels in authorities, as well as a general view of the manager as impersonal and distant, which in turn is related to a high power distance and autocratic leadership styles.
- Although the dynamics of trust between managers and subordinates is not symmetrical, relationships among variables are strong, including when subordinates' trust in managers leads to organizational citizenship behavior (OCB). The strongest relationship is found in the positive influence of managers' trustworthy behavior on subordinates' trust in managers.
- Quantitative results confirmed by our interviews showed that older managers, with higher levels of OCB, are more likely to trust their subordinates.
- Managers with a higher academic level are associated with a lower level of subordinate OCB.
- Factors considered by both sides as important for the development of trust include company size, length of the relationship, and length of tenure.

Historical Perspective

Greek civilization dates back many centuries, with its roots lying in the Minoan civilization in Crete (2400–1100BC) and the Mycenaean civilization in the Peloponnese (1600–1000BC). The period between the eighth and fifth centuries BC is characterized by the rise of the Greek city-states' power and a flourishing of all aspects of Greek culture: philosophy, political science, architecture, sculpture, literature, theatre, mathematics, medicine. The first Olympic Games were held in Olympia in 776 BC and many Greek colonies were established around the Mediterranean and the Black Sea. The new Greek state of Macedonia became progressively more powerful, eventually unifying all the Greek states, and its leader, Alexander the Great, embarked upon a mission to spread Greek civilization to Asia, reaching as far as India. After Alexander's death and the decline of his Empire, Greece was conquered by the Romans in 146BC. During the fourth century AD, the Roman Empire was divided in two and Greece became part of the Byzantine Empire until the fall of Constantinople to the Turks in 1453. Subsequently, Greece was ruled by the Ottoman Turks until the 1820s.

Although Greece had one of the earliest civilizations and led progress in the arts and sciences for many centuries, the 400-year Turkish occupation kept Greece in a state of decline and isolated it from the significant economic and socio-cultural developments that took place in Europe during the Renaissance. However, the Greek language and the Orthodox church managed to survive and the Hellenic/Greek identity was maintained (Clogg, 1992). A long and bitter revolutionary war for independence started in 1821, despite the "Holy Alliance," an institution founded by European monarchs aiming at combating any liberal movements or revolutions. Furthermore, due to certain economic interests, the powerful European states had good relations with the Ottoman Empire at the time (Skoulatou *et al.*, 2003). Later on, the Great Powers changed their attitude toward the Greeks, but only to create a weak state under their protection, encouraged by the Greeks' continuous divisions and quarrels. In 1829, England, France, and Russia signed the London Protocol, which provided for the recognition of an autonomous Greek state. In 1832, 17-year-old Otto, son of the King of Bavaria, was appointed King of Greece. The Greek state took its first loans from foreign powers (England) in 1824, under very costly payment conditions that prevented any future development (History of the Greek Nation, 1975). The Ottoman Empire was replaced by a foreign guardianship. Economic development was slow, taxation was severe, there were no changes in policies, and foreign interventions were often stressful and degrading. In 1843, a revolutionary movement forced the king to consent to the adoption of the Constitution, while the 1862 uprising would compel him to leave Greece. In 1893, the state declared bankruptcy, while a catastrophic war, caused by poor political and diplomatic decisions, led to acceptance of international financial control. The nation felt humiliated and civil power was weakened (Skoulatou *et al.*, 2003).

Until 1890, the economy was pre-capitalist, with agriculture being the dominant sector. The beginning of the last century was marked by a considerable inflow of capital, but the incipient industrialization was disrupted by a series of conflicts, such as the Balkan Wars, the First World War, and the Greek–Turkish war. In the latter, foreign states once again were involved at the expense of Greece, while Greeks were betrayed by their political leaders who did not keep their promise to withdraw from Asia Minor. During the 1920s and 1930s, Greek political life was characterized by military coups and dictatorships. The Italian invasion forced Greek involvement in the Second World War, which subsequently led to a civil war between the communists and the nationalists until 1950, leaving the country in tatters. An ideological, political, and cultural gulf separated the Greek people and created distrust. This ideological divide was again strong in the military coup of 1967, in which many left-wing people were persecuted, while the dictatorship is likely to have affected citizens' trust in the military corps (Skoulatou *et al.*, 2003).

Greece began to industrialize during the 1950s (Georgas, 1993). External capital investment strengthened the Greek economy so that it could now engage in international trade. Several infrastructure developments as well as investments in strategic industries were made and incentives for foreign investment were offered. After 1960, Greece saw impressive economic growth, with an average annual rate of 6.2 percent, one of the highest of the OECD countries (OECD, 1994). GNP increased rapidly—by 7 percent a year between 1950 and 1973. The end of this period coincided with the global oil crisis and the beginning of a long period of economic instability. Unemployment and inflation rose rapidly, the currency was devalued, and domestic and foreign investments were discouraged, leading to a decline in GNP growth. In 1980, Greece became a member of the European Union and its economic policy was forced to adapt to the new requirements. A number of economic indicators were improved; inflation and interest rates fell, while manufacturing output and investment rose. However, unemployment increased and the trade deficit and public debt deteriorated. During the 1980s, output growth was slow, equivalent to only 0.5 percent of GNP per year (Papalexandris, 1992a).

Further reforms, such as the liberalization of capital movements, privatization, and deregulation, together with macroeconomic adjustment policies, led to improvements in economic development and further encouraged foreign direct investment (FDI). Greece's position among other OECD countries was now relatively high in terms of FDI, indicating its strong potential for economic growth (OECD, 1994).

Greece gained admission to the EMU in 2001, and adopted the euro as its new currency in 2002. The public deficit was well below the EU limit of 3 percent of GDP, the country's debt was under control and it was one of Europe's fastest growing economies in 2001, with GDP growth at 4.7 percent. However, unemployment remained high at over 10 percent. Public and private investment was strong in 2003, in preparation for the 2004 Athens Olympic Games.

Institutional Context

Economic Context

Recent years have been difficult for Greece, marked by political and socioeconomic crises. The economy went into recession in 2009 and Greece's growth rate slowed to 2.0 percent as a result of the world financial crisis and its impact on access to credit, world trade, and domestic consumption, which was driving growth in Greece. A high fiscal deficit, mounting aging and entitlement costs, and deteriorating competitiveness resulting from higher than Eurozone-average inflation and rigidities in product and labor markets led to market doubts about the sustainability of Greece's public debt. This resulted in increasingly higher borrowing costs and loss of market access that eventually made the IMF and EU leaders' assistance mandatory. Under the adjustment program, Greece has promised to undertake a major fiscal consolidation, implementing substantial structural reforms in order to put its debt on a more sustainable path, and to improve its competitiveness so that the economy can re-enter a positive growth trajectory.

Social Context

The strict measures imposed—including plans to cut public spending and raise taxes—have caused intense distress and a wave of demonstrations in Greece. Protest activity has escalated, leading to widespread social unrest and anti-government sentiment. The formation of the well-known "Indignant Citizens Movement" marked a series of demonstrations that differ from previous ones, since they were mostly peaceful and had no connection to any political or trade union affiliations. The fact that the movement is independent shows citizens' lack of confidence in traditional ways for claiming their rights. More than two-thirds of the Greek population supported the movement, according to recent surveys (MRB, 2011a; Papapostolou, 2011). People believe that the recent economic crisis and their own financial personal crisis have reached such a point that more citizens should take part in the demonstrations. They view the present as full of dead ends, with "no light at the end of the tunnel," while life plans seem unrealistic and institutions (especially the politicians) have been stripped of glamour and have lost their connection with popular sentiment. Participation in demonstrations symbolizes the transition from the individual to collectivity. It is a common belief amongst Greeks that they cannot be well if fellow citizens are not well. Even though some people have not yet been hit by the crisis, they are aware that they may be next in line. At the same time, derogatory comments coming from the international media seem to have hurt their self-esteem and pride, and people feel a strong sense of injustice at the "immorality" of the political class, which has discredited the image of an entire nation (MRB, 2011b).

As a consequence, Greek citizens seem to have little trust not only in the political and financial systems but also in traditional institutions such as the church. They believe that the politicians bear most responsibility for the recent crisis (98.6 percent), followed by trade union leaders (82.7 percent), business people (76 percent), intellectuals (76 percent), and, lastly, the citizens themselves (43.8 percent). Trust levels are also low in international organizations, as 53.6 percent of the citizens express a negative evaluation of the EU's attitude, and 48.9 percent evaluate negatively the European Central Bank's stance (MRB, 2010a). On a similar note, the Greeks' general optimism index shows a negative trend. The percentage of dissatisfied citizens has reached 81.4 percent, while 45.9 percent consider bankruptcy as very likely. The growing number of unemployed has caused fear and 19 percent believe they will lose their job and will have great difficulty in finding another job. Trust has also been lost in the work of the church, an institution that has always played an important role in civic life. A large percentage of citizens feel that the church's charitable work is less than what could be done with the economic resources available to it (MRB, 2010b).

Leadership and Management Styles

Several studies during the 1980s and early 1990s (Bourantas *et al.*, 1990; Bourantas 1988; Papadakis, 1993) reveal that Greek management is characterized by a concentration of power and control in the hands of top management, which in most companies consists of the owners and their relatives, as well as by a lack of modern systems to support strategic decision-making. Compared to foreign subsidiaries, local firms tend to follow less comprehensive or rational processes, rely less on formal rules, and have less hierarchical decentralization. One of the main characteristics of Greek firms is their small size. Figures reveal that 95 percent of the firms employ less than 100 people and only 14 percent of the manufacturing companies have more than 100 employees (ICAP, 2001). Of this 14 percent, only 2 percent employ more than 500 people. These numbers indicate that Greece has the highest percentage of small businesses compared with other members of the EU. The majority of firms in Greece are family-owned, where the manager (who is usually the owner) makes most of the decisions and is reluctant to delegate authority to his subordinates for fear of losing his power. Even in those cases where the firm grows in size and scope, the owner-manager will prefer to hire people from the in-group, who may be inefficient, rather than trust highly skilled professionals who are strangers (Makridakis *et al.*, 1997). This reflects one of the main characteristics of Greek culture: the strong family bonds. Even though this may be changing in the big cities, the extended family is still the norm in Greece. The father is the center of the family; he is responsible for all its members and the one who makes the final decisions. There is a strict hierarchy and younger members are expected to show respect to the older members. Power is concentrated in a few hands, which is usually accepted, although it does not go unquestioned. It is worth mentioning that the gods in Greek mythology do not guide people on what is right or wrong and justice is rather relative. Consequently, humans are never sure whether they have acted properly or not. Greeks are willing to accept their leaders' mistakes, be it mythical gods, contemporary politicians, or members of the social elite (Peridis, 2009).

This is clearly indicated by the relatively high power distance score for Greece (Hofstede, 1980; Koopman *et al.*, 1999). Moreover, Greeks are generally characterized by a low level of trust toward people unless they belong to one's extended family, which can sometimes include close friends as well as relatives. According to an analysis by Triandis and Vassiliou (1972, cited in Georgas, 1993), Greeks showed a high degree of protection, support, and devotion to their in-group, while being hostile and competitive with members outside of it. Georgas (1993) argues that family/in-group collectivism has critically affected the way Greek firms are organized and managed. Similarly, Hofstede's (1980) study revealed a moderate level of collectivism for Greeks. Even now that most families are nuclear, especially in urban areas such as Athens, relationships are not as individualistic as in Western Europe or North America. Family and background (i.e. roots, position, and origin) are basic characteristics for an individual and society places more importance on these than on skills and achievements. Who you know is much more crucial than what you know (Peridis, 2009). This is reflected in the low GLOBE (*Global Leadership* and Organizational Behavior Effectiveness) score (Koopman *et al.*, 1999) for performance orientation in Greek society. Greek society does not encourage high performance and mistrusts those who achieve individual goals. Even in the cases where achievements receive acknowledgment, this is attributed to the individual rather than to the collective. This again is in line with GLOBE results for institutional Collectivism that put Greece last out of 61 countries, implying a very low score. It is true that the Greeks do not work easily in teams. Team spirit and unity can be achieved only in exceptional cases, as shown by Greek history. People usually give little value to any social practice that would foster collective actions, rewards, or share of resources (Peridis, 2009).

Additionally, Greece scored high in the masculinity and uncertainty avoidance dimensions. The former indicates that status and the need for self-esteem are very important for Greeks. Self-esteem originates from the traditional Greek value of *filotimo*—that is, their sense of pride and honor. According to Peridis (2009), the value of *filotimo* is so strong that one has to target someone's pride and honor in order to get anything done in Greece. He argues that the successful organization of the 2004 Olympic Games had its roots in the fact that they had to honor the venue and its Greek origin, and their pride was more important than possessing resources or technical expertise. This value helps employers secure loyalty in their business (Papalexandris, 1992b). In the case of the uncertainty avoidance dimension, Hofstede's research reveals that Greek society gives great weight to security and formal rules, whereas the GLOBE results show the opposite, reflecting acceptance of ambiguity and inconsistency, an opportunistic culture that relies on broadly stated rules and strategies. "There might be a strong honor code in Greece, but everything else is relative" (Peridis, 2009: 125).

Regarding the future orientation dimension, Greece scores lower than most countries in our sample, except Italy. This reluctance for long-term planning is often attributed to continuous political and economic instability, war, and frequent changes in legislation (Makridakis *et al.*, 1997). Arguably, this explains the short-term planning orientation of many Greek firms (Bourantas & Papadakis, 1996).

Nevertheless, there have been many changes during the last couple of decades. Several external environmental forces as well as socio-cultural, political, and economic developments are likely to have affected management and organization in Greek

Table 3.1 Greece, Mediterranean, and Scandinavian countries' rankings on cultural dimensions by Hofstede (in bold) and GLOBE

Dimensions/Countries	Greece countries	Mediterranean countries	Scandinavian
(1) Power distance	**27 M**	**24–34**	**40–51 L**
	21 M	15–20	47–60 L
(2) Uncertainty avoidance	**1 H**	**2–23**	**31–51 L**
	57 L	37–42	2–12 H
(3) Individualism/ Collectivism	**30 M**	**7–33**	**4–17 H**
3.1 Institutional	61 L	46–56	1–20 H
3.2 In-group	35 M	26–41	54–60 L
(4) Masculinity/Femininity	**18 H**	**4–45**	**47–53 L**
4.1 Gender egalitarianism	29 M	15–52	5–31 H/M
4.2 Assertiveness	60 L	11–46	1–18 H
(5) Confucian dynamism/ Future orientation	51 L	37–56	4–14 H
(6) Performance orientation	61 L	37–55	19–48 M
(7) Humane orientation	59 L	41–60	14–38 H/M

Notes
H= High, L=Low, M=Medium.

companies (Bourantas & Papadakis, 1996). International competition from subsidiaries of foreign companies in Greece, as well as pressures from internationalization on small firms to grow, makes family management dysfunctional. Empirical evidences provide some initial support for this argument (Koufopoulos & Morgan, 1994). Specifically, the majority of the largest manufacturing companies as well as commercial and service firms was found to use professional management, which is distinctively different from the way family-owned firms are run. Before the recent crisis, Greek society underwent major changes, with improvements in economic development and education and a relatively stable political environment (Bourantas & Papadakis, 1996). High-quality management education in Greece and opportunities for studying business administration abroad proved that there were many well-equipped, competent young people. Furthermore, a large number of management training programs funded by the EU and the existence of international training companies operating in Greece increased opportunities for learning about new theories and methods. A recent study that compared HRM practices in Greek companies and foreign subsidiaries located in Greece found several differences (Myloni *et al.*, 2004). The results indicated that the effect of national culture on HRM in Greece is quite prominent. HR practices, such as planning, recruitment, and performance appraisal, are aligned to a great extent with the cultural values of Greek society, implying that Greek firms show a high level of embeddedness in their cultural environment. Practices such as the use of recommendations in recruiting employees, the limited long-term HR planning, and the relatively low implementation of performance appraisal practices are still quite widespread, even in larger Greek companies. However, this study also found certain similarities. Performance appraisal practices in both groups of companies were characterized by a less participative, more top-down approach, reflecting the high power distance and respect for authority in Greek society. Moreover, the relatively high use of references and recommendations in selection and the preference for internal recruitment in both groups probably reflect the high level of in-group/family collectivism. This may suggest that foreign subsidiaries have adapted parent company HRM practices to the local environment to some extent and they may reflect high levels of cultural susceptibility and/or sensitivity to cultural differences.

Literature Review on Trust

Several studies on social capital in Greece conclude that generalized (social) trust is rather low. Generalized trust, one of the main elements of social capital (Putnam *et al.*, 1993), is usually measured through questions about the perceived level of trust and trustworthiness among fellow citizens (Paxton, 1999; Newton & Norris, 2000; Beugelsdijk & van Schaik, 2005). Early research on attitudinal differences among executives in five regional clusters placed Greece at the highest point on the suspiciousness v. trust scale, implying low trust levels—the rest being Spain, Central Europe, Scandinavia, and USA (Cummings *et al.*, 1971). In Bjørnskov's (2006) survey about generalized trust, Greece holds thirty-ninth place—tying with Russia—out of 76 countries, while among the 36 European countries, Greece is twenty-second, showing a medium-to-low level of trust. The Scandinavian countries show especially high levels of trust, at least double compared to most countries, while in large central European countries, trust is slightly higher than in Greece, with the exception of France. On the other hand, there has been a significant drop in social trust levels in Greece when the data of the Eurobarometer 25 in 1986 are compared with the European Values Survey in 1999. In particular, the tendency to trust individuals has fallen from 50.2 percent to 23.7 percent. Furthermore, according to data from the European Social Surveys (rounds one and two, 2002–2004),[1] where social trust was measured with a scale for answers from one to ten, Greece has a mean social trust level of 3.64, the lowest of the countries included in the study (Poortinga, 2006).

These results are also in line with relevant research done by Papanis and Roumeliotou (2007), where only 27.2 percent of Greeks trusted their fellow citizens, while the majority (72.8 percent) showed mistrust. They found that the level of education affects trust. University students, postgraduate degree holders, and technical college graduates systematically exhibited higher levels of trust toward their fellow citizens. Lastly, Medrano's survey (2010) led to the design of a world map,[2] which showed

1 Data is archived at the Norwegian Social Science Data Services (NSD) and is accessible via the ESS data website at http://ess.nsd.uib.no.Social trust at the individual level was assessed with three items. People were asked: "Would you say that most people can be trusted, or that you can't be too careful in dealing with people?," "Do you think that most people would try to take advantage of you if they got the chance, or would they try to be fair?," and "Would you say that most of the time people try to be helpful or that they are mostly looking out for themselves?".

2 Based on the answers given by various countries to a specific question that appears in most international surveys of trust, namely: "Do you believe that most people can be trusted or should one be careful when one deals with other people?" The investigation period lasted from 1995 to 2009 and the five value categories ranged from "more careful" (<20), 20–60, 60–100, 100–140, and "greater trust" (> 140).

that in general people do not trust each other, with the exception of the Scandina-vian countries. Greece, like most countries in the world map, belongs to the category of low interpersonal trust (20–60) while, out of the 117 countries included in the survey, Greece is below the mean (seventy-sixth place).

Regarding trust in certain national (e.g. Parliament, police) and international insti-tutions (e.g. European Parliament, the UN), a general feeling of disappointment has been reported (Dodos *et al.*, 1997; Kafetzis, 1997; Kakepaki, 2006). Indica-tive data for Greece can be derived from a series of Eurobarometer surveys con-ducted since 1999 and the findings of the European Social Surveys (fourth round). First, a general lack of confidence of respondents in political institutions, such as politicians, political parties, and the national and European Parliaments, can be observed. Less than a quarter of the population still trusts their own Parliament and approximately 70 percent do not trust it anymore (European Commission, 2010). Regarding international institutions, although the level of trust (42 per-cent) in the European Parliament has sharply deteriorated, it remains significantly higher than that of the national Parliament, while there is a lower tendency to trust the United Nations (23 percent). On the other hand, non-representative institu-tions, such as the police and the legal system, are trusted more than political insti-tutions, albeit declining as well. Finally, there is significant mistrust in big com-panies (79 percent), while only a minority (40 percent) of citizens trust religious institutions compared with a majority three years before the survey (European Commission, 2011).

According to the relevant literature, social trust may be influenced, among other reasons, by the efficiency of the state, the level of corruption, and the type of net-works dominating the political sphere (Putnam *et al.*, 1993). Consequently, the observed decrease in social trust in Greece over the last 20 years may be related to the traditionally dominant role of the state and the development of vertical clien-telistic networks (Sotiropoulos, 2004), the inefficiency of state bureaucracy, and the widespread individualistic behavior observed since the late 1980s (Jones *et al.*, 2008). The interference from special-interest groups and the lack of credibility and impartiality of contemporary political institutions has weakened the strength of Greek civil society, creating distrust and uncertainty.

Similarly, corruption levels have been shown to have a negative correlation with generalized trust (Uslaner, 2003), so that more trust is associated with less corrup-tion. According to the Corruption Perceptions Index of 2006 (CPI), Greece scores lowest among the old European Union states (Lambsdorff, 2007). Several major incidents of corruption uncovered since the late 1980s may have led to greater distrust. Although efforts have been made to introduce transparency mechanisms, mainly in the public sector, they have not yet succeeded in reducing significantly the level of distrust (Panagiotopoulou & Papliakou, 2007). According to a special Eurobarometer on corruption (European Commission, 2012), respondents in Greece have some of the worst impressions of corruption within individual EU Member States. There is a very widely held belief that corruption is a major problem and that it exists at all institutional levels. Greeks are also the most likely of all Europeans to think that corruption is more widespread in their country than elsewhere in the EU, and more likely than most to think that the level has increased and that corruption forms part of their business culture. Furthermore, they are the most likely to believe there is corruption among national politicians (78 percent) and they hold the least positive perceptions of public officials and public sector workers. The belief that national government efforts to combat the problem are not effective is strongest in Greece (86 percent). However, they do think more positively than they did in 2009 about almost all public sector bodies in terms of their involvement in corrupt activities, most notably the police and the judicial system.

Another factor that may be responsible for the low trust levels is the unequal distribution of income, since it can create a sense of injustice, which in turn may negatively affect trust. Research indicates that trust falls when there is wage discrimination based on non-economic factors and trust is higher in "fair" societies (Zak & Knack, 2001). Greece is located approximately in the middle of the economic equality distribution scale, characterized by greater income inequality than the Scandinavian countries and, accordingly, lower trust levels. Furthermore, trust is linked with optimism and control, which depend on income equality. According to Uslaner (2003), people are optimistic and feel in control when the gap between the rich and the poor is narrow. Eurobarometer 74 reveals that only one out of every three people is satisfied with the life they lead, while Greek people are the most pessimistic about the economic and employment situation in their country and the EU (European Commission, 2011).

We have seen that trust levels in Greece are medium or low compared with other countries. However, trust in foreigners is even lower. In a Eurobarometer survey on European values, only 11 percent of the Greek participants valued the importance of maintaining and enhancing tolerance and openness toward others, the lowest of all European countries. Additionally, 70 percent consider globalization as a threat to national culture, 13 percentage points more than the EU 27 average (European Commission, 2007). Most Greeks show signs of xenophobia: 87 percent of the people—the highest percentage out of the European countries included in the survey—have negative attitudes toward migration and 59 percent resent multiculturality (Alipranti-Maratou, 2007). This may be explained in part by the fact that, in the early 1990s, the country suddenly became a host for immigration and many Greek citizens hold immigrants responsible for the increase in unemployment (EKKE, 2003).

At this point, it is worth emphasizing the elusive boundaries between social trust and its Greek substitute, *filotimo*. The Greek version of individualism and free-riding is counterbalanced by the well-publicized notions of *filotimo*. However, being primarily irrational and non-contractual, it cannot be viewed as a convincing substitute for mutual trust. The fundamental characteristic of clientelistic networks is that decisions are based on personal criteria and are not expressions of abstract rules (Tsoukalas, 1995).

Contextual Factors in Hierarchical Trusting Relationships

In our Greek focus group, there are more participants who believe that *people do not trust their managers* than those who think otherwise. Subordinates believe that it is in the Greeks' nature to not trust authorities ("a leftover from the Ottoman rule," as one respondent put it), to consider the manager as impersonal and distant, and they also believe that managers' behavior usually does not inspire trust. Similarly, most managers feel that this is due to a negative bias toward them, while some admit they are not sufficiently accessible and appear cold to their subordinates. One respondent characteristically mentioned that:

> in Greece, given the predominance of favoritism and clientelistic relationships, things are volatile and labor relations are subject to dispute, since it is well known that, in many cases, senior managerial posts are occupied by members unable to defend their position. Therefore, in this case, one might not enjoy the trust of their subordinates.

On the other hand, those who argue that people trust their managers in Greece attribute this to the fact that Greeks are more prone to open communication and showing emotions, and work best when they feel that they are in a familiar environment.

Participants' beliefs regarding *managers' trust in their subordinates* are divided. Subordinates who disagree attribute this to the managers' authoritarian leadership style, which emphasizes strong control and supervision in order to secure good performance, believing that people in general are lazy and do not like working. Similarly, most managers agree that treating subordinates like people who shun responsibility causes distrust and they believe that this may be due to the manager's inability to cooperate, or "their fear that politeness and cooperation may be a sign of weakness."

Respondents classify the cultural traits that characterize Greeks' tendency to trust other people in hierarchical relationships in three general categories. The first category includes neutral characteristics which, when combined with other parameters, will lead or not lead to trust relationships—for example, Greek moral philosophy, the need for interpersonal relationships, and the strong influence of the family institution. The second category includes all those characteristics that lead to mistrust. Both subordinates and managers consider Greeks to be suspicious of people at different hierarchical levels, unruly, refusing to execute orders, and overly competitive, promoting their individual interests and questioning others' superiority. One supervisor said:

> I would say that Greeks are generally characterized by an "inferiority complex" toward people in higher hierarchical positions and this leads them to not trust them. They believe that the power derived from the higher position can easily lead to violating subordinates' rights and putting their own personal ambitions first.

On the contrary, the third category includes all those characteristics that lead to the development of trust, such as extroversion, friendliness, collective action to achieve common goals, respect for institutions and hierarchy, and generosity.

Regarding the concept of collectivism, our respondents showed a slight inclination toward individualism, with an average of 6.5 on a scale ranging from 1 (very collective) to 10 (very individualistic). Once again, respondents' views are balanced. Others believe that individual interests can be satisfied by meeting collective interests. One subordinate noted that "collectivism is more effective for solving problems and furthering social progress, in contrast to individualism, which prevents development." Others believe that individualism is a key element of Greek culture that is implanted at an early age:

> We live in a country that encourages individuality. From early childhood, Greeks learn to act on the basis of personal interest. The "all for one and one for all" is a utopia that may be applicable in Scandinavia and China. But in the Mediterra-

nean, corruption, patronage in the workplace, and insecurity in general lead to a more individualistic way of thinking.

Some managers stress the importance of a balance between these two dimensions and many respondents imply that individualism is a negative element in society. These results are partly in line with previous research discussed in an earlier section that placed Greece in the middle of the individualism/collectivism continuum.

On another note, the majority of focus group participants consider that company size has a strong influence on the trust relationship. They agree that the larger the company is, the less time is spent in manager–subordinate interactions, which in turn hampers communication between individuals. Similarly, interpersonal relationships become more impersonal. The contrary holds true for small companies (family businesses), which is a major factor in Greek business culture and may contribute to the increased levels of trust in our Greek sample. As we have already pointed out, family networks and informal networks (between friends) are regarded as very dense, which could counterbalance the low levels of social trust (Jones *et al.*, 2008).

Personal Factors in Hierarchical Trusting Relationships

Several personal factors in the manager/subordinate interaction, such as the age difference between the two, gender, the manager's academic level, the duration of their relationship, and the tenure in the company, are likely to affect trust relationships. Our quantitative results indicate the relationships shown in Table 3.2.

Subordinates' organizational citizenship behaviors seem to be more positively affected by the manager's age, less by the age difference between the two, and negatively affected by the manager's academic level. Additionally, the table shows that managers' trust in subordinates is more influenced by the manager's age and much less influenced by the subordinate's gender.

Our focus group respondents claimed there are many reasons why, according to our data, *the older the manager is, the more likely he/she is to trust subordinates and the higher the level of their OCB will be.* A manager's experience makes him/her

Table 3.2 Greece: significant controls (correlations)

	Manager's age	Subordinate's gender (1-> man, 2-> woman)	Manager's academic level	Age difference between manager and subordinate
MTB				
OCB	0.281**		−0.248**	0.233*
MTS	0.317**	0.180*		
STM				

Notes
** Correlation significant at 0.01 level.
* Correlation significant at 0.05 level.
MTB = managerial trustworthy behavior, STM = subordinates' trust in managers, MTS = managers' trust in subordinates, OCB = organizational citizenship behavior.

more capable of assessing the subordinate's value and deciding whether to trust or not. "With experience, you learn that the more you trust your subordinates, the higher their performance and zest for work will be." Furthermore, older managers tend not to engage in competing with their associates and this makes it easier to trust them. It is also plausible that managers close to retirement want to leave a worthy replacement. Again, according to the respondents, manager experience plays a significant role in inducing the development of OCB in subordinates. It enables managers to recognize the importance of a cooperative atmosphere and to assess subordinates' efforts, understand their capabilities, and delegate appropriate responsibilities. Moreover, subordinates suggested that they can benefit from their managers' experience to help them improve. High OCB could also be explained by the higher degree of respect shown to the manager because of his/her age. "For subordinates, this behavior may be due to respect for their supervisor's age, knowledge, and experience, and they want to prove themselves worthy of it." For some, it is important to be acknowledged by a more experienced person with potentially high prestige, so they strive to prove their worthiness.

On the other hand, both managers' and subordinates' views are divided regarding the finding that *the manager's higher academic level leads to less OCB by the subordinate*. Approximately half of the respondents in each groupwere surprised by this result; they thought that the more educated a manager was, the easier it would be to inspire OCB. Simultaneously, subordinates would show higher levels of trust toward higher-educated managers, since the managers' knowledge enables them to give better guidance and at the same time become a role model for subordinates. However, being more educated does not mean being more capable of managing others. Emotional intelligence—that is, being able to handle emotions, speak effectively and appropriately, and give people the opportunity to work together smoothly and harmoniously in order to achieve common goals—is twice as important as purely cognitive abilities for successful performance of the job (Goleman, 2000). Consequently, it is likely that the more educated managers in our quantitative research have not developed the necessary emotional intelligence to generate OCB in their subordinates. Furthermore, those not surprised by this result pointed out that subordinates leave initiatives and important decisions and actions in the hands of highly educated managers and are content to just execute orders. This can happen either because subordinates rely on managers' capabilities or because managers constrain them. Finally, many (mostly subordinates) believe that the more educated somebody is, the more arrogant they become, making them unable to win subordinates' trust. "Highly educated supervisors are usually characterized by centralization. They believe that everything should pass through their hands, and this constrains trust development within their subordinates," one respondent highlighted. Both managers and subordinates agree that gender difference is less likely to affect trust levels.

On the other hand, there is a significant difference between the two sides regarding the duration of the relationship as a factor influencing trust building. While 100 percent of the subordinates consider it to be an important factor, confirming that trust takes time to develop, only 64.28 percent of managers agree. According to both sides, time improves communication and collaboration, since one side comes to know the other side's strengths and weaknesses. Similarly, most participants believe that tenure in the company is a key factor for the development of trust.

For many, trust is something earned and acquired over time, so factors such as the duration of relationship between me and my boss, as well as length of tenure, will certainly affect trust to some extent. When a charismatic leader is receptive to new ideas, he can inspire his subordinates regardless gender and age.

Antecedents and Outcomes of Manager–Subordinate Trust

According to our survey, most subordinates and managers had a similar perception of what constituted a good working relationship. More specifically, smooth

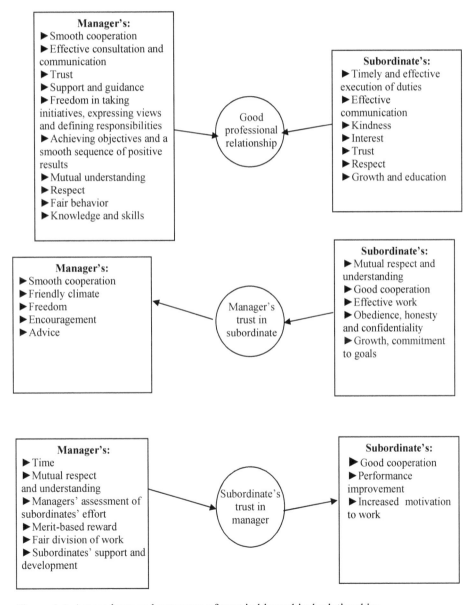

Figure 3.1 Antecedents and outcomes of trust in hierarchical relationships

cooperation and effective consultation–communication were the most important characteristics of a good relationship for the subordinates. Trust came second, while manager support and guidance, freedom in taking initiatives, expressing views and problems, defining responsibilities and, lastly, achieving objectives and a smooth sequence of positive results are mentioned less frequently. Subordinates consider the development of trust as the most crucial prerequisite for achieving a good professional relationship. Mutual understanding and respect, and the manager's fair behavior, knowledge, and skills are also important. Some quotes include: "… consistency from both sides as to the rights and obligations arising from the employment relationship"; "the supervisor has to be right and have professional skills and experience in the field, to be fair and know the daily performance of his subordinates."

Smoothness and efficiency of daily tasks, as well as effective communication, are equally important elements that characterize such a relationship for the managers. Regarding the antecedents, we noticed the existence of two groups. The first focuses on subordinate behavior, stressing the importance of timely and effective execution of duties, as well as interest, effective communication, kindness, etc. The other group focuses on interactive relations, such as trust, communication, respect, subordinate's growth and education, as well as the manager's fair behavior.

A good work relationship can be mainly achieved through good communication. Communication regarding both the way that one handles each task, and if there is any problem, to deal with it. Requirements include the discussion of any problems and joint decisions on this, as teamwork particularly helps work effectiveness.

A prerequisite of this is that both manager and subordinate are on the same page on work issues.

Compared to subordinates, managers focus more on others' behavior as a prerequisite for a good professional relationship. Characteristically, one of them argues that "subordinates must respect work and my efforts, achieve their objectives within the specified timeframe with minimal intervention on my part. In addition, they must have a good character and be an active member of the group they belong to."

Most subordinates show trust in their manager from the beginning of their professional relationship, mainly because their superiors had established a strong reputation for their skills, or because they knew them personally before starting their professional relationship. On the contrary, most managers do not initially trust the subordinate and take time to build such a relationship. "Trust is built day by day, through daily cooperation and friction. It is not required, nor can it be obtained by force." However, there are managers who show trust from the beginning of the relationship, either because they knew them before hiring or because they believe trust is necessary in order to motivate them to act accordingly and become more effective at work. Some of their comments include: "I had confidence from the start. If you show them that you trust them, they make effort to not betray the trust given" and "Initially, you trust your subordinate, so he has an incentive to act accordingly."

According to subordinates' views, trust can be developed through daily activities within a timeframe. Mutual respect and understanding are needed in order to build a relationship of trust.

Trust takes time to build, through the daily interaction between superiors and subordinates. For example, the supervisor begins to trust the subordinate when one is precise in one's work and achieves the objectives assigned. Correspondingly, the subordinate expects the boss to be fair both in the division of labor and the rewards. Therefore, in order to create trust, it is essential for each side to show respect for the other side's personality and integrity.

Managers' assessment of subordinates' effort, merit-based reward, fair division of work, and support and development of subordinates' abilities are also considered important. Summarizing the above, fair and reliable behavior on the part of the manager is essential for building trust in the subordinate.

Managers consider time the most important factor for developing trust. Mutual understanding, mutual respect, and good cooperation are also identified as key antecedents. Furthermore, managers consider that it is important that subordinates have qualities such as effectiveness in the execution of their duties, obedience, confidentiality, honesty, initiative and action when a problem is detected, and commitment to goals and personal growth. "Trust development is based on how subordinates approach their duties. Being correct and consistent, following the rules and conditions defined, and showing goodwill are all necessary in order to build trust." Notably, there were only a few managers who believed that their own responsible (fair) behavior (i.e. treating all employees as equal partners, developing subordinates' abilities and providing continuous learning) was a prerequisite for creating trust.

Managers' trust in subordinates may affect their behavior. It can result in smooth cooperation and a friendly working climate, greater freedom of movement and less control, as well as specific reliable behaviors, such as giving encouragement and advice, taking into account personal problems, and having confidence in the subordinate's abilities. Similarly, subordinates' trust could induce good cooperation, improved performance, and increased motivation to work.

The Dynamics of Trust in Hierarchical Relationships

Table 3.3 shows the quantitative results obtained for Greece. According to this table, the strongest relationship is the positive influence of managerial trustworthy behavior on subordinates' trust in managers. The next strongest confirmed relationship is the positive influence of managers' trust in subordinates on managerial trustworthy behavior and OCB is positively associated with manager trust in subordinates. Finally, subordinates' trust in managers is positively correlated, but to a lesser extent, with OCB. Comparing the Greek scores with the total scores, we note that only the relationship between OCB and MTS is less strong. Although the dynamics of trust between managers and subordinates is not symmetrical, relationships among variables are strong, even in the case of STM, leading to OCB.

The positive relationship between MTB and STM is confirmed by the examples of managerial behavior mentioned by our focus group subordinates, which led them to develop trust. These include reliable and trustworthy behaviors by managers, such as showing impartiality toward subordinates, offering help to solve their problems at work, developing and supporting them, providing information on company

Table 3.3 Standardized regression weights for the trust model in Greece and the overall sample

	OCB–>MTS	MTS–>MTB	MTB–>STM	STM–>OCB
Greece only	0.48**	0.48*	0.91**	0.28*
Complete model	0.68**	0.34**	0.89**	0.08*

Notes
** Regression weight significant at 0.01 level.
* Regression weight significant at 0.05 level.

issues, taking initiative and pointing out mistakes for the subordinates' protection and improvement, and exercising limited control. On the other side, the examples given by managers indicate two groups of subordinate behaviors which lead them to build a trusting relationship: behaviors defined by the work role and actions that go beyond work duties.

The first group includes effective handling of difficult situations, addressing responsibilities with formality, accepting mistakes, providing effective training for new employees, and achieving goals. The second group includes behaviors such as willingness to help the company and colleagues even in situations beyond their responsibilities, dealing with matters concerning the company but not included in their tasks, a desire to develop good work relations, a constant search for solutions for the company's benefit, a constant search for innovation, and, finally, a willingness to work beyond normal working hours, even when this is not paid. All of these behaviors reinforce the positive relationship between OCB and MTS.

On the other hand, according to our subordinates focus group, behaviors that made them aware of their manager's trust in them include the assignment of important and progressively more demanding tasks, the exercise of limited control, and showing respect and interest in their views on important matters. These are also considered fair and reliable behaviors, supporting the positive association between MTS and MTB. Furthermore, managers recognize subordinates' trust by their respect for the managers' views, honesty, interest in their work, assuming responsibilities, initiative, discussing their work and personal problems, good performance, and not questioning orders.

Discussion and Conclusions

Events that have occurred in Greece's history have played a significant role in shaping the factors influencing trust. The almost 400 years of slavery to the Ottoman Empire, the German occupation during the Second World War, the obstacles continuously created by foreign nations, and their economic exploitation by granting loans under onerous terms have all shaped Greeks' skepticism toward foreigners. The heavy-handed intervention of foreign forces in the fate of the Greek state has probably influenced the modern Greeks' trust in foreign nations through stereotypes passed down from one generation to the next. At the same time, it is reasonable to expect that Greeks would show low levels of trust in state power, since Greek history is dominated by conflict between various governmental groups—not for the good of the nation, but for their own interests—or by serious mistakes with disastrous consequences. The disputes and the inability of Greek authorities to look after the interests of the country and its people have created distrust in their leaders. On the contrary, people seem to have more trust in the Greek people, with the idea that only the people can reverse negative situations. Finally, the civil war and the military dictatorship from 1967 influenced people's trust in people or groups with a different political ideology.

In recent years, Greece has experienced acute political, social, and economic difficulties, with the country immersed in an economic crisis. Greek citizens seem to distrust political and economic authorities and traditional institutions. They also show little trust for the support provided by European and global organizations. Trust in all political parties is low. Negative social issues, such as rising unemployment and corruption, cause citizens to lose faith in governments and institutions and also in themselves, since they consider that they too are responsible for this situation. Greece exhibits medium to low levels of social trust compared with many countries worldwide. This may be influenced, among other things, by the state's inefficiency, the level of corruption, and the type of networks dominating the political sphere, as well as income inequality.

Our quantitative research has shown that the strongest positive relationship is between managers' fair behavior and subordinates' trust in managers. The next strongest confirmed relationship is the positive influence between managers' trust in subordinates and managers' fair behavior. There is also a positive association between OCB and managers' trust in subordinates. Finally, subordinates' trust in managers is positively correlated, but to a lesser extent, with OCB. According to our qualitative study, the behaviors that lead to trust development, the descriptions of what is essential and the attitudes developed because of the existence of trust, leave little doubt as to the validity of these assumptions.

Our study has found that a good working relationship between subordinates and superiors is characterized by smooth cooperation, effective communication, and trust. Furthermore, unlike supervisors, most subordinates show trust from the beginning of their professional relationship. Gender has been found to have little effect on the development of trust, while company size, the duration of the relationship between manager and subordinate, and length of tenure are very important factors in building trust. Finally, many more subordinates than managers believe that their country's culture affects trust. More specifically, most believe that, in Greece, people do not trust their managers. When asked if people trust their subordinates, the respondents were divided. The most important cultural traits that characterize Greeks' tendency to trust other people is suspicion of hierarchy and the need for interpersonal relations. Both subordinates and managers agree that the older the manager is, the more easily he/she will trust the subordinate and the more likely it is that subordinates will exhibit OCB. Respondents are divided on the finding that subordinates are less likely to show OCB to more highly educated managers. Finally, respondents ranked Greece as a country that tends toward individualism.

Distrust or lack of trust between managers and subordinates creates problems in work effectiveness for both, as it prevents communication and fair behaviors, such as those proposed by our model. The development of trust between managers and subordinates affects both sides' efficiency in achieving the company's objectives. Therefore, development of trust is a necessary condition for both the employee's and the company's growth.

References

Alipranti-Maratou, L. (2007). Migration to Greece: A new type and emerging problems. In E. Close, M. Tsianikas & G. Couvalis (eds), *Greek Research in Australia: Proceedings of the Sixth Biennial International Conference of Greek Studies, Flinders University, June 2005*, Flinders University Department of Languages, Modern Greek: Adelaide, pp. 185–198.

Beugelsdijk, S. & van Schaik, T. (2005). Differences in social capital between 54 Western European regions. *Regional Studies*, 39(8): 1053–1064.

Bjørnskov, C. (2006). Determinants of generalized trust: A cross-country comparison. *Public Choice*, 130: 1–21.

Bourantas, D. (1988). Leadership styles, need, satisfaction and the organisational commitment of Greek managers. *Scandinavian Journal of Management*, 3(3): 121–134.

Bourantas, D. & Papadakis, V. (1996). Greek management. *International Studies of Management and Organization*, 26(3): 13–32.

Bourantas, D. *Anagnostelis, J., Mantes, Y. & Kefalas, A.G.* (1990). Culture gap in Greek management. *Organisation Studies*, 11(2): 261–283.

Clogg, R. (1992). *A Concise History of Greece.* Cambridge: Cambridge University Press.

Cummings, L.L., Harnett, D.L. & Stevens, O.J. (1971). Risk, fate, conciliation and trust: An international study of attitudinal differences among executives. *The Academy of Management Journal*, 14(3): 285–304.

Dodos, D., Kafetzis, P. & Nikolakopoulos, E. (1996). Elections 1996: Dimensions of political behavior and political culture. *Greek Review of Social Research* (in Greek), 92–93: 241–266.

EKKE (National Centre for Social Research) (2003). *Ελλάδα–Ευρώπη, Κοινωνία–Πολιτική–Αξίες. ποτελέσματα της μεγάλης Ευρωπαϊκής Κοινωνικής Έρευνας* (European Social Survey–ESS). Athens: EKKE.

European Commission (2007). European Cultural Values. *Special Eurobarometer No. 278.*

European Commission (2010). *Standard Eurobarometer No. 73.*

European Commission (2011). Standard Eurobarometer No. 74.

European Commission (2012). Corruption. *Special Eurobarometer No 374.* Retrieved on 1.3.2012 from http://ec.europa.eu/public_opinion/archives/ebs/ebs_374_en.pdf.

European Values Study Group and World Values Survey Association, EVS (2006). *European and World Values Surveys Four-Wave Integrated Data File, 1981–2004, v.20060423, 2006,* www.worldvaluessurvey.org.

Georgas, J. (1993). Management in Greece. In D.J. Hickson (ed.), *Management in Western Europe: Society, Culture and Organization in Twelve Nations.* Berlin: Walter de Gruyter, pp. 109–124.

Goleman D. (2000). *Emotional Intelligence at the Workplace* (in Greek), 3rd edition. Athens: Ellinika Grammata.

History of the Greek Nation (1975). Athens: Ekdotiki Athinon.

Hofstede, G. (1980). *Culture's Consequences: International Differences in Work-Related Values.* Beverly Hills, CA: Sage.

ICAP (2001). *Greek Financial Directory 2001: Greece in Figures.* Athens: ICAP.

Jones, N., Malesios, C., Iosifides, T. & Sophoulis, C. (2008). Social capital in Greece: Measurement and comparative perspectives. *South European Society and Politics*, 13(2): 175–193.

Kafetzis, P. (1997). Political communication, political participation and political crises: The contribution of a two-phase empirical research. *Greek Political Science Review* (in Greek), 9: 168–178.

Kakepaki, M. (2006). Changes in the Greek political culture, 1998–2005: From the generation of political interest to the generation of political disinterest. *Greek Political Science Review* (in Greek), 28: 111–128.

Koopman, P.L., Den Hartog D.N., Konrad, E.& et al. (1999). National culture and leadership profiles in Europe: Some results from the GLOBE study. *European Journal of Work and Organizational Psychology*, 8(4): 503–520.

Koufopoulos, D.N. & Morgan, N.A. (1994). Competitive pressures force Greek entrepreneurs to plan. *Long Range Planning*, 27(4): 12–124.

Lambsdorff, J.G. (2007). Corruption perceptions index. In D. Rodriguez & L. Ehrichs (eds), *Corruption Report 2007*. Transparency International, Cambridge University Press, Cambridge, pp. 324–330.

Makridakis, S., Caloghirou, Y., Papagiannis L. & Trivellas, P. (1997). The dualism of Greek firms and management: Present state and future implications. *European Management Journal*, 15(4): 381–402.

Medrano, J.D. (2010). *World Map of Interpersonal Trust*. Retrieved on 15.5.2011 from www. jdsurvey.net/jds/jdsurveyMaps.jsp?Idioma=I&SeccionTexto=0404&NOID=104.

MRB (2010a). *MRB Poll May 2010* (in Greek). Retrieved on 20.5.2011 fromwww.mrb.gr/Mrb/media/RN05-06-05-2010.pdf.

MRB (2010b). *MRB Poll September 2010* (in Greek). Retrieved on 20.5.2011 from www.mrb. gr/Mrb/media/RN-09-09-09-2010.pdf.

MRB (2011a). *The Citizen in Crisis –Indignant Citizens Movement* (in Greek). Retrieved on 22.12.2011 fromwww.mrb.gr/Mrb/media/TRENDS_JUN_2011_Ο%20ΠΟΛΙΤΗΣ%20ΣΤΗ Ν%20ΚΡΙΣΗ%20&%20ΚΙΝΗΜΑ%20ΑΓΑΝΑΚΤΙΣΜΕΝΩΝ%20ΠΟΛΙΤΩΝ.pdf.

MRB (2011b). *Indignant Citizens Movement – Qualitative Survey Findings* (in Greek). Retrieved on 22.12.2011 from www.mrb.gr/Mrb/media/TRENDS_JUN_2011_ΠΟΙΟΤΙΚΗ%20ΕΡΕΥ ΝΑ%20ΓΙΑ%20ΑΓΑΝΑΚΤΙΣΜΕΝΟΥΣ.pdf.

Myloni, B., Harzing, A.-W. & Mirza, H. (2004). Human resource management in Greece: Have the colours of culture faded away? *International Journal of Cross-Cultural Management*, 4(1): 59–76.

Newton, K. & Norris, P. (2000). Confidence in public institutions: Faith, culture, or performance? In R. Putnam and S.J. Pharr (eds), *Disaffected Democracies: What's Troubling the Trilateral Countries?* Princeton, NJ: Princeton University Press, pp. 52–73.

OECD (1994). *OECD Reviews of Foreign Direct Investment: Greece.* Paris: OECD.

Panagiotopoulou, R. & Papliakou, V. (2007). Facets of social capital formation in Greece. In T. Kafetzis, T. Maloutas & I. Tsiganou (eds), *Politics, Society and Citizens: Data Analysis of the European Social Survey– ESS* (in Greek). EKKE, Athens, pp. 220–267.

Papadakis, V. (1993). *An Empirical Foundation of Strategic Investment Decision-Making Processes: Contextual Influence on Process Characteristics.* Unpublished Ph.D. thesis, University of London, London Business School.

Papalexandris, N. (1992a). Greece. In C. Brewster, T. Lockhart, L. Holden & A. Hegewish (eds), *The European Human Resource Management Guide.* London: Academic Press Limited, pp. 229–260.

Papalexandris, N. (1992b). Human resource management in Greece. *Employee Relations*, 14(4): 38–52.

Papanis, E. & Roumeliotou, M. (2007). Can social trust and participation be reinforced through education? Empirical data from Greece. *Journal of Education and Human Development*, 1(2), retrieved on 1.3.2012 from www.scientificjournals.org/journals2007/articles/1258.pdf.

Papapostolou, A. (2011). Recent study shows strong support for "indignant citizens movement". *Greek Reporter*, accessed on 22.12.2011 from http://greece.greekreporter.com/2011/06/25/recent-study-shows-strong-support-for-indignant-citizens-movement/.

Paxton, P. (1999). Is social capital declining in the United States? A multiple indicator assessment. *American Journal of Sociology*, 105: 88–127.

Peridis, T. (2009). Cultural mythology and global leadership in Greece. In E.H. Kessler, & D.J. Wong-MingJi (eds), *Cultural Mythology and Global Leadership*. Cheltenham, UK: Edward Elgar, pp. 111–126.

Poortinga, W. (2006). Social capital: An individual or collective resource for health? *Social Science and Medicine*, 62: 292–302.

Putnam, R., Leonardi, R. & Nanetti, R.Y. (1993). *Making Democracy Work: Civic Traditions in Modern Italy*. Princeton, NJ: Princeton University Press.

Skoulatou, V., Dimakopoulou, N. & Kondi, S. (2003). *Modern and Contemporary History of Greece 1789-1909* (in Greek), Volume 1. Athens: National Organization of Educational Publications.

Sotiropoulos, D.A. (2004). Southern European public bureaucracies in comparative perspective. *West European Politics*, 27(3); 405–422.

Tsoukalas, C. (1995). Free riders in Wonderland or of Greeks in Greece. In D. Constas and T.G. Stavrou (eds), *Greece Prepares for the Twenty-First century.* Baltimore, MD: Johns Hopkins University Press, pp. 191–219.

Uslaner E. (2003). *Trust and Economic Growth in the Knowledge Society.* Conference on Social Capital, Cabinet of the Government of Japan, March 24–25, Tokyo, Japan.

Zak, P.J. and Knack, S. (2001). Trust and growth. *The Economic Journal*, 111: 295–321.

4 Manager–Subordinate Trust Relationships in Norway

TOR GRENNESS

Introduction

Norway occupies the western half of the Scandinavian peninsula. Two-thirds of Norway is mountainous, and it has a 2000-kilometer coastline. Norway today has a population close to five million, and most of its population is concentrated in the coastal areas and the southern part of the country. In fact, as much as 81 percent of the country is completely uninhabited. The capital of Norway is Oslo, and close to one third of the total population is to be found in and around the larger metropolitan area of the city. Historically, Norway has been joined to both Denmark (from 1380 to 1814) and Sweden (from 1814 to 1905). Particularly as a result of the long union with Denmark, the Norwegian language inevitably became influenced by Danish, and although the Norwegians wanted to eradicate any remaining Danish influence after independence in 1905, the two languages are still pretty similar. Norwegians and Danes understand each other well. The same goes for Norwegians and Swedes. Unlike its two Scandinavian neighbors, Norway is not a member of the European Union. The proposal to apply for membership was rejected in two referendums, in 1972 and 1994. The reasons why Norway has decided to stay outside the Union are mixed, but it has been proposed that a high proportion of the electorate voted against joining the EU on the grounds of Norway's economic strength and a common suspicion of a union strongly influenced by Latin countries, among other reasons (Schramm-Nielsen *et al.*, 2004).

The Norwegian business culture is commonly described as flat and non-hierarchical. Not much research has been done on the Norwegian business culture in particular, but most of what has been written about the Scandinavian business culture is also applicable to Norway. This means that the Norwegian business culture can be characterized as cooperation- and consensus-oriented, the relationship between managers and subordinates is marked by a low power distance, egalitarianism, informality, direct communication, decency, and conflict avoidance (Schramm-Nielsen *et al.*, op. cit.), and the egalitarian attitude can also be seen in the low spread in wages and salaries. Indeed, a cross-cultural study performed by the American consultancy Towers Perrin (2000) shows that Norway's salary gaps are among the lowest in the world. Also, the typical Norwegian manager will invariably credit the team for successful results, knowing that he would be ill-advised to take the credit alone. Based on a replication of the methods used in the GLOBE (2004) study, results for Norway show that Norwegian managers score high on the humane dimension, equally high on gender egalitarianism and low on assertiveness and performance orientation, which means that values such as altruism, benevolence, and promoting equal opportunities are positively loaded, while emphasis on results and showing a tough, dominant behavior are negatively loaded (Warner-Søderholm, 2010).

It is also to be noted that the Norwegian labor market is regulated by The Working Environment Act, legislation promoting workplace democracy, and collective agreements between business and labor (trade unions) A centralized bargaining system (a three-sided bargaining between the state, employers, and employees) is combined with negotiations at company level to set wages, hours, and working conditions under the parameters determined in the central bargaining process. Because of this strict regulation, which also affects the relationship between managers and subordinates, managers' prerogatives are perhaps fewer in Norway than in most other countries.

Together with its Scandinavian neighbors, Norway has developed a uniquely Scandinavian welfare state. It may be argued that the Norwegian welfare state grew out of specific historical conditions. Some pinpoint the relative homogeneity in terms of ethnicity, language, and religion (Baldwin, 1997), and argue that this made it easier to develop a welfare state that covered all citizens. Others refer to the egalitarian class structure as a facilitator of social alliances between the workers and the rural periphery and a political alliance between the labor party and the political center (Esping-Andersen, 1985).

With these introductory remarks, we will continue this chapter by providing a short account of historical developments in Norway, along with a description of the contemporary institutional environment, in particular, the educational, legal, and social systems, as well as an overview of the current economic and social context. We follow with a summary of human resource management practices and developments, and preferred leadership styles. We then move into the substantive area of trust. The literature on multiple aspects of trust relationships—both in the workplace and in society as a whole—is reviewed, followed by the empirical results for Norway based on the cross-cultural study of manager–subordinate trust. The chapter ends with a discussion of the Norwegian results and highlights potential implications for management and leadership practice, along with potential avenues for future research.

Highlights of Manager–Subordinate Trust in Norway

- Norway is definitely a high-trust society. Results from, for example, the World Values Study show that Norway ranks highest of all participating countries when it comes to social trust ("most people can be trusted").
- Managers' trust in subordinates and subordinates' trust in managers rely on a perception of the other party as fair, open, competent, reliable, and concerned.

- While subordinates' trust in managers is of a general type (character), managers' trust in subordinates is of a more specific nature (i.e. trust in skills and competence).
- Female subordinates find it easier to trust a male manager than trust a female manager.
- Both men and women find it easier to trust managers who are older than themselves. The reason given was that older managers were perceived as more experienced and competent.
- This, however, was not the case with managers. Subordinates' age was not important. Again, this may be explained by the more specific nature of managers' trust in their subordinates.
- Length of service is also important. Trust in managers is generally higher among subordinates who have many years' experience in one organization.
- Probably the most important factor for a subordinate's trust in a manager is consistency in the manager's behavior.
- While statements that indicated the importance of benevolence were not untypical among the subordinates, the managers included in the study made no statements referring to benevolence or affect-based trust.
- To be trusted by your manager is decisive for subordinates' motivation and commitment.
- In order to build a lasting trusting relationship between managers and subordinates, developing a high-trust organization culture seems crucial.

Historical Perspective

It is well known that Vikings from Norway raided Scotland, England, Ireland, and France during the ninth century. They even went as far south as Spain, which at that time was in Muslim hands. Following their raids, the Vikings established settlements in the Hebrides (islands west of Scotland), Shetland, and Orkney islands. They also settled on the Isle of Man, as well as Iceland and Greenland (the name Greenland was given by the early settlers to attract people from Norway).

However, in the ninth century, Norway was divided into several kingdoms. Near the end of the century (872 to be exact), Harald Fairhair gained control of the western coast and called himself king of Norway, but it was not until almost 200 years later that the king was in fact the king of the whole of Norway. In 1066, King Harald Hardrada tried to make himself king of England too, but he was killed in the battle of Stamford Bridge. His army fled, and that ended any Norwegian political involvement with England (the Hebrides and the Isle of Man were later sold to the Scottish king).

In 1319, Norway was temporarily united with Sweden and, in 1397, Norway was united to both Denmark and Sweden through the so-called Kalmar Union. Sweden broke away in 1523, but Norway remained united with Denmark until 1814. As a consequence of being on the losing side of the Napoleonic wars, Denmark was forced to surrender Norway to Sweden in January 1814. The Norwegian–Swedish union continued until 1905, when Norway once more gained full independence. In this sense, Norway is exceptional among the Scandinavian countries in having been an independent state only for short periods of time from around the year 1000 until 1319 and again after 1905.

During the First World War, Norway remained neutral. However, as a result of unrestricted German submarine warfare, half of the Norwegian merchant fleet was sunk and about 2000 Norwegian sailors lost their lives. On April 9, 1940, the Germans invaded Norway and the occupation lasted until May 1945. The Norwegian King Haakon, who had been in exile in Britain, returned. Norway is a constitutional monarchy, and the present King Harald succeeded his father, King Olav, in 1991.

Present Norway has a population of five million people, occupies a territory of 324,000 square kilometers and comprises 20 counties (fylker). Norway has two official written languages and, in addition, the Norwegian government has an obligation to ensure that the Sami people can maintain and develop their own language, culture, and way of life.

Institutional Context

Economic Context

It took Norway less than 80 years to transform itself from a rather poor country to one of the most affluent in the world. In spite of the fact that industrialization came later to Norway than to most of Western Europe, the fact that Norway had a plentiful supply of natural resources such as minerals, timber, fish stocks, and, not least, hydroelectric power, and a world-class merchant fleet, helped fuel economic growth. By the 1970s, oil and, some years later, gas from the North Sea had contributed to make Norway one of the wealthiest countries in the world, in terms of GDP per capita (US$ 55,200). At the same time, Norway has developed a particular variety of capitalism, which partly explains Norway's egalitarian state policies and its universalistic welfare system. Historically, the Norwegian economy has lacked large, dominating firms in production and credit supply and, instead, is characterized by many small and medium-sized enterprises. As a consequence of this, the state had to step in to safeguard emerging industries, investing heavily in infrastructure and assisting in the establishment of a national banking system (Gulbrandsen, 2007). The state had thus to compensate for the absence of an "organized capitalism" and became a senior partner to private business. This model has been characterized by a leading Norwegian historian as "democratic capitalism" (Sejersted, 1993)—that is, a state-dominated capitalism tempered by small-scale enterprises and strong norms of popular legitimization. This is particularly evident today, as the state is the major shareholder of the largest oil company (Statoil), the largest bank (Den Norske Bank, DNB), the largest technological company (Telenor), and so forth.

Social Context

Life expectancy at birth currently stands at 80 years in Norway. The total fertility rate is among the highest in Europe (1.78 children per woman in 2010), compared to the EU average of 1.5. Norway is an extensive welfare state (Esping-Andersen,

1990), which means that it differs from the two other main families of welfare states which exist in Europe: the conservative welfare regimes, which are mainly found on the continent, and the liberal welfare regimes, which are found in the UK and Ireland. Among the features of the Norwegian welfare state, it offers citizens:

- a universal system of relatively generous social benefits related to unemployment, sickness, disability, old age, etc.
- an extensive family policy which favors gender equality
- a basic minimum pension for all citizens and income-related supplementary pensions based on years of employment and income
- extensive public health and social services.

(Halvorsen & Stjernø, 2008)

Political and Legal Systems

Norway is a constitutional monarchy. The Norwegian Constitution was signed and dated on May 17, 1814. Today, it is the oldest single-document national constitution in Europe which is still in force. May 17 is now the National Day of Norway. Under the terms of the Constitution, the king himself chooses a Council from among Norwegian citizens entitled to vote. In real terms, however, they are chosen on the basis of political criteria within the Parliament (Storting), from among the political parties included in the parliamentary system, which has been operating since 1864.

The Norwegian National Assembly is called the Storting. Until 2009, the Parliament was a qualified unicameralism with two chambers, the Lagting and the Odelsting. Following the 2009 elections (the next elections will take place in 2013), seven parties are represented in Parliament: the Labor Party (64 representatives), the Progress Party (41), the Conservative Party (30), the Socialist Left Party (11), the Centre Party (11), the Christian Democrat Party (10), and the Liberal Party (2), giving 169 representatives in all. The age for suffrage is 18 (16 will be tested in selected counties in the next elections). State power is formally distributed between the Storting (the legislative power), the government (the executive power), and the courts (the judicial power). The main courts of justice in Norway are: the Supreme Court, the Jury courts, and the District courts. All can rule on both civil and criminal cases.

Educational System

Education in Norway is mandatory for all children aged 6–16. It is estimated that the illiteracy rate for adults (15+) is 0 percent. Public expenditure on education amounts to 16.2 percent of the GDP (2007). The Norwegian school system can be divided into three parts: elementary school (age 6–13), lower secondary school (age 13–16), and upper secondary school (age 16–19). Secondary education in Norway is primarily based on public schools. In 2007, 93 percent of upper secondary school students attended public schools.

Higher education is broadly divided into universities and university colleges. Again, higher education is also based on public institutions, the fraction of students attending private institutions being only about 10 percent. The ECTS credit system was introduced at the beginning of the century and is now used in all Norwegian higher education institutions.

HR Practices

HR policies in Norway were restructured in the present decade for the benefit of both employees and the companies' management. Most companies seem to feel the need to enhance employee productivity to ensure the company's wellbeing. As such, HR policies favoring employee retention are required by companies in order to be profitable, as well as to maintain their reputation.

The Norwegian labor market is characterized by its large public sector; Norway has one of the highest employment rates in Europe, and the participation of women in the labor force is among the highest in the world. The most common working conditions are 37.5 hours of work a week with five weeks holiday. The minimum hourly wage for unskilled workers is NOK 118 (approx. US$ 20). In Norway, there are strict HR policies against any sort of discrimination, be it in the form of gender discrimination or racial discrimination.

As is the case in most European companies, more sophisticated HR practices have been implemented recently in larger Norwegian firms. In particular, the emphasis on strategic HRM—that is, the needto align HR policy and practices with the company's strategy—has received a lot of attention during the last decade. Even so, the most central HR issue in Norway has been compensation practices. In spite of the fact that Norway is commonly labeled as having an individualistic culture, compensation practices tend to be of a more collectivistic nature. Group bonuses are broadly preferred to individual bonuses. Traditionally, in Norway (as in the other Scandinavian countries), pay has been based on collective agreements between employers and unions (Rogaczevska *et al.*, 2004). And even if "the winds of globalization" can be felt in Norway, performance measurement and merit-based compensation practices are still met with skepticism—sometimes open opposition—in Norway. This is partly due also to the fact that unions seem to have strengthened their influence in work organizations, and although union attitudes toward pay based on individual performance have softened over the years, in principle, collective agreements are still preferred.

Leadership Style

Norwegians value the specialized knowledge brought by employees at all levels. In Norway, as in most egalitarian cultures, positions of authority are earned largely on the basis of individual achievement, and people at all levels of the organization are free to aspire to these positions. The role of the leader is to harness the talent of the group and develop any resulting synergies. Research on Norwegian leadership is scarce. However, Hofstede's (1980) theoretical dimensions of culture provide a framework from which a hypothesis regarding Norwegian leadership can be derived. Along with Sweden, Norway's score on masculinity is the lowest of all the countries included in the study. This suggests that great emphasis is placed on cooperation and good working relationships, traditionally seen as feminine values. Norway also scores low on the power distance dimension, referring to the extent to which people accept and expect that power should be unequally distributed. These results suggest that leadership in Norway might be related to the extent to which the manager is perceived as approachable, open-minded, and democratic (Hetland &

Sandal, 2003). Also, the extent to which a leader possesses warmth and sensitivity toward the needs of others appears to be an important attribute. This is in line with much of what has been written about Scandinavian leadership, which is based on the assumption that management in Sweden, Denmark, and Norway is guided by a common philosophy (Schramm-Nielsen *et al.*, 2004). In Norway, like its neighbors, typical management behavior is marked by low power distance, informality, direct communication, decency, conflict avoidance, cooperation, and consensual decision-making. It can be inferred from this that successful leadership in Norway builds on the strengths of the country's culture, context, and history.

Although there is little research on Norwegian leadership, a substantial amount of research has been carried out on Scandinavian management or leadership since the concept was introduced approximately 20 years ago. A review of some of the most recent studies seems to confirm that there is something particular about the "Scandinavian Way." A number of large surveys of Scandinavian (Nordic) managers have been performed during the last decade. For example, a study by Lindell and Arvonen (1996) revealed that Scandinavian managers placed less emphasis on task structuring and were more considerate of their employees than managers from other European nations. Zander (1997) came to a similar conclusion as she found that, compared to samples from other nations, the Scandinavian respondents preferred leadership based on coaching rather than direction. Also, in their recent survey of Scandinavian leaders, Schramm-Nielsen *et al.* (2004) conclude that Scandinavian leaders are softer than their American colleagues, as their main emphasis is more on being credible, honest, and ethical than on being results-oriented and ambitious. Whether this is to be viewed as a strength or a weakness is, however, debatable. It has been proposed that the twenty-first century will be the century of the "knowledge worker." What it takes to lead and motivate knowledge workers is fundamentally different from what it takes to lead manual workers. According to Drucker (2000), less emphasis on external control and more emphasis on intrinsic motivation are needed. This view of leadership seems to align well with the egalitarian Scandinavian societies, with their narrow social differences, flat organizations, and short distance between management and employees.

Literature Review on Trust

Surveys show that generalized trust (i.e. trust which is measured using people's agreement with the statement "most people can be trusted") is very unevenly distributed across the globe. Based on the results of a recent study on generalized or social trust (Delhey &Newton, 2005), Norway can definitely be labeled as a high-trust society. As a matter of fact, results from the World Values Study (2005–2008) have shown that Norway ranks highest in the world in interpersonal or social trust, as more than 60 percent of the population state that most people can be trusted. The high trust level is related to Norway's Protestant tradition and ethnic homogeneity, as well as good government, wealth, and income equality. Citizens' trust in the political institutions has also been quite high (Gulbrandsen, 2007). A broad mass survey from 2001 reveals that Norwegian citizens' support for democracy and the level of trust in public institutions are generally higher than in most other countries (Christensen & Lægreid, 2007). This is confirmed by the results of the recent Edelman Trust Barometer (2011), which shows that Norwegians' trust in government is higher than in most other EU markets. Also a study by Gulbrandsen (2005) of the overall trust of the national elites in the most important private and public institutions in Norway documented that many of the institutions receive relatively high trust from the elites. There is reason to believe that the fact that Norway, contrary to most other European countries, has not been severely affected by the economic crisis has a definite impact on these results. At the same time, Norwegians' trust in business is rather low, and the percentage who trust CEOs as credible spokespeople is very low (14 percent) (Edelman, op. cit.) As for Norwegians' trust in the EU as an institution, no direct measures are available, but public opinion polls clearly indicate that the general attitude toward the EU has gone from mild skepticism to open distrust. Obviously, this is a consequence of the recent crisis in EU countries such as Greece and Spain. These particular features of Norwegian society make Norway an interesting case in intra-organizational trust—for example, trust between managers and subordinates. The high-trust culture can also be expected to provide fertile ground for mutual trust between managers and subordinates. At the same time, generalized trust is more abstract than personal trust, and it requires greater cognitive skills to handle it. Personal trust is more easily understood because it is strongest in small, face-to-face communities where people know each other. This leads to the assumption that generalized and personal trust are two different kinds of trust. However, as was mentioned above, the assumption would be that generalized trust is strongest when we have something in common with others, especially when we are from the same ethnic background. But this similarity-attraction paradigm is often associated with personal trust as well (Thomas & Ravlin, 1995), which may lead to the assumption that generalized and personal trust are somehow associated. Consequently, we will suggest that widespread trust in people in general, as well as in society's main institutions, should lead to the hypothesis that manager–subordinate trust in Norway is high.

Contextual Factors in Hierarchical Trusting Relationships

There seems to be a general opinion among Norwegians that Norwegian work life is based on trust—that is, managers trust employees, and employees trust managers. One reason for this assumed high mutual trust is the existence of a large number of micro firms and small companies in Norway. Combined with a low power distance, this indicates a close and often friendly relationship between managers and employees (Rogaczewska *et al.*, 2004). This was confirmed by the Norwegian focus group participants, where there seem to be only minor differences between managers and subordinates regarding their opinions on trust (what it is) and what it takes to create a trusting relationship. Both groups emphasized fairness, openness, competence, reliability, and concern as trust antecedents.

Another finding worth mentioning is that while subordinates' trust in managers is more general, managers' trust in subordinates is more specific. Managers seem to trust subordinates based on the knowledge or assumption that a particular subordinate has the necessary competence or skills, while subordinates' trust in managers seems to be less about specific skills and competences and more about their general impression of the person's character or truthfulness. While subordinates came up with statements such as "she is very honest," "I have a feeling that he supports me," or " he makes me feel valuable," typical statements from the managers are:

"I trust him because he is able to …," or "she is a very responsible person," or "he has never disappointed me." In many ways, it seems that it is the subordinates' performance which creates the basis for the development of trust.

By and large, the Norwegian Delphi experts confirmed this description. However, the two experts who had practical experience from the business context (they both work as management consultants) were somewhat less inclined to support the assumption of a high level of mutual trust. Their experience was that the recent tendency among leaders to put more emphasis on using their prerogatives to make decisions has created a sort of "them and us" atmosphere, which does not support trust. At the same time, it has to be said that these experts' experiences came predominately from some of the largest Norwegian companies, and they admitted that the situation in most (medium and small) companies was probably different.

The Delphi experts also pointed out that in Norway, as is the case in the other Scandinavian countries, interpersonal organizational behavior is marked by cooperation (both vertically and horizontally), consensual decision-making, informality, direct communication (not only top-down, but bottom-up as well), decency, and conflict avoidance, which—put together—make up fertile ground for mutual trust. The ongoing globalization process, on the other hand, which has led to several Norwegian companies being acquired by foreign MNCs (even Chinese), may—again, according to the Delphi experts—lead to less mutual trust because of perceived differences of beliefs, values, and norms between the Norwegian employees and the foreign owners/managers.

In terms of the cultural dimensions of trust, participants were asked to evaluate Norway's standing along the individualism–collectivism and power distance dimensions. In the case of the *individualism–collectivism dimension*, the participants were somewhat mixed in their opinions. This may be due in part to their different perceptions of collectivism, which in many ways reflect the GLOBE study's distinction between institutional collectivism and in-group collectivism (Gupta, 2002). Both the respondents and the Delphi experts characterized Norway as rather collectivistic, meaning that societal collectivism is strong. Their reasoning is based on the fact that both organizational and societal institutions' practices encourage and reward collective distribution of resources and collective action (see also Schramm-Nielsen *et al.*, 2004). However, at the same time, in-group collectivism is weaker, personal needs and attitudes are important determinants of social behavior, rationality is emphasized, and there is little distinction between so-called in-groups and out-groups. A leading Norwegian anthropologist has called the typical Norwegian individualism "egalitarian individualism," meaning that, even if Norwegians are individualists, this individualism (score of 71 on Hofstede's measure) is different from the archetypical US individualism (Hylland Eriksen, 1993). Contrary to North Americans, Norwegians have a firm belief in the society they are part of and are also willing to contribute to the common welfare through the taxation system.

The view on *power distance*, however, was identical, as all agreed that the low power distance mixed with egalitarian values was perhaps the prime reason for the high levels of interpersonal trust among Norwegians. The lack of hierarchies facilitates the use of cross-functional teams, which are given extended authority and responsibility from management. This is a clear expression of trust on the part of management. But this also leads to expectations that those upon whom this trust is bestowed will live up to the team's collective responsibility, which demands trust and cooperation among the team members. In this way, one may say that trust leads to more trust.

Personal Factors in Hierarchical Trusting Relationships

Results from the qualitative interviews clearly show that several personal factors can influence a trustful relationship between managers and subordinates. In particular, gender and age were mentioned as important variables. For example, the two female participates admitted that for them it was easier to trust a male manager than a female manager. They had no real explanation for this; it was, they said, "just the way it is." That this view is expressed in egalitarian Norway is perhaps somewhat surprising. One possible explanation could be that female managers are perhaps not perceived (by their female subordinates) to be as "professional" as a manager as a man—that is, less inclined to act objectively and non-emotionally. As for age, there was a general agreement that it was easier to build trust in a manager who was older than you. The explanation for this was that managers who were older than you were seen as more competent and experienced, and hence easier to trust. Length of service within the company was also perceived as a significant factor. All of the participants agreed that subordinates who had worked for a long time in the same company trusted their managers more. This was partly explained as a consequence of the length of the manager–subordinate relationship, but it was also mentioned that being part of the same company for a long time makes you more committed. Also, the company's culture will have a stronger effect when one has worked there for some time.

They were also asked to comment on the findings of the quantitative study on the significance of personal variables that account for variations in trust (see Table 4.1).

On one hand, the data indicate that there is a *negative correlation between the age difference between manager and subordinate and managerial trustworthy behaviors*. The participants' explanation for this, as was also mentioned above, was that it is, from a subordinate's point of view, more difficult to trust a manager who is younger than you than someone who is about the same age or older. This probably

Table 4.1 Norway: significant controls (correlations)

	Gender manager (1–> man, 2–> woman)	Age subordinate	Gender subordinate	Academic level subordinate	Age difference
MTB		0.324**	–0.229*		–0.188*
OCB	–0.364**	0.227*		–0.182*	
MTS	–0.208*	0.242**	–0.215*		
STM		0.189*	–0.204*		–0.186*

Notes
** Correlation significant at 0.01 level.
* Correlation significant at 0.05 level.
MTB = managerial trustworthy behavior, STM = subordinates' trust in managers, MTS = managers' trust in subordinates, OCB = organizational citizenship behavior.

has to do with a feeling that younger people do not have the necessary experience or wisdom needed in order to trust them. Obviously, the lack of trust could also be seen as a consequence of a "generation gap"—that is, older employees simply have difficulties in understanding and accepting younger managers' attitudes and priorities and hence find it hard to trust them. They simply belong to two different cultures.

On the other hand, none of the managers had problems in trusting young subordinates. Again, a possible explanation for this would be that trust in subordinates is more about trust in a person's ability to perform and deliver, and as long as he/she does what is expected of him/her, there is no reason not to trust this person. Age is of little importance here.

The study also showed that *the older the subordinate, the higher the manager's trust*. The Norwegian participants did not think that this was typical for Norway. Again they referred to their general opinion that managers' trust in subordinates was linked to their perception of the subordinate's competence and ability to perform. Trust in subordinates is closer to "cognition-based trust" than a more relational-based form of trust. Consequently, age is of less importance than merit. Also, the finding that *subordinates with a higher educational background show less proactive behaviors* was commented on in the sense that none of the participants were able to explain why. On the contrary, all agreed that in Norway there is a demand for more education among employees ("life-long learning"). Furthermore, both private and public employers encourage their employees to continue their education, and it is quite normal to provide both the necessary economic support and more flexible working hours. So the finding that subordinates with higher education (which is almost the normal situation in Norway) show less proactive behaviors was simply not accepted by the Norwegian participants. Rather, they were inclined to believe that it was the other way around.

Antecedents and Outcomes of Manager–Subordinate Trust

Both the participating managers and subordinates viewed trust as a key factor in the relationship between managers and subordinates. Also, the dominating opinion among the participants was that the Norwegian work culture, being based on open communication, involvement, delegation, and equality, made it easier to build trust between managers and subordinates than in cultures where inequality and hierarchies were typical. As for the more precise question of how trust is formed in a manager–subordinate relationship, the subordinates emphasized such things as openness, fairness, consideration, and support, but they also stressed that this was in itself not sufficient. Showing behavioral consistency and integrity, as well as professional competence, was decisive for their perceptions of managerial trustworthiness. In short, this means that subordinates trust managers who are consistent in their behavior—both when it comes to consistent behavior over time and across situations, and consistency between words and actions. Managers, on the other hand, tend to evaluate their trust in subordinates on the basis of experiences from work situations rather than from a more general impression of the person. Statements like "I trust him because he is able to …," or "She is a very responsible person," or "He has never disappointed me" are typical examples. There were almost no statements referring to, for example, benevolence or affect-based forms of trust. The subordinates, on the other hand, came up with statements such as "… a feeling that he supports me," or "… makes me feel that I am important," or "… makes me feel valuable," which clearly indicate that benevolence is also an element of Norwegian subordinates' trust in their managers.

As for the positive outcomes of manager–subordinate trust, the managers emphasized that having trust in their subordinates, which from the managers' point of view means that they regard their subordinates as able and willing to do the work they are assigned to do, reduced the need for close control and thus allowed them to focus on more strategic matters. The managers also pointed out that by showing trust in their subordinates—for example, by letting subordinates decide on matters which were closely linked to their jobs—the subordinates' level of job satisfaction and organizational commitment also increased. This was supported by the subordinates who stated that, for them, feeling that they were trusted by their managers was decisive in maintaining their motivation and their sense of being appreciated. One respondent even said that:

> For me, if I had any doubt as to whether my manager trusted me, I would probably not have been able to work with that person. For me, to know that you are trusted is the most important aspect of all in a work situation.

The importance of having a trusting relationship between managers and subordinates was underscored by both parties. However, because subordinates' trust in managers tends to be of a more general nature, while the managers' trust in subordinates is a more "limited" kind of trust, perceived outcomes of trust in these relationships tend to vary too. Again, managers focused more on direct job-related outcomes, such as not having to monitor subordinates' work and consequently being able to concentrate on more "meaningful" tasks, such as planning and strategy, while subordinates regarded a more general feeling of wellbeing, satisfaction, and being competent as the main outcome of a trusting relationship.

Figure 4.1 provides a diagrammatic summary of the major antecedents and consequences of trust in the manager–subordinate relationship arising from thequalitative data generated from the focus groups and expert panels in Norway:

As can be seen from Figure 4.1, a good professional relationship between managers and subordinates in Norway is characterized by the manager's ability to delegate, to communicate openly with her/his subordinates, and to act in a fair manner. Also of importance is consistency (i.e. for the manager to behave in a consistent manner). A good relationship between managers and subordinates is also dependent on the manager's positive perception of the subordinate's skills and competence, and of the subordinate's willingness and ability to contribute. When managers trust their subordinates, they delegate tasks and responsibility and receive in return motivated, satisfied, and committed subordinates. Managers who trust subordinates, and thus establish a level of equality in a power-based relationship, are expressing benevolence—that is, they give their subordinates the impression that they are concerned about the subordinate's welfare and will have her or his best interests at heart. When subordinates perceive managerial behavior to be benevolent, trust is built.

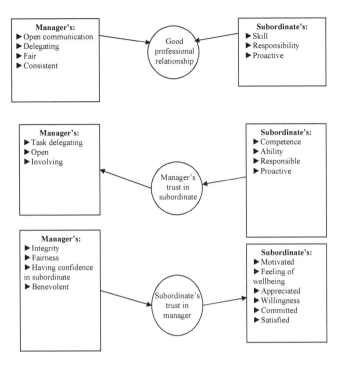

Figure 4.1 Antecedents and outcomes of trust in hierarchical relationships

The Dynamics of Trust in Hierarchical Relationships

Trusting someone is not an "either-or." Nor is it natural for someone to trust another person; he or she must know that person or that person's professional experience. In fact, several studies (Kramer, 1994, Meyerson *et al.*, 1996) show that, even when there is no interaction history, participants often show a remarkably high level of trust in each other. Although this "initial trust" is partly grounded in personality factors, some societal cultures still tend to be more trusting than others. According to Whitener *et al.* (2000), Norwegians have a high propensity to trust others. This was confirmed by the Norwegian participants, who said that their trust in the other party did not necessarily begin at a zero baseline. It is more like they actively *wanted* to trust the other party from day one. Distrust, on the other hand, arises when the other party does not fulfill expectations. For example, managers who do not involve, do not give feedback, or are not acting in a consistent manner will lose the trust that subordinates had from the start of their relationship. The same goes for subordinates who are not performing well or who lack initiative. Both parties regarded this as a pretty serious situation. According to the managers, if they could not trust their subordinates, they had to switch to a management style based more on close control and monitoring, which they were not comfortable with. One even expressed that not trusting subordinates made it almost impossible to continue working with them. As managers, they were simply not prepared to manage in situations in which there was little or even no trust. The answer given by the participating subordinates to the question of what would happen if you do not trust your manager was that "… in that case, we cannot continue to work together." When the topic of coaching was brought up as a possible management approach, the answer from the same manager was that "I cannot coach someone I do not trust."

Although both managers and subordinates agreed that, in Norway, initial trust was typical of the manager–subordinate relationship, they nonetheless admitted that the way they interacted changed as they became better acquainted and initial trust was confirmed. Especially the subordinates admitted that, when they started to work with a new manager, they were more restrained and less inclined to "lower their guard." If the manager, however, proved his or her trustworthiness, the initial circumstance that they were two people who were supposed to work together evolved into a (trust-based) relationship. In these matters, it is also important to bear in mind that the Norwegian work culture is characterized by informality, equality, mutual trust, and cooperation—not only between managers and subordinates, but also between the state, employers, and unions. This was especially mentioned by the Delphi experts as something one had to take into consideration when the topic of trust in organizations was discussed.

Our quantitative data offers interesting insights into the dynamics of trust (see Table 4.2). When the results from Norway are compared with the overall findings among the 18 countries included in the study, we find both similarities and differences.

As the figures show, the relationship between organizational citizenship behavior (OCB) and managers' trust in subordinates (MTS) is stronger in Norway than in the overall sample. From the literature on trust, we know that OCB acts as an antecedent to managers' trust in subordinates (Podsakoff et al., 2000). The strong relationship in Norway between OCB and MTS is somewhat surprising, as this relationship was not particularly mentioned, neither by the focus group nor by the experts. One reason for this could be that the term "organizational citizenship" is not well known or commonly used in Norway. On the other hand, the Norwegian expression "medarbeiderskap," which can be loosely translated as "employee responsibility," was both explicitly and implicitly mentioned several times during the interviews. "Medarbeiderskap" is about showing commitment, loyalty, and initiative, but it also means to show stewardship—that is, that you as an employee are looking after (the welfare of) your subordinates. There was general agreement that showing "medarbeiderskap" will increase manager's goodwill and, hence, his/her level of trust. Also, the relationship between the managers' trust in subordinates (MTS) and managerial trustworthy behavior (MTB) is stronger than in the overall sample. Why this is so was not quite clear, but some of the participants suggested that when a manager trusts subordinates he/she tends to act in ways that subordinates find trustworthy. It is a common assumption that trustworthiness commonly begets trust. Acting in a trustworthy manner is, again according to the participants, easier when you trust your subordinates because then there is less risk in being open, showing concern, and being available (i.e. behaving in a trustworthy manner) than if one does not trust the other party.

Table 4.2 Standardized regression weights for the trust model in Norway and the overall sample

	OCB–>MTS	MTS–>MTB	MTB–>STM	STM–>OCB
Norway only	0.93**	0.57**	0.94**	−0.25
Complete model	0.68**	0.34**	0.89**	0.08*

Notes
** Regression weight significant at 0.01 level.
* Regression weight significant at 0.05 level.

The relationship between managerial trustworthy behavior (MTB) and subordinates' trust in managers (STM) is quite similar to that of the overall sample. However, while the more general findings indicate that managers' trustworthy behaviors seem to lead to higher levels of subordinates' trust in managers than the effect that subordinates' OCB has on managers' trust in subordinates, the Norwegian results show that these two relationships are almost equally strong. The participants' opinion was that this was probably a consequence of the flat, open, equality-based work culture which dominates most Norwegian work organizations. At the same time, one must also bear in mind that the results of the cross-cultural study showed that the Norwegian subordinates' trust in managers was the lowest of all. As we have pointed out above, according to several other studies, Norway is a high-trust country (see, for example, the World Values Survey, 2000). The low scores on subordinates' trust in managers are therefore somewhat surprising. However, both the focus group participants and the experts believed that the trust measure used in the study, which measures affective-based trust, was probably the explanation for the low Norwegian scores. There is ample evidence that relations between managers and subordinates vary across cultures (Javidan *et al.*, 2006; Hofstede, 2007). According to the focus group participants, in Norway, trust in your manager is based less on emotions and respect than on whether you trust the manager's competence and ability. Thus, this trust measure did not fit in with the Norwegian work culture.

Finally, the effects of subordinates' trust in managers (STM) on subordinates' organizational citizenship behaviors are not statistically significant. The reason(s) for this lack of significance (i.e. why the correlation, albeit a weak negative correlation (−.25), may have occurred by chance) is not easy to explain. Again, according to the participants in the qualitative interviews, even if their behavior is influenced by the level of trust they have in the manager, this behavior does not necessarily align with how OCB is generally conceptualized. The concept is, as has been mentioned above, relatively unknown in Norway, and the answers given by the Norwegian sample on the OCB items in the questionnaire may reflect this.

Discussion and Conclusions

The results of our study of manager–subordinate trust in Norway by and large confirm the main findings in the trust literature. Both managers and subordinates agreed that trust is decisive in order to develop a positive work culture, which in Norway means a culture based on open dialogue, delegation of responsibility, and involvement of employees. Although it was also agreed that trust building needs time, the Norwegian participants nonetheless pointed out that both managers and subordinates are inclined to trust the other party from day one. This means that, in a Norwegian work relationship, you do not have to "earn trust." There will be initial trust from the beginning, but depending on your attitudes and behavior, this initial trust will subsequently grow stronger or disappear. Also, the results of the Norwegian study clearly support the hypothesis that the trustworthy behavior of a person (e.g. the manager) leads subordinates to trust the manager even more. Trustworthiness refers to the accumulated positive experiences that lead a person to trust another person (Mayer *et al.*, 1995). Trust and trustworthiness are sometimes used interchangeably. In order to get a deeper understanding of what it takes to trust another person, we think that the difference between the two can be defined as follows: trustworthiness is the perception of the trustor that the trustee can be trusted. This distinction is vitally important and is clearly mirrored in the discussions both with the participants of the qualitative interviews and with the experts, as the focus was on antecedents and outcomes of trust, not on trust itself. Subordinates' perceptions of trustworthy behavior on the part of the managers included such things as openness, fairness, consideration, and support. But, although necessary, this was not sufficient in itself. The real acid test is whether this behavior is perceived to be consistent. As for outcomes, the subordinates' experience that having a trusting relationship with your manager leads to improved job satisfaction, higher levels of commitment, and organizational citizenship behavior (or rather, as they expressed it, "medarbeiderskap") aligns with what is found in the literature (see, for example, Kodish, 2006). Lack of trust, on the other hand, obviously led to less interaction and more emphasis on "minding my own business." Ultimately, however, lack of trust in a subordinate-manager relationship would probably lead to the subordinate trying to find another job. As for the managers, having trust in subordinates reduces the need to monitor subordinates and allows them to work on more strategic and longer-term issues.

The cultural variables discussed provide a deeper understanding of the behaviors observed and the characteristics of manager–subordinate relationships in Norway, typified by a low power distance, a high level of societal collectivism, and a lower level of in-group collectivism (House *et al.*, 2004), and not least, a profound egalitarianism. Hierarchical relationships are more affected by competence and behavior than by power and position. When, for example, Schramm-Nielsen *et al.* (2004) focus on the relationship between managers and subordinates in Scandinavia, the subordinates' attitudes to the "higher ups" are described as non-deferential, and loyalty to the decision process may in many cases be stronger than loyalty to a particular manager. The same authors also point out that trust in managers is based less on emotions and respect than on whether one trusts the manager's competence and ability. This was certainly confirmed by the participants in the qualitative study, who, when asked what it takes for a manager to be trusted, stressed in particular such aspects as professionalism, ability to manage, and competence, among others, as being decisive.

The relatively strong relationship between subordinates' organizational citizenship behavior and managers' trust in subordinates has been discussed above. However, this can also be seen as a consequence of the rather strong value-focus of many Norwegian organizations. It is quite common for Norwegian work organizations to have a vision and a mission, and there is generally a strong emphasis on building strong, positive corporate cultures. One of the participants explained that, in her organization, even the physical lay-out of the work space (an open flexible work space design) was chosen because it was thought to reflect the organization's values. When vision, mission, and codes of conduct are clearly communicated, behaving according to a common set of "rules" is easier, and the link between expected behavior and actual behavior is strengthened, which in turn creates fertile ground for mutual trust.

As is the case in most European companies, more sophisticated HR practices have recently been implemented in most (larger) Norwegian firms. In particular, a more strategic emphasis on HRM has been evident in academic writing. This means that HRM practices should be aligned with the company's strategy. In order to strengthen employees' trust in management, it is recommended to inform openly at an early stage about strategic choices, explaining the reasons why and the possible consequences. As for Norwegian employees, they usually expect to be actively involved in the early stages of strategy development and to play an active part in the implementation process. A "top-down" approach is the fastest road to distrusting employees. And most managers know this. All the participants expressed agreement with the idea that managers and subordinates are "in the same boat." Accordingly, one practical implication of the qualitative study is that, if managers are to be trusted by their subordinates, they must communicate a "we are in this together" attitude, meaning that "I am just as dependent on you, as you are dependent on me." This aligns with the Norwegian egalitarian, low power distance culture, and consequently will also fit in with what subordinates expect from a manager. In short, development of an empowering culture is perhaps the most effective means to establish an organization characterized by a high level of manager–subordinate trust.

No studies on organizational behavior are without limitations. The results of the current study are based on qualitative interviews of a rather limited number of respondents, supplemented by a Delphi study with an even smaller number of experts. Also, all the respondents worked in relatively large Norwegian firms, and all were quite well educated. In spite of this, we think that the current study has shed valuable light on manager–subordinate trust in Norway. Obviously, the nature of trust and trust relationships between managers and subordinates varies across organizations and occupations. For example, it was suggested by one of the experts (who himself worked at a university) that trust may take forms in institutions such as universities that are different from more ordinary work organizations. The need for more research on this important matter is obvious. Still, we think that the combined results from the quantitative and qualitative studies have provided valuable knowledge about the important issue of manager–subordinate trust in organizations.

References

Baldwin, P. (1997). State and citizenship in the age of globalization. InP. Koslowski & A. Føllesdal (eds), *Restructuring the Welfare State. Theory of Reform of Social Policy*. London: Springer.

Christensen, T. & Lægreid, P. (2007). Trust in government; The relative importance of service satisfaction, political factors and democracy. Paper. Stein Rokkan Centre for Social Studies, Bergen, Norway.

Delhey, J. & Newton, K. (2005). Predicting cross-national levels of social trust: Global pattern or Nordic exceptionalism? *European Sociological Review*, 21(4): 311–327.

Drucker, P. (2000). *Management Challenges for the 21st Century*. London: Butterworth Heinemann.

Edelman Trust Barometer (2011). Retrieved on 12.2.2011 from www.edelman.com/trust/2011/.

Esping-Andersen, G. (1985). *Politics Against Markets. The Social-Democratic Road to Power*. Princeton: Princeton University Press.

Esping-Andersen, G. (1990). *The Three Worlds of Welfare Capitalism*. Cambridge: Polity Press.

Gulbrandsen, T. (2005). Elite integration and Institutional trust in Norway. *Comparative Sociology*, 6: 190–214.

Gulbrandsen, T. (2007). Elite integration and institutional trust in Norway. *Comparative Sociology*, 6: 190–214.

Gupta, V. (2002). Cultural clusters: Methodology and findings. *Journal of World Business*, 37: 11–15.

Halvorsen, K & Stjernø, S (2008). *Work, Oil and Welfare. The Welfare State in Norway*. Oslo: Universitetsforlaget.

Hetland, H. & Sandal, G. (2003). Transormational leadership in Norway: outcomes and personality correlates. *European Journal of Work and Organizational Psychology*, 12(2): 147–170.

Hofstede, G. (1980). *Culture's Consequences*. Beverly Hills, CA: SAGE Publications.

Hofstede, G. (2007). A European in Asia. *Asian Journal of Social Psychology*, 10(1): 16–21.

House, R.J., Hanges, P.J., Javidan, M., Dorfman, P.W. & Gupta, V (2004). *Culture, Leadership and Organizations. The Globe Studies of 62 Societies*. London: SAGE Publications.

Hylland Eriksen, T. (1993). Being Norwegian in a shrinking world. In A. Cohen Kiel (ed.), *Continuity and Change: Aspects of Modern Norway*. Oslo: Scandinavian University Press.

Javidan, M., Dorman, P. W., de Luque, M.S. & House, R. (2006). In the eye of the beholder: Cultural lessons of Project Globe. *Academy of Management Perspective*, February: 67–90.

Kodish, S. (2006). Antecedents of organizational trust. Working Paper presented at the International Communication Association.

Kramer, R.M. (1994). The sinister attribution error: Paranoid cognition and collective distrust in organizations. *Motivation and Emotion*, 18: 199–230.

Lindell, M. & Arvonen, J. (1996). The Nordic management style in a European context. *International Studies of Management and Organization*, 26(3): 73–92

Mayer, R.C., Davis, J.H., & Schoorman, D. (1995). An integrative model of organizational trust. *Academy of Management Review*, 20: 709–734.

Meyerson, D., Weick, K. & Kramer, R. (1996). Swift trust and temporary groups. In R. Kramer and T.R. Tyler (eds), *Trust in Organizations: Frontiers of Theory and Research*. Thousand Oaks, CA: SAGE Publications, pp. 166–195.

Podsakoff, P.M., MacKenzie, S. B., Lee, J.Y., & Podsakoff, N.P. (2003). Common method biases in behavioral research: A critical review of the literature and recommended remedies. *Journal of Applied Psychology*, 88: 879–903.

Rogaczewska, A.P., Larsen, H.H., Nordhaug, O., Døving, E. & Gjelsvik, M. (2004). Denmark and Norway: Siblings or cousins. In C. Brewster, W. Mayrhofer & M. Morley (eds), *Human Resource Management in Europe: Evidence of Convergence*. London: Elsevier-Butterworth/Heinemann.

Schramm-Nielsen, J., Lawrence, P. & Sivesind, K.H. (2004). *Management in Scandinavia. Culture, Context, and Change*. Cheltenham, UK: Edward Elgar.

Sejersted, F.(1993). *Demokratisk Kapitalisme*. Oslo: Universitetsforlaget.

Thomas, D.C. & Ravlin, E.C., (1995): Responses of employees to cultural adaption by foreign managers. *Journal of Applied Psychology*, 80: 132–176.

Towers Perrin (2000). *The 2000 Worldwide Total Remuneration*.

Warner-Søderholm, G (2010). *Understanding Perceptions of Culture and Intracultural Societal Practices and Values of Norwegian Managers*. DBA Thesis, Henley Business School, University of Reading.

Whitener, E.M., Maznevski, M., Hua W., Sæbø, S.R. & Ekelund, B. (2001). *Testing the Cultural Boundaries of a Model of Trust: Subordinate-Manager Relationships in China, Norway and the US*. UCLA: Asia Institute.

Zander, L. (1997). *The Licence to Lead: An 18 Country Study of the Relationship between Employees' Preferences Regarding Interpersonal Leadership and National Culture*. Institute of International Business, Stockholm School of Economics.

5 Manager–Subordinate Trust Relationships in Spain

OLENA STEPANOVA

Introduction

Spain, officially the Kingdom of Spain, is situated on the Iberian Peninsula in southwest Europe. It is the second largest country in the European Union (EU), after France. Its territory also includes the Balearic Islands in the Mediterranean, the Canary Islands in the Atlantic Ocean, and the autonomous cities of Ceuta and Melilla in North Africa. Spain was a highly influential country between the fifteenth and eighteenth centuries and became a global empire with numerous colonies. As a consequence of this historical reach, Spanish remains the second most spoken language in the world today, with an estimated 500 million speakers. Spain is a democratic constitutional monarchy. Spain's mixed capitalist economy is the twelfth largest in the world, with one of the highest quality of life levels. In the twentieth century, the country transitioned peacefully to democracy after Franco's death in 1975. The country joined the European Union in 1986 and its economy experienced significant growth up to 2007. With the onset of the global financial crisis, the economy underwent a protracted period of stagnation, accompanied by a significant rise in unemployment from 8 percent to an estimated 20 percent.

Spain's business culture has been characterized as being hierarchical with relatively high levels of power distance. As a result, managers are more often seen as directors than as leaders (O'Connell *et al.*, 2007). Nevertheless, Spanish managers describe a leader as someone inspirational with a collectivist orientation and a capacity for team integration. Valued traits include a strong performance orientation, integrity in business dealings, capacity for vision, administrative competence, decisiveness, and diplomacy. Conversely, traits such as self-centeredness, malevolence, an autocratic style, or a need to save face are viewed as negative in a leader (O'Connell *et al.*, 2007). At the organizational level, the human resource management function has evolved over the past decades from a largely administrative role, charged with handling recruitment and payroll, toward a more strategic role as business partner, with evidence of the adoption of practices from abroad (Quintanilla *et al.*, 2009).

This chapter opens with a brief account of historical developments in Spain, along with a description of the contemporary institutional environment, in particular, the educational, legal, and social systems, and an overview of the current economic and social context. We then present a summary of human resource management practices and developments, and preferred leadership styles in the organizational context. Subsequently, we move to the substantive area of trust. Extant literature on multiple aspects of trust relationships in the workplace context in Spain are reviewed, before presenting our empirical results. The chapter concludes with a discussion of some of the main results obtained in the context of the extant literature and highlights potential implications for management and leadership practice, together with potential avenues for future research.

Highlights of Manager–Subordinate Trust in Spain

- The Spanish participants in our study did not show unanimity concerning whether managers were trusted. They suggested that managers' degree of proximity to subordinates plays an important role in determining trust.
- Historically, the existence of a large number of small family businesses affected the perception that managers make decisions not necessarily because of their expertise, but because they are the owners or represent the owner of the company.
- The experts believed that managers tend to exert control over employees' work, emphasizing the transactionality of the hierarchical relationship and the importance of the work output, more than the underlying trust dynamic.
- Study respondents pointed to the importance of the organization's culture in establishing trust relationships across levels, with a culture of communication being viewed as particularly important. The experts argued that, in bigger companies, the organizational culture is more consolidated and HR functions are more advanced, which ultimately influences the existing leadership styles that have an important impact on trust building.
- Among the personal factors that influence trust building in the Spanish context, respondents pointed to the importance of age proximity, where individuals have more experiences they share in common. However, professionalism is deemed more important than any personal factor.
- Finally, our participants note that intensive communication, the possibility of working closely together, and a certain degree of seniority support trust building.

Historical Perspective

Iberia was a term created by the nomads traveling from Sahara to the north of Spain to describe what is now known as Spain and Portugal (O'Connell *et al.*, 2007). It was also known as *Sepharad*, a Hebrew name mentioned in the Bible; *Hispania*, a Latin name introduced during the Roman Empire; and *Al Andalus*, the Arab name used between the eighth and sixteenth centuries. The many names reflect the country's heterogeneous background. Over the centuries, a variety of cultures occupied the territory (Tartessians, Celts, Phoenicians, Greeks, etc.) until 711, when almost the entire peninsula was conquered by the Islamic Moors, whose reign lasted for around 800 years. The Northern Christian Kingdoms started the process of winning back their territories (called *Reconquista*), which was completed in 1492 with the fall of Granada. Once the Christian kingdoms started gaining control of the territory, a peculiar social structure was established: key governance and military positions were occupied by Christians; Sephardic Jews specialized in professions requiring prolonged training; and the Moorish worked as farmers and builders. This arrangement broadly provided for a peaceful coexistence of these distinct cultural and religious beliefs over a period spanning two centuries (O'Connell *et al.*, 2007).

The unification of the Kingdom of Castile and the Kingdom of Aragon led to the foundation of the Kingdom of Spain in 1492. The same year, Christopher Columbus arrived in the New World. The establishment of the Inquisition forced Jews and Muslims to decide between conversion to Christianity or face expulsion from the country. During the next three centuries, Spain's economy and culture flourished. It was the world's largest colonial power in the Americas and the Western Pacific. Its literature, fine arts, and philosophy thrived. The wealth arriving from its colonies allowed it to take part in European wars, although this ultimately led to the decline of power at the end of the seventeenth century, under the Habsburg rule. After an internal war for the Spanish Succession, in the eighteenth century, the Bourbons became the new dynasty and worked toward restoring state institutions. The end of this century and the beginning of the new century marked a period of general disarray in Europe, with the French Revolution and Napoleonic Wars, which led to French occupation of Spain in the early nineteenth century. The war for independence devastated the country and led to the independence of the Spanish colonies, the last of them—Cuba and the Philippines—in 1898.

Political instability at the beginning of the twentieth century led Spain to becoming a republic, which culminated in 1936 in a bloody civil war. After the war, in 1939, General Francisco Franco proclaimed himself leader of the country and governed Spain as a dictator until his death in 1975. Under his rule, Catholicism became the official religion, the regions were prohibited from using their respective languages, and strict censorship was imposed on all the media. After Franco's death, the Bourbon monarchy was restored, headed by King Juan Carlos. Modern Spain is a constitutional monarchy and became part of the European Union in 1986. It has a population of 45 million people and occupies a territory of 505,988 square kilometers, comprising 18 Autonomous Communities. Spanish (Castilian) is the official language, along with Catalan, Galician, and Basque in some of the Autonomous Communities. Approximately 77 percent of the Spanish population lives in urban environments and some 94 percent of the population are Roman Catholics.

Institutional Context

Economic Context

After the death of Franco in 1975, Spain transitioned peacefully to democracy and experienced significant economic growth. Currently, Spain is ranked fourteenth in the world in terms of GDP, currently standing at US$ 1.359 trillion. After a 15-year period of GDP growth, the Spanish economy slowed down at the end of 2007, entering into recession in the second quarter of 2008. The unemployment rate rose from 8 percent (2007) to 20.6 percent as of October 2010 (Eurostat, 2010), double the EU average. Its fiscal deficit increased from 3.8 percent of GDP in 2008 to 7.9 percent in 2009. In the context of the world economic crisis, the economic decline in Spain was due to the collapse of the construction sector, an oversupply of housing, and a decrease in consumer spending and exports. Growth is forecast to resume slowly in 2011.

Social Context

Life expectancy at birth stands at 81 years. The total fertility rate is one of the lowest in Europe (1.39 children per woman in 2008), compared to the EU average of 1.5 and the international average of 2.7. Spain is a conservative welfare state (Esping-Andersen, 2000), where state provisions are mostly based on pensions, and the level of social assistance is low and mainly directed to employees within the regular market (Ferrera, 1996). The social security system provides unemployment benefits, sick leave, maternity leave, and free healthcare to all those legally employed and making monthly contributions to the public pension fund. Such provisions as leave policies, childcare services, and financial allowances are guaranteed by law, while flexibility arrangements and social provisions depend on companies' discretion.

Political and Legal Systems

Spain is a constitutional monarchy. The executive branch of government consists of the Chief of State (King Juan Carlos I, the Head of Government), the President of the government (equivalent to Prime Minister), and the Council of Ministers, appointed by the President. The monarchy is hereditary, while the President is proposed by the winning party or coalition and elected by the National Assembly. The legislative branch is bicameral. The General Courts (National Assembly) consist of the Senate (264 seats in 2008) and the Congress of Deputies (350 seats). Finally, the judiciary branch is represented by the Supreme Court. Among the political parties are the Spanish Socialist Workers Party (PSOE), the Popular Party (PP), and the United Left (IU) coalition. Key regional parties include Convergence and Union (CIU) in Catalonia and the Basque Nationalist Party (PNV) in the Basque country. The voting age is 18. Spain's legal structure is based on a civil law system with comprehensive legal codes and laws, a judiciary organization that combines courts and tribunals, and a legal body composed of judges and magistrates.

Educational System

Education between the age of 6 and 16 is compulsory. The percentage of the population over 15 who can read and write is 97.9. In 2007, the government allocated 4.4 percent of the GDP for expenditure on education. Education is structured on four levels: pre-school (3–5 years), primary school (6–11 years), secondary education (12–15 years), and post-compulsory schooling, *bachillerato* (16–17 years). Pre-school attendance is optional and free of charge. Completion of the post-compulsory studies gives the option of taking the University Entrance Exam. Those who leave school at the age of 15 can opt for vocational training.

HR Practices

The Spanish workforce comprises a core group of permanent employees, protected by an employment contract, along with a cohort of precarious employees with temporary contracts, particularly blue-collar workers in the construction industry (Quintanilla *et al.*, 2009). Temporary employment in Spain is the highest in the EU (OECD) and characterized by instability and involuntary turnover. Nevertheless, recently there have been moves toward obliterating this dual labor market (Amuedo-Dorantes, 2000). HRM is considered an important source of competitive advantage for companies (Camelo *et al.*, 2004). HR practices in Spain have evolved over recent decades and the specialist function has developed to occupy a more strategic position, involved in a broad range of value-adding activities, including succession planning, managerial coaching, and performance management (Quintanilla *et al.*, 2004). The implementation of new practices for talent development and empowerment also seems to be more commonplace than before (García-Olaverri *et al.*, 2006).

In large, multinational corporations, more sophisticated HR practices are in evidence than in small and medium-sized enterprises, though the latter have also experienced change (Quintanilla *et al.*, 2009). A study carried out in 195 Spanish companies showed that high-performance HR practices positively influenced organizational learning, which, in turn, positively affected business performance (Perez *et al.*, 2005). Hence, companies are more preoccupied about employees' commitment and their perceptions of belonging to the company than 15 years ago. The change in the Spanish HR system has also been prompted by its malleability—that is, flexibility in the adoption of "best practices" from other companies.

A study of 130 Spanish industrial companies (Camelo *et al.*, 2004) identified a total of 15 different HR practices, including training content and context, career design, remuneration system, recruitment and selection profiles, employment contracts, and evaluation systems. Based on these HR practices, three models of HR management were identified. In the first model (23 percent of the sample), HR management was not very well developed and functioned reactively, focused on reducing conflict and cost. Practices such as career planning, training, evaluation, and remuneration were not well defined. The second model (30 percent of the sample) reflected a higher degree of planning in training focused on productivity improvement and remuneration policies. Finally, the third model (39 percent of the sample) was characterized by a high level of organization and coherence of the human resources management system, focused on enhancing efficiency. However, certain HRM practices were used in all three models. For instance, all companies relied more on promoting from within than on recruiting from the external market; also, compensation policies were focused on job position. This can be explained by the historical influence of trade unions that promoted the employment stability. Interestingly, in none of the companies was HR management directly aligned with the companies' strategies, reflecting a lack of positioning of HR as a strategic partner.

Leadership Style

Spanish relationships have traditionally been characterized by loose time management enriched by a certain degree of creativity and intuition, and its society is characterized by strong family and geographical cohesion, leading to low domestic (and, even less, international) mobility. These characteristics reflect the so-called "Latino style." In terms of cultural values, Spain can be considered as an individualistic society with strong power distance, where employees are not very engaged in participation and expect relatively autocratic leadership (Hofstede, 1991). High power distance and uncertainty avoidance reinforce the existence of pyramidal organizational structures (Trompenaars, 1993), with leaders taking responsibility and subordinates exercising high levels of risk aversion (Boldy *et al.*, 1993). In the last two decades, Spain has shown a higher propensity to participation (McFarlin *et al.*, 1993), though it is still comparatively low (Page & Wiseman, 1993). This reality contrasts with individual values about preferred management styles. For instance, a comparative study on management style shows that Spanish top managers praise values such as personal esteem and job fulfillment, reflecting the importance of respect for subordinates and colleagues, and advocate a balance between professional effectiveness and warm relationships and joy for living (Rivera & Verna, 1996). Also, managers describe a leader as someone who is an inspirational, team-oriented integrator (O'Connell *et al.*, 2007).

In the GLOBE study (Chhokar *et al.*, 2007), with a sample of 60 countries, Spain is below average on performance orientation. In social relationships, middle-managers are reported to be slightly above average in assertiveness, though conciliation is often the preferred style for negotiating. Managers describe their culture as rather individualistic but wish it were more institutionally collective. As for gender egalitarianism, the culture tends toward "masculine-oriented standards," though desirability of a stronger presence of women in the workforce and fewer gender role differences was reported. Spain is ranked very low on the humane orientation—that is, a propensity to being generous, altruistic, and fair to others. However, it was also along these dimensions that managers indicated the importance and desirability of change. On the power distance dimension, Spain ranks very high. This is also reflected in the language, where there is a special form (*usted*) to address those in authority or customers. As for in-group collectivism, level of cohesiveness in one's organization and family, Spain scores average in the international comparison without an explicit desirability for change. Finally, managers report average uncertainty avoidance compared to the international sample. Overall, managers put most emphasis on the need to practice more gender egalitarianism and move toward a more compassionate society (humane orientation).

Content analysis of media, focus groups, and several interviews conducted as part of this study (ibid.) offered additional insights into the perceptions of leadership in Spain. The media analysis showed that the term "leader" is not used when describing companies' top management or CEOs, preferring "executive, general director, and boss." The term leadership is only used in connection with trade unions, religious leaders, political groups, or sport "leaders." Managers do not define themselves as leaders, or charismatic figures, but see themselves instead as "executives," "supervisors," and "bosses." The discussion of leadership in a focus group showed that leaders differ from managers in that they act more for the long term and are friendly, while managers tend to be bound to hierarchies, the short term, and tasks. According to the interviewees, the leadership style is expected to be hard and demanding, while acknowledging that it can combine both softness and self-confidence at the same time. Overall, they identified with the idea that leaders are chosen by their subordinates, while managers are imposed by the hierarchy.

Literature Review on Trust

In a 12-country European study of social trust, Spain is positioned at the bottom of the list in terms of social trust exhibited by its citizens (Montero *et al.*, 2008). More specifically, 67 percent of Spaniards perceive the country's membership of the EU positively. Their trust in the EU as an institution increased compared to 2008, standing at 56 percent (five points higher than the EU27 average), while trust in the European Central Bank stands at 46 percent (Eurobarómetro, 2009). As for the Spanish government and the Congress of Deputies, only 29 percent trust these institutions. These data show a clear decline in public opinion in 2009, which could be attributed to the economic crisis and Spain's difficulty in coming out of it. Most think that the country's government has a greater influence on their standard of living than the European, regional, or local authorities. Overall, Spaniards place more trust in the police and the army than in political institutions.

A comparative study of public and private home-based and residential social services in Spain showed that the sources of cross-sector distrust were institutional (Saz-Carranza & Serra, 2009). It was found that insufficient regulation and legislation, lack of business certification, and low local government administrative capacity lead to distrust. Trust is granted mostly to the family and, to a lesser extent, to other social groups. Thus, within the company's network, trust is granted to people close to the family, which hinders the incorporation of new partners (Gúzman *et al.*, 1995), and thus new opportunities for business might be missed (Cáceres, 1999). From the clients' perspective, a long-lasting commitment to companies is granted once there is trust in the company's intentions and values, which is more important than any economic variables (San Martín *et al.*, 2004). A recent study on trust in business agents showed that, in 2009, Spain was one of the countries where trust in companies decreased and it was the second country in the EU after Italy with the highest trust loss (Edelman Trust Barometer, 2009). Fewer than 50 percent of people between the ages of 25 and 64 trusted companies. Nevertheless, trust in business was higher than trust in the government. Even so, trust in general managers was at an all-time low (20 percent). Out of the four institutions (NGOs, companies, media, and government), NGOs were the most trusted.

According to the World Values Survey (2005–2008), Spain is placed below the median trust and is included with the countries tending to show lower interpersonal trust. However, an international study of attitudinal differences among managers conducted in five regional clusters (Cummings *et al.*, 1971) pointed out that, in Spain, managers tend to be the most conciliatory (understanding and friendly) among the groups studied (Greece, Spain, Central Europe, Scandinavia, and USA).

In the organizational context, García and Valle (2003) looked into whether the variables that generate trust and affect trust behaviors were the same in environments where social exchange has a stronger influence than economic exchange, focusing on the particular case of university professors. Based on an extensive literature review, they found that efficiency of communication, empowerment, and shared values were the antecedents of trust, while organizational citizenship behavior and turnover intention were seen as its consequences. It was also found that, in the university context, the supervisor gained the trust of subordinates (professors) through appropriate, exact, and valid communication, as well as through shared values. At the same time, empowerment, which is an important factor in the economic context for trust generation, was not applicable to the university context, as subordinates (professors, in this case) had much more autonomy in their daily tasks (teaching and research). Moreover, relationships based on trust did not lead to extra-role behaviors, as was the case for economic exchanges.

Finally, interfunctional trust was found to be critical for performance in new product development (García et al., 2007). A study conducted among R&D directors of innovative Spanish firms showed that the existence of affective bonds among product innovation participants was key for successful innovation, and trust between marketing and R&D directly affected new product performance. In line with this research, in a study of professional elite athletes, team member trust and a trusting environment affected team performance, thereby contributing to achieving organizational goals (Mach et al., 2010). In addition, trust in the coach was positively related to team cohesion, emphasizing the importance of the leader for the team's common work and outcomes. In the case of self-managed work teams, a study conducted among teams working in 12 Spanish companies, mostly multinationals, revealed that mutual trust within the work team and access to resources were the main factors for knowledge exchange and transfer (Zárraga & Bonache, 2003). The role of the leader was central for the existence of these two factors. Therefore, trust in colleagues within the same team, across departments, and in a variety of companies was shown to be important for the general climate, for product innovation, and for knowledge exchange and transfer. The role of team leader was paramount for trust creation.

Contextual Factors in Hierarchical Trusting Relationships

We now turn to the results of our research. Our Spanish focus group participants believed that the manager's perceived proximity is important in generating trust. In addition, a close working relationship, visibility in the workplace, and also the specific hierarchical position may affect the level of trust. Research participants mentioned the traditional existence of a large number of SMEs, many of which are family-owned, where it was understood that employees have to heed the manager-owner. This style of "manager-as-boss" is still found in many modern organizations. On the other hand, focus group participants believed that the subordinate is usually trusted and that the ability to trust one's subordinate is an essential quality of the manager, especially if he/she wants to be successful. Mutual trust is essential for a good professional relationship, and that requires that employees feel part of a team. In general, Spaniards tend to trust, unless the other person proves otherwise, in which case it is difficult to regain trust.

Our Delphi experts, on the other hand, believed that the level of trust between managers and subordinates was modest. Some of them believed that there is a general attitude between managers and subordinates that ranges from distrust to indifference. The professional relationship is not established along the trust–distrust continuum, but rather along the line of work done–not done (or results–no results). One of the experts posited that, in general, the attitudes and factors included in the model usually only have a small weight in the professional environment, which makes them even more necessary. These experts argued that most subordinates have an attitude of submission and delegation of decisions to other levels. Managers, they believed, have a tendency to supervise subordinates' work excessively, assert control without explanation, and invest little in training and developing their people. An important step in the right direction would be to change the name of "subordinate" to "collaborator." Subordinates obey managers out of fear, rather than out of trust. Sometimes, double standards are applied: the manager is rated differently behind his back than when face to face. Relationships are very transactional and trust depends significantly on the final results. In general, managers seem to experience problems with delegation and communication.

Several factors were given as possible explanations for the different levels of trust in hierarchical relationships:

1 *Organizational culture*: Most companies are SMEs with less than 15 employees, run by family owners rather than businessmen. This leads to a bossy style of manager. Regions with a longer business and industrial tradition, such as the Basque Country and Catalonia, tend to have higher levels of trust between managers and subordinates. The level of trust is also higher in the Community of Madrid, due to a higher concentration of large companies with more sophisticated corporate cultures.
2 *Sector*: In the services sector and high-tech start-up companies, the underlying levels of trust were perceived to be higher.
3 *Company size*: The company's size was believed to play a role in building trust by means of different (and sometimes counterbalancing) processes. In smaller companies, employees were perceived as having more task interdependencies, which leads to them interacting and working closer together. As one subordinate put it: "Trust is induced faster in small companies, because you work 'elbow to elbow' with colleagues and you support each other." This close communication can be lost when the company becomes larger. Commenting on a post-merger experience, one subordinate noted: "Before the merger, the final decision was in the hands of the General Manager in Spain, who allowed substantial participation and input from managers and subordinates. After the merger … this communication changed and was much more restricted." On the other hand, larger companies have more consolidated company cultures and HR policies, which influences the leadership style and ultimately increases trust.

In terms of the cultural dimensions of trust, participants were asked to evaluate Spain's standing along such dimensions as individualism–collectivism and power distance. Along the *individualism–collectivism dimension*, the focus group participants characterized Spain as rather individualistic, while as a society it is characterized as collectivistic. Our experts agreed with the latter classification and attributed it to the weak welfare system, strong family ties, and the support provided by the extended family to its members. Circumstances arising from the economic crisis in which the family has had to support unemployed relatives was cited as an example of this tendency toward social collectivism.

Our experts' views on *power distance* were mixed. Trust in hierarchical relationships was perceived to be very influenced by position, authority, and leadership. The leadership model in Spain is characterized as showing a preference for hierarchy, founded more on potential distrust than on axiomatic trust. Managers tend to distrust, which is exhibited as excessive control and centralization in the decision-making process. Finally, the presence of powerful unions in companies was viewed as something which increases the level of distrust.

Personal Factors in Hierarchical Trusting Relationships

Among our participants, both managers and subordinates believed that several personal factors can influence a trusting relationship. For example, both groups agreed that similarity in age can strengthen trust as employees will have more experiences in common, which reinforces empathy and communication. Nevertheless, professionalism was seen as crucial for a working relationship and could attenuate the effects of the age differences. As one manager put it: "I agree that one shares more things in common [with people of the same age], but ultimately, this is a professional relationship, so it's important that everybody is moving in the same direction." The subordinates emphasized that the duration of the relationship and the manager's and subordinate's seniority in the company have a positive influence on trust. With respect to *gender*, managers considered that having a gender mix was positive. Female employees were viewed as having better professional profiles and the ability to identify more closely with the team. One of the subordinates mentioned that, in homogeneous female teams, she observed a higher level of conflict than in gender-heterogeneous or homogenous male teams. On balance, however, both managers and subordinates agreed that professionalism, regardless of gender, was paramount and a skill set encompassing personal characteristics such as extroversion, transparency, good listening skills, a strong work ethic, and good communication skills, particularly when negative feedback has to be given, were important for good professional relationships and for fostering trust.

The expert group ranked the length of the relationship, age, and seniority in the company as the most important factors, while gender was seen as less significant. The experts viewed that the length of the relationship was important as trust is built over time on the basis of met expectations. As one noted: "I feel more comfortable with those I know better: he knows all the shortcuts, you can be frank with him, he can cover my mistakes and I will cover his." Age similarity was also seen as important because, by belonging to the same generation, people have more experiences in common and may relate better to each other. Seniority was seen as having the potential to breed trust, particularly among colleagues, as it transmitted the message that the person knew how things are done in the company. While the length of the relationship was seen as more important than seniority, the latter was also seen as important.

The focus group participants were asked to comment on the findings of the quantitative study regarding the significance of the personal factors that account for variations in trust (see Table 5.1).

Our data indicate that the *age difference between manager and subordinate is negatively correlated with managerial trustworthy behaviors*. Our participants suggested various explanations for this result. They suggested that the traditional promotion system based on seniority rather than merit may lead to distrust toward younger subordinates. Participants indicated that as merit becomes more important for promotion, the younger subordinates can be seen as a threat. Also, the cultural difference between the generations was seen as a potential explanation. One of the managers illustrated this by recounting his experience of working with younger subordinates who surprised him with what he observed as their lack of motivation and dedication to work and their marked preference for more leisure time.

Table 5.1 Spain: significant controls (correlations)

	Gender manager (1–> man, 2–> woman)	Age subordinate	Gender subordinate	Academic level subordinate	Age difference
MTB		0.324**	−0.229*		−0.188*
OCB	−0.364**	0.227*		−0.182*	
MTS	−0.208*	0.242**	−0.215*		
STM		0.189*	−0.204*		−0.186*

Notes
** Correlation significant at 0.01 level.
* Correlation significant at 0.05 level.
MTB = managerial trustworthy behavior, STM = subordinates' trust in managers, MTS = managers' trust in subordinates, OCB = organizational citizenship behavior.

The study also showed that *managers have more trust in older subordinates*, which participants attributed to cultural and generational differences. Culturally, they indicated that it can often be seen as unacceptable to promote and thus place trust in a young person, even if he or she is highly competent. One of the underlying assumptions was that a young person is less experienced and can make more mistakes. Conversely, older subordinates, because of their experience, are more trusted generally.

Subordinates with a higher educational background show less proactive behaviors. Our participants explained this effect by pointing out that the environment often is not merit-focused enough and the experience of seniority-based promotion may be more frustrating for those with a higher education. This frustration can lead more highly educated subordinates to be less engaged.

Antecedents and Outcomes of Manager–Subordinate Trust

Both managers and their subordinates viewed trust as an essential pillar for building a good professional relationship. From the subordinate's point of view, a good professional relationship meant open communication and the ability to exchange ideas, contribute to the decision-making process, and give mutual feedback. Managers indicated that subordinates should be able to fulfill the tasks that cannot be done by the manager. To make this possible, feedback was seen as crucial, as it ensures employees' motivation, proactivity, and good communication. According to the managers, a trustworthy person shows professionalism, loyalty toward the projects' objectives, and sound ethics. Furthermore, the degree of professional and personal communication was seen as important for trust building. Finally, managers say that trust is generated when the subordinate is proactive, motivated, shows respect, goes beyond what is asked, and can be delegated to.

Various behaviors may generate subordinates' trust in their managers. From the subordinate's point of view, it was seen to be important that the manager accept the subordinate's way of managing his work and should be open to his suggestions.

Besides manager's transparency, coherent and consistent behavior and communication were viewed as essential. Subordinates considered that their own consistency toward their co-workers was also important. They also valued open communication, and emphasized the importance of being able to delegate. One subordinate put it this way: "The capability to delegate things gave me security and peace of mind, this increased my responsibility, and this capability surprised me."

Subordinates trusted managers who were consistent in their behaviors and objectives. As one respondent put it: "One thing that discourages the team a lot is when the boss gives instructions and, within three months, he changes them." Trust is also seen to be greater in managers who accept feedback and suggestions, communicate openly, delegate tasks, and publicly recognize the subordinate's job. One subordinate noted: "When the manager says in public about me, 'This person is an expert,' it gives me a lot of trust because the manager is telling others that I am an expert." Finally, subordinates emphasized the characteristic of extroversion, which was seen as offering the potential for openness in the collaboration, engagement in the project, and meaningful feedback.

Interestingly, in our individual interviews, we found a similar list of behaviors that may generate trust: faithfulness to commitments, professionalism, responsibility, honesty, and fulfillment of work expectations. For example, as one interviewee points out:

> when the manager does what she says, I know that she is reliable, she sticks to her commitments. It is not a question of never changing criteria but of having a good reason for changing and being able to explain it.

Managers and subordinates suggested that trust has various positive outcomes for the professional relationship. From the subordinates' point of view, the manager's trust gives a feeling of security, which the subordinate can then transmit to his own team. In addition, it was seen to have a positive spillover to the company overall, as it engendered organizational commitment. As one committed subordinate put it: "I am the company."

Trust is closely related to employees' proactivity in situations where trust is reciprocated between manager and subordinate—that is, higher trust engenders extra discretionary effort. A similar situation seemed to apply to delegation by the manager, which acted as a conduit to effort. The downside of this situation was that managers' trust could, on occasion, lead to excessive delegation, resulting in excessive work demands.

Figure 5.1 provides a diagrammatic summary of the major antecedents and consequences of trust in the manager–subordinate relationship arising from the qualitative data generated by our focus groups and expert panels in Spain.

Our qualitative data indicate that a good professional relationship is characterized, on one hand, by a manager's ability to engage in substantive and meaningful communication, where ideas are combined and exchanged, meaningful feedback is provided, and engagement and motivation are the hallmarks of their managerial effort. From the subordinate's perspective, a positive professional relationship is evidenced by the ability to attain the objectives that have been set. Subordinates' proactivity, motivation, and task fulfillment generate managers' trust, which in turn leads to a more open, frank communication and higher levels of delegation. Similarly, managers'

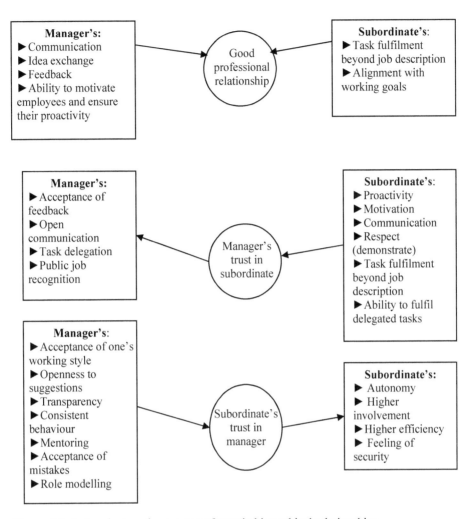

Figure 5.1 Antecedents and outcomes of trust in hierarchical relationships

acceptance of individual working styles, extensive communication, and consistent behavior engender subordinates' trust, which results in a higher level of subordinate engagement. Therefore, both managers' and subordinates' communication skills and ability to fulfill their respective job expectations support trust building.

The Dynamics of Trust in Hierarchical Relationships

Both managers and subordinates were clear in their view that trust evolves over time. While the individual's previous professional experience is seen to offer a certain initial platform for establishing trust with colleagues, it is recognized that trust is also an on-going, evolving process. In this evolution, several conditions may contribute to trust building. Managers emphasize the history and duration of the relationship, the results achieved, and the level of proactivity on the part of subordinates. One of the managers explained that trust was essential for generating autonomy in a subordinate, which potentially leads to higher job engagement. This in turn has the potential to generate higher satisfaction among employees.

Trust is transmitted not only verbally, but also at the non-verbal level. As one respondent noted:

> It is transmitted even "energetically." If you have the trust of your supervisor, the subordinate feels it, and also if you are not trusted, even if he comes one day and congratulates the team, it [the lack of trust] is also seen.

Subordinates underscored the importance of giving feedback to the manager, especially in situations where there are conflicting views. An initial level of trust allows the subordinate to speak up and debate with the manager with the goal of ensuring the project's success. One participant noted: "The courage to give this feedback is very valued by your supervisor. If you see that something is wrong, it is also your responsibility to try to give feedback and tell him." As indicated earlier, such behaviors are often appreciated by the manager, but are frequently only possible when a certain level of trust has been established.

While all interviewees emphasized that trust evolves over time, by their own volition, managers and subordinates experience this evolution differently. One manager prefers to "start the relationship by granting full trust to the person at the beginning." If subsequently difficulties arise, this is seen as a signal that some trust should be taken back and this person needs more of the manager's time and attention. Another manager opts for controlling the employees at the beginning of the relationship and giving more flexibility over time. It can take the form of closer employee follow-up or coaching. For instance, at the beginning, one manager schedules weekly coaching sessions, then biweekly sessions, and then gradually spaces them further over time. Finally, for another manager, at the beginning of a relationship, when he does not yet know his subordinate, trust is based on two factors: efficiency and professional respect. Managers emphasize the importance of perceiving the subordinate as a real talent, not just as a task executor, who "can enrich the process through his knowledge and skills." They also highlight the importance of building a good relationship with the subordinate, which at times is not easy, if the personalities are very different. As one manager puts it: "… depending on the subordinate, you need to win him over." Managers value proactive subordinates who search for creative solutions and this is often only possible when they are satisfied and motivated.

Subordinates outlined three different ways of interacting with a supervisor with whom they have yet to build a deep level of trust. First, there is the possibility of adopting a closed stance, where the employee shares only the necessary information while negotiating advantages for his work (cell phone use etc.). Second, a more transparent approach might be favored which seeks to understand the manager's personality and his way of working. Third, a more "forthright" posture, in which the subordinate positions himself as a valued resource, leveraging the fact that he is already part of the company and possesses insider knowledge, may be possible. All subordinates agreed that, until they get to know the manager, it is important to be prudent and draw a clear line between relationships and work. A new manager gains the subordinate's trust if he respects past actions and previously built trust. To conclude, reciprocal trust is essential in a manager–subordinate relationship. As one subordinate said: "Trust should be mutual, it is up-down, down-up, and sometimes in circles."

Our quantitative data offer interesting insights into the dynamics of trust (see Table 5.2). Comparing Spain with the overall findings among the 18 countries, we find a similar relationship between organizational citizenship behavior and managers' trust in subordinates. The Spanish data are also similar to the total sample as regards the relationship between managerial trustworthy behaviors and subordinates' trust in managers. Managers' trust in subordinates leads to a higher exercise of managerial trustworthy behaviors than in the overall model. Finally, in Spain, the effects of subordinates' trust in managers on their organizational citizenship behaviors are not statistically significant.

The dynamics of trust between managers and subordinates is not symmetrical, as managerial trustworthy behaviors seem to lead to higher subordinate trust in managers than the subordinates' OCB leads to managers' trust in subordinates. Nevertheless, in the focus groups, the importance of proactivity was mentioned by both managers and employees. The focus group participants explained this relationship in various ways. First, it was noted that, if identification with the project is high enough, the subordinate exhibits proactivity and does not necessarily need the manager's trust for that to occur. Besides, there are some job positions where employees do not interact closely with the manager and, thus, the proactive behaviors are less observed. Initially, there is little trust between the manager and the subordinate but people show more or less proactivity depending on their motivation and personality. Another possible explanation is that, in Spain, compared with Anglo-Saxon countries, companies do not have clearly articulated mission/vision statements and this might play a significant role in explaining the absence of a culture underpinned by concrete, tangible, agreed objectives. In many instances, employees could therefore be seen as left to their own devices.

The Delphi panel experts also provided valuable insights into the model. They agreed that the model is applicable to Spain and is universal, but that it could be enriched and extended. Of note, personal factors, such as personal traits, biases, and expectations, were viewed as potentially significant. In addition, positive and negative contextual factors, including family situations, were also seen as offering potential explanatory input to relationships: mood, work environment, the existing incentive system, and the nature of the work itself. While it was acknowledged that these are more difficult factors to measure, they were seen as enriching understanding of trust relationships. They suggested that trust represents a meta-value that must be fostered by the manager to create a general trusting environment, which only then would lead to OCB. The manager must be capable of showing a range of behaviors in order to attain this, such as professional capability, awareness of oneself and the subordinate, clarity, work fulfillment, and consistency. Additionally,

Table 5.2 Standardized regression weights for the trust model in Spain and the overall sample

	OCB–>MTS	MTS–>MTB	MTB–>STM	STM–>OCB
Spain only	0.54**	0.57**	0.81**	−0.01
Complete model	0.68**	0.34**	0.89**	0.08*

Notes
** Regression weight significant at 0.01 level.
* Regression weight significant at 0.05 level.

trust is reciprocal. A manager's trusting attitude is just as important as his trustworthy behavior and the subordinate's trusting attitude also plays a role in establishing trust.

Discussion and Conclusions

The results of our study in Spain confirm some of the main findings in the extant literature. Both managers and subordinates believe that trust is essential for building and then maintaining good professional working relationships (García, 2004). In this sense, the trust building process is viewed as a dynamic process that evolves over time (Peterson & Behfar, 2003). While the professional credentials that an employee possesses when starting in a new company are important in the initial stages of relationship building, trust is forged through on-going interpersonal exchanges (Williams, 2001). Moreover, trust itself is seen to be mutually reinforcing as one person's trustworthy behaviors lead to higher levels of trust on the part of the other (Coyle-Shapiro, 2002). For instance, managers argue that their ability to delegate leads to higher levels of subordinate autonomy and satisfaction, which allows the manager to direct his attention elsewhere, as was also evidenced in previous research (Long & Sitkin, 2006). At the same time, a lack of trust in the manager directly affects the subordinate's behavior, making him/her act in a more cautious manner, trying to "get a feeling" of the other person before making any suggestions, and setting clear limits between work and personal life. Once trust is established, the work–personal life boundaries can at times be voluntarily moved by the subordinate, motivated by the positive relationship that exists or the enhanced commitment to the task at hand. Our research shows that an excess of trust can also have potentially negative effects on the relationship, as the manager may delegate too much, leading to possible work and role overload.

The cultural variables discussed provide a deeper understanding of the behaviors observed and existing manager–subordinate relationships. Similar to the GLOBE findings, our study participants contend that the organizational environment tends to be individualistic, while at the societal level, Spain is rather collectivistic. Experts argue that trust in hierarchical relationships is strongly affected by one's position, authority, and leadership (Rivera & Verna, 1996). The peculiarity of the Spanish context characterized by a high power distance, is evoked by the example of giving feedback to one's manager, which is perceived as an act of bravery, as the employee risks having his feedback perceived by the manager as a threat or criticism. Nonetheless, existing trust can moderate this risk-taking, as employees who have established trusting relationships with their manager view this behavior as a responsibility and a sign of loyalty to the manager.

Interestingly, the results of our study showed no significant relationship between subordinates' trust in their managers and their organizational citizenship behavior. Study participants emphasized individual agency to explain these results, as employees' interest and involvement in the project may be sufficient motivation to generate proactive behavior, without depending on the interaction with the manager, which might be scarce at times. Finally, the lack of a company vision or an overview of strategic goals in some companies might limit employees' scope of action and, thus, their proactive behaviors.

Current research on HR practice has pointed out that the HR function has evolved over the last decades in Spain, adopting more strategic developmental characteristics (Quintanilla *et al.*, 2004). HR practices can play a key role in enhancing employees' motivation and attracting more skilled, committed individuals (García-Olaverri *et al.*, 2006) who will ultimately influence the company's performance. Furthermore, a number of actions can be takento improve trusting relationships between managers and subordinates. Organizational communication can enhance trust and employees' awareness of organizational actions and strategy (Tzafrir *et al.*, 2004). HR can contribute to the establishment of a fair justice system, as fairness was found to be one of the key antecedents of trust (Cohen-Charash & Spector, 2001), also affecting employees' extra-role behaviors.

Our study also provides several practical implications. Participants believed that talent exists at all organizational levels and, by encouraging exchanges across different hierarchical levels, managers and subordinates benefit from the knowledge transfer facilitated by enhanced intra-organizational networks.

As the focus group participants highlighted, it is important that the training provided by the organization be aligned with the organization's culture and existing employee participation practices. Otherwise, the skills and knowledge acquired are not applied, which can be a frustrating experience for employees and eventually lead to general distrust toward organizational actions. Consequently, we advocate implementing training opportunities that offer potential for enhanced employee empowerment and development. In this effort, it is important that employee selection and inclusion in training programs be guided by the principles of fairness and equitability (Tzafrir *et al.*, 2004). The creation of an empowering culture, based on open communication and fairness, might, in itself, contribute further to establishing trusting relationships between managers and subordinates.

Overall, while we have attempted to gain a representative picture of manager–subordinate relationships in Spain, it should be acknowledged that the study sample was confined to respondents residing in Northeastern Spain, mostly in Catalonia. Future research might explore differences in other geographical regions. In addition, it is plausible that manager–subordinate relationships might be different among various occupational groups and further insights into trust building could be provided by including a more diverse occupational spread in the sample. Beyond occupational group, the issue of gender clearly deserves further study. The higher participation of women in management could shed new light on our knowledge of appropriate managerial style and effective workplace relationship building between managers and subordinates. Consequently, we would encourage future research on the role of gender in trust building.

References

Amuedo-Dorantes, C. (2000). Work transitions into and out of involuntary employment in a segmented market: Evidence from Spain. *Industrial and Labour Relations Review*, 52(2): 309–326.

Boldy, J., Jain, S. & Northey, K. (1993). What makes an effective European manager? A case study of Sweden, Belgium, Germany, and Spain. *Management International Review*, 33: 157–169.

Caceres, F.R. (1999). *Función empresarial y emergencia empresarial. Un análisis empírico sobre losfactores económicos y socio-institucionales que explican la aparición de empresarios en Andalucía Occidental*, Ph.D. thesis, Universidad de Sevilla.

Camelo, C., Martín, F., Romero, P.M. & Valle, R. (2004). Human resource management in Spain: Is it possible to speak of a typical model? *International Journal of Human Resource Management*, 15(6): 935–958.

Chhokar, J.S., Brodbeck, F.C. & House, R.J. (2007). *Culture and Leadership Across the World: The GLOBE book of In-Depth Studies of 25 Societies*. Manhaw: Lawrence Erlbaum Associates.

Cohen-Charash, Y. & Spector, P.E. (2001). The role of justice in organizations: A meta-analysis. *Organizational Behavior and Human Decision Processes*, 86: 278–321.

Coyle-Shapiro, J.A. (2002). A psychological contract perspective on organizational citizenship behavior. *Journal of Organizational Behavior*, 23: 927–946.

Cummings, L.L., Harnett, D.L., & Stevens, O.L. (1971). Risk, fate, conciliation, and trust: An international study of attitudinal differences among executives. *Academy of Management Journal*, 14: 285–304.

Edelman Trust Barometer (2009). Retrieved on 7.12.10 from www.edelman.com/speak_up/blog/ Trust_Barometer_Executive_Summary_FINAL.pdf.

Esping-Andersen, G. (2000). *Fundamentos sociales de las economías postindustriales*. Barcelona: Ariel.

Euromarómetro (2009). Informe Nacional: España. Standard 72, Otoño.

Eurostat (2010). Harmonised unemployment rate by gender. Retrieved on 7.12.10 fromhttp://epp.eurostat.ec.europa.eu/tgm/table.do?tab=table&language=en&pcode=teilm020&tableSelection=1&plugin=1.

Ferrera, M. (1996). The "Southern Model" of Welfare in Social Europe. *Journal of European Social Policy*, 6: 17–37.

García, J. (2004). *Análisis de la confianza organizacional mediante un enfoque de metaanálisis: marcos teóricos, disciplinas subyacentes, conceptualizaciones, antecedentes y consecuencias*. Document presented at the 14th Congress of the Scientific Association of Economics and Business Administration (ACEDE), September, Murcia, Spain.

García, R. & Valle, J. (2003). La generación de confianza y sus efectos sobre el comportamiento. Retrieved on 15.11.2010 from http://dialnet.unirioja.es/servlet/articulo?codigo=2712267.

García-Olaverri, M.C., Huerta-Arribas, E. & Larraza-Kintana, M. (2006). Human and organizational capital: Typologies among Spanish firms. *The International Journal of Human Resource Management*, 17(2): 316–330.

García Rodríguez, N., Sanzo Pérez, M.J. & Trespalacios Gutiérrez, J.A. (2007) Interfunctional trust as a determining factor of a new product performance. *European Journal of Marketing*, 41(5/6): 678–702.

Gúzman, J., Santos, J. & Cáceres, F.R. (1995): Small and medium-sized enterprises, family business and the enterprise culture in Spain. In *Conference on Business Development in Central and Eastern Europe and its Implications for the Economic Integration of the CEEC in a Wider Europe*, 1st ed. Brno (Czech Republic), Technical University of Brno, pp. 126–134.

Hofstede, G. (1991). *Cultures and Organizations: Software on the Mind*. London: McGraw-Hill.

Long, C.P. & Sitkin, S.B. (2006). Trust in the balance: how managers integrate trust-building and task control. In R. Bachmann & A. Zaheer (eds), *Handbook of Trust Research*. Cheltenham: Edward Elgar, pp. 87–106.

McFarlin, D.B., Sweeney, P.D. & Cotton, J.L. (1993). Attitudes toward employee participation in decision-making: A comparison of European and American managers in a United States multinational company, *Human Resource Management*, 31(4): 363–383.

Mach, M., Dolan, S.L. & Tzafrir, S. (2010). The differential effect of team members' trust on team performance: The mediation role of team cohesion. *Journal of Occupational and Organizational Psychology*, 83: 771–794.

Montero, J.R., Zmerli, S. & Newton, K. (2008). Confianza social, confianza política y satisfacción con la democracia [Social trust, political confidence, and satisfaction with democracy]. *Revista Española de Investigaciones Sociológicas (Reis)*, 122: 11–54.

O'Connell, J.J., Prieto, J.M. & Gutierrez, C. (2007). Managerial culture and leadership in Spain. In J.S. Chhokar, F.C. Broadbeck & R. J. House (eds), *Culture and Leadership, Across the World: the GLOBE Book of In-depth Studies of 25 Societies.* Mahwah: Lawrence Erlbaum Associates, pp. 623–654.

Page, N.R. & Wiseman, R.L. (1993). Supervisory behavior and worker satisfaction in the United States, Mexico, and Spain. *The Journal of Business Communication*, 30(2): 161–180.

Pérez, S., Montes, J. & Vásquez, C. (2005). Human resources practices, organizational learning and business performance. *Human Resource Development International*, 8: 147–164.

Peterson, R. & Behfar, K.J. (2003). The dynamic relationship between performance feedback, trust and conflict in groups: A longitudinal study. *Organizational Behavior and Human Decision Processes*, 92: 102–112.

Quintanilla, J., Sánchez-Runde, C. & Cardona, P. (2004). *Competencias de la dirección de personas. Un análisis desde la alta dirección.* Madrid: Pearson/Prentice Hall.

Quintanilla, J., Belizón, M.J., Susaeta, L. & Sánchez-Mangas, R. (2009). Malleability in Spain: The influence of US Human Resource Development Models. In C. Hansen & Y. Lee (eds), *The Cultural Context of Human Resource Development*. Hampshire: Palgrave Macmillan.

Rivera Camino, J. & Verna, G. (1996). The Spanish management style: An exploratory comparison with the French managers. *Working Paper 96–35. Business Economics Series*, May.

San Martín, S., Gutiérrez, J. & Camarero, K. (2004). Trust as the key to relational commitment. *Journal of Relationship Marketing*, 3(1): 53–77.

Saz-Carranza, A. & Serra, A. (2009). Institutional sources of distrust in government contracting. A comparison between home-based and residential social services in Spain. *Public Management Review, 11*(3): 263–279.

Trompenaars, F. (1993). *Riding the Wave of Culture: Understanding Diversity in Business.* London: Economist Books.

Tzafrir, S.S., Harel, G., Baruch, Y. & Dolan, L.S. (2004). The consequences of emerging HRM practices for employees' trust in their managers. *Personnel Review*, 33(6): 628–647.

Williams, M. (2001). In whom we trust: Group membership as an affective context for trust development. *Academy of Management Review*, 26(3): 377–396.

Zárraga, C. & Bonache, J. (2003). Assessing the team environment for knowledge sharing: An empirical analysis. *International Journal of Human Resource Management*, 14(7): 1227–1245.

6 Manager–Subordinate Trust Relationships in Poland

KONRAD JAMRO

Introduction

> Poland is the most easterly portion of Western Europe, the outpost of the West so to speak. [...]
> A sentinel on a wall, a guard on an outpost, it acquired an acute perception and recognition of
> what is foreign, what is alien, menacing and dangerous.

The outpost reality, as expressed above by a German philosopher (Hilckman, 1962), greatly influenced 11 centuries of Poland's history. The combination of Slavic character and Roman Catholic faith created a specific Polish culture and soul: inherently individualistic with a strong aversion to imposed authority, and permeated with the spirit of liberty, magnanimity, and manhood (Chesterton, 1922). One of its most characteristic heritages was the Polish–Lithuanian Commonwealth, the largest and one of the wealthiest countries in Europe, a democratic federation of *the free with the free, and equals with equals*, with unprecedented religious and personal liberties in pre-Enlightenment Europe (Davis, 2007; Łojek, 1996).

In the twentieth century, the Polish soul manifested strongly in the hard times. For example, the violent occupation by Nazi Germany during the Second World War led Poles to create the largest underground state, with police, courts, schools, and universities, together with the Home Army, the largest resistance movement in occupied Europe; and a unique Council to Aid Jews, even though concealing Jews was considered by the German occupiers to be a crime punishable by death (Davis, 2006; Davis, 2009; Connelly, 2005; Korboński, 2009; Lucas, 2001; Szpytma, 2009). Again, in the 1980s, accumulated abuses of civil and political rights by the communist regime, and a bankrupt centrally planned economy led almost one third of Polish people to join *Solidarity*[1], an independent trade union and unique civic movement, which, through peaceful protests, resistance, and pressure, helped bring about democratic changes that spread quickly to other Soviet-controlled communist countries (Ash, 1989, 1991; Łojek, 1996).

---

1 Full name: The Independent and Self-Governing Trade Union Solidarność (*Solidarity*).

Although there is no doubt that those civic movements required an exceptionally high level of trust between their members, it is less clear whether this heritage has still any influence on trust relationships in the stable political and economic environment of contemporary Poland. In this chapter, the author seeks to shed more light on this question, looking at the forces currently prevailing in Polish society that affect these relationships, particularly in hierarchical organizations. Above all, particular attention is paid to individual experiences of trust in professional relationships between managers and subordinates.

The chapter is organized into five main sections. The first consists of a brief historical perspective of the development of the Polish state and society, highlighting macro-societal factors that are conducive to the emergence of a culture of trust (Sztompka, 1999). The second briefly describes the current social, economic, and political context and provides a few macro data that are connected with the climate of trust. The third reviews contemporary domestic and international studies on trust in Poland at the societal, organizational, and individual level. The fourth presents the results of empirical studies on manager–subordinate trust relationships in Poland. The fifth section discusses the study's findings and suggests implications for practice and future research.

Highlights of Manager–Subordinate Trust in Poland

- Trust between managers and subordinates is not symmetrical. Managers tend to trust more upfront, while subordinates are rather distanced and usually have a lower affective trust in managers.
- Managers and subordinates underscore the influence of age differences on the initial level of trust. The bigger the age difference, the lower the initial level of trust, mainly due to stereotypes that young employees are less worthy and older employees are closed to collaboration and inflexible.
- Managers trust subordinates who are, first and foremost, reliable—that is, highly skilled and knowledgeable. Managers also stress the importance of subordinates' credibility and integrity.
- Subordinates trust managers who have, first and foremost, consistent and predictable behaviors. Subordinates also stress the importance of managers' loyalty, concern, and integrity.
- Managerial trustworthy behaviors do not seem to facilitate subordinates' organizational citizenship behaviors. Instead, they seem to be important for interpersonal and task related citizenship behaviors.
- In general, trust has to be earned, and Poles put their trust in people they already know well, especially the closest family, friends, co-workers, and business partners. For historical reasons, there is little general confidence in strangers or in state institutions.

Historical Perspective

The baptism of Mieszko I, the ruler of the Piast dynasty, in 966 and consequent adoption of Catholicism by his people was a symbolic beginning of the Polish state. Within a few centuries, the Kingdom of Poland evolved into the Polish–Lithuanian

Commonwealth, the union of the free with the free, and equals with equals, officially proclaimed in 1569 (Łojek, 1996).

The free and equals pertained to all classes of the numerous Polish and Lithuanian nobility, who enjoyed many personal and civil rights, including a remarkable veto right in the Diet. These unprecedented civil rights of the nobility slowly became a curse for Poland (Bocheński, 1996; Jasienica, 1988; Łojek, 1996). Power struggles between magnates and the kings and lack of state reforms led gradually to the downfall of the largest and one of the wealthiest countries in Europe. The last spectacular attempt to reform the state took place in 1791, when the May 3 Constitution was adopted. Soon after, Poland disappeared from the political map of Europe.

For almost 200 years, since the final partition in 1795 until the fall of communism in 1989, with the exception of two decades of independence between the World Wars, the Polish people have lived unwillingly under imposed authorities. Many people emigrated, and some of them—driven by the motto "for our freedom and yours"—took part in various independence movements around the world, and those who stayed were involved in endless protests, boycotts, resistance movements, and dramatic uprisings.

During the First World War, the civic and military engagement of many Poles, and the diplomatic efforts of eminent Polish emigrants, bore fruit in 1918 when Poland regained its independence. Faced with an exhausting military effort to stabilize its eastern borders (D'Abernon, 1931; Pobóg-Malinowski, 1953), and a difficult economic reality, the young Republic of Poland was developing slower than most European countries, reaching in the late 1930s just one third of the European average GDP per capita (Żarnowski, 1999).

Deprived of their state in 1939 after the German Nazi invasion followed by the Soviet aggression, Poles once again went underground, and fought for our freedom and yours on almost every European front of the Second World War (Davis, 2007; Olson & Cloud, 2003). That war brought traumatic consequences as more than 5.3 million people were exterminated, and a huge part of its material assets were devastated and plundered (Davis, 2006). Finally, at the end of the Second World War, Poland was ceded to the Soviet sphere of influence (Bliss Lane, 2008), and until 1989, Poles lived under a communist regime.

The essence of the communist regime was a shocking disparity between political theory and practice; between written constitutional laws and deprivation of civil, political, and economic rights in real life. All the nonsense and waste of the centrally-planned economy, which was also used to support the Soviet industry, led to a permanent economic crisis (Łojek, 1996). The differences between the values held by society and those promoted by the state were extreme and created a lot of suffering (state terror, murders, and victimization), huge moral pressures (dual morality, i.e. decline of the work ethos in state enterprises, and no care for public good; vulnerability to blackmail in exchange for basic civil rights and goods), as well as social disintegration and alienation (cynical attitude toward the state, sense of hopelessness). The public life created by the propaganda and state ideology was fictitious (Legutko, 2008).

The people of Poland rose against the communist regime several times, including mass protests in 1956–1957, 1968, 1970, and 1980–1981, which finally led to a peaceful downfall of the regime in 1989. Scholars (Davis, 2006; Legutko, 2008;

Lukowski & Zawadzki, 2006) highlight the catalytic role of the Catholic Church, especially the election of Cardinal Wojtyła to the Papacy in 1978. A landmark visit to his native Poland a year later was cathartic for many Poles, and created a foundation for a mass movement of national and political renaissance, known throughout the world as Solidarity.

Institutional Context

Economic Context

Twenty-three years of transformation after the fall of the communist regime in 1989 has been the longest period of continuous development in the last 200 years, without a war or other shocks. Today, Poland is the sixth largest economy in the European Union, with a GDP per capita (PPP) equal to US$ 19,000 (IMF, 2010). The service sector comprises 64 percent of GDP, industry 31 percent, and agriculture 5 percent. As the only EU country with GDP growth in 2009, Poland is regarded as a very attractive place for foreign investments, mainly due to a strong internal market, relatively low labor costs, and highly qualified young workers. In the record year of 2007, Poland received almost 17 billion EUR in direct foreign investments (The World Bank Group). Poland's exports comprise 37 percent of its GDP, while imports account for 40 percent (GUS). The biggest trading partner and investor is Germany, accounting for 30 percent of overall trade and 16 percent of direct foreign investment.

Since 1989, major reforms have been undertaken to facilitate the transition from a centrally planned economy and central government to a free market and democratic state. However, there are still urgent challenges, especially to increase the quality and efficiency of taxes, laws, and public institutions, create a favorable environment for an innovative economy, and create more favorable conditions for social development (Ministry of Economy, 2008; Polish Chamber of Commerce, 2006). These challenges may be the reason why the black economy accounts for 15 or even 25 percent of the GDP (Barszcz, 2010; CBOS, 2009).

Political System

Poland is a democratic country with an elected President as Head of State. Most of the executive power is concentrated in the government, led by a Prime Minister. Legislative power corresponds to the elected Parliament, consisting of a Lower and Upper House. As of 2011, the political scene is dominated by two parties: Civic Platform (PO), which rules the government in a coalition with the much smaller Polish People's Party (PSL); and Law and Justice (PiS), which is the largest opposition party.

The last two decades have witnessed major political achievements, such as joining NATO in 1999 and the European Union in 2004. On the other hand, the lack of a transparent lustration and in-depth decommunization of state institutions has been widely criticized and identified as one of the major weaknesses of the transformation process (Kieżuń, 2004; Pejovich, 2005; Śpiewak, 2009; Szczęsny, 2010; Wildstein, 2005). First, it maintained the informal connections and influence of people who were involved in the communist regime, which was particularly harmful during the privatization of state-run companies. Second, new people joining state institutions were nolens volens invited to continue the bad formal practices of the old system. Third, it did not allow for complete and coherent state reforms.

Sociological Context

Polish scholars point out several vital sociological and demographic processes. First, its population growth of 0.1 percent and the fertility rate of 1.4 are one of the lowest in the world (GUS). Second, the unemployment rate of 11.6 percent is still very high, although it has improved from 20 percent in 2003 (GUS). Third, for the past 20 years, emigration for work decreased the population by 0.5 percent each year. Fourth, the work ethos, destroyed during the communist system, is being rebuilt according to the traditional values of utility and necessity, but younger generations also add self-realization and creativity (Jacher & Świadźba, 2008; Jezior, 2001). Fifth, morality still plays an important role among the younger generations, but it is considered part of private life, leading to moral permissiveness in public life (Świda-Ziemba, 2008). Finally, civic society is being built very slowly, as the legitimization of the central government and other state institutions is relatively weak (Śpiewak, 2009).

HR Practices

HR practices in Poland have evolved significantly during the past two decades of state and economic transformations, including, among others, a transition from a closed, centrally planned economy where private initiative was suppressed to an open market with freely competing people and enterprises.

One of the most important events was privatization. From almost 8500 state companies at the beginning of the transformation, only 174 remained in 2010 (Ministry of the Treasury, 2010). Around 2000 state-run companies were wound up, but at the same time almost three million small and medium-sized private companies were created. Almost 95 percent of these new companies are micro-enterprises, hiring less than ten workers, a further 5 percent are small and medium-sized enterprises with less than 250 employees (Tarnawa, 2009). As a result, 60 percent of employees in Poland work on permanent contracts, while the other 40 percent are either self-employed or work on different types of temporary assignments, usually without the benefits which permanent positions qualify for (Central Statistical Office, 2011).

Recent studies of 54 medium-sized and large companies in the production, FMCG, finance, and sales sectors (Hay Group, 2009, 2011) show that HR departments in 59 percent of the firms still play a mainly administrative role. However, there are a growing number of companies that treat their HR departments as strategic partners (29 percent), or change agents (14 percent). HR departments' strategic role is implemented in 58 percent of companies with foreign capital, and 28 percent of firms with a majority of domestic ownership. More than 50 percent of the firms run talent management programs, and two thirds offer e-learning opportunities for their employees. More than 90 percent of the executives are aware that the HR strategy chosen has a direct impact on the bottom line. Interestingly, it is measured not only by return from investment in human capital, but also by balanced scorecards.

Other studies (Borkowska, 2007) show that HR practices in the largest Polish companies usually match those of foreign competitors. It confirms also that executives are aware of the importance of human resource management for profitable business. However, not many of them really treat HR strategically. The HR departments in small and medium-sized companies still play a mainly administrative role, and rarely focus on talent management. Nevertheless, HR executives are at least aware that their firm's lack of competitive advantage is due in part to poor human resource practices.

Recent work on changes in HR practices (Puchalski, 2010) shows that companies do not implement human resource management in a comprehensive manner, which may hinder organizational knowledge creation and accumulation. Executives pay attention to selection, retention, and competence development, including pay-for-performance, coaching, mentoring, complex performance appraisals, and career plans, but these practices are usually tactical and not connected with the organization's overall strategy.

Literature Review on Trust

Generalized Trust and Social Capital

According to the CBOS survey on generalized trust (CBOS, 2010a), 26 percent of respondents agreed that most people can be trusted, and it seems to be a growing trend over the past few years. With this result, Poland is included in the group of countries with a low interpersonal trust (World Values Survey, Trust Index 1999–2007; Reeskens & Hooghe, 2008).

On the other hand, it contrasts with other results (ESS Round 4, 2008). For example, Poles are much less afraid about their home being robbed, or about being a victim of a violent crime, than most other Europeans. The same goes with the feeling of safety of walking alone in a local area after dark. These feelings are some of the necessary elements for the *environment of trust*, which precedes development of a *culture of trust* (Sztompka, 2007).

Scholars (Fukuyama, 1995; Putnam, 1993, 2000) have already identified a strong correlation between generalized trust and social capital, which in turn conditions societies' wellbeing and competitiveness. However, a study on rural communities in Poland (Fedyszak-Radziejowska, 2007) shows that social capital might be high despite low interpersonal trust. The author found that, despite the deficit of trust created in the past by the communist regime, social capital is built by local elites, which creates more and more active organizations and associations, which in turn leads to restoration of interpersonal trust.

Nevertheless, studies show that that civic engagement of Poles is relatively low, as only 12 to 28 percent[2] of the society belongs to any civic organization (ESS Round

---

2 Czapinski & Panek (2009) explained this significant discrepancy by the fact that studies used various methodologies. And, for example, Social Diagnosis had only one general question about membership of organizations, whereas CBOS included more than 30 questions about different kinds of organizations.

4, 2008; CBOS, 2010b; Gumkowska *et al.*, 2007). The level of civic engagement varies in different social groups—for example, managers, specialists with higher education, farmers, and students represent the highest level of engagement. On the individual level, civic engagement is positively correlated with the level of education and income (Czapinski & Panek, 2009), as well as the frequency of attending religious services (CBOS, 2010b).

Trust in Institutions

Poles exhibit various levels of trust toward different institutions (CBOS, 2010a). About 80 percent of Poles trust charities (The Great Orchestra of Christmas Charity; Caritas; and the Polish Red Cross), the Catholic Church, and the Army. About 60 percent of the people trust international institutions, such as the European Union, the United Nations, and NATO. Slightly more than half of the people trust local authorities, the Ombudsman, and the Institution of National Remembrance. On the other side of the scale are the political parties, the Parliament, central government, public administration, and courts, which are distrusted by most citizens.

Such a low level of trust toward central government, courts, and the Parliament is explained by the fact that Poles do not identify themselves with the state or its structures (Domanski, 2005). Domanski claims that such low legitimization cannot be attributed to immature democracy, low civic culture, or relatively low average living standards. It is rather the fact that citizens are disappointed with the leaders and elites, who are often blamed for sustaining and creating more informal and pathological ties between politics, media, and business. Moreover, the transition period from a communist regime to democracy gave rise to a common distrust of state agencies due to the blurred accountability of local and central governments, and unclear separation of powers.

Trust in Business Agents

A recent Edelman Trust Barometer (2010) shows that general trust in business is moderate (54 percent), with a positive trend over the past few years. The perception of a businessman in Poland has also changed positively in the last few years (Kolarska-Bobińska, 2009; Biały, 2009). However, still almost half of the people think that businessmen in general do not care about employees and are not honest in paying taxes or adhering to the law.

In a study of 26 countries in transition, Raiser *et al.* (2003) introduced a robust measure of trust between firms: the level of prepayment demanded by suppliers from their customers in advance of delivery. All in all, Polish and Czech companies require the smallest prepayment among all 26 countries under study, which is a sign of relatively high trust between business partners in these two countries.

In another empirical study of firms in Poland, Tridico (2006) built six governance indexes and tested their impact on the productivity of firms in two macro-regions of Poland (West and East). One of these indexes is trust, including trust between business agents as well as trust in foreign investors and public institutions. Even though the reverse causality effect cannot be completely excluded, the trust index has the strongest influence on companies' economic performance and is clearly higher in the West than in the East.

Trust at Work

In a four-country study (Costigan *et al.*, 2006), scholars examined the effects of an employee's affect-based and cognition-based trust in the supervisor on that employee's citizenship behaviors. For all countries under study (Poland, Russia, Turkey, and the US), these effects are significant although modest. In addition, the average employee's trust in his/her supervisor is lowest in Poland, compared with other countries, although the difference does not exceed 10 percent.

Another study shows that the level of trust among employees with temporary contracts and people who are generally not favored in the market (e.g. mothers, fresh graduates, and elderly people) is very low (Skrzek-Lubasińska, 2009). Generally, employees do not trust employers and vice-versa, and neither of them trust government institutions. A worrying lack of trust between employees was also found. This is a consequence of different kinds of stereotypes and the continuous pressure of competition and rivalry to keep a job or receive a promotion.

Such a low level of trust in this sector of the Polish labor market is explained by the transformation processes from a centrally planned economy to a free market (Sójka, 1999). According to Sójka, transformation processes are generally distrusted. For example, in the case of Poland, a national privatization program was recognized as a process against workers, resulting in massive layoffs and lower wages, and benefitting only a few.

Trust in the Family

The family is the leading institution for Poles (Grabowska & Roguska, 2008). Most Poles generally trust their nearest and dearest—that is, the closest family (96 percent), friends (90 percent), other relatives (87 percent), co-workers (84 percent) and neighbors (74 percent). This high position held by the family in Poland has been stable for generations and is reflected in the high level of trust toward relatives and other people that are known well (CBOS, 2010a; Czapinski & Panek, 2009).

Contextual Factors in Hierarchical Trusting Relationships

We now turn to the results of our study. First of all, trust levels are not balanced (i.e. managers tend to trust more than subordinates do). Practitioners participating in focus groups explain that it is the manager who has power over the subordinate, especially when promoting and firing. Second, it could be a consequence of communism, where the boss often represented or legitimized the regime. This effect could be stronger in public companies or firms that were recently privatized. Lastly, managers often participate in training sessions, conferences, and post-graduate studies, where they become more aware of the importance of trust, and subsequently take the lead in trust building. On the other hand, subordinates are more distanced from their bosses and organizations as a whole, and thus express lower trust.

Practitioners believe that, in general, subordinates trust managers and vice-versa. They emphasize that trust depends on the type of industry, whether the company is private, public, or state-owned, multinational or domestic, based in a smaller or bigger town, etc. One of the middle managers explained:

I would say that generally subordinates trust managers and vice-versa. However, trust is a grayscale, and in a private, modern company there might be quite a high level of mutual trust, but in a state monopoly, trust might be very low or even non-existent—for example, in a coal mine where recent fatal accidents have completely destroyed the trust of line workers in the management.

On the other hand, most Delphi panel experts say that there is little trust in general between employees and their bosses, even though there are more and more positive exceptions of organizations with a prevailing culture of trust, as in an example given by one of the experts:

A company I know has been on the market for ten years; it started in a garage, and over the years it has grown considerably. Recently, due to difficulties in the market, the company hit the bottom. However, employees who still remembered "the garage stage" volunteered to waive 25 percent of their wages to develop new products and markets, and to save other employees and the company itself.

Experts from academia recall different studies showing that Poles have relatively low trust toward other people (Czapinski & Panek, 2009; CBOS, 2010a) and state agents (Domanski, 2005; CBOS, 2010a), as well as between employees and employers (Skrzek-Lubasińska, 2009). They indicate competition in the labor market as one of the reasons for low trust levels between managers and subordinates as well as among employees. Experts also emphasize the influence of recent history on the trust culture in Poland, including two World Wars, more than 40 years under the influence of the former Soviet Union, and the last 20 years of transformation. One of the experts said:

Generally, there is no trust between the two sides of the labor relationship. The roots of this general lack of trust in Poland are buried deep in its history. Poles do not trust any formal authority. In practice, it means an eternal distrust of the state and the state's laws. Managers are representatives of another authority—the owners—and as such, cannot be trusted either.

Another added:

I think that there are a couple of reasons. First, there is the heritage of the communist past: homo sovieticus with no culture of collaboration in trust. Second, there is a lack of experience in the free-market economy, which is still underdeveloped, with pathologies such as corruption, nepotism, and dishonesty.

In addition, experts underline that general trust between employees and their managers also depends on the firm and its culture, styles of leadership, transparency, etc.

In terms of cultural dimensions, experts agree that Poles are very individualistic and their individual wellbeing and that of their closest family is much more important than the goals of the wider group or society. One of the reasons could be the "Polish soul," historical events, and current transformation processes where Poland is trying to catch up with the wealthier countries. One of the experts summarized:

Poles can be very active, they can show good entrepreneurship abilities but only when they act or work for themselves, or for their closest family. The lack of generalized trust prevents Poles from building cohesive groups on a large scale.

In terms of power distance, experts agree that there is little acceptance of power distance in Poland, which is heightened by the country's history and democratic heritage. However, the current reality might be different from what people like, expect, or accept—for example, when differences in social status and a degree of aversion toward successful businessmen are taken into account. One of the experts summarized:

> In Poland, historically, kings seldom had a strong power, as it was distributed among the nobility, and there was no acceptance of an unequal power distribution. Also today, people in Poland are rebelling against those who, in their opinion, have too much power. This also applies, to some extent, to relations in the work place.

Another added: "Poles hate dictators, and in the organizational setting, workers want clear rules, more autonomy, flexibility, and no distance in the relationships."

The experts also mention a few national traits, which influence trust at work, such as: individualism, impulsiveness, not much respect for authority, formal rules treated very flexibly, strong family orientation, and a strict distinction between positions in public and private life.

Personal Factors in Hierarchical Trusting Relationships

As for personal factors, the quantitative study showed interesting relationships with some control variables, as depicted in Table 6.1. While some of the correlations seemed to be intuitive, there were others that needed more attention. Therefore, we asked all the interviewees (i.e. managers and subordinates as well as the Delphi panel experts) to comment on and explain the most significant correlations.

First of all, it is surprising that no correlation has been found between trust (both MTS and STM) and the length of the relationship, even though managers, subordinates, and experts agree that it is the best predictor of mutual trust. They assume probably that it is a freely made decision between the manager and the subordinate to work together on a long-term basis. However, the reality might be different (i.e. people who participated in the quantitative study often had to work together regardless of the trust levels between them). It also might be a consequence of the limited sample size.

As for the correlation between the number of employees in the company and subordinates' citizenship behaviors, most interviewees admit that, in a smaller company, it is much easier to have closer and deeper relationships, and to see how one's effort is reflected directly in the company's results. Both factors may facilitate citizenship behaviors toward the organization. In addition, a significant proportion of the smaller companies included in the study were start-ups or family-owned businesses where employees are usually highly motivated and engage more eagerly in citizenship behaviors.

Third, managers and subordinates underscore the influence of age differences on the initial level of trust. The larger the age difference, the lower the initial level of trust, mainly due to stereotypes that young employees are less worthy and older employees are closed to collaboration and inflexible. It was suggested that these stereotypes are stronger in relationships between opposite genders, or when a person is still strongly influenced by the communist past. Furthermore, experts say that age or

Table 6.1 Poland: significant controls (correlations)

	Gender: subordinate	Org. tenure: subordinate	Gender: manager	Age: subordinate	Number of employees	Age difference
MTB: fairness	−0.212*					
OCB: loyalty to the firm		0.240**	−0.284**		−0.288**	
MTS		0.393**		0.295**		
STM						−0.220*

Notes
** Pearson correlation significant at 0.01 level.
* Pearson correlation significant at 0.05 level.
MTB = managerial trustworthy behavior, STM = subordinates' trust in managers, MTS = managers' trust in subordinates, OCB = organizational citizenship behavior.

the age difference is usually more important for trust building in large, state-owned companies where managerial careers depend significantly on age and tenure. On the other hand, in smaller, private organizations, it is not rare to see people in their thirties who are already members of executive teams.

As for the gender, when asked to comment on the negative correlation between gender and managerial trustworthy behaviors, managers and subordinates pointed out that women probably have more difficulty in accessing managerial careers. This means that female managers are worried more often about maintaining their hard-won positions, and these concerns might negatively influence their trustworthy behaviors. In addition, experts argue that women have more trust in male managers, and they also prefer to work with male colleagues. On the other hand, women are still perceived by many Polish employers as more "difficult" to work with—for example, due to expected maternity leaves, but also due to stereotypes of emotional instability.

In addition to variables which we did not control, managers and subordinates highlight the influence of one's own personality and value system on the trust-building process, as someone commented: "The most important thing in trust building is the manager's character and personality. The kind of a person he or she is—i.e. cold or warm, flexible or rigid, etc.—is very important."

All interviewees also mention nationality as a possible factor that may influence trust building. There are three elements: first of all, the differences in management and communication styles resulting from different cultures may lead to difficult moments at the beginning of the relationship. Second, people hold stereotypes about other cultures, confirmed or not by their experience, which are used almost unconsciously when projecting future relationships. Third, the national culture might have an influence on one's propensity to trust other people.

Antecedents and Outcomes of Manager–Subordinate Trust

The picture of trust emerging from the qualitative studies is very clear. Trust is a foundation for a good relationship between a manager and a subordinate, and often a sine qua non condition for their cooperation. From the managers' viewpoint, trust means sincerity in the relationship, and makes delegation possible, reducing the need for control of task implementation, but it also requires giving responsibility to employees. From the subordinates' viewpoint, trust also means sincerity, and the increased delegation brings fulfillment, but it requires a certain level of proactivity in the relationship with the manager.

Managers trust subordinates who are, first and foremost, reliable (i.e. highly skilled and knowledgeable), as one manager put it:

> Trust is described by the situation where I have only one precious bag of seeds to be sowed in the autumn. For whatever reason, I cannot do it by myself, so I put my trust in another person. I entrust this bag to her and, counting on her sowing skills, I hope the seeds will sprout, as I do not have any more bags.

Managers also stress the importance of subordinates' credibility and integrity. Interestingly, female managers also pay attention to their subordinates' loyalty and reciprocity.

Subordinates trust managers who are, first and foremost, consistent, as one commented: "If I trust my manager, it means that I know that he will behave in this or that way." Subordinates also stress the importance of managers' loyalty, concern, and last but not least, integrity.

Both managers and subordinates perceive trust as a necessary condition at work, and both highlight important implications not only for a manager–subordinate relationship, but also for the organization as a whole.

On the relationship level, it is beneficial for both parties in different ways. First, managers who trust their subordinates are more efficient and effective. They are able to exercise less control and monitoring over how a delegated task is implemented, and thus have more time and energy to focus on strategic issues and other things strictly related to management. Second, the manager's rigid delegating style based on small, clearly defined tasks evolves toward a more participative decision-making style, where she invites a subordinate to discuss possible solutions for complex problems, and leaves tasks definition, planning, and execution to the subordinate. As one manager summarized:

> I believe that people work most efficiently when they are highly delegated and have a feeling of constant support from their boss, i.e., the boss is not a controller, but a tool for an independent subordinate. On the one hand, it means that the subordinate can always count on my support in terms of my knowledge, skills, experience but also on my power to push decisions in the company. On the other hand, the subordinate feels independence because I do not ask how he is planning his work, what his subordinates are doing, etc.

Finally, decision-making processes require less time, as managers are confident that subordinates have done their homework and proposed the best alternative. In extreme cases, trust leads to a situation where managers sign propositions prepared by subordinates without even reading their justification.

A subordinate who trusts his boss is more motivated and effective, which in turn brings other visible results, such as promotions, bonuses, or salary increases. A subordinate who trusts his boss does not hesitate to ask for advice rather than for a solution. He does not fear his manager and is able not only to express his own opinions, but also to speak openly about work-related problems and difficulties as soon as they arise, and admit his own errors instead of sweeping them under the carpet. On the other hand, the subordinate has a sense of constant support from his manager, and—if he makes a mistake—is confident that the manager will be fair and constructive in her feedback, and will never make him a scapegoat. Moreover, reassured by the manager's support and trust, the subordinate feels more responsible and committed, since he does not want to let her down. Since this commitment comes from a greater satisfaction, it does not mean just overtime work, but rather constant interest in and care about the business, even during leisure time.

Overall, mutual trust helps create a healthy, high-quality manager–subordinate relationship, and a constructive, two-way feedback loop. Both parties share work-related information freely and sincerely, as they know that it will not be used against them, but rather will be used to improve the diagnosis of work-related issues and find more effective joint solutions.

However, managers point to the risk of too much trust; building a friendship relationship is dangerous, because emotional bonding could be destructive at work. For example, people who have a friendship relationship tend to push the professional relationship to the limits (often unconsciously) and test their boss's power.

Another potential danger related with trust is that managers may overload the subordinates they trust the most. Moreover, instead of increasing their trust networks, managers may purposefully (but for a wide range of reasons) count on only a few entrusted subordinates.

On the organizational level, trust brings long-term results, sometimes not very clearly visible or measurable, but extremely valuable nonetheless. One example is a good atmosphere at work, or in a wider sense, a strong corporate culture. Without trust, it is hard to build effective teams and a good atmosphere at work because then affairs are run by politics and hypocrisy, which is detrimental to the whole organization. Another example is when trust networks are built across teams and departments, or even between organizations. This happens when entrusted subordinates are empowered enough to represent their manager in contacts with other stakeholders, inside and outside of a parent organization.

The behavioral antecedents and consequences of trust as seen by Polish managers and subordinates are summarized in Figure 6.1.

The Dynamics of Trust in Hierarchical Trusting Relationships

Both managers and subordinates paint a similar picture of trust dynamics, with some interesting details, which are pointed out in this section. First of all, a trust relationship is dynamic and trust building does not depend only on time, but on the frequency and

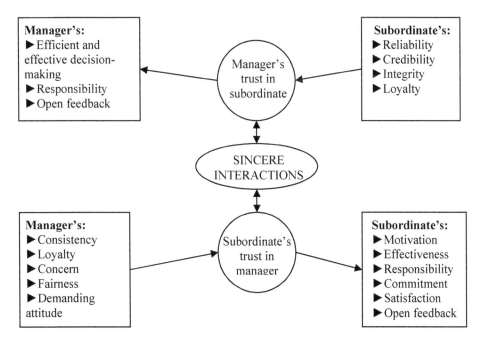

Figure 6.1 Trust at work, its antecedents and consequences

quality of interactions. Second, there are many levels of trust in professional relationships, but it never goes as high as in private relationships. Third, mutual trust is not balanced, and the trust-building process, although reciprocal, is not symmetrical.

Managers and subordinates agree that there are a few conditions for building a trust relationship. First, the rules of cooperation and mutual expectations have to be clearly defined at the very beginning. Second, both parties have to show a constant attitude of mutual understanding and respect. Due to his privileged position, it is the manager who takes the lead in defining these norms and expectations, and who is responsible for the consequences of a chosen management style. Managers stress that it is their responsibility to ensure that subordinates are aware of what is expected from them and that they have the possibility to give feedback all the time. Managers emphasize that mutual understanding and respect is not only related with delegation and empowerment, but must be shown on a human or personal level, as one of them said:

> I give flexibility and understanding, and, for example, my subordinate does not need to explain why his lunch took longer than usual (maybe he had to see the doctor, or wanted to buy a gift for his wife). But on the other hand, we have an unwritten agreement that, if the business situation requires, we are willing to face the challenge and work on it for as long as may be needed.

Although it depends on personality, managers usually start the relationship with quite a high level of trust in subordinates; in other words, they believe in subordinates' good intentions and competencies. Initially, it is connected with higher control. However, when trust is not abused, monitoring becomes less intense with time. With shared experiences, the manager–subordinate relationship becomes better and deeper: there is more mutual understanding and respect, strengths and weaknesses are better known, expectations are better recognized, and the sense of duty is higher. Besides subordinates' contractual duties, there are behaviors that are important for building managers' trust in subordinates, as one leader exemplified:

> It was crucial for me to see how my subordinate interacts with his people during an offsite company event. It became evident that my subordinate built his team just as I would do it: without power distance or arrogance, and with a high level of acceptance from the team members.

Another manager said:

> It is essential for me that my subordinate has lots of ideas about doing new things or improving existing processes, and that he shows enthusiasm for cooperation with people, not only from his own team, but also from other departments and offices. I also appreciate it if he can cope actively with different assignments, even without prior experience.

As for subordinates, although it depends on personality, they are usually more wary and begin the relationship with a low level of trust in the manager. Trust develops through common experiences and many repeated situations, but subordinates stress that it rarely achieves 100 percent. They underscore the importance of respecting the rules of play, which were established at the beginning of the relationship, and the importance of honesty and fairness on the part of the manager. This provides a necessary level of perceived reliability and predictability of the manager, which in turn facilitates trust building, as one subordinate explained:

We have common arrangements in the project, but as time goes by, we may encounter some difficulties and confrontations. And there arises the question of whether both parties keep their arrangements or one is hung up to dry in front of others in the company.

Another person added: "One of the strongest trustworthy behaviors of my boss is when the time of confrontation comes and she does not use any of the sensitive information against me, even though this might give her some short-term benefits."

Interestingly, subordinates who are higher in the hierarchy or those who have their own team are not afraid to be proactive in the relationship and are able to begin it with quite a high level of trust in their manager. Thus, they have an important influence in the initial process of trust building, as one subordinate commented: "When I am proactive at the beginning, I can influence my future relationship. Otherwise, my boss will decide everything. Moreover, the initial level of trust depends on his track record and reputation, which I can get to know beforehand."

Both quantitative and qualitative data suggest that there are different levels of managers' and subordinates' trust. Most managers and subordinates interviewed identify these levels depending on the type and depth of the relationship, as one of the participants commented:

There are different levels of trust, showing the depth of the relationship: the lowest level concerns only the professional relationship with that particular person; the middle level is when you can talk with this person also about other co-workers' behavior, problems at work, etc.; and the highest level when you can talk about anything that is important to you: life, family, work, society, your country.

Another added: "There are levels of trust, which depend on the complexity and importance of the tasks delegated and on the competencies of the person who is doing that task." On the other hand, there are people who treat trust as a binary construct—that is, for them, trust either exists or it does not exist.

Our quantitative data offer interesting insights into the dynamics of trust (see Table 6.2). Comparing Poland to the overall model with the full sample, and to the regional model for Central-Eastern Europe (CEE), subordinates' organizational citizenship behaviors have a weaker relationship with managers' trust in subordinates. In addition, the relationship between subordinates' trust in managers and subordinates' citizenship behaviors is very weak and statistically not significant.

Table 6.2 Standardized regression weights for the trust model in Poland, CEE, and the overall sample

	OCB–>MTS	MTS–>MTB	MTB–>STM	STM–>OCB
Poland only	0.42**	0.26*	0.81**	0.13
CEE (Romania and Russia)	0.77**	0.28*	0.60*	0.27*
Complete model	0.68**	0.34**	0.89**	0.08*

Notes
** Significant at 0.01 level.
* Significant at 0.05 level.

Evidently, in this model, trust building is not symmetrical, as subordinates' organizational citizenship behaviors have a much lower influence on managers' trust in subordinates than managerial trustworthy behaviors have on subordinates' trust in managers. This lack of symmetry is also clearly seen in the interviews. Managers highlight subordinates' reliability and integrity as a source of trust in employees, rather than their citizenship behaviors toward organizations. On the other hand, subordinates give great importance to managerial trustworthy behaviors, such as fairness, concern, and consistency.

The Delphi panel experts agree that it is a universal but simplified model, as trust building in dyad relationships in hierarchical organizations is more complicated and is influenced by personality, the organization's specific culture (its current strategy, policies and practices, reputation, customers, etc.), and the country's culture (its history, traditions, authorities, laws, current economic situation, stage of development, etc.). Moreover, these factors are also dynamic—that is, at a given moment, the most influential factor for building trust relationships might be a perception of an upcoming economic crisis or threat of unemployment, whereas in another period it might be a change in the firm's strategy.

As for the model, the experts proposed an additional relationship between existing constructs. For example, they suggested direct two-way links between behaviors, as well as between manager and subordinate. The experts also expressed doubts as to whether trust has a significant effect on behaviors. They argue that, for example, subordinates' citizenship behaviors are more likely to be consequences of upbringing, value systems, personality, and peer pressure than a result of subordinates' trust in managers.

Discussion and Conclusions

The results of our study in Poland confirm some of the main conclusions from the existing literature. Trust is fundamental for good relationships between the manager and the subordinate (Dirks & Ferrin, 2001). The process of trust building is reciprocal—that is, the manager's trust in the subordinate reinforces the subordinate's trust in the manager (Dirks & Ferrin, 2002). It is the manager who initiates the trust-building process, primarily by his or her consistent, loyal behavior and by showing concern about the employee (Whitener et al., 1998). Managers tend to trust subordinates in advance, so to speak, whereas subordinates build trust in managers through repeated positive interactions, even though the initial level of subordinates' trust in managers might be often based on the latter's reputation. Interestingly, in Poland, this initial asymmetry of trust levels prevails over the course of the relationship and might be explained in various ways. First of all, it is the manager who has the power over the subordinate. Second, it is influenced by recent history, including the communist past, where managers were often perceived as agents of the hated regime, and the transformation processes after 1989, in which the employees suffered the most. Third, it might be a typical feature of countries with moderate to high collectivism (as defined by Hofstede) for people to have less trust in any formal authority (Huff & Kelley, 2003).

The process of trust building is reciprocal, but not symmetrical. On one hand, the influence of managerial trustworthy behaviors (i.e. fairness) on subordinates' trust in managers is much stronger than the impact of subordinates' citizenship behaviors (i.e. loyalty to the organization) on managers' trust in subordinates. This difference is bigger in Poland than in the full sample. This may be due to the fact that subordinates' citizenship behaviors toward the organization are not easily observed by managers. Moreover, we found that Polish managers pay far more attention to behaviors that are directly connected with subordinates' and teams' tasks and responsibilities than to any behavior related toward the organization as a whole.

On the other hand, managers' trust in subordinates has a significant relation with managerial fairness, but subordinates' trust in managers does not translate into subordinates' citizenship behaviors toward the organization. The former seems natural and in line with existing research (Gómez & Rosen, 2001; Lewicki & Bunker, 1996), but the latter needs more explanation in the Polish context. First, as is pointed out by Polish scholars, people do not trust and do not identify with most of the state institutions (Czapinski & Panek, 2009; Nasierowski & Mikuła, 1998; Śpiewak, 2009). We might extend this observation also to work settings where employees do not have confidence in the company and do not identify with it. Second, even though studies show that managers' behaviors are important factors in motivating employees to reciprocate with citizenship behavior (Konovsky & Pugh, 1994; Korsgaard *et al.*, 2002), it might be the case for Poland that it is related with citizenship behaviors toward specific individuals or tasks, rather than toward an organization. Data from the focus groups and interviews with managers suggest that this could be a valid explanation.

The trust-building process is complex, and managers have to be aware that subordinates are very sensitive to managerial behaviors such as delegation, fairness, and consistency. Lack of these behaviors leads simply to distrust among subordinates. On the other hand, managerial trustworthy behaviors are not enough to promote subordinates' citizenship behaviors toward an organization. The organizational and societal context, including company rules and norms and the climate of trust prevailing in society, also seems to be important.

Subordinates expect managers to lead the trust-building process. Managers have to be aware that the level of subordinates' trust in them will be moderate or even fairly low. However, this does not mean that employees will not perform their tasks or will not exhibit citizenship behaviors.

As for the limitations of this study, we have to be aware that participants were chosen mostly from high-tech and service companies in the Warsaw and Krakow areas, which implies limitations when drawing general conclusions. In addition, only 14 percent of managers were females. Thus, future studies may explore further the role of gender in building and maintaining trust relationships at work. We also encourage further studies of the importance and relative strength of the organizational context (including, but not limited to, organizational values and culture, ownership type, and office location) in trust building in dyad relationships. Lastly, future research may look further into different kinds of citizenship behaviors and determine which are really important for Polish managers and subordinates.

Summing up, in Poland, trust has to be earned, and Poles put their trust in people they already know well, especially the closest family, friends, co-workers, and business partners. For historical reasons, there is little general confidence in others or in state institutions. Even though there has been an observable trend toward increased generalized trust in the last ten years, the social and civic involvement of Poles is still relatively low, and they prefer to fulfill themselves in private spheres.

References

Ash, T.G. (1989). Revolution in Hungary and Poland. *The New York Review of Books*. 36(13), August 17.

Ash, T.G. (1991). Poland after solidarity. *The New York Review of Books*. 38(11), June 13.

Barszcz, M. (2010). *Szara strefa* [Grey Market]. Business Centre Club Report.

Biały, A. (2009). Businessmen are more and more appreciated. *Rzeczpospolita* daily, November 21.

Bliss Lane, A. (2008). *Widziałem Polskę zdradzoną* [I Saw Poland Betrayed]. Warszawa: Fronda.

Bocheński, A. (1996). *Dzieje głupoty w Polsce* [The History of Inanity in Poland]. Warszawa: Świat Książki.

Borkowska S. (ed.) (2007). *Zarządzanie zasobami ludzkimi w Polsce. Przeszłość, teraźniejszość, przyszłość* [Human Resource Management in Poland. Past, Present, Future]. Kraków: Wolters Kluwer Polska.

CBOS (2009). *Black Market*. CBOS Research Report BS/6/2009.

CBOS (2010a). *Social Trust*. CBOS Research Report BS/29/2010.

CBOS (2010b). *Civic Engagement of Poles between 1998 and 2010*. CBOS Research Report BS/16/2010

Central Statistical Office. (2011). Quarterly information on the labour market. Warszawa: Central Statistical Office.

Chesterton, G.K. (1922). Introduction. In C. Sarolea, *Letters on Polish Affairs*. Edinburgh: Oliver and Boyd.

Connelly, J. (2005). Why the Poles collaborated so little: And why that is no reason for nationalist hubris. *Slavic Review*, 64(4): 771–781.

Costigan, R.D., Insinga, R.C., Berman, J.J., Ilter, S.S., Kranas, G. & Kureshov, V.A. (2006). The effect of employee trust of the supervisor on enterprising behavior: A cross-cultural comparison. *Journal of Business and Psychology*, 21(2): 273–291.

Czapinski, J. & Panek, T. (2009). *Diagnoza Społeczna 2009. Conditions and Quality of Life of Poles*. Warszawa: Rada Monitoringu Społecznego.

D'Abernon, E.V. (1931). *The Eighteenth Decisive Battle of the World: Warsaw, 1920*. London: Hodder & Stoughton.

Davies, N. (2006). *Boze igrzysko: historia Polski* [God's Playground: History of Poland]. Krakow: Znak.

Davies, N. (2007). *Europa. Między Wschodem a Zachodem* [Europe: A History]. Kraków: Wydawnictwo Znak.

Davies, N. (2009). *Powstanie '44* [Rising '44: The Battle for Warsaw]. Kraków: Znak.

Dirks, K.T.& Ferrin, D.L. (2001). The role of trust in organizational settings. *Organization Science*, 12: 450–467.

Dirks, K.T.& Ferrin, D.L. (2002). Trust in leadership: meta-analytic findings and implications for research and practice. *Journal of Applied Psychology*, 87: 611–628.

Domański, H. (2005). The Polish transformation: Structural changes and new tensions. *European Journal of Social Theory*, 8(4): 453–470.

European Social Survey (2010). Round 4 Edition 3.0.

Fedyszak-Radziejowska, B. (2007). Czy kapitał społeczny bez społecznego zaufania jest możliwy? Przykłady polskich gmin wiejskich. In T. Kaźmierczak, M. Rymsza (eds), *Kapitał społeczny. Ekonomia społeczna* [Social Capital. Social Economy]. Warszawa: Instytut Spraw Publicznych.

Fukuyama, F. (1995). *Trust: The Social Virtues and the Creation of Prosperity*. New York: Free Press.

Gómez, C. & Rosen, B. (2001). The leader–member exchange as a link between managerial trust and employee empowerment, *Group & Organization Management*, 26: 53–69.

Grabowska, M.& Roguska, B. (eds) (2008). Changes in the life of a Polish family. *Polish Public Opinion* (CBOS monthly report), March.

Gumkowska, M., Herbst, J., Szołajska, J. & Wygnanski, J. (2007). *Index of the Civic Society 2007*. Warszawa: Klon/Jawor Association.

GUS (n.d.). Annual macroeconomic indicators. www.stat.gov.pl/gus/5207_ENG_HTML.htm.

Hay Group. (2009–2011). Nawigator HR.

Hilckman, A. (1962). Introduction. In F. Koneczny, *On the Plurality of Civilizations*. London: Polonica Publications.

Huff, L.& Kelley, L. (2003). Levels of organizational trust in individualist versus collectivist societies: A seven-nation study. *Organization Science*, 14(1): 81–90.

IMF, International Monetary Fund (2010). *World Economic Outlook Database*, October. Washington: IMF.

Jacher, W.& Świadźba, U. (2008). Etos pracy w Polsce [Work ethos in Poland]. In J. Mariański & L. Smyczek (eds), *Wartości, postawy i więzi moralne w zmieniającym się społeczeństwie* [Values, Attitudes and Moral Ties in a Changing Society]. Kraków: Wydawnictwo WAM.

Jasienica, P. (1988). *Polska anarchia* [The Polish Anarchy]. Kraków: Wydawnictwo Literackie.

Jezior, J. (2001). Work in the system of values from the perspective of investigations in the region of Central-Eastern Poland. *Annales Universitatis Mariae Curie-Skłodowska*, Sect. I: 89–109.

Kieżuń, W. (2004). Struktury i kierunki zarządzania państwem [Structures and management of a state]. In W. Kieżun & J. Kubin (eds), *Dobre państwo* [A Good State]. Warszawa: Wydawnictwo WSPiZ.

Kolarska-Bobińska, L. (2009). Polscy przedsiębiorcy wobec integracji. Polska i polscy przedsiębiorcy w oczach mieszkańców„starej" UE [Polish businessmen in view of the integration. Poland and Polish businessmen in the eyes of citizens of the "old" EU]. In A. Żołnierski (ed.), *Report on MSE in Poland between 2007 and 2008*. Warszawa: PARP.

Konovsky, M.A. & Pugh, S.D. (1994). Citizenship behavior and social exchange. *Academy of Management Journal*, 37: 656–669.

Korboński, S. (2009). *Polskie Państwo Podziemne* [The Polish Underground State]. Warszawa: Świat Książki.

Korsgaard, A., Brodt, S. & Whitener, E. (2002). Trust in the face of conflict: The role of managerial trustworthy behavior and organizational context. *Journal of Applied Psychology*, 87: 312–319.

Legutko, R. (2008). *Społeczeństwo otwarte a idea solidarności* [The Open Society and Solidarity]. Kraków: Ośrodek Myśli Politycznej.

Lewicki, R.J. & Bunker, B.B. (1996). Developing and maintaining trust in work relationships. In R. Kramer & T.R. Tyler (eds), *Trust in Organizations: Frontiers of Theory and Research*. Thousand Oaks, CA: Sage, pp. 114–139.

Łojek, J. (1996). *Kalendarz historyczny. Polemiczna historia Polski* [Historical Calendar. A Polemic History of Poland]. Warszawa: Alfa-Wero.

Lucas, R.C. (2001). *The Forgotten Holocaust: the Poles under German Occupation, 1939–1944*. New York: Hippocrene.

Lukowski, J. & Zawadzki, H. (2006). *A Concise History of Poland*. Cambridge: Cambridge University Press.

Ministry of Economy (2008). National Reform Program for 2008–2011. www.mg.gov.pl.

Ministry of the Treasury (2010). Przekształcenia własnościowe przedsiębiorstw państwowych. [Ownership Transformation of State Enterprises]. www.msp.gov.pl.

Nasierowski, W.& Mikula, B. (1998). Culture dimensions of Polish managers: Hofstede's indices. *Organization Studies*, 19: 495–509.

Olson, L.& Cloud S. (2003). *A Question of Honor. The Kościuszko Squadron: Forgotten Heroes of World War II*. New York: Random House.

Pejovich, S. (2005). On the privatization of "stolen goods" in Central and Eastern Europe. *The Independent Review*, Vol. X, No 2.

Pobóg-Malinowski, W. (1953). *Przygody z historią* [Adventures with History]. Paryż.

Polish Chamber of Commerce (KIG) (2006). Raport z badania warunków dla funkcjonowania firm z sektora MSP [Report from studies on the conditions for MSE], research report.

Puchalski, J. (2010). *Zmiany w zarządzaniu zasobami ludzkimi* [Changes in Human Resource Management]. Wyższa Szkoła Handlowa: Wrocław.

Putnam, R. (1993). *Making Democracy Work: Civic Traditions in Modern Italy*. Princeton: Princeton University Press.

Putnam, R. (2000). *Bowling Alone: Collapse and Revival of American Community*. New York: Simon and Schuster.

Raiser, M., Rousso, A. & Steves, F. (2003). Trust in transition: cross-country and firm evidence. *EBRD working paper*, No. 82.

Reeskens, T.& Hooghe, M. (2008). Cross-cultural measurement equivalence of generalized trust. Evidence from the European Social Survey (2002 and 2004). *Social Indicators Research*, 85(3): 515–532.

Skrzek-Lubasińska, M. (2009). *Wpływ niestandardowych form zatrudnienia na poziom kapitału społecznego* [The Influence of Non-Standard Forms of Employment on the Level of Social Capital]. Ph.D. Thesis, Akademia Leona Koźmińskiego, Warsaw.

Sójka, J. (1999). The impact of trust on employee participation in Poland. *Journal of Business Ethics*, 21(2/3): 229–236.

Śpiewak, P. (2009). Kilka uwag o reformie państwa [Few notes about the state reform]. In A. Żołnierski (ed.), *Report on MSE in Poland between 2007 and 2008*. Warszawa: PARP.

Świda-Ziemba, H. (2008). Paradoksy postaw etycznych młodzieży licealnej i studenckiej [Paradoxes of ethical attitudes of high school and university students]. In J. Mariański & L. Smyczek (eds), *Wartości, postawy i więzi moralne w zmieniającym się społeczeństwie* [Values, Attitudes and Moral Ties in a Changing Society]. Kraków: Wydawnictwo WAM.

Szczęsny, J. (2010). Postpolska, czyli „jaśni" i "ciemni" [Post-Poland]. *Rzeczpospolita* daily, July 27.

Szpytma, M. (2009). *The Risk of Survival. The Rescue of the Jews by the Poles and the Tragic Consequences for the Ulma Family from Markowa*. Warszawa: Institute of National Remembrance, Commission of the Prosecution of Crimes against the Polish Nation.

Sztompka, P. (1999). *Trust. A Sociological Theory*. Cambridge: Cambridge University Press.

Sztompka P. (2007). *Zaufanie. Fundament społeczeństwa* [Trust. The Foundation of Society]. Warszawa: Wydawnictwo Znak.

Tarnawa, A. (2009). Makroekonomiczna sytuacja Polski w 2008 roku. [A macroeconomic situation of Poland in 2008]. In A. Żołnierski (ed.), *Report on MSE in Poland between 2007 and 2008*. Warszawa: PARP.

Tridico, P. (2006). Institutional change and governance indexes in transition economies: The case of Poland. *The European Journal of Comparative Economics*, 3(2): 197–238.

Whitener, E., Brodt, S., Korsgaard, M.A.& Werner, J. (1998). Managers as initiators of trust: An exchange relationship framework for understanding managerial trustworthy behavior. *Academy of Management Review*, 23: 513–530.

Wildstein, B. (2005). *Długi cień PRL-u, czyli dekomunizacja, której nie było* [Decommunization Which Has Not Been Done]. Kraków: Arcana.

The World Bank Group (n.d.). Foreign direct investment, net inflows.http://data.worldbank.org/indicator/BX.KLT.DINV.CD.WD.

Żarnowski, J. (1999). *Polska 1918–1939 Praca Technika Społeczeństwo* [Poland 1918–1939 Work Technology Society]. Warszawa: Książka i Wiedza.

7

Manager–Subordinate Trust Relationships in Romania

DAN V. CAPRAR AND ANDREA BUDEAN

Introduction

Romania is a European Union (EU) Member State situated in southeast Europe. It contains a vast swath of the Carpathian Mountains and is bordered to the south and east by the Danube and the Black Sea. Its Latin origins are strongly reflected in the Romance language and a culture that is closer in nature to other Latin-based cultures than to neighboring Slav and Hungarian cultures. Yet, having been over time in the path of many migrating populations, alternately pressed between the Ottoman, Austro-Hungarian, and Russian powers, and at a crossroads between Catholicism and Orthodoxism, Romania developed a culture with many flavors, occasionally struggling to reaffirm its identity against assumptions based on its location and its inclusion in the former Eastern communist bloc. This struggle perhaps explains the occasional occurrence of nationalism (Livezeanu, 2000). However, Romanians were eager to join the EU in 2007, and contemporary Romanians are inclined to emphasize a European rather than a national identity.

After the abolition of communism in December 1989, Romania returned to a multi-party political system and a market economy. It experienced an unprecedented economic boom in the years before the global financial crisis (GFC) of the late 2000s, fueled by intensive foreign investment. Romania was not only a new market, but a land of opportunities with cheap skilled labor, important natural and human resources, and a consumer base highly receptive to new products and services after years of austerity. Post-GFC Romania struggles with an increasing current-account deficit; many businesses have had to cease their activity, and unemployment is growing.

The political and economic change has had significant impact on the culture. The most common framework of characterizing cultures as relevant to business, offered by Hofstede (1991), defines Romania as a high power distance, collectivistic, and relatively feminine culture with a very high level of uncertainty avoidance. However, a more recent study based on the same methodology (Neculaesei & Tătărusanu, 2008) revealed important regional differences, especially with regard to uncertainty avoidance. The inter-regional cultural differences are confirmed by how Romanians define themselves: the strong, unique identities of individual regions are uniformly acknowledged and agreed upon throughout the country, and are consistent with differences in regional history (detailed in the "Historical Perspective" section). Moreover, an ethnography of workers in MNCs revealed that these workers may not be representative of the local culture (Caprar, 2011), and in general, generational differences are expected to switch the ratings on the traditional Hofstede dimensions.

We explore the particular findings related to the trust relationship between managers and subordinates in Romania in the context of the aforementioned complex history, while also taking into account current developments. The historical context and the contemporary institutional environment are presented as relevant antecedents to how Romanians view trust in general, and how this view is translated in perceptions of trust in the work context. In particular, the ambivalence toward leadership and mixed views on the role of managers in organizations are explored in the sections about leadership and HR practices, along with insights from existing literature on trust in Romania, in both international and locally conducted studies. Empirical results, and especially an evaluation of the quantitative results through the perspective of Romanian managers and subordinates, make up the main parts of the chapter. The findings are concluded with overall remarks and implications for both future research and practice.

Highlights on Manager–Subordinate Trust in Romania

- Trust is a complex matter for Romanians: the locals challenge the very definition of the concept as applied to the work context. Most believe that trust is something specific to non-work relationships (friendship and family) and that its presence in the work context is conditioned by developing a very personal (as opposed to professional) relationship.
- Romanians also emphasize trust as a subjective feeling, rather than an objective characteristic; there was a strong distinction made between "really" trusting and displaying trust-related behaviors. Efforts toward showing trust (especially declaration of trust) are viewed with suspicion, and the ultimate test of trust is in the "eye of the beholder."
- The history of communism is relevant to the way Romanians view trust in society and in the work setting: in general, there is a low level of trust outside very close relationships, and trust can only be established in such close relationships, which must be developed over time.
- Subordinates perceive managers as controlling, and managers admit having ambivalent views on how they relate to subordinates: some believe being perceived as a trustworthy manager is good, but others insist, consistent with the traditional culture, that distance between the manager and the subordinate is important: such distance precludes the possibility of developing relationships of real trust at work.
- Special relationships are developed at work, either in the form of friendships (transcending the pure professional relationship) or in the form of identifying special employees who become protégés of the manager. However, the nature of the relationships in organizations varies widely with the type and size of the company, with visible trends of change toward a new culture that is yet to be defined.

Historical Perspective

The history of Romania remains fraught with uncertainty, many of its major events a debating ground for historians with different vantage points. The Romanian identity has been repeatedly challenged, but perhaps nothing had a more profound impact on what Romania is today than its almost five decades of communism. Indeed, in spite of a name claiming Latin origins (Fox, 1996), Romania is often seen as a former Eastern European communist bloc country; its history, however, has many more chapters.

The earliest written evidence of people living in the territory of the present-day Romania comes from Herodotus in his book written in 440 BCE, which mentions the Dacians, a branch of Thracians. The Dacian kingdom became a powerful state that threatened the regional interests of the Romans during their expansion toward the east. Although early attempts to conquer Dacia failed, Emperor Trajan eventually defeated the Dacians in two campaigns (101 CE and 105 CE). The Romans heavily colonized the province, and the Vulgar Latin became the proto-Romanian language. The Roman Empire withdrew from Roman Dacia around 271 CE, after which different migratory populations (e.g. Goths, Huns, etc.) invaded the area or settled and lived alongside the local population.

There is continuing debate on whether Romanians always lived within the territory occupied by contemporary Romania, or whether some or all of the first Romanians migrated from the region south of the Danube. There is agreement, however, that in the Middle Ages, three main regions covering the former Dacian territory were inhabited by Romanians: Wallachia, Moldavia, and Transylvania. While Wallachia and Moldavia maintained their independence from the Ottoman Empire until the fifteenth century, Transylvania has been an autonomous part of the Kingdom of Hungary since the eleventh century. The three principalities regained their independence in 1600, when for the first time in their history, they elected a common ruler, Michael the Brave; however, the new ruler was promptly assassinated, and the dream of a united Romania was again just a dream. Later, Transylvania became part of the Habsburg Empire, and Wallachia and Moldavia were under Ottoman suzerainty until the eighteenth century.

The re-unification of Romanians started in 1859 when Moldavia and Wallachia elected a common ruler and formed the Kingdom of Romania. In 1918, after the First World War, Transylvania and two other northeastern regions, Bukovina and Bessarabia, joined this burgeoning state to form Greater Romania. Between the two World Wars, Romania underwent rapid development, including the beginnings of its modern political life. However, the end of the Second World War and the Warsaw Pact placed Romania under Soviet influence and the era of communism began. Later, the Romanian leaders managed to limit the Soviet influence (Farlow, 1964), while simultaneously developing one of the most draconic regimes in the world. It is estimated that two million people were direct victims of oppression under the Romanian communist regime (Romanian Presidency, 2006).

After the fall of Ceauşescu, the famous communist dictator, in 1989, Romania became a semi-presidential republic with a political system based on multi-party democracy. Romania joined the North Atlantic Treaty Organization in 2004 and the European Union on January 1, 2007.

Institutional Context

Economic Context

After the transition to democracy that began in 1989, Romania's economy developed, slowly at first and then at a much brisker pace in 2006–2008. It is considered to be one of the former communist states that adopted a more liberal economic model, as opposed to a more coordinated model (Lane, 2007). In 2010, Romania was ranked twenty-first among 46 European states in terms of nominal GDP, at US$ 158 billion (International Monetary Fund [IMF], 2011). Inflation in 2011 was 3.1 percent, down from previous years, and the unemployment rate was 7 percent, much lower than the rates of other middle-sized or large European countries. The account balance in 2011 held a deficit of US$ 6.35 billion (IMF, 2011). As it prepares to enter the Eurozone by 2014, Romania is planning to budget a deficit of up to 3 percent. The average gross wage per month in Romania was €442.48 (US$ 627.70) in May 2009, the year that the Romanian economy started to contract as a result of the global economic downturn.

Social Context

The Romanian population is estimated at 21 million (Romanian Census, 2011), with a life expectancy at birth of 73.98 years. The country's population is expected to decline in the near future due to the low fertility rate (1.29 children born per woman in 2011) and emigration. Employed persons with an individual work contract receive state benefits, including old-age pension, sickness and maternity leave, unemployment benefits, and free healthcare.

Political and Legal Systems

Romania is a republic in which executive functions are held by both the government and the President. The Parliament consists of two chambers: the Senate and the Chamber of Deputies. Romania has a multi-party system and political parties must work with each other to form coalition governments. The present political parties with parliamentary representation are: the Democratic Liberal Party, Social Democratic Party, National Liberal Party, Democratic Union of Hungarians in Romania, National Union for the Advancement of Romania, and the Conservative Party. In addition, ethnic minorities have guaranteed seats, one for each recognized minority. The justice system is based on civil law and comprises a hierarchical system of courts, culminating in the High Court of Cassation and Justice, which is the Supreme Court in Romania.

Educational System

Education is structured in four levels: pre-school (3–6 years old), primary school (four grades, ages 6 to 10–11), secondary school (four grades, ages 10 to 15–16) and high school (four or five grades). The completion of ten grades (ages 6–16) is compulsory. At the end of the eighth grade, the pupils must pass an exam in order to be accepted into high school. In the same manner, at the end of the fourth year of high school, students take an exam which has a major impact on their chances of being accepted to a college or university. In recent years, higher education was reorganized according to the Bologna Process, which sets compatible and coherent standards for higher education across Europe. Although the educational system has been under continuous reform since the revolution in 1989, the educational performance of the graduates is still among the lowest in the EU (UNESCO, 2008). Many attribute this to the education system becoming less rigorous and less competitive after the fall of the communist regime.

HR Practices

One of the numerous changes that have taken place in Romania since 1990 is the development of the human resources management (HRM) field, which was practically non-existent under communist rule. Under the totalitarian regime, the party made all the personnel decisions in an organization. The Romanian management system is still a traditional one to a great extent; in many local companies, remaining highly centralized and thus with limited support for the development of standardized modern HR policies at the national level.

The results of a questionnaire administered in two phases, 1999 and 2003, revealed that most managers lack basic knowledge on HRM and do not hire experts in this area (Constantin *et al.*, 2006). However, the results varied with the size of the company. Medium and large organizations were found to be more likely to hire and use internal HR specialists, work with consulting firms, and ask for training services, compared to small enterprises, which rarely use such services. The respondents invoked a lack of financial resources as the main reason for not investing in modern HR practices.

The most often required consulting services are those for personnel selection, personnel evaluation, and analysis of the organizational climate. Regarding personnel selection, Ispas *et al.* (2010) noted that less than 40 percent of their Romanian respondents reported being assessed based on their resume and an interview. This result is discrepant with findings in Western Europe and the Americas, where the interview is one of the most common selection methods. When asked about their level of trust in different selection procedures, Romanians rated more favorably work samples, ability tests, personal references, biographical information, personality tests, and integrity tests than did employees from the United States, Singapore, and Greece. Conversely, they provided significantly lower ratings for personal contacts, graphology, and ethnicity relative to their counterparts in the other countries (Ispas *et al.*, 2010). The authors posited that the differences in personnel management between Romania and other countries are a hold over from the uncontrollable selection processes of the communist regime, which have yet to be replaced with sufficiently fair and efficient procedures.

When it comes to training, managers in Romania think that improving job-specific skills is most important, due to their strong belief that the success of a firm depends on productivity. Training in technical skills is followed in importance by interpersonal relations, marketing, leadership, and promoting the firm image (Constantin *et al.*, 2006).

Overall, a process of "gradual Westernization" of HRM policies and practices is observed in Romania (Nicolae *et al.*, 2006; Gross *et al.*, 2007). Multinational companies (MNCs) in particular have played an active and important role in this development. MNCs conduct their HRM using efficient models developed at headquarters (Plesoianu *et al.*, 2011) and usually provide clear guidelines and resources for their subsidiaries. The 16 MNCs included in the aforementioned study considered employee communication to be the most critical factor, followed by recruitment and selection—clearly a switch from the communism era, when the focus was mainly on payroll and purely administrative management.

Although the human resources development practices have a long way to go before being efficient and mature (Brewster & Viegas Bennett, 2010), the annual survey conducted by Danis Consulting (a Romanian consulting and research firm) indicates an improvement in the managers' perception of the role played by HRM in the company. The proactivity, credibility, and strategic partner role of HRM were all positively evaluated, with ratings increasing every year (Danis Consulting, 2011).

Leadership Style

The Romanian manager is traditionally described as having an autocratic style, mainly due to the economic centralization imposed by the communist regime (Aioanei, 2006; Dalton & Kennedy, 2007). A smaller percentage of managers, however, display more democratic behaviors. The autocratic dimension is more prevalent in the state-owned organizations, but irrespective of the organization, Romanian managers tend to retain the final decision, without involving their subordinates in the process. They tend to make use of coercion and expect obedience from the workforce. Due to the relatively high level of power distance in Romania (Hofstede, 1991), the disparity in authority between high- and low-status members of a group or organization is readily accepted by most employees.

Romanian leaders are more task-oriented than relationship-oriented, with men being more task-oriented than women (Aioanei, 2006). Many managers perceive themselves more as "fixers" of anomalies in a process than creators of an alternative future, and report feeling rather uncomfortable when dealing with ambiguous and unstructured problems (Dalton & Kennedy, 2007). They are also less comfortable with risk-taking and nonconformist behavior. This attitude toward ill-defined situations is also supported by the cultural trait of uncertainty avoidance (Hofstede, 1991). There is a strong need for written rules and regulations in organizations, and employees appreciate job security and a clear task structure. The main obstacles faced by managers in supporting and developing their firms are the lack of strategic thinking and planning and the lack of teamwork abilities (Danis Consulting, 2011).

A study conducted by Fein *et al.* (2010) noted that, contrary to expectations, Romanian managers aged 35 and over manifested a strong preference for transformational leadership behaviors, while younger managers preferred a more autocratic, transactional style of leadership. The authors explain this preference of the young managers by taking into account the economic decline after the fall of communism, an atmosphere in which a transactional leadership style would seem to promote faster change.

In a study comparing preferred leadership behaviors in Romania, Germany, and the UK, Littrell and Valentin (2005) identified two outlying traits of Romanian managers: a high level of demand reconciliation and a low level of persuasiveness. The first trait reflects the ability of the manager to reconcile conflicting demands and to reduce the disorder in a system. Romanians rated this trait as significantly more desirable than did participants from Germany or the UK. The results are in line with the aforementioned high score on uncertainty avoidance. Persuasiveness indicates the extent to which a manager uses oral persuasion and argument effectively. This behavior received the lowest desirability score from the Romanian sample, significantly lower than the German and UK scores. This result is consistent with the high power distance accepted in Romania, which reduces the relevance of oral persuasion as a managerial tool.

In spite of the identified characteristics of Romanian leaders, according to Aioanei (2006), Romanians would like to have leaders with a stronger democratic (95 percent of respondents) than authoritarian (5 percent) orientation, as well as managers with a greater relationship orientation. Cătană and Cătană (2010) noted that the first two leadership preferences of Romanian prospective leaders are team-oriented leadership and charismatic/value-based leadership. Finally, Caprar (2011) showed that MNCs have a strong influence on their local employees, who seem to display preferences that are not consistent with the local culture, and suggested that such culture change may spread to non-MNC employees as well.

Literature Review on Trust

According to the survey data from the New Democracies Barometer (Mishler & Rose, 1997), the levels of trust in various institutions in Romania and Bulgaria are lower than those of the other nine countries included in the survey. Romanians have a high level of distrust in political parties, Parliament, and the media, reserving their highest levels of trust for the army and the church. The authors attribute these low levels of trust to the impact of the former communist regime, which was extremely repressive in terms of human rights and individual freedoms. A low level of trust in other citizens, as well as in the political authorities, was also reported by Bădescu et al. (2004) and by Letki and Evans (2005), with the latter authors noting that, despite its high levels of support for democracy and the free market at the time of the survey, Romania registered the lowest score on the index of social trust among the 11 countries included in the study. According to the Standard Eurobarometer (2011) results, the optimism index for the next 12 months in Romania is negative. Although in Romania the transition to democracy has been slow and difficult at times, trust in the European Union predominates, with Romania displaying the highest level of EU trust (62 percent) among the countries participating in the survey.

The lack of trust among Romanians for their fellow citizens and institutions also extends to the Romanian healthcare system. Compared to other European countries, in which this issue is not a predominant concern, in Romania there has been a rise in preoccupation with healthcare, according to the Standard Eurobarometer (2011) results. People's general perceptions and attitudes toward the Romanian healthcare system are among the lowest in Europe, despite the efforts to improve the system in recent years (Sava & Menon, 2008). A working paper on trust and distrust in the patient–physician relationship in Romania (Andrei et al., 2012) revealed that patients evaluate their condition as rendering them vulnerable and dependent on various characteristics of their physician, including his or her reputation, benevolence, competence, and integrity. While the interpersonal competence of a physician was related more with trust, the technical competence (or more exactly, concern for the lack of it) was associated with distrust. A core element determining the level of trust or distrust was the integrity of physicians, which the respondents considered to be compromised by the cultural practice of providing financial enticement to doctors. The study reported duality in the way the respondents related to this issue.

Bribery is not reserved to the healthcare system: it occurs in many other public and private services in Romania, thereby hindering the development of trust in the context of work. Su and Richelieu (1999) conducted a study on perceptions regarding business ethics of 50 Western managers working in Romania. Their results suggest that there are differences between the ethics of foreign managers and those of their Romanian counterparts, especially when it comes to bribery. Shockley-Zaback *et al.* (2010) explored why Romanian managers fail to build trust in the competence of the organizations they lead. The conclusion is captured by the comment of a Romanian engineer: "They don't see trust as a priority. They have other priorities—like obtaining profit without caring too much about their employees" (p. 63).

Although studies on trust in management have shown that Romanians have only moderate levels of trust in the management of various Romanian organizations (Budean & Pitariu, 2009; Pitariu & Rus, 2010), even this level of trust has clearly positive consequences on Romanian employees. Results obtained for teams of students working on a project (Andrei *et al.*, 2010) and medical emergency intervention teams (Oţoiu *et al.*, 2012) in Romania illustrate that trust improves coordination processes and facilitates behaviors related to team effectiveness and performance. Budean and Pitariu (2009) observed a direct effect of trust in management on attitudes toward the company's acquisition by a foreign investor and turnover intention. Pitariu and Rus (2010) have shown that trust in a supervisor negatively predicted organizational and interpersonal counterproductive work behavior, while trust in an organization was a negative predictor of interpersonal counterproductive behaviors and a positive predictor of employees' positive emotions. Moreover, the same authors observed that trust in a supervisor moderated the correlation between daily workplace frustrations and interpersonal counterproductive behaviors, while trust in an organization moderated the correlation between the organizational climate and interpersonal counterproductive behaviors.

Contextual Factors in Hierarchical Trusting Relationships

We conducted interviews and two focus groups with managers and subordinates from different industries and at different levels in the organization in order to capture the current perception of trust in manager–subordinate relationships.

As the interviews and focus groups were conducted in Romanian, several particularities of the concept of trust in Romanian culture were brought to attention right away. In Romanian, the concept of trust is mainly translated as a feeling of sureness and lack of doubt with regard to another person: a sense that one can rely on another. "To trust" is usually translated as "*to have* trust in someone," indicating that trust is very much "located" in the person trusting, rather than the person being trusted. A person can have the characteristic of "being a person of trust" (i.e.

a person that can be trusted), but what really matters is how others perceive this person—and perceptions can vary significantly. In other words, the participants emphasized the subjective nature of trust. Thus the most common way to define a trustworthy person is "someone you can rely on," or "someone you are sure of," and the participants emphasized that such an assessment is very personal and cannot be objectively measured.

Participants in both interviews and focus groups had a hard time providing an example of trust from the work setting, because many believe "real" trust is a characteristic of friendship and family relationships, not something that defines work relationships. Although many admitted to having real trust relationships at work as well, in most cases these were with co-workers who were also friends outside of the work context. Some spoke about the trust one can have in someone's work abilities, but they considered this to be a different type of trust. This is rather interesting given the fact that the Romania culture is rather diffuse (i.e. no separation between work, and personal issues and relationships). This idea was expressed by some in an absolute manner ("I only trust my family and my friends—who else can you trust?"); others offered a more nuanced analysis, yet in essence not very different:

> Well, I can say I trust Ion, who is always on time, never misses work, does every thing well that I give him to do, and doesn't bad-mouth the company. But to me, that's just a good employee! Do I trust him? I could say that, but it's not the right use of the word. I trust my friends. And I trust that Ion would do good work. Well, yes, maybe it is trust … kind of …

Both managers and subordinates also believed that behaviors can be misleading. That is, people can purposely display trustworthy behaviors, but that does not mean they really are trustworthy or that they trust you. Under communism, it was required, and was common practice, to display trust and loyalty even if these sentiments were not felt. Our results suggested that this dissociation is still common in the current workplace (and perhaps in other cultures as well, as pointed out by one of the interviewees: "In every society, people put on a mask when at work or in public settings"). Interestingly, when trust is established, it has a halo effect on how behaviors are interpreted in general: a behavior that may seem suspicious, but comes from a trusted person, is dismissed as irrelevant (i.e. "there is an explanation for it"). In contrast, normal (or positive) behavior of a non-trusted person is viewed with suspicion. As one of the focus group participants put it:

> I don't think that doing what appears to be trustworthy is enough—yes, I expect that those people I trust would do certain things, but even if they don't, it doesn't matter, I know they have a reason … while others, who I don't trust, they can do all the right things, I would still wonder whether they want something from me, and still have my guard on—I can never know what is really behind it!

A commonly agreed upon theme in both interviews and focus groups was that trust can be defined in terms of "how much you can disclose," or what kind of information you can share with a certain person. This complements the view that trust can only exist in very close relationships, and that there is a distinction between displaying behaviors of trust and *really* trusting. A similar distinction was made between "agreement" and "trust," suggesting people might agree with you (for the sake of social conformity), but that does not mean you can trust them. Honesty came up as an essential dimension of trust: keeping one's word, and guaranteeing and respecting confidentiality are very important. These ideas are reflected in the following comment:

> It really comes down to what I can talk with you about: if I can tell you whatever goes through my mind, without me worrying how you will be using this information, or who else is going to find out what I said, that means I can trust you. Of course, I also expect you would do the same, including telling me exactly what you think about what I said, no matter how much that would be agreeing with me or telling me otherwise.

Many examples illustrated the fact that trust cannot happen without enough time and deep interaction, which allows for getting to know a person very well. Again, this theme is related to previously presented insights, as it explains why real trust can only be achieved with family members and very close (long-term) friends. While some interviewees described trusting relationships at work, they usually also defined these relationships in terms of friendship and especially in terms of having been tested over time:

> I chose this person as an example of a person who I trust because I have known him for a very long time… I have worked with this person in the past, and that experience tells me about him: I have plenty of examples in which he took initiative in helping me, and was available when I needed him. In other words we had a true relationship.

Concluding that Romanians do not trust each other outside of family or friendship relationships might be inadequate—perhaps, as some of the interviewees suggested, what is labeled trust in other cultures (reliability, polite behavior, or organizational citizenship) does not suffice to engender trust in Romanians. Trust is very personal in this culture, and as a result it is difficult to define in the work context, or when a different type of relationship (friendship or family relationship) is not present. Another way to understand these insights is perhaps by considering that, when Romanians trust someone at work, they become friends: in other words, trust in working relationships is possible, but it changes the nature of the relationship from purely professional to a more personal one. This insight may apply to other cultures, but the unique definition of trust and its connection with a certain type of relationship seems to be rather essential in the way Romanians relate to the concept.

Personal Factors in Hierarchical Trusting Relationships

Because our quantitative data suggested that certain personal factors might be relevant to the trust relationship between managers and subordinates, we explored this idea with the participants in the focus groups. We first asked the participants to generate their own list of personal factors that may be relevant, then presented them with the findings from the quantitative study, and asked them to comment on it.

In both focus groups, the main factors listed were the age difference between manager and subordinate and the age of both in general, the duration of the relationship, a match in personality, and interestingly, the region of birth (some regions in Romania being attributed with more trust than others). Gender was brought into the discussion, but there was no clear consensus that gender influences trust, and other factors were considered to be much more important. These opinions overlapped to a large extent with the quantitative findings, as presented in Table 7.1.

Table 7.1 Romania: significant controls (correlations)

and	Age of manager	Age of subordinate	Age difference between manager and subordinate	Organizational tenure: manager	Organizational tenure: subordinate	Time manager subordinate worked together
MTB						
OCB	0.189*			0.166*	0.244**	0.304**
MTS						0.219**
STM		0.306**	−0.314**		0.202*	0.202*

Notes
** Correlation significant at the 0.01 level.
* Correlation significant at the 0.05 level.
MTB = managerial trustworthy behavior, STM = subordinates' trust in managers, MTS = managers' trust in subordinates, OCB = organizational citizenship behavior.

Consistent with the preliminary observations made by the focus groups, the quantitative data revealed that the age difference between the manager and subordinate is one of the most important personal factors associated with trust relationships. More specifically, the age difference was negatively correlated with the trust of a subordinate in his or her manager. The participants suggested that these findings could be explained by the aforementioned observation that younger generations do not appreciate the style of older managers, and older subordinates resent having to report to a younger manager. This explanation was also supported by the finding that the age of the subordinate was positively correlated with the subordinate's trust in a manager: the older the subordinates were, the more they trusted their manager. It is important to note that, in the sample used for the quantitative data, the average age in the subordinate group was lower (32 years) than the average age in the manager group (39 years), which was the typical relation in the workplaces of participants in the focus groups—although exceptions were noted. This difference may further explain why the age of subordinates is associated with their trust in managers, while the age of the managers seems to have less relevance. When the subordinate is younger, issues related to power distance and generational differences can impede the trust the subordinate has in the manager, but the reverse is not necessarily true.

The length of the relationship seems to be particularly important, as was also noted in the preliminary comments. Moreover, the data show that the length of the relationship affects several components of the trust model derived from the quantitative data. The positive impact of the length of the relationship on the subordinate organizational citizenship behavior and the managers' trustworthy behaviors was explained by the fact that long-lasting relationships "oblige" the parties to commit to each other; in contrast, parties in new (shorter) relationships may still be in the "exploration" phase, attempting to figure out how much to "invest" in each other, and therefore showing fewer citizenship and trustworthy behaviors. The participants found it surprising, though, that the length of the relationship was positively associated with the trust of subordinates in their managers but not with the trust of managers in their subordinates. The participants suggested that the paradox may have been due to the tendency for managers to hire new workers who they already trust or *feel* they can trust, and thus the length of the relationship would not have as much impact on whether the manager trusts the subordinate. However, newly hired subordinates do not necessarily trust their manager before they get to know them better, hence the positive correlation between length of relationship and trust in the manager.

The tenure of both managers and subordinates was positively associated with the subordinate organizational citizenship behaviors. The participants explained that this finding was more an effect of the manager and subordinate working together for a longer time, rather than either necessarily working for the company longer. In the Romanian culture, they explained, the loyalty is to the people in the company, not to the company itself. Therefore, they believe that the effect of tenure actually works through the effect of the longer relationship between the manager and the subordinate, not independently. This argument is supported by the observation that longer tenure of a manager did not influence the trustworthy behavior of a manager or the manager's trust in the subordinate (such trust does not depend on how long the manager has been with the company, but rather on how long the manager has been working with certain subordinates), nor was longer tenure for the manager associated with a subordinate's trust in the manager (i.e. a manager with long tenure, but who the subordinate did not know for a long time, was not necessarily trusted more by the subordinate). However, a subordinate that has been with the company longer is more likely to also show more trust in the manager because, as the participants explained, that subordinate probably had more time to get to know the manager.

Antecedents and Outcomes of Manager–Subordinate Trust

A common theme in the focus groups was the idea that trust develops naturally, over time, and that one cannot force trust to happen. We challenged this idea by asking which factors could lead to the development of trust.

Interestingly, both managers and subordinates listed a series of trusting behaviors as antecedents of "feeling" trust toward each other. Managers suggested that employees who are reliable, those they can count on in any situation, are definitely the first to benefit from their trust. They listed work-related behaviors (e.g. completing tasks on time, providing quality work, etc.), but agreed that a very important element is that the subordinates they trust (or who they will trust in the future) are those who do not engage in gossiping (i.e. talking about their manager behind their backs). All managers agreed that this is an essential factor. They see it as a sign of honesty—which is an important requirement for trusting someone—as well as a sign of loyalty and proof that their employees trust them. Moreover, beyond refraining from gossip, subordinates who informed the manager about any issues arising in the team were also highly prized, since such information was considered an important factor in facilitating the work of the manager. However, some managers, but especially subordinates, interpreted the strong reaction against gossiping as a manifestation of a manager's desire to be in control. As one subordinate explained, "They want to know about everything that is happening, and most of them are paranoid." Another suggested, "They are very insecure and immature, and afraid of losing their power." Some associated the behavior of subordinates who constantly report to the "boss" with the behavior of the typical "informers" common under communism: the system had a widespread formal and informal political police, with "recruits" in all layers of the society. Some subordinates further insisted that managers only trust those who perform this role.

Managers also appreciate employees who support their decisions and who take their side whenever a dispute occurs. Again, subordinates had mixed feelings about their fellow subordinates who seemed too eager to be "on good terms with the boss."

Subordinates appreciate information and open communication from the manager as an antecedent of trust. They suggested that they will trust a manager who is honest and open, and who provides them with information beyond what is officially required. They also seem to trust managers who leave aside formalities, and are more direct, unofficial, and personal. They appreciated fairness, but soon the opinions converged toward the idea that subordinates will trust a manager who treats them fairly, but who also provides them (but not others) with special treatment (benefits, rewards, information, etc.). In other words, the subordinates defined a trusting relationship between managers and subordinates as only typical for the cases in which the employee is a protégé of the manager. Most subordinates agreed that they would only trust a manager if he or she acted in a way that substantiated that trust (i.e. by offering promotions, special opportunities, etc.). Appreciation of work was also mentioned as an antecedent of trust, but the subordinates insisted that they might discount (i.e. distrust) declarative appreciation if it is not backed up with corresponding behaviors/actions. In fact, some subordinates believed that praise and, in general, non-monetary rewards are manipulative techniques that make them trust the manager even less.

These antecedents, along with outcomes of trust from the perspective of both manager and subordinates, are summarized in Figure 7.1.

From the perspective of the manager, the main outcome of trusting a subordinate seems to be that the manager will indeed prioritize a trusted employee both in terms of responsibilities and rewards. Offering more opportunities to a trusted employee will "promote" the employee to a special status, which inevitably will allow him or her to justify this special status because they will, indeed, benefit from the enhanced opportunities to stand out. Subordinates also observed such outcomes, but focused more on the trusted subordinate becoming more motivated by their increased opportunities and developing a sense of obligation toward the trusting manager, making them more committed and, eventually, better performers.

Both managers and subordinates agreed that trust ends up being reciprocal (and indeed that it cannot function otherwise) and that a trusting relationship means a better working relationship overall. They insisted that such a relationship will be a closer one, perhaps going beyond the formal work relationship: if trust develops between the manager and subordinates, it means that they have become "friends,"

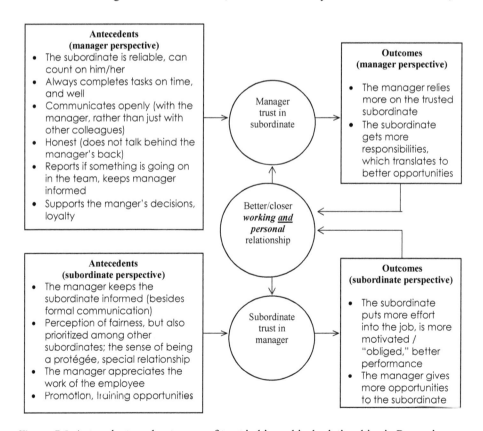

Figure 7.1 Antecedents and outcomes of trust in hierarchical relationships in Romania

or that they trust each other because they were friends. It was difficult to agree on a causality direction (whether trust leads to friendship or friendship leads to trust), with most suggesting that they develop simultaneously, being in fact facets of the same phenomena. Again, the fact that "real" trust can only develop if such a closer relationship is achieved was emphasized, with most participants restating the idea that purely professional, manager–subordinate trust is not real trust.

The Dynamics of Trust in Hierarchical Relationships

In discussing the way trust develops between managers and subordinates, the participants emphasized the importance of a long history together. "It needs to get personal," suggested one of the participants, and this statement seems to capture what most participants believed. Having a connection outside of work helps a lot and, historically, that connection is, in many cases, what secured the job for a new candidate. This is not necessarily the case any more, especially in large companies, but remains an important feature in smaller and medium enterprises, according to those working in these sectors.

The professional relationship turned into friendship theme re-occurred: participants believed that the way trust is formed is that the manager and the subordinate will eventually socialize outside work and that the relationship will become one that is more complex than a simple work relationship. Some participants reacted, insisting that in some organizations this is less common—but agreement was reached in suggesting that a purely professional relationship is not one based on trust. They suggested the possibility of a respectful reciprocal relationship, but again, this respect (professional or even personal) is not what trust really is in their opinion.

We separately asked managers and subordinates how they initiate a trusting relationship and if they are at all preoccupied with developing trusting relationships at work. Managers suggested that they indeed make an effort in this regard, and it starts with whom they hire. Many admitted that, if they had a great candidate for a job that they felt they could not trust, they would probably hire the next best candidate. Again, the personal connection was emphasized. However, when they cannot directly select their employees, some managers suggested that they would try to develop a trusting relationship with all employees. Others insisted that they would be very selective, keeping it professional with most, and having a closer, trusting relationship with just a few. Managers of both camps suggested that they would try to present themselves as someone the employees could trust, even if they considered this difficult to achieve: some were rather skeptical about the idea of developing such relationships with their subordinates, believing that it was important to keep some distance with all subordinates. This last category included especially managers with longer work experience.

Subordinates, on the other hand, suggested that they all try to make sure the managers believe they can be trusted, by showing commitment to work, by showing "friendliness," and by trying to be part of what they called the manager's "circle of friends" (i.e. the in-group). But many suggested that their efforts depend a lot on whether a manager signals a desire to develop such a relationship and, if they do not see such signals, they will also maintain distance.

Most managers and subordinates agreed that one cannot trust another before getting to know the person: "You cannot just trust someone the first time you meet them—it takes time; trusting too early can get you into troubles, especially at work." This attitude is consistent with the studies suggesting a low level of trust in Romania in general.

Although the dynamic of trust has some particularities in Romania, overall the processes are very similar to those in any other culture: reciprocal trust reinforces the relationship, and behaviors that induce trust on the part of both mangers and the subordinate generate a virtuous cycle, leading to more trust on both sides. The quantitative data for Romania support the general model in which the subordinate's organizational citizenship behavior (OCB) leads to a manager trusting the subordinate (MTS), associated with the display of trustworthy behaviors on the part of the manager (MTB), which induces the subordinate's trust in the manager (STM), as indicated in Table 7.2. However, the link between STM and OCB was not significant. This pattern was actually found in several countries, but we wanted to see how the focus group participants interpreted it in the context of Romania.

The strongest association in the model for the Romanian sample (and for the 18-country sample as well) was the association between MTB and STM. This finding was consistent with the observations of participants that it is very important for managers to signal trust in their subordinates, in order for the subordinates to trust their managers. The weaker association between STM and OCB was explained by the fact that subordinates would attempt to display OCB even when they did not trust their managers, in an attempt to gain their trust. In other words, the only way the subordinate can actually attempt to build a relationship with the manager is by showing good OCB. The relatively strong association between the subordinate's OCB and the manager's trust in the subordinate was contested by participants: they believe that the manager's trust is not always triggered by the subordinate's OCB (at least the group of subordinates strongly believed so). Indeed, while the association suggested by the quantitative data is a positive one, it is not a perfect relationship. Participants suggested that we would need to explore the relationship over time: if the subordinate displays OCB and the manager does not respond with trust in the subordinate and managerial trustworthy behavior, eventually the subordinate will stop displaying OCB. An alternative explanation offered, especially by managers, was that once the manager trusts the subordinate and displays managerial trustworthy behaviors, the subordinate will trust the manager as expected, but will also feel "safe" (i.e. protected, "in good terms with the manager"), and therefore will feel less need or pressure to show OCB. Many participants viewed OCB more as a display of behaviors meant to get the attention of the manager and a privileged position

Table 7.2 Standardized regression weights for the trust model in Romania and the overall sample

	OCB–>MTS	MTS–>MTB	MTB–>STM	STM–>OCB
Romania only	0.56**	0.67**	0.77**	0.11
Complete model	0.68**	0.34**	0.89**	0.08*

Notes
* Regression weight significant at the 0.05 level.
** Regression weight significant at the 0.01 level.

in the work group (part of the manager's in-group). Of course, proper conclusions with regard to this dynamic can only be obtained with longitudinal data in future studies.

Discussion and Conclusions

Although considerable time has passed since the 1989 revolution that constitutes the major event in modern Romanian history, the country's economy and especially its social structures are still in a transitioning phase. Communism eroded trust at both the interpersonal and institutional levels throughout the Eastern bloc states (Kornai *et al.*, 2004). In Romania in particular, the message conveyed through state propaganda was that one must appear to trust the leadership of the country in spite of the evident economic, social, and political problems. As in many communist states, this requirement may have facilitated the generally negative attitude of Romanians toward individuals in positions of authority. Consequently, managers may face attitudes of suspicion, skepticism, and ultimately distrust simply because of their positions.

Among our findings, the observation that Romanians struggled with defining the concept of trust in work settings was of particular interest. This phenomenon likely arose from the historical challenges summarized above. The fact that, under communist rule, people had a public, official life related to work and institutions, and a private, personal life that was only available to friends and relatives seems directly related to the distinction between the formal trust, displayed at work, and the real trust, specific to close relationships. Under communism, the public life (including work) required formalism, compliance, and a high degree of dissembling. One could never be totally open with just anyone, especially when it came to politics, and thus *real* trust could only be achieved with close friends and family. This tendency to trust only friends is actually typical for post-communist societies: a study in eight former Soviet countries (not including Romania) showed that people in these countries trusted their friends and relatives the most, followed by non-related individuals, while politicians and institutions were trusted the least (Sapsford & Abbott, 2006). Does this mean that trust between subordinates and managers is not to be expected in these countries? Our findings show otherwise: the quantitative study revealed a model of trust between subordinates and managers that was very similar to that in the 18-country sample (i.e. the subordinate's organizational citizenship behavior leads to the manager trusting the subordinate and showing trusting behaviors, which facilitates the subordinate trust in the manager). How, then, can this finding be explained in relation to the other observations about the Romanian context?

While it has been revealed that Romanians show a lower level of social trust, it appears that they satisfy their need to trust and be trusted within close relationships. Even under communism, the Romanians developed alternative informal trusting relationships in order to solve their problems: for example, obtaining a product or service in an economy of austerity required "special relationships," where what was available was offered based on priorities defined by such relationships. In other words, getting what you needed was about who you knew. In this way, Romanians may have found a solution to both low social trust and poor customer service by building close ties with those who had access to certain resources. The findings from our study (i.e. subordinates attempted to replace the formal relationship with an informal, closer relationship with the manager) seem to be consistent with this notion. Indeed, Brewster and Viegas Bennett (2010) found that, even recently, Romania had one of the lowest customer service ratings among the six former communist countries they studied, and that good professional relationships are not automatically dictated by the status of a customer or work colleague. They could not explain the paradox of, on the one hand, the strong relationships observed among Romanians and, on the other hand, the poor service. Our results further explain that good relationships are based on trust, which is only achieved in the context of closer ties that go beyond the basic business relationship: once such ties exist, proper service becomes extremely important, but it is reserved for these special situations.

In the context of the manager–subordinate relationship, good "service" is reflected in organizational citizenship behavior. Findings of a study comparing OCB in Romania and the US (Turnipseed & Murkison, 2000) suggest that the construct of OCB may be different in the two cultures and, therefore, culturally defined. We second this observation based on the fact that the concerns expressed in our focus groups were similar to those observed in this previous study; moreover, our quantitative data shows, surprisingly, a weak link between the trust of subordinates in the manager and their propensity to engage in OCB. As noted earlier, the particularities of the Romanian context (the "special relationship" focus) may explain this finding, but it could also be attributed to problems with the definitions of trust. In fact, several measures presented lower reliability in the Romanian sample than in other samples. Future research should further explore the content and the validity of the OCB construct (and the other constructs used in this study) across different cultural contexts.

The dynamics of trust in the Romanian culture should be of particular interest for future research. As we have already noted, the historical context is changing rapidly, and along with these changes may come changes in the way trust is formed and the way trust influences work. Since contemporary Romania is characterized by, on the one hand, fundamental low social trust and potential distance between levels in organization and, on the other, new trends and models in the business culture and the society in general, approaches focused on process (i.e. longitudinal data) would certainly reveal interesting insights and a more complete picture on the role of trust in organizations.

For the moment, we have presented a model that suggests a reciprocal effect of trust between managers and subordinates, along with specifying significant personal correlates (such as the age of the subordinate and manager and the age difference between them, the tenure with the organization for both manager and subordinate, and the amount of time they worked together). These findings should provide a starting point for researchers interested in further exploring the role and dynamics of trust in the Romanian work context, but could also be the basis for formulating preliminary practical implications. Both managers and subordinates would benefit from reflecting on what drives their behavior and, in particular, their attitudes toward each other. Questioning implicit beliefs would increase the chances for capitalizing on the positive potential of the reciprocal cycle, while avoiding potential breakdowns in the process. Perhaps an important insight is that, for the most part, both the manager and subordinate can initiate the trust formation process or correct the potential interruptions. Deliberate analysis, feedback, and monitoring of perceptions and assumptions seem to be particularly useful in a context in which historically determined tendencies and modern approaches intersect, with potential for confusion and misinterpretations. Finally, both managers and subordinates may need to approach their reciprocal relationship with patience, allowing the time that seems to be needed for building a working (*and* personal) relationship based on trust.

References

Aioanei, I. (2006). Leadership in Romania. *Journal of Organizational Change Management*, 19(6): 705–710.

Andrei, D., Isailă, S., Oţoiu, C. & Băban, A. (2012). Trust and distrust in patient-physician relationship in Romania: a grounded approach. Working Paper, 'Babes-Bolyai University, Cluj-Napoca, Romania.

Andrei, D., Oţoiu, C., Isăilă, Ş. & Băban, A. (2010). What does it mean to trust your team colleague? An exploratory study using grounded theory. *Cognition, Brain, Behavior. An Interdisciplinary Journal*, XIV(2): 121–140.

Bădescu, G., Sum, P. & Uslaner, E.M. (2004). Civil society development and democratic values in Romania and Moldova. *East European Politics and Societies*, 18(2): 316–341.

Brewster, C. & Viegas Bennett, C. (2010). Perceptions of business cultures in eastern Europe and their implications for international HRM. *The International Journal of Human Resource Management*, 21(14): 2568–2588.

Budean, A. & Pitariu, H. (2009). Relaţia dintre încrederea în management şi atitudinile faţă de schimbare în contextul unei achiziţii internaţionale [The relationship between trust in management and attitude towards change in the context of an international acquisition]. *Psihologia Resurselor Umane* [*The Psychology of Human Resources*], 7(1): 29–42.

Caprar, D.V. (2011). Foreign locals: A cautionary tale on the culture of MNC local employees. *Journal of International Business Studies*, 42(5), Special Issue: Qualitative Research in International Business: 608–628.

Cătană, G. & Cătană, D. (2010). Prospective Romanians' leaders view on leadership dimensions. *Analele Universităţii din Oradea. Fascicula Ştiinţe Economice*, Tom XIX(1): 645–650.

Constantin, T., Pop, D. & Stoica-Constantin, A. (2006). Romanian managers and human resources managers. *Journal of Organizational Change Management*, 19(6): 760–765.

Dalton, K. & Kennedy, L. (2007). Management culture in Romania: Patterns of change and resistance. *Journal of East European Management Studies*, 12(3): 232–259.

Danis Consulting (2011). Annual Survey: Management challenges and development of organizations. Research Report.

Farlow, R. (1964). Romania's foreign policy. A case of partial alignment. *Problems of Communism*, 13(2): 14–24.

Fein, E.C., Tziner, A., Vasiliu, C. (2010). Age cohort effects, gender and Romanian leadership preferences. *Journal of Management Development*, 29(4): 364–376.

Fox, C.R. (1996). What, if anything, is a Byzantine? *Celator*, 10(3): 36–41.

Gross, A., Plesoianu, G. &Poor, J. (2007). Human resource management in Central-East Europe: policies and practices. *Romanian Statistical Review*, 12: 60–69.

Hofstede, G. (1991). *Cultures and Organizations: Software of the Mind*. London: McGraw-Hill.

International Monetary Fund, (2011). *World Economic Outlook. Tensions from the Two-Speed Recovery. Unemployment, Commodities and Capital Flows*. Retrieved on November 29, 2011 from www.imf.org/external/pubs/ft/weo/2011/01/pdf/text.pdf.

Ispas, D., Ilie, A., Iliescu, D., Johnson, R.E. & Harris, M.M. (2010). Fairness reaction to selection methods: A Romanian study. *International Journal of Selection and Assessment*, 18(1): 102–110.

Kornai, J., Rothstein, B. & Rose-Ackerman, S. (2004). *Creating Social Trust in Post-Socialist Transition.* New York: Palgrave Macmillan.

Lane, D. (2007). Post state socialism: A diversity of capitalisms? In D. Lane and M. Myant (eds), *Varieties of Capitalism in Post Communist Countries.* London: Palgrave, pp. 13–39.

Letki, N. & Evans, G. (2005). Endogenizing social trust: Democratization in East-Central Europe. *British Journal of Political Science,* 35: 515–529.

Littrell, R.F. & Valentin, L.N. (2005). Preferred leadership behaviors: exploratory results from Romania, Germany, and the UK. *Journal of Management Development,* 24(5): 421–442.

Livezeanu, I. (2000). *Cultural Politics in Greater Romania: Regionalism, Nation Building, and Ethnic Struggle, 1918–1930.* New York: Cornell Paperbacks.

Mishler, W. & Rose, R. (1997). Trust, distrust and skepticism: Popular evaluations of civil and political institutions in post-communist societies. *The Journal of Politics,* 59: 418–451.

Neculaesei, A.N. & Tătărusanu, M. (2008). Romania – Cultural and regional differences. *Analele Ştiinţifice ale Universităţii „Alexandru Ioan Cuza" din Iaşi, Ştiinţe Economice,* Tomul LV: 198–204.

Nicolae, O., Plesoianu, G. & Poor, J. (2006), *Case Handbook on International Human Resource Management in Emerging and Developed Countries of Europe.* Bucharest: Editura Olimp.

Oţoiu, C., Andrei, D. & Băban, A. (2012). Cross-understanding and trust formation within medical emergency intervention teams. *Procedia – Social and Behavioral Sciences,* 33: 875–879.

Pitariu, H. & Rus, C. (2010). Rolul moderator al încrederii organizaţionale în relaţia stresori – reacţii la stres [The moderating role of organizational trust on the relationship between stressors and the reaction to stress]. *Psihologia Resurselor Umane [The Psychology of Human Resources],* 8(1): 39–49.

Plesoianu, G., Poor, J., Farcas, F. & Kerekes, K. (2011). Human resource management practices of large multinational firms in Romania, in the light of a Central and Eastern European Survey 2009–2010. *Managerial Challenges of the Contemporary Society,* 2: 146–150.

Romanian Census (2011). *Comunicat de presa priving rezultatele provisorii ale Recensamantului Populatiei si Locuintelor* [Press release regarding provisional census data]. Retrieved on April 13, 2011 from www.recensamantromania.ro/wp-content/uploads/2012/02/Comunicat_DATE_PROVIZORII_RPL_2011_.pdf.

Romanian Presidency (2006). *Raportul Comisiei Prezidenţiale pentru Analiza Dictaturii Comuniste din România* [Final Report on Communist Dictatorship in Romania]. Retrieved on November 30, 2011 from www.presidency.ro/static/ordine/RAPORT_FINAL_CPADCR.pdf.

Sapsford, R. & Abbott, P. (2006). Trust, confidence, and social environment in post-communist societies. *Communist and Post-Communist Studies,* 39: 59–71.

Sava, D. & Menon, R. (2008). România. Sectorul de sănătate. Studiu de politica sectorială. [Romania. Healthcare sector. A study of sectorial policy]. Retrieved on November 29, 2011 from http://siteresources.worldbank.org/INTROMANIAINROMANIAN/Resources/HealthSectorPolicyNoteRomanian.pdf.

Shockley-Zaback, P., Morreale, S.P. & Hackman, M.Z. (2010). *Building the High-Trust Organization. Strategies for Supporting the Five Key Dimensions of Trust.* San Francisco: Jossey-Bass.

Standard Eurobarometer (2011). *Public opinion in the European Union.* Retrieved on November 29, 2011 from http://ec.europa.eu/public_opinion/archives/eb/eb75/eb75_publ_en.pdf.

Su, Z. & Richelieu, A. (1999). Western managers working in Romania: Perceptions and attitudes regarding business ethics. *Journal of Business Ethics,* 20(2): 133–144.

Turnipseed, D.L. & Murkison, E. (2000). A bi-cultural comparison of organization citizenship behavior: Does the OCB phenomenon transcend national culture? *The International Journal of Organizational Analysis,* 8(2): 200–222.

UNESCO (2008). *The Romanian Educational Policy in Transition.* Retrieved on December 1, 2011 from www.unesco.org/education/wef/countryreports/romania/rapport_1.html.

8

Manager–Subordinate Trust Relationships in Russia

ALEXEY SVISHCHEV

Introduction

Russia, officially known as the Russian Federation (briefly RF), is located in Eastern Europe and Northern Asia. It is the largest country in the world in terms of area (17,075,400 square kilometers, 11.46 percent of the Earth's land surface, or 12.65 percent of the inhabited land surface, and double the size of the next largest country, Canada). It also includes the Kaliningrad region, which is separated from the rest of Russia by the Baltic countries. The total population amounts to 142,914,136 people (according to the 2011 census) and it is the world's ninth most populated country. Russia is a federative state consisting of 83 constituent entities of the Federation. Russia is a very cosmopolitan country. Among the 83 constituent entities of the Federation, there are 23 with official languages other than Russian, which is spoken all over the country. Russia has common borders with 18 independent countries (the highest number in the world).

After the collapse of the Soviet Union at the end of 1991, the Russian Federation was recognized as the official successor of the Soviet Union, with all the consequences deriving from that (including membership of all international organizations). According to some experts (Zorkin, 2003; Elgie, 2007; Shugart, 2005), Russia is considered to be a democratic federative presidential-parliamentary state with wide powers for the President.

Russia joined the group of countries with a high level of human development in 2007. According to Newsweek, Russia is fifty-first in the list of "The World's Best Countries." This is a complex indicator which consists of the following ratings: Education—thirty-first place, Health—seventy-fifth place, Quality of Life—fiftieth place, Economic Dynamics—thirty-sixth place, and Political Situation—seventy-fifth place. According to the World Economic Forum (2010–2011), Russia holds sixty-third place in the list of the world's most competitive countries.

According to the IMF, the Russian nominal GDP in 2010 amounted to 44.5 trillion Russian rubles and the GDP per PPP was $2.23 trillion (sixth in the world). The Russian economy accounts for about 3 percent of the world economy. With the onset of the global financial crisis, the economy experienced a protracted period of stagnation. Russia has a relatively modest official level of unemployment (about 6.5 percent in 2010). However, the problem is that the unofficial unemployment rate is much higher. Some local experts say that it is about 14–15 percent. The inflation rate in 2010 was 8.7 percent. The official external state debt was $37.6 billion (i.e. 3 percent of the GDP) in 2010. The economic growth rate was about 4 percent (according to different sources).

Russia's traditionally hierarchical business culture was formed after many years of absolutism and the Soviet Union's highly centralized system. However, nowadays, work relations tend to keep in line with the changes that are taking place in Russia and, particularly, in its economy. This is due to a reappraisal of values with the transition to a free market. Currently, centralization, obedience, discipline, career, and strong power are being replaced by personal identity, focus on real needs, collectivism, innovation, and decentralization. In many respects, the Russian business culture is the outcome of a high instability and volatility in which it is very difficult to plan and make concrete management decisions. One of the particularities of the Soviet economy that still persists is the high level of paternalism within companies. At the organizational level, human resource management functions and aims have changed significantly during recent decades. Nowadays, companies are aware of the need not only to attract new talent but to retain existing talent as valuable capital.

In this chapter, we begin with a short account of historical developments in Russia, along with a description of the contemporary institutional environment, in particular, the educational, legal, and social systems, as well as an overview of the current economic and social context. This is followed by a summary of human resource management practices and developments, and preferred leadership styles in the organizational context. We then move to the substantive area of trust. Extant literature on multiple aspects of trust relationships in the workplace context in Russia is reviewed before presenting our empirical results. The chapter concludes with a discussion of some of the main results in the context of the extant literature and highlights potential implications for management and leadership practice, along with potential avenues for future research.

Highlights of Manager–Subordinate Trust in Russia

- As in many countries in this study, the Russian participants did not show total unanimity concerning whether managers were trusted. The general tendency in Russia is that the longer a manager and his/her subordinate know each other, the more trust they have in their work or interpersonal relations.
- Historically, the Russian model of trust has undergone significant transformation. The twentieth century is marked by three very distinct periods: before the Great October Revolution, the Soviet Union Era, and the Post-Soviet Era. The modern situation can be described as a transition period from the Soviet business culture to a new culture, called the "new capitalist approach" by many experts.
- The experts participating in our study tend to believe that trust itself is more likely to be found in everyday life than in business environments. Furthermore, business results are more important for Russian managers than the underlying trust dynamic.

- Our study respondents pointed out that, in modern Russia, advanced managerial tools such as organization culture were just starting to become established in Russian companies, so it was too early to talk about the use of sophisticated tools in HR practices. The experts believed that foreign companies play a big and, probably, decisive role in HR practices in Russia. It was also considered that trust in work relationships should be viewed as a continuation of interpersonal relations between people in companies. Company size is not considered to be an influential factor in terms of trust building.
- Among the personal factors that influence trust building in the Russian context, our experts mentioned a manager's or subordinate's tenure in a company. Professionalism was not considered to be more important than other personal factors.
- The Russian experts highlighted that there was a big difference between trust at work and trust in private life. Trust at work was not as important as trust in private life. Managers believe that the job description means more than trust at work.
- Another very interesting finding was that the managers in higher positions usually divided trust into two parts: trust in business partners and trust in subordinates, saying that these were two different types of trust at work. Of course, there exists the third type of trust—the trust of a subordinate in his superior. In this study, we have addressed all types of trust.

Historical Perspective

According to the many archeological remains that have been found, the first settlements in what is now Russia date from 1–1.5 million years BC. The term "Russia" is found for the first time in the writings of Emperor Constantine as the Greek name of Rus' (A.V. Soloviev, 1957). Afterwards, the term "Russia" was used for northeastern Russia—that is, the territories which were not part of Poland and the Grand Duchy of Lithuania and were united by Moscovia. This name was used by Western Europe (but not Russia) for the Russian state in the sixteenth and seventeenth centuries, while the people were called Moscovites (Jasque Margeret, 2004). In the fifth century, Russia was inhabited by Slavic tribes, including the territory of Poland and the Eastern Baltics. New inhabitants also entered Russian territories, settling in the Dniester and Volga River basins. However, these tribes were pushed out by the nomads and formed the so-called "northern" tribes.

The Old Russian state was formed in the ninth century with the amalgamation of all the eastern Slavic tribes. According to the Russian Primary Chronicle, Prince Rurik was invited to head the union of tribes. His origins are still the subject of debate by historians but there is general agreement that he was invited because he was a neutral person among the conflicting parties and he had enough power to resist the invasions of the Varangians. After 882, the Rurikovich dynasty reigned in Kiev. In 988, Russia adopted Orthodox Christianity. The Kiev princes initiated prosperous trade relations with the Western countries and fought against the steppe nomads.

In the mid-twelfth century, Kievan Russia split into 15 independent principalities, while maintaining a dynastic and religious unity. One century later, most of these principalities, Bulgaria, and several other European countries were occupied by the Tatars, saving Western Europe from a destructive invasion. The centuries under Mongolian occupation put Russia behind in development compared with other European countries. Prince Vladimir was chosen by the Khan of Mongolia, who used the squabbling between pretenders to the throne to maintain occupation of Russia. Only in the fifteenth century did Moscow become independent, shaking off the colonial yoke (in 1480) and, at the beginning of the sixteenth century, the territory comprising the Russian centralized state was formed.

In 1613, after a long period of instability and war with Poland and Lithuania, the Romanov dynasty came to power and ruled the country until the twentieth century. The end of the seventeenth century and beginning of the eighteenth century were marked by the rule of the famous reformer Peter the Great. It was a time of major social and economic change for Russia. The victory in the Great Northern War (1700–1721) gave the country an exit to the Baltic Sea and the new capital, Saint Petersburg, was built in 1703 on the River Neva. Since then, Russia has been an active player in all the world's political events. It took part in the world's three greatest wars (the War against Napoleon, the First World War, and the Second World War) and was victorious in all of them.

In 1917, the monarchy was deposed and a new period in Russian history began. For more than 70 years (until the 1990s), Russia was part of the Soviet Union as one of its Republics. Ruled by the Communist Party, the USSR tried to build a socialist state with a closed, self-sufficient economy. This effort failed in 1991 with the collapse of the Soviet Union and the emergence of independent states out of 15 former Republics. Subsequently, the Russian Federation was declared successor of the USSR by the international community and took the latter's membership in the United Nations Security Council (Federal Law of July 15, 1995, No. 101-FZ). In 1993, Soviet government institutions were dismantled and the present Constitution of the Russian Federation was adopted.

The modern Russian Federation is a democratic Republic. As of 2011, it has a population of about 143 million people (Rosstat, 2011). Russia is the largest country in the world. Approximately 73 percent of the Russian population lives in urban areas. Russia is a secular state, but 75 percent of the population declare themselves to be Orthodox Christians (All-Russian Public Opinion Research Center, 2009).

Institutional Context

Economic Context

The Russian so-called "new economy" has been under construction from 1991 to the present day. The main feature of the Soviet economy was the attempt by the Soviet government to build a totally self-sufficient economy. Even now, 20 years after the collapse of the Soviet Union, Russia is still living with the "legacy" of that attempt. During the 1990s, the Russian economy could be described as a "transition period" economy. In 1998, Russia experienced a financial crisis which resulted in an internal economic default. After that, Russia enjoyed significant economic growth until 2008. Russia is ranked sixth in the world in terms of GDP per PPP, which currently stands at $2.23 trillion. After a ten-year period of GDP growth, the Russian economy slowed down at the end of 2008, entering into recession in the second quarter of 2008. The official unemployment rate rose from 5.9 percent (in May 2007) to 6.5 percent as of September 2010 (Rosstat, 2010), but still lower than many developed countries. The state budget deficit in 2010 totaled $64.8 billion (4.3 percent of the GDP), despite the fact that Russia had a budget surplus until 2008. The Russian economy is excessively dependent on the commodities markets (particularly, oil and gas). In the context of the world economic crisis, Russia's main macroeconomic indicators do not look too bad (especially when compared with other countries), but this situation is mainly due to the favorable situation of the world commodities markets. The Russian economy's main problem is still the very inefficient structure of the national economy, which is why forecasts for the Russian economy are not very positive.

Social Context

Life expectancy at birth stands at 66.2 years (one-hundred and sixtieth in the world ranking) (CIA, 2010). The total fertility rate is very low for a country that wants to increase its population (1.537 children per woman in 2009) (Rosstat, 2010), compared with the EU average of 1.5 and the global average of 2.7. Russia is a social, secular state (Russian Constitution). In the social context, Russia is considered to be a state in "a transition period" (Chichkanov, 2005). During the Soviet Union era, the government created a totally socially responsible state. Modern Russian social policy is based on market principles, where state provisions mostly consist of pensions (the level of these pensions is very low), and the general level of social assistance is very low. The social security system provides for a limited number of childcare services, elementary education for everybody, limited free places for higher education, some basic provision for sick leave, maternity leave, and free healthcare for all citizens officially registered in Russia. Provisions such as leave policies, unemployment benefits, and financial allowances are guaranteed by law, while flexibility arrangements and social provisions are increasingly left to companies' discretion.

Political and Legal Systems

Russia is a democratic federative presidential-parliamentary state with wide powers for the President, like a constitutional monarchy. State power in the Russian Federation is officially divided into three branches: legislative, executive, and judicial power. Each branch is totally independent of the others. The Head of State is the President. He is elected by a nationwide ballot for a six-year period (according to the new amendments to the 2008 Constitution). The state's legislative branch is called the Federal Assembly, consisting of an upper house (the Federation Council) and a lower house (the State Duma or the Russian Parliament). The Federation Council consists of two representatives from each of the constituent entities of the Federation (giving a current total of 166). The State Duma has 450 seats. The representatives are elected on a proportional basis (by party lists) for a five-year period. The chairman of the government (the Prime Minister) is appointed by the President. The members of the government are appointed by the President at the suggestion of the Prime Minister. Finally, the judicial branch is represented by the

Constitutional Court, the Supreme Court, and the Supreme Arbitration Court. The judges of these courts are appointed by the Federal Assembly at the suggestion of the President. Public Prosecution is independent of all the branches of state power. The head of Public Prosecution is the Prosecutor-General and is appointed by the Federal Assembly at the suggestion of the President. According to the Ministry of Justice (as of June 25, 2011), there are seven registered political parties in Russia. Four of them now form the State Duma: "United Russia" Party (315 seats in the State Duma), Communist Party of the Russian Federation (57), Liberal Democratic Party of the Russian Federation (40), and "Just Russia" Party (38). The voting age is 18. Russia's legal structure is based on a civil law system with comprehensive legal codes and laws, a judiciary organization that combines courts and tribunals, and a legal body composed of judges and magistrates.

Educational System

Education in Russia is no longer compulsory but the state provides to its citizens a certain number of places at every level of education absolutely free of charge. More than 99 percent of the population over the age of 15 can read and write (Rosstat, 2010). In 2010 (Rosstat, 2010), the government allocated 5.1 percent of the GDP to expenditure on education. Education is structured on four levels: pre-school education (1–7 years); general education (7–15 or 17 years), professional education (includes studies at universities—that is, six years of education), and postgraduate professional studies (Ph.D., MBA, etc.). Preschool attendance is optional and a number of places are available free of charge. The same situation is found at every level of education. At every level, there are educational services that are free of charge (provided by the state) and others that charge tuition fees (provided by commercial enterprises).

HR Practices

According to the Federal Service for Labor and Employment, most of the Russian workforce (81 percent) is protected by a permanent employment contract, while only 10 percent have temporary contracts. This is due to the country's—and the labor market's—historical development. In the state-planned economy, all company–employee relations were determined and controlled by the state. Even today, staff have no trust in temporary contracts, as the traditional way of regulating labor relations seems to be more stable and trustworthy. Another point is that a large part of the population works illegally, without a contract, or has illegal earnings from different kinds of activities.

Companies in Russia can be divided into different groups, depending on the HRM practice they use. Large multinational companies are actively entering the Russian market, bringing with them foreign practices of doing business and managing their personnel. A large part of business activity is still under government control and, while the largest companies try not to fall behind the foreign companies in their HR practices, with the small companies, it is not in the state's interest and they cannot afford it. Generally speaking, HR practices have evolved considerably during recent decades, together with the scope of specialists' professional functions. Large international companies adopt common foreign practices in their activities, such as

personnel career development, coaching, team-building, and performance development, among others. Furthermore, companies are starting to realize the need to not
just attract qualified personnel. In addition to motivation and training programs,
large companies are starting to implement a more individual approach to employees, developing personal integration and career development programs. Finally,
companies are becoming increasingly preoccupied about employees' commitment
and their feelings of belonging to the company. The more an employee associates
himself with the company and the better his perception of the company and its
values, the more appeal the company will have for consumers and skilled workers.
However, only the largest companies can afford this; the rest continue doing business as before, with so-called "grey salaries" (not official to avoid taxes) and personal relations with employees.

A study of 100 Russian companies (Morgulis-Yakushev, 2004) distinguished several important HR practices, such as high salaries, variable components, profit-
sharing, career progression, staff training, and performance appraisal, among
others. The study has analyzed the use in practice of each of the above-mentioned
factors in the context of their efficiency. It was found that the most efficient methods for improving employees' competencies, motivation, and performance in
Russia include training, development, and performance appraisals of employees'
activities and abilities. For employee motivation, the most useful are career progression within the company, compensation, and communication. Furthermore, the
research brought to light a synergistic effect between employees' motivation and
competencies: the effect of their joint influence is greater than the result of the separate effects of other factors on the company's performance. This is really important
for practice as not even the top-level professional will produce good results at work
if he is not motivated. And not even well-motivated employees will give good
results if they are not rewarded.

Leadership Style

The Russian way of doing business is unique; it is a mix of chaotic order, a lack of
structured or planned decisions, and a high degree of creativity in problem-
solving. Russian society, on the other hand, is characterized by an unequal distribution in terms of employment, which forces people to move to the central regions,
where salaries are higher and working conditions are better, leading to a high level
of domestic and international mobility. In terms of cultural values, Russia can be
considered as a society in transition from collectivism to individualism, with a high
power distance in which employees have a low level of engagement in participative
activities and expect a relatively autocratic leadership. The pyramidal organizational structure is typical for Russian companies.

One of the main features of Russia is its very short management history. Until the
beginning of the 1990s, the economy was administered centrally. This was followed
by a period of transition and a series of crises. Only during the last decade has Russia started to adapt to current developments in HR practices. Consequently, Russian
managers lack practice and background but the level of expectation from them is
high. There are several important areas in which they lag far behind their foreign
colleagues and which can be summarized as lack of strategic planning, insufficient

adaptation to change, and lack of expertise in mentoring and guidance. Therefore, Russians are basically results-driven leaders.

In the GLOBE study (Chokar *et al.*, 2007), with a sample of 60 countries, Russia is below average on participative orientation, autonomy, and team orientation. Managers describe their culture as in transition to an individualistic approach. As for gender egalitarianism, there is a significant presence of women in management, which is attributable to a specific feature of the country's transition to a market economy: women were better at adapting to the changes, while men had difficulties in coping with the new ways of doing business. Today, many management positions are occupied by women. Russia is ranked very low on the humane orientation—that is, a propensity to be generous, altruistic, and fair to others. However, this aspect is becoming increasingly important for employees. Management ethics has undergone substantial change, accompanied by a reappraisal of values. Today, values such as obedience/malleability, discipline, career, centralization, and power have been replaced by values such as self-determination, collectivism, participation, orientation toward needs, personality and personality development, creativity, innovation, ability to meet halfway, and decentralization. These changes have led to profound modifications in business ethics and management theory and practice. The role of ethical norms and principles has increased notably in Russia in both business dealings and labor relations.

The survey performed in 2007 in 300 companies from different industries showed that there are three general models of relationships between managers and subordinates (Levada-center-research on conflict's influence on productivity in organization. www.fira.ru). About one-third of the companies have a paternalistic relationship with employees on different levels, which means that all of them feel part of a single community. However, about 30 percent of the companies suffer from latent conflicts, where employees are not considered partners and are not rewarded appropriately. The remaining companies operate in a situation of open conflict, where employees refuse to carry out the tasks assigned by the managers and managers complain about the difficulties in managing their employees. Interestingly, the level of trust in the managers in the companies in the last category is much higher than in the first two categories.

When discussing employees' trust in their bosses, most of our experts stated that the subject has not been studied methodically in Russia, but the usual reason for trusting someone is the existence of a long-term relationship. One expert notes that "the special trait that marks people in Russia is adherence to hierarchical relationships at the managerial level, in the business sphere, and predominantly horizontal relationships in interpersonal relationships." However, to be a real leader, the manager must be a charismatic person.

Literature Review on Trust

During the global financial crisis of 2007–2010, trust in social institutions and the government deteriorated and Russia was no exception. According to the All-Russian Public Opinion Research Center (VCIOM), trust in the President was at the lowest level for the last decade. Trust in business also fell from 45 percent to 41 percent. As regards trust in the media, Russia held third place from the bottom, with

37 percent. Non-governmental organizations are not favored by people either. However, out of the state authorities, the highest level of trust is held by the President, with 66 percent. This has a historical explanation: in Russia, people always believed in the Tsar, then in the Party and now in the President, as the power coming "from above," while the government was believed to be a destructive force.

A comparative study of public and private home-based and residential social services in Russia shows a lack of belief in social security, which people attribute to the high level of corruption and lack of legislation (Polling Research Statistics, All-Russian Public Opinion Research Center, 2007–2011). Even though they are entitled to medical insurance, education, and other social benefits, those who have the possibility prefer to use independent paying services. Furthermore, the largest companies offer a comprehensive benefits package to their employees and their families, which strengthens company–employee interdependence and acts as a guarantee for a long-term relationship. A recent study showed that trust in businesses fell 10 percent between 2009 and 2010 (Polling Research Statistics, All-Russian Public Opinion Research Center, 2007–2011). This can be explained by the fact that the crisis, which started in 2007, has still not ended and companies seeking to reduce costs are shedding excess workforce. Although Russia is third from the bottom, above France and Germany, the difference is that the trend in the latter countries is moving in the opposite direction. An interesting point is that people under 34 years old showed more trust in business and the media than older people. Moreover, people are more likely to believe the company's CEO than their managers.

According to the surveys, the nation is characterized by a lack of interpersonal trust. According to the reports published by the All-Russian Public Opinion Research Center (VCIOM) in 2006, Russians have greatest trust in the members of their family. In second place, respondents indicated their work colleagues, with a trust level of 26 percent. In spite of this, Russia is a very open-minded, communicative nation.

Unfortunately, the issue of interpersonal trust has not been studied in Russia. In 2003, the well-known Russian specialist E.S. Yahontova conducted one of the first studies on trust between managers and subordinates, focusing on companies undergoing restructuring processes. The aim of this study (Yahontova, 2003) was to identify the problems existing in this field and find solutions that could be implemented in practice. The factors that limited trust between managers and subordinates included the political system, the psychological climate, type of leadership, etc. Individual managers' willingness to trust employees was evaluated in order to determine the risk of dependence on employees, evaluating the level of trust in manager–subordinate relationships in terms of their responsibilities. The analysis of the results showed a lack of correlation between subordinates' and managers' opinions and between those of managers on different levels. This differentiation can be explained by the difference in the possibility of using interpersonal communication. Higher-level managers have more freedom to define the level of trust, while their lower-level colleagues are more dependent on rules, norms, and procedures. In general, the level of trust, based on the evaluations given by all the respondents, has been determined as average. However, managers on all levels consider their willingness to trust to be excellent, while their subordinates think otherwise. If this contradiction is not resolved, it can lead to serious problems.

Another interesting study was conducted in 2007 by Tatiana Kovaleva, who analyzed the interdependence of trust and organizational culture based on two assumptions: law and authority, and appropriate behavior. This author was one of the first to investigate the problem of trust between owners and hired top managers as a controlling factor in their relationship. She concluded that Russian companies face a huge challenge: they need to develop a practice of procedural trust to increase management performance and be able to survive in the global market. Finally, there is another famous author who has studied the problems of HRM practices in Russia and the issue of trust in particular: Igor Gurkov. In his study, performed in 2007, he points out that the corporate culture of Russian companies has evolved considerably in recent decades. The CEOs of leading companies are trying to solve an important problem—how to bring their corporate culture in line with the highest world's standards while maintaining the best practices of Russian HRM and employee trust.

Contextual Factors in Hierarchical Trusting Relationships

We now turn to the results of our research. Our Delphi experts noted that trust between managers and subordinates was not very strong in modern Russian society. Some Russian experts believe that subordinates' level of trust in their bosses depends on the sector of activity. Other experts observed that, as a general rule, people in Russia only had a limited trust in their bosses.

However, business experts think that people in Russia do tend to trust their bosses, although this depends on the situation and reciprocity. If subordinates feel that their trust does not bring them any benefits and, in fact, is used as a tool to the detriment of their interests, trust diminishes. However, the general idea held by these experts confirms the opinion expressed by our focus group participants and described above: Russians are now much less prone to trusting people than they were in the Soviet Union.

Several factors were given as a possible explanation for the different levels of trust in hierarchical relationships:

1. *Organizational culture*: As mentioned earlier, organizational culture is a relatively new concept, which is just taking starting to gain acceptance in modern Russian companies. During the Soviet era, it did not exist—and, in any case, there was no need for it. Now, foreign companies are showing that the idea of building an organizational culture (team-building, sharing common values, etc.) can be very profitable in all senses of the word. But then a conflict arises: companies must go against the Russian mentality, which is not ready for these "new" ideas. The regional factor is also very important here. Trust between managers and subordinates in the more developed regions (Moscow, Saint-Petersburg, etc.) is not as high as in more remote areas. However, most experts say that this factor (organizational culture) is gaining in importance every year in Russia and, in the near future, it will play a significant role in building trust.
2. *Sector*: In sectors where there is a high level of creativity, the underlying levels of trust were perceived to be much higher. In these sectors, trust is supported and driven mostly with the help of original approaches to work. The level of trust in culture and education is also considered to be very high. Unfortunately,

in industries that are important for the national economy, such as oil, gas, and energy, companies are characterized by an extremely low level of trust!

3. ***Origin of the company***: Russian companies (with Russian ownership) have a higher level of trust compared with international companies. Foreign companies impose their human resources management models, which are often alien to the local models. Russian companies, especially if they have their roots in the Soviet Union, provide much higher levels of trust between all hierarchical levels, as this was an innate need of all the Soviet people. International companies are considered to be a good place to work but it is very hard to stay there for long, and this causes serious mistrust at all levels of management.

4. ***Size of the company***: The company's size was considered to play a significant role in building trust between different hierarchical levels. In smaller companies, where employees know each other well, the level of trust is obviously much higher as people feel the responsibilities deriving not only from their job description but also from their personal relationships. The fact that larger companies have a more consolidated organizational culture and HR policies does not guarantee that this will inspire Russian employees to show higher levels of loyalty and trust. The simple explanation for this is that Russian people do not have this culture and are not used to it. These processes are only just starting to gain ground and cannot be described as fully accepted.

Along the *individualism–collectivism dimension*, the focus group participants and Delphi panel experts characterized Russia as a country in a transition period. This means that Russia is changing its attitude toward this dimension, moving from the very high level of collectivism which existed in the Soviet Union (probably the highest level in the world) to the extremely high level of individualism, which is becoming more commonplace in Russia, mainly influenced by foreign general and business culture. Many experts tend to think that modern Russia can already be included among the countries with a high level of individualism. However, most of our experts disagreed with this view and said that, although family ties were losing strength, with less support from the extended family, Russia was increasingly consolidating its welfare system. However, if we compare the two types of collectivism, we see that business collectivism is very low and social collectivism still exists but is tending to diminish.

Our experts' views on *power distance* were very similar and univocal. Russia is considered to be a country with an extremely high level of power distance. The high level of corruption existing in Russia, the so-called "administrative resources," is widely accepted by all Russian citizens. People do not like it but they accept it and consider this unequal distribution of power to be unavoidable. The leadership model in Russia is characterized by a preference for hierarchy, in which the people in power are not fully trusted but nevertheless obeyed. Some recent affairs, such as the "Yukos case" and others, have made people afraid to say anything against authorities and officials. Generally speaking, managers in all spheres of life tend to be distrusted, which in turn leads to excessive control and centralization in the decision-making process. Finally, the absence of powerful, effective trade unions in companies is viewed as a factor that helps employees come together, with growth of trust on a horizontal level, while reducing the level of trust in vertical employment relationships.

Personal Factors in Hierarchical Trusting Relationships

Among our participants, both managers and subordinates believed that several personal factors can influence a trusting relationship. For example, both groups agreed that some non-business relationships between colleagues can strengthen trust, as employees will have more common interests and a greater understanding of each other, which ultimately strengthens empathy and communication. Nevertheless, the most important personal factor which positively influences the level of trust between a manager and a subordinate is the duration of the relationship between them. There is a proverb in Russia that says "to eat a pound of salt together," meaning "to know somebody really well." As one manager put it: "The duration of the relationship is traditionally acknowledged as the best way of knowing whether a person is worth trusting or not. Trust can never be built in the first few days ..." Some managers emphasized that people of the same age often found it easier to find common ground. As has been said earlier, Russia is in a period of transition, which means that people born and brought up in the Soviet Union have very different values and principles from the young people born and brought up in modern Russia. This is why it is extremely difficult for the two groups not only to build trust but also just to understand each other. With respect to gender, managers considered that having a gender mix was positive, but with male prevalence. Many experts believe that Russian females are no good at managing companies (of course, with some exceptions) but make better subordinates than males. Female employees are viewed as having better professional profiles and the capacity to identify with the team more closely. Two managers from the focus group and one of the subordinates mentioned that all-female teams could never be created in Russia as the level of conflict would be too high and such teams would never work. However, both managers and subordinates agreed that true professionalism, regardless of gender, age, and other factors, was one of the main factors that helped establish trust between managers and subordinates. It was considered that skills and personal traits, such as willingness to help others, openness, transparency, good listening skills, a strong work ethic, good communication skills, and example-setting in attitudes to work, can overcome other barriers and foster trust among all employees, both vertically and horizontally.

The expert group ranked the duration of the relationship, the existence of non-business relationships, and age as the most important factors, while gender was seen as less significant. The experts were absolutely convinced that trust was impossible if people had not known each other for a minimum period of time! As one noted: "Shared values and habits can never appear between people who have not known each other for long enough. And trust can never exist without them!" It is interesting to note that the experts do not consider age, tenure in the company, or seniority to be important factors that help managers and subordinates build trust. Age sometimes helps people understand each other quicker and better but it is not a guarantee that trust will develop in the relationship. Tenure in the company is viewed more often as a negative factor for trusting relationships than as a positive factor, as people who have been working for a long time in the same company tend to become very arrogant, and this does not foster trust. Seniority usually causes dependence and very rarely trust. Summarizing all the above, we can see that the views expressed by experts and focus groups are broadly similar.

The focus group participants were asked to comment on the findings of the quantitative study on the significance of personal factors when accounting for variations in trust (see Table 8.1).

Table 8.1 Russia: significant controls (correlations)

	Time manager and subordinate worked together	Organizational tenure: subordinate	Gender: manager (1-> man, 2-> woman)	Number of employees in firm	Academic level subordinate
MTB					−0.230**
OCB			0.181*		
MTS	0.164*		0.171*		
STM		−0.174*		−0.203*	−0.235**

Notes
** Correlation significant at 0.01 level.
* Correlation significant at 0.05 level.
MTB = managerial trustworthy behavior, STM = subordinates' trust in managers, MTS = managers' trust in subordinates, OCB = organizational citizenship behavior.

Our data indicate that *organizational tenure is negatively correlated with subordinates' trust in managers*. Our participants suggested an explanation for this result. Some of them suggested that the longer a manager works at a certain company, the more uncompromising he/she becomes. Usually such managers do not allow subordinates to make mistakes, saying that they (the managers) have been working at the company for many years and the fact that they are still there shows that they do not make many mistakes. Sometimes, managers with this outlook do not notice new trends and new people and do not let young colleagues grow professionally.

We were also struck by the fact that *subordinates with a higher educational background show fewer proactive behaviors*. What is more, the correlation was quite strong. The focus group participants explained this effect by pointing out that the environment is often not merit-focused enough and the experience of seniority-based promotion may be more frustrating for those who are more highly educated. This frustration can lead more highly educated subordinates to be less engaged. But the most interesting fact is that a high level of subordinate education affects managers' trust in them. This is often found in situations where the manager is very close to his/her subordinates and is afraid of being replaced by a well-educated subordinate.

The study also showed that the *more employees there are in a company, the less subordinates trust their managers*. The explanation comes from the fact that, in large companies, the level of responsibility is lower as it is difficult to determine who is to blame if a mistake is made. And this means that subordinates do not try too hard to do anything above the minimum level of their responsibilities as they do not expect the feedback. They also think that their managers do not know them personally and that is why the level of trust is very low in this case. As has been mentioned, Russians link trust with personal relationships.

Antecedents and Outcomes of Manager–Subordinate Trust

Trust in Russia is a special aspect of people's relationships which is not considered an inevitable part of work relationships between managers and subordinates. Both managers and subordinates view trust as a very helpful but not vital part of the business process. They stated that trust was more important in everyday life than in business. Managers indicate that subordinates should be able to reach a set of established goals on time, without additional control or pressure. They also want their subordinates to be able to carry out the tasks that cannot be done by the manager or, at least, to be a reliable support for them. For all this to be possible, mutual feedback was seen as crucial, as it ensures employees' motivation, proactivity, and good communication. According to managers, a trustworthy person first of all shows loyalty toward the projects' objectives, sound ethics, and a high level of responsibility, in both private and business life. The level of communication in all spheres of people's lives—professional and personal—was seen as important for trust building. Finally, managers say that trust is generated when the subordinate is proactive and motivated, shows respect, goes beyond what is asked, and can be delegated to.

Various behaviors may help generate subordinates' trust in their managers. From the subordinate's point of view, it was considered important that the manager spend a lot of time working with the same subordinate, even if he/she makes mistakes. One manager put it this way: "If the organization has existed for all this time, it could indicate that its people trust each other." If subordinates feel that their trust does not bring them any benefits but, on the contrary, is used as a tool to the detriment of their interests, trust decreases. In addition to transparency on the part of the manager, coherent and consistent behavior and communication were viewed as essential. As one subordinate put it: "I can trust a manager who behaves absolutely transparently toward me, giving me not only work tasks but also personal contact …" However, it is still true that, in Russia, trust is more common in horizontal work relationships than in vertical relationships, since the latter were the dominant relationship in the country for many decades and people are tired of them. When the focus group members were asked to give an example of trust in their work relationships, *no one* gave an example of a manager–subordinate relationship, only horizontal relationships!

Trust is also seen to be greater in managers who welcome feedback and suggestions, communicate openly, delegate tasks, and publicly recognize the subordinate's success, but it is important to go a little bit further, such as having lunch with subordinates, spending some free time with them, skating, bowling, etc. It is also very important that the manager demand the same level of responsibility from himself/herself as he/she demands from his/her subordinates. One subordinate noted: "I would never trust a manager who leaves work two hours before me while at the same time giving me a load of tasks to do before he left."

Interestingly, in our individual interviews, we found a similar list of behaviors that may generate trust: credibility, reliability, integrity, loyalty, and reciprocity. Concepts such as constituency and commitment were not mentioned by *any* of the interviewees. For example, as one interviewee points out:

> when you expect a behavior from a manager which will not disappoint you, which will not go against your own values and moral principles, when you don't have to control this behavior because you know and are absolutely sure that this person is thinking the same way you are.

Managers and subordinates suggested that trust has various positive outcomes for the professional relationship. From the subordinates' point of view, managers' trust gives an internal calmness, confidence in success, and a responsibility, which can then be shared with other colleagues. In addition, it was seen to have a positive impact on the company as a whole, as several cases of mutual manager–subordinate trust can have a synergistic effect on the whole company. Others, seeing this effect and how it can benefit them, can start trying to implement it in their own business activities. One subordinate put it this way: "If my friend has this, I want to be in the same position."

Figure 8.1 provides a diagrammatic summary of the major antecedents and consequences of trust in the manager–subordinate relationship arising from the qualitative data generated from our focus groups and expert panels in Russia.

Our qualitative data indicate that a good professional relationship is characterized, on one hand, by a manager's existing skills and expertise in a certain range of activities, his/her ability to create an atmosphere where there is a free exchange of ideas and his/her desire for communication via mutual feedback. In addition, showing interest in the subordinate's private life and some off-work relations

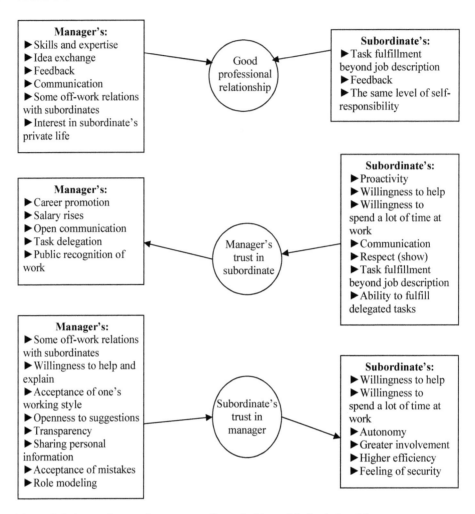

Figure 8.1 Antecedents and outcomes of trust in hierarchical relationships

with subordinates (going to the cinema, parties, etc.) will enhance the quality of professional relationships. From the subordinate's perspective, a positive professional relationship is shown by the ability to achieve the objectives that have been set within an environment of mutual feedback and a desire to work beyond the responsibilities given in the job description. An equal level of self-responsibility is also desirable. Subordinates' proactivity, a willingness to help and spend more time at work, and fulfillment of tasks generate the manager's trust, which in turn leads to more open and freer communication, higher levels of delegation, and, sometimes, promotion and/or salary rises for the subordinate. Similarly, a manager's willingness to spend spare time with a subordinate, acceptance of individual working styles, willingness to help and coach a subordinate, and ability to accept mistakes engender subordinates' trust, which results in a higher level of engagement on their part. Therefore, both managers' and subordinates' communication skills and ability to fulfill their respective job expectations support trust building and strengthening.

The Dynamics of Trust in Hierarchical Relationships

Both managers and subordinates were clear that trust evolves over time. Many Russian participants stressed that previous professional experience can never be seen as a platform for initially establishing trust with colleagues at a new workplace. It is fully acknowledged that trust is a very difficult, on-going, evolving process. They also stated that trust can never be built on the same principles and approaches if a manager (subordinate) changes job, in spite of having had very trustworthy relations at a previous job. In the course of this process, several conditions must be honored and these can contribute to trust building. Managers highlight the history and duration of the relationship, the results achieved, a willingness to help and stay longer at work, and fulfilling tasks beyond the responsibilities stated in the job description.

Trust is not only transmitted verbally but also non-verbally. As one respondent noted: "Trust is a feeling of confidence in someone else, as if you have jumped into the water from a tower being absolutely sure you won't die." Or:

> It is a feeling inside when you are not afraid of looking silly or ugly in someone's else opinion. When you are ready to share everything with a person without fearing that this person could change his/her opinion about you.

So, it is very important not to neglect the non-verbal side of trust.

Many managers who participated in the survey observed that they allowed all subordinates to give their opinion, trying to create something like a brainstorming process, and only after that took the final decision. This can only be done when there is a certain level of trust in a group. And, looked at from the other direction, this practice reinforces the existing level of trust between the participants. However, it is too early to say that such a pattern of behavior is widely spread and used in Russia. This can partly be explained by the fact that many managers still adore the power they have and do not want to share it with someone else.

While all interviewees emphasized that trust evolves over time, managers and subordinates experience this evolution differently. Managers are not willing to give a high level of freedom to subordinates right from the start. As one manager put it: "They have to deserve it!" In real life, this can take the form of a very tight initial control of all aspects of the subordinate's job; this control is gradually loosened, managers give more flexibility, and subordinates start to feel more freedom. This can only be done if trust has been established within their relationship. In this case, managers act more like coaches than mentors. The other approach, where managers totally trust their subordinates right from the beginning and then start to limit their trust in a certain subordinate until the appropriate level is found, is very rare in Russia. Trust in Russia is something that grows stronger with time—that is, as the relationship's duration increases. Managers emphasize the importance of perceiving the subordinate as a separate part of the process, not just as a task executor, who "can add something personal using his knowledge and skills." They also stress the importance of building close relationships with subordinates. This is not always easy as everybody has different personalities. As one manager said: "... depending on the subordinate, you need to find the best way to approach him/her." This becomes particularly important in the case of a subordinate who is very valuable for the company but has a very difficult personality.

From the subordinates' point of view, there are several ways of behaving toward managers with whom no deep level of trust has yet been built. Many Russian subordinates want to build close, trusting relationships with their direct managers. The first way consists of showing their loyalty by spending a lot of time at work, showing their willingness to help, even in activities that are outside their job description. And then, depending on the feedback received from the manager, they adjust their behavior. The second way of behaving is quite different from the first one. Subordinates are more guarded at the beginning, waiting for the first steps from the manager, while at the same time trying to get as many benefits for themselves as possible (time off, mobile phone, etc.). As a third way, the subordinates can first of all try to gain the attention, support, and, if they succeed, trust of their peers. After that, they start talking with their managers as if they were one of the company's most valuable resources, holding insider knowledge, which is why they deserve trust. However, most subordinates agree that trust does not appear by itself and never from the very beginning of a relationship. If a new manager joins the group, he/she can only gain the subordinates' trust if he/she respects common past actions and previously built trust. To conclude, reciprocal trust is essential in a manager–subordinate relationship. As one subordinate put it: "There is no 'one-way' trust. And my perception is that two people must work hard to be rewarded with trust. To my mind, in business it is just like in private life—no difference at all …"

Our quantitative data offer interesting insights into the dynamics of trust (see Table 8.2). Comparing Russia with the overall findings among the 18 countries, we find that the general trends are more or less the same. However, it is worth mentioning that organizational citizenship behavior leads to significantly higher managers' trust in subordinates than in the overall model. The Russian data are almost identical to the complete sample for the relationship between managers' trust in subordinates and managerial trustworthy behaviors. However, according to the same data, managerial trustworthy behaviors do not lead to the same level of subordinates' trust in managers as in the overall model. Finally, in Russia, subordinates' trust in managers has a much greater effect on their organizational citizenship behaviors than in the global sample.

The trust dynamics between managers and subordinates is not symmetrical, as subordinates' OCB seems to lead to a significantly higher level of managers' trust in subordinates than managerial trustworthy behaviors does with respect to subordinates' trust in managers. Nevertheless, in the focus groups, the importance of trustworthy behaviors by the manager was mentioned by managers and subordinates alike. The explanation given by the focus group participants for this relationship is as follows: It should be remembered that Russia is still very influenced by its Soviet past, when the whole HRM system was completely different. Now that the situation is changing, subordinates mostly want to keep their job and that is why

Table 8.2 Standardized regression weights for the trust model in Russia and the overall sample

	OCB–>MTS	MTS–>MTB	MTB–>STM	STM–>OCB
Russia only	0.91**	0.23**	0.55**	0.26
Complete model	0.68**	0.34**	0.89**	0.08*

Notes
** Regression weight significant at 0.01 level.
* Regression weight significant at 0.05 level.

they are willing to start moving closer to the manager in particular and the company in general. They are mentally prepared to be initiators of trust with their bosses. It should also be remembered that Russia has a very high power distance (from 9 to 10, according to our experts). This means that managers are viewed a priori as very important and intelligent people and subordinates are willing to obey them. It is also interesting to note that subordinates' trust in managers leads to a higher level of subordinates' OCB behaviors than in the complete sample. It is like looking at the reverse side of the same coin. Thus, Russian subordinates do not expect trust to appear at the very beginning of the relationship but are willing to be the first to initiate it. So, when trust appears, subordinates are motivated to make even more effort to show their loyalty to the company and to work in general. It has been in the nature of the Russian people for a very long time. Russians were always ready to fight "for their bosses": tsars, communist leaders, military heads, etc. As one subordinate put it: "I love my boss. He is like my second father to me."

The Delphi panel experts also provided valuable insights into the model. They agreed that the model is applicable to Russia without any limitations and is universal, but they also added that nobody has paid any serious attention to such models in Russia. Here, the informal network is very important for organizational success. And trust is one of the major components of the informal network's social capital. Even though formal regulations are very important, most managers would seek to build trust with subordinates because it is a proven method for increasing people's efficiency and loyalty, which in turn is important for the company's performance and the manager's position, respectively. Moreover, a more loyal attitude toward managers and the company makes subordinates feel safer in the workplace.

Discussion and Conclusions

The results of our study in Russia confirm some of the main findings in the existing literature. Just like in many other countries, both managers and subordinates believe that trust is essential, first to build and then to maintain a good professional relationship (García, 2004). It was also proved that the trust-building process is viewed as a dynamic process that evolves over time (Peterson & Behfar, 2003). One of the most valuable results of this study was that one person's trustworthy behaviors can lead to higher levels of trust from another person. And it was observed that the trust-building process is like a spiral, moving upwards at an ever faster rate, once initiated. For instance, according to our data, both managers and subordinates argue that trust can start and be reinforced by a subordinate's willingness to help his/her boss or other horizontal colleagues and to spend more time at work, performing beyond their job description. Such behavior leads to the appearance of trust and, if trust has already formed at a low level, to the growth of trust. The important point here is that this process is mutual. At the same time, in Russia, lack of trust in the manager does not directly affect the subordinate's behavior, particularly at the beginning of their working together. High power distances and the Soviet past create an atmosphere where subordinates can continue to work with a certain manager, even when the level of trust within their relationship is low. Attaining a high level of trust in Russia is impossible without adding some personal relationship to the work relationship. Otherwise, people will normally not open themselves to others. Once trust is established, the work–personal life boundaries can at times be voluntarily moved by the subordinate, based on the positive relationship or enhanced commitment to the task at hand. However, caution is required, as our study shows that too much trust can also have negative effects on the relationship; trust becomes difficult to control and can ultimately lead to an imbalance in the relationship, with too little work-related interaction and too much personal-related interaction, which is not good for either side.

The cultural variables discussed provide a deeper understanding of the behaviors observed and existing manager–subordinate relationships. Similar to the GLOBE findings and the results for some other countries, our study participants stress that Russia is in a period of transition, moving from an extremely collectivistic approach (as existed in the USSR) to an individualistic approach. We can say that the organizational environment is becoming increasingly individualistic every year, while, at the societal level, Russia is still rather collectivistic, even though the level of collectivism is diminishing. The word "trust" is perceived as a concept from individuals' private life rather than from business life. When talking about trust in manager–subordinate relationships, it is clear that there tends to be a high level of trust on a horizontal level in Russia and not much trust on a vertical level. It is important to understand that this takes place in a context of high power distances, which means that, in Russia, even though managers and subordinates do not have a stable level of trust between each other, they can still be effective in their work because their performance is based on other perceptions provided by subordinates. Both sides point out that trust can help reduce the risk of a decision-taking process, as employees who have established trusting relationships with their manager see this behavior as their responsibility and a sign of loyalty to the manager.

Interestingly, the results of our study showed that Russia had one of the highest correlations in the world between subordinates' OCBs and their managers' trust in them. The explanation for this is that, most of the time, it is the subordinates who take the first steps toward trustworthy-behavior building. At the same time, the subordinate's trust in the manager does not necessarily trigger a desire in the subordinate to develop OCBs. Certain objective factors, such as lack of a company vision or overview of strategic goals, may contribute to creating a situation in which trust is a matter of personal effort and nothing more.

In spite of the lack of literature on this subject in Russia, since no researchers have studied this issue, it is still possible to draw some conclusions. Current research on HR practice has shown that the HR function has evolved over recent decades in Russia, shifting from Soviet approaches to new "market-oriented" approaches. HR, as it is, is only just starting to gain ground in Russia and, in most cases, Russian HR managers do not invent anything new but simply try to implement ready-made, well-known practices in Russian reality. It is obvious that not everything will work with Russian employees, and HR managers still need time to prove the effectiveness of these practices. As regards possible ways for improving trust relationships between managers and subordinates, a number of options are open. First of all, companies must enhance trust and employees' awareness of organizational actions and strategy. Second, HR can help create a more transparent and fairer system, with the idea that, when the employees see how it works and how it can benefit them personally, they will want to contribute to the system themselves. And third, working together, providing support, discussing, explaining, and spending time doing things together can bring more trust to the relationship between managers and subordinates.

Our study also provides several practical implications. As the focus group participants highlighted, it was important for Russia to end the transition period and start building a new HRM system that takes into account the Russian people's past and mentality. For those wanting to build trustworthy behaviors that will contribute significantly to the company's success, it should be remembered that Russian people always demand something more than just a work relationship in order to establish a certain (even low) level of trust. The training programs provided by the organization must be closely aligned with the organizational culture and existing employee participation practices. Thus, existing training schemes must be adjusted to include specific ideas which will help Russian people become involved in the trust-building process. The creation of an empowering culture, based on open communication and fairness, might, in itself, contribute to establishing trusting relationships between managers and subordinates.

To conclude, we have attempted to provide a representative picture of manager–subordinate relationships in Russia. However, the study sample was not totally representative because Russia is a huge country and it is impossible to assure full coverage. However, our sample did try to take into consideration all regions, from Kaliningrad to Vladivostok. Potential future research could explore differences in *all* Russian regions in more detail. It is plausible that manager–subordinate relationships might be different among different occupational groups and further insights into trust building could be provided by including a more diverse occupational spread in the sample. Beyond occupational group, the issue of gender clearly deserves further study. The higher participation of women in management could shed new light on our knowledge of appropriate management styles and effective workplace relationship building between managers and subordinates. Consequently, we would encourage future research on the role of gender and age in trust building. In the specific case of Russia, it is necessary to follow closely the changes in the dynamics as the transition period is drawing to a close and forthcoming membership of the WTO will accelerate the process toward the next, as yet unpredictable, level.

References

All-Russian Public Opinion Research Center (2009). *Annual Report*. Available http://wciom. ru/ratings-state-institutions.

Bondarenko N. (2010). Particularities of Russian HR policies in crisis of 2008-2010, *Public Opinion Reporter* 4(106), October-December.

Chhokar, J.S., Brodbeck, F.C.& House, R.J. (2007). *Culture and Leadership Across the World: The GLOBE book of In-Depth Studies of 25 Societies*. Manhaw: Lawrence Erlbaum Associates, Publishers.

Chichkanov A.V. (2005). *Social relations in the contemporizing society (Social analysis)*, Moscow: Russian Academy of State Service.

CIA (2010). The World Factbook: Russia. Retrieved on 9.7.12 from www.cia. gov/library/ publications/the-world-factbook/geos/rs.html.

Clifford, C. (1971). Cooperation, trust, and perceived intentions in a 2 person game. *Dissertation Abstracts International*, 32(5-a): 2797–2798.

Domsch, M.& Lidokhover, T. (2007). *Human Resource Management in Russia*. Farnham: Ashgate Publishing Limited.

Edelman Trust Barometer, (2009). Retrieved on 7.12.10 from www.edelman.com/trust/2009/.

Eldgie R. (2007) Semi-Presidentialism Outside Europe, London: Routledge.

Emelianov, E.N.& Povarnitsina, S.N. Psychology of business.www.hrm.ru.

Filonovich, S.P. (2000). *Leadership and Practical Skills of Good Manager: 17–module Program for Managers*, Module 9. Moscow: INFRA-M.

Gurkov, I. (2007). Mapping HRM in Russia: The results of repeated surveys of CEOs. Paper for V Chemnitz East Forum on HRM Management.

Hiel, L. & Zigler, D. (2007). *The Theory of Personality*. Saint-Petersburg: Piter.

Immelman, P. (2005). *Boss: Incomparable or Useless*. Moscow: Institute of Aggregated Strategic Research.

Kalabin, A. *The Archetypes in Communication. Techniques of Positioning*. www.stratateg.ru.

Kovaleva T.V. (2007). Economic Relations in the system of propriety relations, Conference on Innovational Development of Russia, Moscow, HSE.

Kozlov, V.V. (2009). *Corporate Culture*. Moscow: Alfa-press.

Lialina, A.M. & Rumiantseva, M. (eds) (2009). *The Theory and Art of Management*. Moscow: State University of Management.

Majaret, J. (1982). *L'Etat de l'Empire de Russie et de grand principauté de Russie, Moscou*, Moscow: Russian Academy of Science.

Malik, F. (2008). *Manage. Work. Live.* Moscow: Dobraya kniga.

Morgulis-Yakushev, S.V. (2004). Six efficient methods of human resources management in Russia. *Human Resource Management Guide*, No. 4.

Prigogin, A.I. (2007). *Disorganization: Reasons, Types, Overcoming*. Moscow: Alpina Business Book.

Rosstat (2011) *Annual Review*. Russian Federal State Statistics Service. Available http://www.gks.ru/wps/wcm/connect/rosstat/rosstatsite/main/ and http://www.gks.ru/free_doc/new_site/population/urov/kn-ujn/tabl2.html.

Shadrina, O. (2008). Suvorov's trajectory through the office. Expert Sibir, No. 29.

Shein, E. (2008). *The Corporate Culture and Leadership*. Saint-Petersburg: Piter.

Sho, R.B. (2000). *Key to Confidence in Organization. Effectiveness. Ethics. Attentiveness.* Moscow: Delo.

Shugart M. (2005). Semi-presidential systems: dual executive and mixed authority patterns, *French Politics* 3(3): 323–351.

Skott, K. (1998). *The Psychology of the Estimation and Decision–making*. Moscow: Filin.

Soloviev A. V. (1957). The Byzantine name of Russia /The Byzantine chronicles no. 12. Available http://www.hist.msu.ru/Byzantine/BB%2012%20(1957)/BB%2012%20(1957)%20136.pdf (in ancient Russian).

Tolkatchev, E.V. (2007). Ethology as a support to organizational behavior. *Management in Russia and Abroad*, No. 6.

World Values Surveys (n.d.). Data analyses. www.worldvaluessurvey.org/index_html.

Yahontova, E.S. (2002). *The Effectiveness of the Managerial Leadership*. Moscow: TEIS.

Yahontova, E.S. (2003). *Efficient Technologies of Human Resources Management*. Saint-Petersburg: Piter.

Yahontova E.S. (2004). *Social Technologies of Personnel Leadership Potential Optimization*. Moscow: State University of Management.

Zorkin V.D. (2003). The Constitutional court chairman report at the anniversary conference in Russian Academy of Science "Constitution of Russian Federation", http://www.ksrf.ru/ru/News/Speech/Pages/ViewItem.aspx?ParamId=8 (in Russian).

9   Manager–Subordinate Trust Relationships in Brazil

DIOGO ZANATA AND CESAR FURTADO C. BULLARA

Introduction

Brazil, officially the Federative Republic of Brazil, is the largest country in South America and the world's fifth largest country, both by geographical area (with more than 8.5 million square kilometers) and by population (with more than 195 million people in 2011). It borders all other South American countries except Ecuador and Chile. Geographically, Brazil is mostly located between the two tropics, which gives a very stable climate throughout the year with a predominance of high temperatures. Brazil was a Portuguese colony from 1500 until 1815. It declared independence in 1822 and, in 1889, became a presidential republic, with the current Constitution dating back to 1988. It is also the only Portuguese-speaking country in the Americas and the largest Portuguese-speaking country in the world. The Brazilian economy is the sixth largest in the world by nominal GDP and one of the world's fastest growing major economies. Economic reforms, mainly after 1994, have given the country more stability, inflation control, and international recognition. Brazil is a founding member of the United Nations, G20, Mercosul, and one of the most influential countries in South America.

Brazilian business culture is similar to many other Latin American countries when analyzed by Hofstede's dimensions (Hofstede, 1991), although there are some particularities and trends that may distinguish Brazil from these other countries. In a study performed in 2004, O'Keefe and O'Keefe (2004) found that there are indicators to support a high power distance score for Brazilian culture. Hess and DaMatta (1995) classified Brazil as an "intermediate society" whose members were often in a middle position between collectivistic and individualistic influences (Sledge *et al.*, 2008). Although leadership is still viewed as a transactional relationship, today many organizations, especially multinational companies, are challenging this concept, promoting long-term results, relationship-oriented behaviors, trust, and commitment. The development of trust between manager and subordinate is viewed as a long-term relationship that evolves over time and is strongly influenced by leader–member experience and personal values.

In this chapter, we will provide a short overview of historical developments in Brazil and describe the current institutional environment (including the educational, legal, and social systems), followed by an overview of the economic and social context. The following section summarizes human resource management practices and leadership styles in the organizational context. Trust is then introduced with a literature review of multiple aspects of trust relationships in the workplace and our empirical results are presented. The remainder of the chapter presents a discussion of the results and highlights potential implications for management and leadership practice. Finally, the chapter ends with potential areas for future research.

Highlights of Manager–Subordinate Trust in Brazil

- Participants agree that there is a general disposition in Brazil to trust each other, even when there is little mutual knowledge and previous experience.
- All the managers, subordinates, and experts who participated in our study associated the development of trust with the evaluation of perceived personal values and time working together, with cooperation and collaboration in joint activities.
- Experts believe that, because of the acceptance of high power differences in Brazil, managers tend to exert greater control over employees' work, enjoy more benefits from their seniority, and undermine proactivity and meritocratic behavior.
- Our qualitative study reported that trust is associated with similar outcomes for managers and subordinates, in the form of open communication and job commitment, although the perceived antecedents of trust differ between them. On one hand, from the managers' viewpoint, trust development is associated with performance, efficiency, and subordinate proactivity. On the other hand, for subordinates, trust development is more sensitive to the perceived values of managers, such as respect, integrity, and transparency.
- Among the personal factors that influence trust building in Brazil, our quantitative study pointed to the importance of the manager's age, the time that manager and subordinate have worked together, and the subordinate's gender and organizational tenure as the main variables that affect trust development.
- Finally, our participants also noted that high levels of trust take time to develop and untrustworthy behavior can both destroy trust and make it much harder to be rebuild once undermined.

Historical Perspective

Archeological remains found in many places around Brazil show evidence that the area has been inhabited for at least 8000 years by indigenous people. When the country was discovered by the Europeans, these original inhabitants were called erroneously "Indians." Since these nomadic tribes never developed written records or monumental architecture, very little is known about the history of Brazil before 1500. When the Portuguese arrived, there was an initial period of miscegenation with the original populations, although diseases spread quickly along the indigenous trade routes and whole tribes were probably annihilated. Today, the number of natives is very small and reduced to the north part of the country, especially the Amazon forest; furthermore, native descendants constitute a small percentage of the population.

From 1500 until 1815, Brazil was a Portuguese colony and then a Portuguese kingdom. More specifically, in 1808, after the invasion of Portugal by Napoleon Bonaparte, the city of Rio de Janeiro became the capital of the entire Portuguese Empire and seat of the Royal Family and most of the Portuguese nobility. In 1822, after a failed attempt to return Brazil to being a colony, the Brazilians refused to yield and Prince Pedro stood by them, declaring the country's independence from Portugal. He was subsequently declared the first Emperor of Brazil, which was governed by a constitutional monarchy and parliamentary system that lasted until 1889, when Brazil became a republic. The country then entered a prolonged cycle of financial, social, and political instability that would continue until the 1920s. In 1930, the defeated presidential candidate Getúlio Vargas, supported by the majority of the military, led a coup d'état to impose a dictatorship. After the Allied victory in 1945 and the end of the Nazi-Fascist regimes in Europe, Vargas' position became untenable and, in 1954, he committed suicide. There followed a succession of short-lived interim governments, some of which, such as that of Juscelino Kubitscheck, adopted conciliatory postures. This was a period of remarkable economic and industrial growth, culminating in the construction of the country's new capital, Brasilia, in 1960. The military regime became increasingly closed in on itself and a full dictatorship was re-imposed. The extraordinary economic growth during this period is known as the "economic miracle," and the regime enjoyed a high level of popularity, in spite of the political repression.

In 1985, after a long transitional period to full democracy, civilians returned to power with José Sarney as the first President. However, reeling under a severe recession and spiraling inflation, the new government became extremely unpopular. In 1992, the Minister of Finance, Fernando Henrique Cardoso, implemented a highly successful plan that gave stability to the Brazilian economy and he subsequently became President in 1994. With the peaceful transition of power to Luís Inácio Lula da Silva, who was elected in 2002 and re-elected in 2006, Brazil had finally succeeded in achieving its long-sought political stability. Lula was succeeded in 2011 by the current President, Dilma Rousseff.

Institutional Context

Economic Context

Currently, Brazil's economy is the seventh largest in the world (by GDP), presently standing at $2.172 trillion (in 2010), and the largest of the Latin American countries. Brazil is one of the fastest-growing major economies in the world, with an average annual GDP growth rate of over 5 percent. Since 2003, Brazil has steadily improved its macroeconomic stability, building up foreign reserves and reducing its debt profile. In September 2008, the global financial crisis hit Brazil and it entered into recession for two quarters. However, Brazil was also one of the first emerging markets to come out of the recession. GDP growth became positive again in 2010, boosted by the recovery in exports. As a consequence of the large capital inflows, its currency rapidly appreciated, which led the government to raise taxes on some foreign investments. The unemployment rate stood at about 6 percent in 2010 (one of the lowest in the country's history) and forecast inflation is about 7 percent, controlled by fiscal policies implemented by the Central Bank. Its fiscal deficit has increased in recent years to 59 percent of the GDP (2010). According to analysts, these recent events signal a deceleration of the country's growth.

Social Context

Brazil's population is expected to top 200 million in 2012, increasing at an annual rate of 1.1 percent. The population is heavily concentrated in the east along the coast. Life expectancy at birth stands at 73 years. The total fertility rate is 2.18 children per woman (2010) and has been decreasing in recent years, which puts Brazil below the international average of 2.7. After the end of the military regime in the country, the pro-democracy mobilization led to the creation of a social security system regarded as a social right, along with education, health, work, leisure, safety, and maternity and childhood welfare. However, even today, corruption and privileges restrict access to the state bureaucracy, which is governed by patron–client relations mediated through politicians, middlemen, or members of the local elite.

Political and Legal Systems

Brazil is a democratic republic with a presidential system. The President is both Head of State and Head of Government of the Union and is elected for a four-year term, with the possibility of re-election for a second successive term. The President appoints the Ministers of State, who assist in government. Legislative houses in each political entity are the main sources of law in Brazil. The National Congress is the Federation's bicameral legislature, consisting of the Chamber of Deputies and the Federal Senate. Judiciary authorities exercise jurisdictional duties almost exclusively. The voting age is 18. Brazil's legal structure is based on a civil law system with comprehensive legal codes and laws, a judiciary organization that combines courts and tribunals, and a legal body composed of judges and magistrates.

Educational System

The Brazilian education system still presents a number of deficiencies and social and regional disparities, like other large middle-income countries. In 2006, 4.3 percent of the GDP was allocated to education and the federal government aims to gradually increase this amount. About 90 percent of people aged 15 or older are considered able to read and write their own names, but the literacy rate increases to 97.5 percent for people aged 6 to 14. The level of education in Brazil is considered low compared with developed countries, especially in public education. Formal education averages 7.2 years (8.4 years for white people, 6.1 years for black people) and 5.1 years in the northeast versus 7.2 years in the southeast. Access to higher education is growing fast, with an increasing offering from the private and public sectors. Today, Brazil struggles to improve the level of public primary education and maintain the high standards offered by the public universities.

HR Practices

The Brazilian labor market is currently undergoing a maturing process that has a substantial impact on how human resource policies and practices are implemented in the organizational environment. In addition to an aging population, the last two decades have been shaped by significant socio-economic transitions, driven by major macroeconomic reforms, a number of economic and financial crises (regional and global), deeper integration with the world economy, with increased trade and investment, and the spread of new technologies (Neri, 2010). After the 2008 global crisis, Brazil implemented a number of macroeconomic reforms and policies that restored growth rates and considerably reduced unemployment rates.

Because of the size of its population and its economic maturity, the Brazilian labor market has certain features that set it apart from other Latin American countries. From 1999 to 2009, women's participation in the labor force increased significantly in all age groups, reflecting increased economic opportunities, lifestyle changes, and the lowering of social barriers. However, the increase in the female labor force has not been accompanied by a redefinition of gender roles in terms of domestic responsibilities; as a result, women in general work "double shifts."

At 70.7 percent in 2009, Brazil's labor force participation rate exceeded both the world average (64.7 percent) and the regional average (65.4 percent in Latin America). This higher participation holds both for the total labor force and for each of the two sexes. The 2008 economic crisis had a very short-lasting impact on the employment rates in Brazil and, unlike many other countries, its labor market recovered quickly, with unemployment rates returning to pre-crisis levels by the last quarter of 2009, and falling below the pre-crisis levels in 2010. Today, some sectors and industries suffer from a scarcity of employees, especially for the more highly skilled jobs. This in turn is driving up salaries and also triggering changes in recruitment and training practices and talent retention policies.

There are other factors that have affected the Brazilian labor force. First, the absolute working population has increased, leading to an increase in the labor force. During the last decade, Brazil's labor force has increased by nearly 20 million people due to immigration and population aging. Despite this increase, net employment creation in Brazil over the last decade has risen faster than the increase in the working population. Second, structural demographic changes, such as an aging working population, extension of the retirement age (due to social security reforms), and an increase in the proportion of blacks, women, and immigrants in the working population, create challenges for current HR practices. Third, the level of education has increased in the last decade, associated with a higher demand for more highly skilled employees, which has also impacted on training and development practices. Finally, the level of economic development (per capita income) creates pressure to raise salaries and benefits, driving changes in promotion polices in the organizational environment.

The HR policies implemented in Brazil tend to be fairly simple and reasonably beneficial for the employee. This being so, they are expected to adhere to them and only in a few specific sectors do labor unions have enough power to seek benefits for their members. Regarding recruitment policies, organizations are implementing a more specialized process for candidate selection, employee retention, training, and skill development. Companies are more worried about employees' commitment and performance, due to the high turnover rates and competitive pressure from international markets. Apart from seniority, all employees with the same job profile are treated equally and paid a similar compensation. In addition, the pay scale is generally assessed on the basis of an employee's job profile, experience, and qualifications. Finally, termination policies are quite formalized and the companies must carry out a specific procedure for it to become official. The employment agreement can be terminated either by the employee or by the employer. However, the employee must give 30 days' notice to the organization in order to obtain entitlement to all the official benefits.

Leadership Style

According to Hofstede (1991), manager–subordinate relationships in Brazil are similar to those found in many Latin American countries and, in terms of cultural values, Brazil can be characterized as a collectivistic society with high power distance and uncertainty avoidance, a medium score for masculinity, and long-termorientation. This gives a good overview of the underlying drivers of Brazilian culture, organizational policies, and leadership styles. First, as a collectivistic society, people are integrated in strong, cohesive groups (including the extended family) that shape their decision processes. In the work environment, leaders seek to build trustworthy, long-lasting relationships, and prefer a communication style that is context-rich, with a prevalence of harmony, over discordance and confrontation. Leaders usually adopt a paternalistic behavior toward their subordinates, expecting loyalty from them in return.

With the high power distance, hierarchies are respected and inequalities between people are readily accepted, generally resulting in the creation of pyramidal organizational structures. Power differences are used to justify the fact that some people (power holders) enjoy more benefits than the less powerful in society. In the business environment, leaders expect respect from their subordinates and there is usually only one boss who takes on full responsibility. The symbols of power play a very important role in indicating social position and "communicating" the respect that should be shown. Reflecting the high uncertainty avoidance, people have a strong need for rules, even though individuals' need to obey these laws may be weak. Consequently, bureaucracy, rules, and regulations are common in organizational environments. Leaders usually prefer to follow a transactional pattern with clear expected behaviors and rewards, combined with a broad acceptance of the need to change schedules and redesign tasks.

Brazilian culture also has a long-term orientation (as the only non-Asian society) and the famous Brazilian way ("jeitinho brasileiro") of doing things shows how people look for alternatives to doing things considered impossible. Like Asians, Brazilians accept more than one truth and easily accept change as part of life. Finally, Brazil is low (neutral) in the masculinity dimension, which gives greater emphasis to softer aspects, such as seeking common ground with others and consensus, instead of competition and achievement-oriented behavior. However, since it is also low in femininity, there is not a clear dominance of quality of life or not standing out from the crowd, as would be expected in societies with a high femininity score. In the business environment, cooperation and competition alternate, leading to alternating approaches to worker motivation, sometimes emphasizing masculinity aspects, such as a drive to excel over others, and sometimes emphasizing femininity aspects, such as improving work relations and people's tasks.

Interviews with managers, subordinates, and experts invited to participate in this study offered additional insights into leadership styles in Brazil. Participants highlighted that organizational leaders generally do not have the necessary preparation to follow the behavior expected from a leader in Brazilian culture. According to our respondents, there is a prevalence of individual values and personality traits that shape management styles. For example, leaders are expected to be more transactional in industry, which is more results-driven, and more transformational in sectors which are more client-oriented (such as services). Furthermore, managers describe a leader as someone who tends to be hierarchical, with a short-term outlook and who is task-oriented. This in turn leads to a more demanding and assertive behavior which can be identified with Hofstede's dimensions of individuality and masculinity.

Literature Review on Trust

According to the World Values Survey (1995–2008), Brazil ranks in the bottom 10 percent of countries on the interpersonal trust scale, among countries such as Kenya, Ghana, Malaysia, and Indonesia. It also has one of the lowest scores among Latin American countries, which in general show a low level of interpersonal trust. This shows a general tendency among the population to think that one can never be too careful when dealing with others.

Data from the Latinobarómetro (2010) give more information about the general level of trust in Brazil. The interpersonal trust indicator used by the World Values Survey (WVS) was designed by Ronald Inglehart and was proved to be strongly correlated with a country's level of development. The paradox of Latin America is that some countries reconcile growth and a low level of interpersonal trust, contradicting Inglehart's assumption (Latinobarómetro, 2010). One possible explanation is that, being collectivistic societies, these countries usually have a trust network that includes the family and close group members, but not institutions or people from other groups. In other words, trust exists but among people who are known. Contrasting with the low level of interpersonal trust, Brazil has a high level of trust in institutions compared with other Latin American countries, especially the government, the Congress of Deputies, the judicial power, the army, and political parties. This data can be explained by the fact that Brazil has a more mature democracy, with a strong middle class and strong economic growth in recent years. However, corruption and recent political scandals explain why Brazilians place more trust in the army and the police than in political parties and government institutions.

Finally, according to the Edelman Trust Barometer (2011), Brazil has the highest level of trust in business institutions, with 19 points more than 2010 and surpassing other countries such as China and India. Although Brazil also shows a high level of trust in government, media, and NGOs, they are still less trusted than business institutions. Within the business category, industry and services are considered more trustworthy than companies operating in the financial sector (such as insurance and banks), probably as a consequence of the recent financial crisis.

Another important distinction found in the literature concerns attitudinal and behavioral trust. Attitudinal measures of trust, such as the WVS/GSS scale, have been shown to be correlated with important country-level variables reflecting economic and institutional development (Knack & Kiefer, 1997). Also, attitudinal measures of trust do not significantly explain trusting behavior, but do explain trustworthy behavior, since individuals who affirm to be more trusting are actually less inclined to act opportunistically (Lazzarini *et al.*, 2004). Based on this, one might be tempted to conclude that Brazilians are less trustworthy instead of less trusting. One possible explanation is that the WVS scale may be capturing the effectiveness of legal enforcement across countries, and respondents may simply be expressing their perception of the country's institutional environment, leading to more or less cooperation. In fact, the inefficiency of the Brazilian law system is well documented. Another possible explanation for the low level of trust exhibited by Brazil is that respondents may be influenced by stereotypes of the Brazilian culture. Thus, when answering whether they trust "people in general," Brazilians may provide a biased assessment based on popular types such as the "malandro": a person who is supposed to achieve social status solely by acting in his or her self-interest (DaMatta, 1991). Thus, our results presented in the following sections explain differences on trust measures and analyses based on attitudinal and behavioral measures of trust.

Contextual Factors in Hierarchical Trusting Relationships

This section gives the results of our empirical research in Brazil, consisting of focus groups with managers and employees and a Delphi panel with invited experts. The Brazilian focus group participants believed that one of the most important factors in generating trust is experience and previous mutual knowledge between manager and subordinate. Participants commented that in Brazil, on one hand, there is usually an initial tendency to trust people (even without previous knowledge) and, on the other hand, a distrusting behavior regarding formal rules and institutions, which are usually viewed as impersonal and unknown. This concurs with the general perception that people are trustworthy, even after only a short period of interaction, since they are not hidden behind an institutional mask. The participants explained that, historically, in Brazil, the informal contract (based on a mutual verbal agreement between two parties) predominated over the formal written contract. In this sense, it is usual to find that people are more committed to an informal agreement made face-to-face than to a formal signed contract with an institutional representative. There is also a popular expression that reflects the idea of a person who accepts a contract that he is not committed to (because it is done on behalf of a third party). Therefore, managers are usually likely to develop trusting behavior with their partners and workers if they can interact with them personally (in a face-to-face relationship).

The experts on the Delphi panel also agree that experience and mutual knowledge are essential for developing trust among people. However, they drew attention to the role played by personal values (such as honesty, sincerity, and friendship) in the initial tendency to trust a person at the beginning of a new interaction, when there is no previous experience between partners. When analyzing the focus group's comments about the Brazilian disposition to trust other people and not institutions, they also mentioned the concept of "face" from sociological studies. According to them, Brazilians (and Latin Americans) can sometimes be labeled as prone to taking advantage of others. However, this does not happen when there is mutual knowledge. In actual fact, people try to behave honorably to not betray the trust initially placed in them, especially if the other person is in a powerful position (such as manager or boss). In Brazil, people care about their self-image, delineated in terms of approved social attributes, and generating a bad social appraisal will destroy their self-image (face). Sometimes, from an external observer's viewpoint, this pattern of action can lead to passivity and obedience, lack of innovation, and divergence of opinions within teams.

In hierarchical relationships, there are various factors that can possibly account for different levels of trust. Among them, our participants considered the most important to be company size, sector and capital origin. *Company size* appears to be one of the more important factors that affects trust behavior. According to the participants, the small number of people in teams and the more horizontal organizational structure in SMEs benefit trust among workers and enable a deeply personal contact among employees to develop. Another important factor is the *sector* in which the company does business; industry usually tends to have lower levels of trust and in the services sector (such as banking and consultancy), firms tend to show higher levels of trust. Finally, *capital origin* is also a relevant factor since multinationals are perceived to be more formal organizations with formal polices, and consolidated teams tend to be more trustworthy. Companies with national capital, especially among large firms, where the proportion of public companies is higher, the level of trust decreases, and control and authority-based leadership styles are more usual.

Participants were also asked to evaluate Brazil's standing in terms of cultural dimensions of trust such as individualism–collectivism and power distance. Along the *individualism–collectivism dimension*, Brazil is usually characterized as a collectivistic society. The participants highlighted changes in recent decades with the emergence of individualistic trends, probably influenced by Anglo-Saxon culture. This classification can be attributed to strong family ties and to the support provided by the extended family to its members. Nowadays, the decreasing size of families and the growing urban social life (open social networks) result in fewer connections within the family and extended relationships and a lower dependence on a specific group. There is still a high level of loyalty and long-term commitment to the group, which sometimes overrides other social rules. Participants mentioned some of the effects of this dimension as important for understanding their influence on how Brazilians perceive problems, generate strategies and solutions, and choose what to implement. It also influences how people negotiate deals that benefit and are accepted by their primary group (distinction among people who are group members and those who are not) and the primacy of cooperation over competition when group members are involved.

Along the *power distance* dimension, experts and managers show more concern about the problems for leadership and trust relationships. Brazil is broadly considered to have a high power distance culture in which a greater amount of inequality is accepted, especially when compared to the United States. Business people in Brazil expect and accept the fact that there are organizational hierarchies and superiors may have more benefits (inequalities) as a result. According to the participants, seniority is viewed as a superiority trait and even talented people show passivity and lack of initiative until they have acquired tenure. Managers mentioned that, particularly in organizations that do not reward by meritocracy, there is a feeling of

unfairness about recognition and this leads to non-proactivity and political maneu-
vering instead of results-oriented action. Acceptance of this power distance usually
leads to lack of trust, with an increased need for control and monitoring, frequent
problems for employee autonomy, and a strong defense of personal territory to the
detriment of collaboration.

Personal Factors in Hierarchical Trusting Relationships

Our quantitative study shows evidence that several personal factors are relevant for
building trust in Brazil. According to this study, the manager's age, the time that
manager and subordinate have been working together, the subordinate's gender, and
organizational tenure have a significant impact on at least two of the four stages of
the trust cycle. The participants in our study were asked to analyze and comment on
the following relationships shown in Table 9.1.

The *manager's age* appeared as a significant variable affecting positively both the
level of manager–subordinate trust and the subordinate's OCB. According to our
participants, the older the manager is, the more likely he is to trust his subordinates.
First, more experienced managers are able to create a less competitive and more
cooperative work climate, where trust comes as a natural consequence. Second,
these managers are usually looking for a replacement for their own function or after
retiring, which fosters assessments of subordinates' value and trust. Finally, older
managers are also more familiar with the idea that trust relationships start when one
of the parties takes a risk and becomes vulnerable to the other, and they decide to
take the initiative.

Correspondingly, as managers age, their appreciation for OCB increases and they
cease to be purely results-oriented. This appreciation also encourages subordinates
to show OCB, since it is now acknowledged and evaluated by their managers. In
addition, our study also analyzed other related factors, such as the subordinate's
age and the age difference between manager and subordinate, but the results
were not significant, which gives added validity to the reasons highlighted by our
participants.

Table 9.1 Brazil: significant controls (correlations)

	Age: manager	Time manager and subordinate have worked together	Gender: subordinate (1–> man, 2–> woman)	Organizational tenure: subordinate
MTB				0.184*
OCB	0.201*	0.175*	−0.177*	0.217*
MTS	0.244**	0.278**	−0.185*	0.209*
STM		0.220*		

Notes
** Correlation significant at 0.01 level.
* Correlation significant at 0.05 level.
MTB = managerial trustworthy behavior, STM = subordinates' trust in managers, MTS = managers' trust in
subordinates, OCB = organizational citizenship behavior.

The participants also commented that the *subordinate's gender* also affects manager's trust behavior and OCB. Our participants were surprised that this variable had a significant effect on trust, and they view it as a leftover from a predominantly masculine environment. As these variables have the lowest values in Table 9.1, it would appear that male subordinates are more likely to receive trust from their managers. The reasons for this are that male employees are subjectively perceived as more committed to their job (which promotes a higher level of trust from their immediate superiors) and male employees are more proactive within organizations and take more risks, which can explain the higher OCB. In the words of one participant, "this behavior should be expected to change, since the proportion of women in high positions will grow over the next few decades." In spite of the general surprise expressed by the participants regarding the significance of this personal factor, we could find similar results in many other countries in our global study, from very different regions and cultural areas.

The study also shows that the *time spent working together* has a great impact on the trust level both for managers and for subordinates and also on the subordinates' OCB. Participants agree that this is probably one of the most significant variables affecting trust, since it is a dynamic relationship that changes with time and grows (or decreases) as the experience between partners is positively (or negatively) reinforced. Spending time working together allows partners to know each other and predict future behavior under different circumstances. Longer relationships reduce risk and uncertainty in the relationship, since it provides a better basis for judging trustworthiness. Likewise, longer relationships also promote more involvement of the subordinate with their colleagues and managers, which is expected to increase OCB.

Finally, the *subordinates' organizational tenure* positively affects managers' trust, subordinates' OCB, and managerial trustworthy behavior. According to the participants, longer employment affects three key aspects of the relationship. First, it shows loyalty from both sides (employee and organization), which is considered to be a very important value since it reduces uncertainty. Second, tenure usually leads to increased knowledge and experience about organizational practices and policies. And finally, tenure is strongly associated with networking, which increases a person's involvement with the organization as a whole. These three reasons support managers' behavior, fostering trust in their subordinates and a broader use of managerial behaviors. Also, from the subordinate's point of view, a greater involvement in the organization due to personal networking and greater organizational knowledge promotes OCB.

In summary, all four personal factors analyzed (manager's age, subordinate's gender and tenure, and time working together) are expected to have a positive effect on subordinates' OCB and managers' trust in subordinates (MTS), since these two variables are strongly correlated. Participants affirmed that subordinates' OCB is also a manifestation of the subordinates' values and beliefs and this fosters managers' trust, since it is a source of information for a new relationship. From the subordinate's viewpoint, a longer time spent working together increases mutual knowledge, which in turn fosters subordinates' trust in managers (STM). Finally, a subordinate's tenure increases managerial trustworthy behavior (MTB), seen as a behavioral response from managers in response to the subordinate's experience and knowledge both about his job and about the organization.

Antecedents and Outcomes of Manager–Subordinate Trust

According to our study and the data obtained from interviews with managers, subordinates, and experts, trust is considered to be both an essential condition for developing a good professional relationship between managers and subordinates and also a natural consequence of a good relationship.

As requirements for creating and maintaining a good professional relationship, subordinates commented that it is important that managers maintain open communication and information exchange, delegate and give responsibility, are fair when giving feedback and rewards, and also respect how subordinates go about their work. On the other hand, managers commented that subordinates should show efficiency and responsibility in the tasks delegated and also job-related skills in order to be trustworthy and competent. In the words of one manager, "Delegating is not as easy as we think. Subordinates must show professionalism and proactivity to convince us to give them more responsibility in a project."

Similarly, when analyzing behaviors that generate subordinates' trust in their managers, subordinates mentioned that it helps them to feel support and protection from their managers in their work environment (influence, conditions, and approval). Personal values play a very important role in building this kind of trust and subordinates commented that, when they see integrity, consistency, and transparency from their managers, they are naturally prone to trust them. Also, the manager's performance and mentoring were highlighted by subordinates as important for this relationship. As one subordinate said, "It's common to see our colleagues talking about and analyzing our manager's behavior, even about actions unrelated to our job. What they do has a strong influence on our motivation to commit ourselves to a task."

From the manager's point of view, they are more likely to trust their subordinates when they see positive job-related attitudes, such as competence, motivation, and proactivity. As one manager said, "When I trust someone and give him more responsibility in a project, I need to know that I'll not be let down and that he has the minimum abilities required to do this task." However, also according to the managers, this is not enough and subordinates must show certain aptitudes that promote trustworthy behavior, such as cooperation and open communication, which complement the first set of minimum requirements.

When asked about the positive outcomes of trust for their professional relationship, managers commented that a good relationship can be identified as a mutual understanding between manager and subordinate, which manifests as open communication and feedback. Additional outcomes are increased delegation from the manager's side and commitment to goals from the subordinate's side, and finally a motivation to work together and share successes and failures. One manager said, "When there is trust between us, it's easy to see, we talk often and communicate even without words, just a glance is enough. I can see whether she needs more support and help or whether everything is OK!"

Subordinates made very similar comments about the positive outcomes of a trusting relationship, which make us think that, while they may have different preferences for starting and developing trust, the outcomes are similar for both and the most important outcomes are shared by both. Subordinates commented that a good relationship increases their commitment to their job and to the organization, the efficiency in obtaining results, and the motivation to work together and overcome problems.

In summary, our qualitative data indicate that a good professional relationship is characterized, on one hand, by a manager's ability to show values that attract and engage the subordinate's goodwill and give them a perception of being supported and fairly valued, and, on the other hand, subordinates must show certain aptitudes to be considered trustworthy, such as competence, commitment, efficiency, and proactivity. When asked about the negative aspects that destroy or discourage trust, both said that a bad experience either suffered personally or witnessed as a third party will lead them to avoid exposure to vulnerability.

Figure 9.1 provides a diagrammatic summary of the major antecedents and consequences of trust in the manager–subordinate relationship, as evidenced by the qualitative data obtained from the focus group and expert panel in Brazil.

The Dynamics of Trust in Hierarchical Relationships

From our study and also from the literature review, it is clear that trust is a dynamic variable that evolves over time. Thus, trust is an on-going, evolving process that

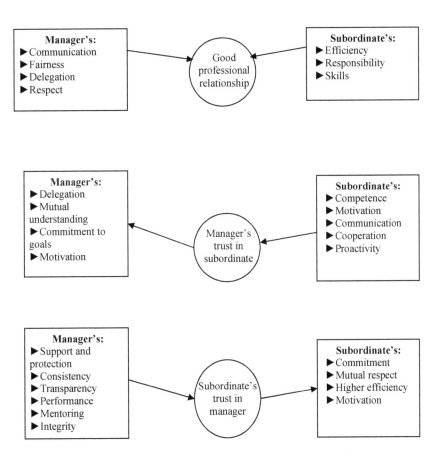

Figure 9.1 Antecedents and outcomes of trust in hierarchical relationships

starts from an initial belief in and acceptance of each other (based mainly on a subjective and personal evaluation of the other party) and evolves on the basis of subsequent professional experience.

When asked about how trust starts in a new relationship, where people do not have too much mutual knowledge, our participants mentioned the importance of perceived match and appreciation of values. Demographic similarities are considered to be a facilitator for developing trust. Thus, similarities in age, education, race, gender, religion, political views, organizational experience, etc. break down initial barriers and bring up common points. As one manager said, "When you first meet someone, it's difficult to have an open posture and trust him. Usually we Brazilians are considered open and free-talking, but it's talking about soccer or the weather and not personal stuff."

Another important condition is personal values and traits. People with similar values have an advantage in starting a new relationship, but our participants also mentioned that these should be "good" values and "good" personality traits. Otherwise, these aspects can affect the early relationship, creating barriers and fostering distance and prejudice. As a participant commented, "Sometimes a young manager is similar to you in many aspects, but if he is jealous or insecure about his position, this breaks the relation." Another participant highlighted the importance of an initial open posture, with managers taking the risks and starting to become involved with others. He said:

> As they are usually older and more experienced, managers should trust people they have just met, and take the risk. If this person lets you down, taking advantage of something, this means that he doesn't deserve to be trusted, but at least we have tried our best.

Another participant complemented this idea by showing how receiving good references about a new person creates high expectations and induces people to be more open and trusting in the early contacts. And, like a self-fulfilling prophecy, an initial predisposition to trust others often creates a positive work environment that fosters reciprocal trust.

Table 9.2 gives the quantitative analysis for the trust circle model. Analyzing this table can provide valuable insights into the trust dynamics in Brazil compared with the global model (including all 18 countries participating in this study).

According to the results presented in Table 9.2, the quantitative data for Brazil are consistent and reliable. It is possible to identify three strong, significant correlations in the model and a last correlation that is weak and not significant. Comparing with

Table 9.2 Standardized regression weights for the trust model in Brazil and the overall sample

	OCB–>MTS	MTS–>MTB	MTB–>STM	STM–>OCB
Brazil only	0.66**	0.50**	0.58**	0.07
Complete model	0.68**	0.34**	0.89**	0.08*

Notes
** Regression weight significant at 0.01 level.
* Regression weight significant at 0.05 level.

the complete model, many common characteristics and similarities can be identified that highlight the generalization of the model across cultures.

According to the first correlation, a subordinate showing organizational citizenship behavior (OCB) increases a manager's willingness to trust him. When asked about this relationship, the experts commented that managers probably see the subordinate's OCB as a proxy for commitment to the organization, efficiency, and proactivity. In the literature, showing OCB is usually associated with people perceived as being more valuable and this also affects their personal evaluation. OCB is not a measure of efficiency, initiative, or ability, but is perceived as a proxy since people who are more involved with the organization are more likely to put the organization first. As one participant said, "When we see a person defending or showing loyalty to and pride in the organization, this makes us feel that we can rely on that person, but this could only be goodwill and not real results."

The next relationship proposed in the model is that managers' trust in subordinates positively influences managers' trustworthy behavior. And considering the previous relation, we can say that both behaviors—the subordinate's OCB and the manager's trustworthy behavior—are mediated by the manager's trust. Or in other words, in the presence of a trusting relationship in which manager and subordinate share ideas, feelings, and hopes and are emotionally involved, it is easy to see more trustworthy behavior, such as transparent communication, autonomy and delegation, mutual interest and concern, and consistent, predictable behavior. When asked about this relationship, participants commented that trust has many positive outcomes that benefit and improve working, but many of them are less noticeable than more delegation, respect, and autonomy. In the words of one participant:

> The people I trust are often the first I think of to do a task, and usually those who demand less time from management since I don't need to be calling, controlling, and asking them all the time to have feedback.

Following the proposed model, the third relationship shows managerial trustworthy behavior to be a positive influence on subordinates' trust in managers. Subordinates participating in the qualitative interview gave broad support for this relationship, since they consider that the manager's behavior is fundamental in developing trust. Trust is a personal relationship and grows with mutual knowledge. Subordinates are more likely to trust their managers when they see consistent behavior across different conditions, real concern and interest from their superiors, and honesty and integrity in their behavior. One subordinate emphasized that:

> when we perceive support from our partners, such as providing information or defending the team, this generates a feeling of union among us and with our leader. It is when times are difficult that one sees how the other person really is.

Finally, subordinates' trust in managers is positively correlated, but to a lesser, non-significant extent, with subordinates' OCB. Comparing the Brazilian scores with the global results, we note that the relationship is weak. Since trust is essentially a personal characteristic, it requires involvement and acceptance of each party in the relationship to allow oneself to become vulnerable to the other. Consequently, the trust dynamic between managers and subordinates is not symmetrical; it develops in different ways and can achieve different levels, depending on personal traits and the perceived evaluation. However, the two parties are not completely independent and development of trust on one side fosters (but does not determine) trust development on the other side. This explains the complexity of trust development and the changes in dynamics observed in a relationship.

When asked to comment on why subordinates' trust in management was poorly correlated to subordinates' OCB, the experts explained that there was a difference in the level of perception and the level of action. OCB should be observed (actions) when subordinates are deeply committed to the organization through clear acceptance of values and mission, perception of organizational support, or a feeling of gratitude for the organization itself. And this is not determined by the relationship with the immediate supervisor, although this relationship does affect the perception. As one participant said:

> People show good behaviors such as loyalty, defending the organization's image, or proposing improvements when they really feel part or in debt to the company, even when they have problems with their managers. Usually this is the only tie that makes a subordinate remain in an organization when facing direct distrust; they really believe in the structure and that things will change when the supervisor is changed.

As we have seen, the dynamics of trust are very rich and complex. Trust development depends on a myriad of factors and conditions, and personal traits and values also affect this relationship. The participants provided valuable insights into the model and they agreed that it can be generalized to countries other than Brazil. The weak tie in the model can still be considered part of the model, completing the trust cycle. Perhaps, OCB should be considered more related to members of the team and associated with tasks such as helping partners and sharing information in a group. Another possibility is the association of the manager with the organizational image; subordinates who associate their superiors strongly with the organizational image are expected to show more OCB.

Discussion and Conclusions

Brazil is going through a rapid process of modernization and internationalization. Markets are becoming increasingly competitive and organizations need to adapt and develop competitive advantages in order to achieve sustainable growth and long-term results. HR departments are becoming more strategically important, especially in the current labor market, which has become more highly skilled and more demanding. The participants invited to take part in our research emphasized the importance of positive outcomes obtained through a good relationship between manager and subordinate and how this can improve team performance, unit results, and the organization as a whole. Leadership is changing and more skills are required from managers. Results themselves are no longer the only goal; how they are obtained is also important and impacts employees' commitment, proactivity, innovation, etc.

Our study was able to bring together the academic discussion on trust (as presented in the literature review) and the practical wisdom and experience of the managers and subordinates who are facing the challenges of developing trust in work environments. To generalize our conclusions and proposed model, we tested and collected data from many different regions inside Brazil (since, as in many large developing countries, regional differences matter) and submitted these findings to a group of invited experts with different backgrounds, such as social researchers, professors, journalists, and top managers.

The results are quite consistent and clear, and many questions were answered in this study. As a general overview, our study confirms the notion of trust as context-dependent shaped by cultural characteristics. Brazil has many similarities with Latin American countries, but also some particularities. As a collectivistic society, leaders working in Brazil should foster a long-term relationship, with open, flexible communication, and be aware of the importance of group membership. Also, as a high power distance society, Brazilian leaders experience respect and hierarchy privileges, but this should not encourage distance and non-approachability by employees. Leaders not used to flexibility and adaptation can be surprised by subordinates' commitment and effort to overcome difficulties and carry out tasks sometimes considered impossible by other people who are more bounded by rules.

Contrary to global studies such as WVS and Latinobarómetro that classify Brazilians as low in interpersonal trust, our study shed new light for understanding and contextualizing trust development. In line with these findings, people develop a high level of attachment, especially when face-to-face communication is used. In addition, interviews with managers, subordinates, and experts invited to participate in this study offered additional insights into leadership styles in Brazil. Participants also commented that leaders should be more willing to develop trusting relationships. Individual values and personality traits, perceived by the subordinates, have a strong influence on people's willingness to initiate trust.

In general, this study summarizes many ideas about how trust affects people in work environments and tries to synthesize the core idea and essential elements that characterize trust in Brazil today. Although we have invited participants from different sectors, firm sizes, and geographical regions, there is a predominance of respondents from São Paulo (where there is also a higher concentration of businesses). Future research should focus on the role of trust development when women hold the top positions; this was clearly under represented in our study. Furthermore, the development of organizational citizenship behavior within organizations was insufficiently explained by subordinates' trust in managers. Perhaps a more detailed explanation of how subordinates associate their superiors with the organization and how leadership shapes this relationship can bring new insights on trust.

References

DaMatta, R. (1991). *O que faz o brasil, Brasil?* (4th ed.). Rio de Janeiro: Rocco.

Edelman Trust Barometer (2011). Retrieved on 9.5.11 from http://trust.edelman.com/trust-download/executive-summary/.

Hess, D. & DaMatta, R. (1995). *The Brazilian Puzzle: Culture on the Borderlands of the Western World.* New York: Columbia University Press.

Hofstede, G. (1991). *Cultures and Organizations: Software on the Mind.* London: McGraw-Hill.

Knack, S. & Kiefer, P. (1997). Does social capital have an economic payoff? A cross-country examination. *Quarterly Journal of Economics*, 112: 1251–1288.

Latinobarómetro (2010). Retrieved on 14.5.11 from www.latinobarometro.org/latino/LATContenidos.jsp.

Lazzarini, S., Madalozzo, R., Artes, R. & Siqueira, J. (2004). Measuring trust: An experiment in Brazil. *IBEC Working Paper*, WPE 01–2004.

Neri, M.C. (2010). The decade of falling income inequality and formal employment generation in Brazil. In OECD, *Tackling Inequalities in Brazil, China, India and South Africa: The Role of Labour Market and Social Policies*. Paris: OECD Publishing.

O'Keefe, H. & O'Keefe, W. (2004). Business behaviors in Brazil and the USA: Understanding the gaps. *International Journal of Social Economics*, 31: 614–624.

Sledge, S., Miles, A. & Coppage, S. (2008). What role does culture play? A look at motivation and job satisfaction among hotel workers in Brazil. *The International Journal of Human Resource Management*, 19(9): 1667–1682.

10 Manager–Subordinate Trust Relationships in Colombia

SANDRA IDROVO CARLIER, ALEJANDRO MORENO
SALAMANCA, AND PAMELA LEYVA TOWNSEND

Introduction

Colombia is situated in the northwest corner of South America, bathed by the waters of the Caribbean Sea at the north and the Pacific Ocean at the west. Its favorable geographical location has been used since colonial times to transport merchandise to Europe. Cartagena de Indias was the port from which gold, silver, and precious goods coming from all over South America were sent to Spain. Today, it is one of the country's main growth areas. The Republic of Colombia, with slightly more than 45 million inhabitants, is the third most populated country in Latin America and the twenty-ninth most populated in the world. By area, it is the third largest in South America and the twenty-fifth largest in the world. After the severe economic crisis of the 1990s and due to a high level of violence related with sociopolitical events, with confrontation between armed groups fighting for power and control of the illicit drug traffic and for land control (Patti & Cepeda, 2007), Colombia entered the twenty-first century with the goal of establishing peace and security within its borders. The citizen security policy enacted in the last nine years has enabled the levels of insecurity and violence to be significantly reduced in almost all parts of the country. The first decade of the new century shows a country with an average growth rate of 4.36 percent over the last five years and similar growth prospects for the next 20 years. However, the Gini coefficient, which measures the level of inequality, has increased from 0.55 to 0.58, also in the last five years, which makes Colombia the most unequal country in Latin America and the fourth most unequal in the world. As at May 2011, unemployment was still high, at 11.2 percent.

The Colombian business culture is hierarchical, with a high distance between those who have power and those who do not. This inequality is defined from below and it is maintained by followers and leaders alike (Hofstede PDI = 67). With respect to leadership, measured with 21 scales, Latin American managers, including Colombian managers, comprise a very homogenous group that shows a clear preference for leaders who are focused on achieving a high level of performance, skilled in team-building, willing to cooperate with the group, competent administrators, and willing to sacrifice their personal interests for those of the organization (Ogliastri et al., 1999). The leader is seen as a person who has the necessary adaptability, creativity, and open-mindedness to transform each experience, whether positive or negative, into a learning process (Sepúlveda *et al.*, 2009). As in the rest of the world, leadership is associated with criteria such as the ability to inspire others, have a clear forward-looking vision, personal integrity, decisiveness, diplomacy, and humility. The self-reliant or individualistic leader is rated very poorly (Ogliastri *et al.*, 1999). At the same time, in the organizational sphere, the human resources departments have evolved from performing operational and functional roles at the end of the last century to being currently viewed as an area that generates value for the organization (Calderón *et al.*, 2008), with practices that acknowledge the employee as a person and a source of success for the company (Calderón *et al.*, 2010).

This chapter begins with a brief account of historic developments in Colombia and a description of the current institutional framework, focusing on education and employment, together with an overview of the economic and social institutional context. This is followed by a review of human resources practices directly related to leadership within organizations and the development of trust. The review of extant literature contributes to the discussion of the results of the study performed and the analysis of its implications for managerial practice.

Highlights of Manager–Subordinate Trust in Colombia

- Participants in the study agree that there are scenarios in which there is trust between managers and subordinates and others in which distrust prevails. They highlight authoritarian behaviors by some managers as related to lack of trust and experience of such behavior by subordinates as the reason for maintaining this lack of trust.
- Trust differences in hierarchical relationships are explained by corporate culture (power distance), company size, and historical circumstances of distrust due to internal intelligence mechanisms developed by companies to prevent infiltration by members of terrorists groups.
- Managers and subordinates agree that key personal factors that influence trust building are: getting to know the other person (his/her motivations, personal and family issues), respectful communication, and duration of the relationship.
- Age is not a significant factor in trust for subordinates but it is for managers who find that if their subordinates are older than they are, it is more difficult for them to gain trust.
- Respondents and experts agree that academic level is an important factor for building trust, especially from the manager's perspective. Due to the hierarchical relationship and power distance, managers are expected to take, and assume the responsibility of taking, the first step in building trust.
- Subordinate's trust in manager is highly correlated with subordinate's organizational citizenship behaviors.

Historical Perspective

Originally inhabited by native tribes, chief among which were the Chibchas, Colombia was the seat of the Viceroyalty of New Granada, belonging to the Spanish Empire, until the nineteenth century when, along with other independence movements of the time, it declared its independence on July 20, 1810. Another decade was required to consolidate this independence. In 1821, the Republic of Colombia was established as a representative democracy agglutinating what are now Venezuela, Colombia, and Ecuador, following the ideals of Simon Bolívar. Great Colombia came to an end in 1830 with the secession of Venezuela and Ecuador, and the Republic of Colombia embarked upon a series of political changes that took it from a Confederation to its current form as a Republic.

In the twentieth century, Colombia was a traditional, aristocratic, agrarian society centered on the rural estate and commerce. Conservative and liberal governments alternated in power. "If the legacy of the '60s and '70s was the violence of the guerilla movements […] the '80s brought the violence of drug trafficking, terrorism and paramilitary militias" (Ocampo, 1997:338). In spite of the strong economic growth, social inequality and violence increased. The 1990s began with the approval of a new Constitution for Colombia and the country gradually began to open its economy, although this did not prevent it from plunging into a deep economic recession at the end of the decade (Santos, 2009:293). The new Constitution, which replaced the 1886 Constitution, introduced a series of changes, among which perhaps the most significant was the creation of areas for citizen participation, signaling a transition from a representative democracy to a participative democracy. Together with these changes, mechanisms were established to protect basic rights, such as tutelage. The Constitution recognizes the freedom of worship, in which all religious confessions and churches are equally free before the law, and the freedom of religious education and suspends the civil effects of Catholic marriage with the possibility of divorce. The Catholic religion ceases to be the "religion of the nation," as it was called in the Constitution of 1886.

With the beginning of the twenty-first century, the government has intensified its offensive against the insurgent groups, strengthened the military, established government presence in a major part of the country, and the citizen security policy has started to bear fruit. Although it is true that the left-wing guerilla groups FARC (Revolutionary Armed Forces of Colombia) and the ELN (National Liberation Army) have lost a lot of territory and presence, and the paramilitary groups (AUC, illegal armed groups loyal to landowners fighting in self-defense against the guerilla groups) have been demobilized under the 2005 Justice and Peace Act, the conflict persists. Although armed confrontations have fallen by more than 50 percent since 2002, incidents with anti-personnel mines have increased in the critical areas (Angulo *et al.*, 2009). The clashes have forced a large number of people to move from the country to the cities, where they have not been able to integrate satisfactorily. The number of displaced people ranges between 3.5 and 5 million people, depending on the source (government or NGOs). Most of them are women and children and 94 percent of them live below the poverty line. According to the 2009 report submitted by the Internal Displacement Monitoring Centre (IDMC) to the United Nations, after 25 years of conflict, Colombia is the second country with more internally displaced people in the world, only surpassed by Sudan. In June 2011, the Colombian Congress passed the Victims Act, which creates an institutional framework for providing financial redress to the victims of the conflict, and offers a mechanism for returning land to slightly more than half a million people.

Furthermore, according to the High Presidential Council for Reintegration (Alta Consejería para la Reintegración, n.d.), there are more than 50,000 demobilized guerrilla and paramilitary fighters who have put down their arms between 2002 and 2009 and are now part of the population looking for work. One of the social consequences of it is an increased level of urban violence, in a country where more than 75 percent of the total population lives in cities (DANE, 2010).

Institutional Context

Economic Context

According to the 2001 report released by the Central Bank of Colombia, economic growth in Colombia during the twentieth century has been within the average for Latin America. GDP growth for the period 1905–1924 was 5.36 percent, 4.2 percent for 1925–1981, and 3.85 percent for 1982–1997, which is fairly similar to Brazil and Mexico during the same periods. Venezuela, Chile, and Argentina had higher sustained growth than Colombia. However, it is also true that growth in Colombia was considerably below that of the Asian countries during these periods. From 1998 to 2002, average GDP growth was barely 0.78 percent, as Colombia suffered a severe recession during this period, perhaps the deepest since the 1930s. From 2003 to 2010, the Colombian economy recovered, with an average GDP growth rate of 5.32 percent, according to IMF and WEF data. The 2008 crisis caused a shortfall in growth but its impact in Colombia, as in the other developing countries, was less devastating than in the developed economies. For 2011, the growth prospects suggest figures above 5 percent, with inflation ranging between 3.5 and 4 percent. Unemployment has fallen to a level that has ranged between 15.6 and 9.9 percent in the last ten years. At the end of 2010, unemployment stood at 12 percent according to the IMF and fell to 10.8 percent by December 2011.

Social Context

Life expectancy at birth in Colombia for 2010 was 74 years. The fertility rate for the same year was 2.2 and the crude birth rate was 17.76 for every 1000 inhabitants. Colombia has a comprehensive social security system with four basic pillars: pensions, health, occupational hazards, and complementary social services. The pension system assures coverage for the population of the risks or contingencies derived from old age, invalidity, and death. It covers employees who are formally registered and, therefore, contribute each month to the system. For its part, the health system allows participation of the private sector in providing health services to Colombian workers. In addition to the Institute of Social Security (ISS), the health system provides for the creation of the Solidarity and Guarantee Fund to assure the provision of health services to the unemployed and/or vulnerable sectors of the population, and gives all workers the possibility of choosing their health provider. The occupational hazards system regulates management of events arising from labor-related accidents, with separate funding from common diseases. Membership is compulsory for the employer and it covers all health expenses arising from occupational injuries or diseases and also the payment of sick leave. In 2007, social security coverage in Colombia for its population stood at 80–85 percent. The mission of the Mandatory Health Plan is to preserve health and prevent and cure disease. It includes medicines for the worker affiliated to the Plan and his family and the payment of sickness and maternity benefits.

Political and Legal System

Colombia is a presidential republic, where the President is Head of State, Head of the government, supreme administrative authority and Chief of the Armed Forces. It is the President who appoints his cabinet: Ministers, Deputy Ministers, and senior advisers. The President is elected for a four-year term and, until October 2005, re-election was not allowed. The legislative body is a bicameral Congress composed of the Senate (102 members) and the House of Representatives (166 representatives). The members of the Congress are elected by popular vote for a four-year period and can be re-elected indefinitely. The judicial system consists of the Attorney General of the Nation, created in 1991; the Constitutional Court, which interprets the constitutionality of different laws; the Supreme Court of Justice, the State Council which guarantees the legality of administrative processes; and the Higher Council of the Judiciary, which regulates the conduct and function of legal counsel and government officials in the judiciary branch.

There are two bodies which do not come under the executive, legislative, or judiciary branches and are represented at national, department, and municipal level. They are the Comptroller's Office, which audits the state's spending, applying efficiency, economy, equity, and environmental cost criteria; and the Ombudsman's Office, which is responsible for fostering respect for human rights, defending the public interest, ensuring observance of laws and regulations, and performing disciplinary investigations of the conduct of government officials and public sector employees in general, including members of the security forces.

For 150 years, since the second half of the nineteenth century, there were only two political parties: the Conservatives and the Liberals. In recent years, this has evolved toward a multiparty system and, currently, 16 parties have seats in the Congress. In 2002, Álvaro Uribe Vélez became the country's first independent President.

Education System

In 2006, 4.7 percent of the GDP was invested in education. The pupil–teacher ratio that year was 30:1. Primary education from age 6 to 12 and up to a total of nine years is free and compulsory. Secondary education starts at age 11 and lasts for six years. Those who graduate leave with the equivalent of a high-school diploma. According to the 2005 census, 50.3 percent of children aged 3–5 years were enrolled in pre-school education; 90.7 percent of those aged 6–10 years were enrolled in primary education; and 79.9 percent of those aged 11–17 years were enrolled in secondary education. The literacy rate in 2008 stood at 93 percent of the population. The ratio between public and private primary and secondary schools was 3:1. However, for higher education, the ratio is reversed, with the private sector surpassing the public sector with a ratio of 2.4:1.

HR Practices

The Colombian labor force has the following features: a) it is composed mostly of men, although the proportion of women is growing; b) there is a growing migration from the country to the city; and c) there is a high average age due to the increased life expectancy and smaller family sizes. As at 2006, 60 percent of the labor force was skilled—that is, completed secondary school. Another feature of the labor system is its rigidity, and non-wage payments account for 50 percent of the minimum wage. These payments include vacations, pensions, health insurance, unemployment benefits, and occupational hazard insurance. They also include contributions to family welfare programs (Colombian Family Institute), vocational training programs (SENA, National Learning Service), and family benefit programs. The percentage of these payments is one of the highest in the region and comparable with those of developed countries. This high rigidity and high labor costs encourage the development of an informal sector (with no contractual relationship with an employer), which accounts for about 50 percent of the GDP and 60 percent of total employment in the cities. The high proportion of the informal sector in Colombia is one of the main challenges facing the economy and the social and business sector.

Within this context, human resources management in Colombia has managed to position itself within companies as an area that generates value on five dimensions: organization projection (strategic orientation), change management, organization infrastructure (efficiency and effectiveness), people leadership, and social responsibility (Calderón, 2008). However, in Colombia, generally speaking, research in human capital management is "incipient, scarce, with significant gaps in the subject areas addressed, the establishment of an academic community and in its response to the needs of companies and regions" (Malaver et al., 2004, in Calderón et al., 2007).

Historically, the human capital management areas, a term that is currently preferred to "human resources," have been responsible for recruitment and retention; skill-building with a view to implementing management by competencies; career plans, which are currently changing to adapt to flatter organization structures; and assessment processes tied to compensation processes. At present, their added functions include change management, corporate culture, assisted career disengagement, process management, knowledge and learning management, social responsibility, life–work balance, and work flexibility (Calderón et al., 2010).

In a study performed by Calderón et al. (2010) in 273 Colombian companies, 73 percent of which had more than 200 employees, a level of maturity in the human capital management areas was identified by the high level of qualification of their managers, an extensive experience in this field, and diversity of work experience. As regards practices, human capital managers were asked to order a list of ten practices, recognized by the specialized literature as strategic, by order of importance, and then to list the three that they considered were working well and the three that needed to be improved on. More than 40 percent ranked talent management, change management, and leadership development as the three most importance practices. Other practices, such as having a human talent strategy, performing strategic alignment, and developing strategy design and implementation skills, are only acknowledged as priority practices by 28.6 percent of the companies. The remaining four practices—social responsibility management, human capital management metrics, social capital building, and globalization and diversity management—are accepted as priority practices by less than 20 percent of the respondents. When listing the practices that were best structured, talent and change management are still included, although the percentage of companies mentioning them falls, leadership development falls to seventh place and social responsibility management rises to third place. The three practices requiring immediate improvement are: life–work balance (in 37.7 percent of the companies), organizational learning (28.9 percent), and talent management (28.6 percent). It is worth highlighting that this last practice was also considered well-structured by a substantial proportion of companies (27.5 percent). A cluster analysis identifies two clearly differentiated groups. The first group, consisting of 70 percent of the companies, shows significant progress in its strategic practices, except leadership development. Considerable effort has been devoted to life–work balance, globalization management and social responsibility, measurement systems, and social capital building. The second group, consisting of the remaining 30 percent of companies, has lower scores in all strategic practices except change management and leadership development, and considers most critical those mentioned earlier. The respondents also identified two issues that had yet to be satisfactorily addressed in human capital management: adequate measurement of results and the low contribution to technological capital formation.

It must be remembered that most of the sample consisted of large companies. A study of human capital management practices in SMEs and micro-businesses might give different results. Large multinational companies or government organizations have rational and "bureaucratic" rules and regulations that integrate innovations in management practices and state-of-the-art technology, while small and medium-sized companies, and also family-owned businesses, apply paternalist approaches and a short-term view permeates the entire human talent process: from selection to training (Ogliastri *et al.*, 2005).

Leadership Style

Colombia shares a series of cultural characteristics with the other Latin American countries, which can also be found in Latin Europe, namely, an organization culture characterized by a high power distance or elitism (Hofstede, 2001). The elitism, also present in other Latin American countries, can also be explained by the historic structure of these societies: hierarchical and closed, which, in addition to elitism, also generate envy and even violence (Ogliastri *et al.*, 1999). However, Colombia holds first place out of the 64 countries that took part in the GLOBE study on culture and leadership in its wish for a less elitist society (Ogliastri *et al.*, 1999). To this must be added the fact that Colombia has the highest uncertainty avoidance index in Latin America (80 on Hofstede's scale), which in turn leads to attempts to minimize this uncertainty by adopting and implementing strict rules, laws, policies, and regulations; everything has to be controlled so that anything unexpected is eliminated or avoided. This creates a risk-adverse society that has difficulty in accepting change. However, a distinction must be made between uncertainty avoidance and ambiguity tolerance. As Ogliastri *et al.* suggest, it is necessary to distinguish three things: "one is that a country's people live in uncertainty, another is that they are able to tolerate situations of ambiguity, and the last is that they want (or do not want) to change the situation" (1999: 37). As these authors suggest, there is a desire among executives in Latin American countries, including Colombia, to reduce uncertainty in their societies. However, at the same time, they show a high degree of tolerance of ambiguity, which is "one of the great virtues of living in these cultures" (Ogliastri *et al.*, 1999: 37).

The GLOBE study mentioned previously shows a fairly strong cultural and leadership homogeneity for Latin America. For Latin Americans, the elements that contribute to leadership are: being performance-oriented, team builders, competent administrators, decisive, diplomatic, hard-working, and status-aware. For the Colombian managers interviewed in the study, one of the necessary traits of a leader is being a visionary. Of the ten Latin American countries that took part in the study, the Colombians rated this feature higher than the other Latin Americans. With the other Latin American countries, except Brazil, Colombia would add humaneness. And with the exception of Mexico and Venezuela, the Latin Americans would include integrity and being inspiring and a visionary. Among the managers in the region, the Colombians are those who rate face-saving most unfavorably and, in fact, they consider it antagonistic to leadership. Together with Brazil, Ecuador, and Costa Rica, Colombia includes modesty and equanimity among the features of a good leader, unlike the international vision where this item does not have much impact (Ogliastri *et al.*, 1999). As we have already said, in Colombia, the leader is also seen as someone who has the necessary adaptability, creativity, and open-mindedness to transform each experience, whether positive or negative, into a learning process (Sepúlveda *et al.*, 2009).

Within this context, the following features stand out in Colombian leaders: maintaining direct communication with all levels of the organization and teaching teamwork by making it known that group interests come before personal interests (Guerrero, 2009).

Literature Review on Trust

Trust in Latin America, and Colombia is not an exception within the region, is based on trust networks: people trust those they know by personal contact and this trust grows with experience. Thus, more than half of the people in the countries surveyed trust the Fire Brigade, the Catholic Church, the police, the poor, the radio, the neighbor, and the Armed Forces (Latinobarómetro, 2007). They strongly distrust political parties, foreigners, the Congress, and the judiciary power. They distrust those who have power because they can do harm. The situation remains unchanged in 2009, when the Latinobarómetro report puts the same players, in slightly different positions, at the top of those most trusted by people. That year, the Catholic Church had first place. However, this distrust in the institutions does not include the President. According to the Latinobarómetro report (2007), Álvaro Uribe Vélez, the Colombian President at that time, was trusted by 57 percent of the population, and was the third most trusted President in the region, while barely 41 percent of the Colombian population trusted his government. Perhaps the biggest trust losers within the public institutions have been the political parties. Barely 18 percent of the Colombian population say that they trust political parties somewhat or a lot (Latinobarómetro, 2007). This configures a map in which trust in the President strengthens, while trust in the mechanisms of representation weakens. To this must be added the low level of trust in the judiciary system: only 23 percent of Colombians think that there is equal access to justice for all.

The 2009 Latinobarómetro shows that only 19 percent of Colombians think that most people can be trusted. This percentage is below the regional average

(18 countries), which is 21 percent. These data confirm those obtained in the World Values Survey (2005), which reports that only 17.2 percent of Colombians would fully trust a person they know personally; 76.1 percent would trust a little or not much, and 6.7 percent would not trust at all. It also reports that 33.3 percent of Colombians would have no trust in a foreigner and 26.3 percent would have no trust in someone with another religion. It should be pointed out that, unlike other countries, it seems that trust in Latin America, and in Colombia, is not linked to economic growth: countries grow irrespective of the distrust there may be between people; and it does not seem to change over time, at least it does not change during the period 1996–2009. Neither does it seem to be affected by growth or recessions or by different attitudes toward democracy. This is very different from what happens in the First World.

One figure that comes out strengthened in the Latin American evaluation, and which also applies to Colombians, is that of the entrepreneur: 46 percent of Latin Americans rate entrepreneurs highly or very highly (Latinobarómetro, 2007). In addition, 44 percent trust banks a lot or somewhat, and 42 percent trust private enterprise a lot or somewhat (Latinobarómetro, 2009). And according to the same report, 51 percent of Colombians agree or agree a lot that private enterprise is indispensable for the country's development.

Colombians have strong family and friendship ties and, in this sense, they are collectivistic, limiting their endogroup to the family and close friends (Ogliastri *et al.*, 1999). Consequently, behind an easygoing, superficially warm behavior, Colombians have a low level of generalized trust (Cuéllar, 2000) and establish hierarchical differences. As Salgado suggests, if one learns:

> a prescribed way of relating with others – tightly closed groups and distrust of people who are not known – they will replicate it in other situations and will not use the possibilities offered by other spheres of social life, associations, etc., to facilitate transmission of trust to other people in society.
>
> (2005:98)

At the organizational level, when Salgado and Chaparro (2006) reproduced a study performed in Mexico and the United States, they found that the subordinate's trust in his/her manager was positively correlated with organizational citizenship behaviors, except on the dimensions of sportsmanship 1 and sportsmanship 2; and in fact, it predicts all the dimensions of organizational citizenship behaviors, except sportsmanship 2. However, in this study, the subordinate's trust in the manager does not perform a mediating role, as other studies have proposed and found (Konovsky *et al.*, 2001).

In a study performed to determine the importance of the company's reputation, fairness at work, care and concern for employees, trust in employees, and resources available, for deciding whether or not to stay with the company, Bernardi and Guptill (2008) found that Colombians, Ecuadorians, and South Africans attributed greater importance to these items than the group composed of students from Canada, Hong Kong, and Ireland.

As Salgado (2005) suggests, it is important to look closely at the issue of generalized trust in Colombia and study the features of individualized trust, such as trust in one's boss.

Contextual Factors in Hierarchical Trusting Relationships

We now come to the empirical results of our research. The Delphi panel experts qualify the statement about trust between managers and subordinates. They say that there are scenarios in which there is trust and others in which distrust prevails. They highlight authoritarian behaviors by some managers as related with lack of trust, and experience of such behavior by subordinates as the reason for maintaining this lack of trust. One expert in particular pointed out that there is a tendency for bosses to breathe down their subordinates' necks and delegate incompletely and non-functionally. In some organizations, the lack of trust leads to control mechanisms that are perceived as excessive and interpreted as distrust. When explaining trust differences in hierarchical relationships, several factors are mentioned. One of them is *corporate culture*. In Colombia, most jobs are created by small and micro-companies that are often family businesses. This adds the pressure of family dynamics to professional environments, contributing proximity in some cases but distance and demanding expectations in other cases. Another factor is *company size*, which influences in different ways and with different results. In the opinion of one of the experts, small companies in Colombia have more flexible structures and "the clear recognition of the command structures, familiarity with and closeness to the managers facilitates more open communication and the creation of trust through closer personal ties." However, both managers and subordinates mention that, while the formal atmosphere and the reliance on processes in large and/or multinational companies may interfere with the interpersonal relationships required to foster trust, it is still possible to find this proximity, as the unit, area, or department can become like a family group. As one subordinate says:

> We are divided into units but in my unit we are like a family. So that would be my company for me. Sometimes we compare ourselves with the other units and we say "We're the best." Because we're very close and we trust each other a lot.

The change happens when an employee ceases to be a person and becomes a tool, a number, or a letter, and when, after becoming used to seeing your boss once a week, you never see him at all.

When asked whether Colombia was an individualistic or collectivistic society, the participants in the focus groups answered that it was highly individualistic as a country. However, within the family and with friends, it is collectivistic: the family comes first and family members help each other. You respect your parents and you do not criticize them; parents will sacrifice all they can for their children (Encuesta Nacional de Valores, 2006). The experts agree with this opinion: Colombia is an extremely individualistic country that comes together on very specific occasions, when faced with tragedy and adversity. The universal rejection of the insurgent groups and the demonstrations that have united the country in recent years are evidence of such collectivistic actions.

However, the experts are not unanimous in their opinion about power distance. Some think that Colombians accept that someone has to hold power and that that person enjoys certain benefits, often excessive. Others think that organizations are moving toward more participative models but, being a vertical society, this trend goes counter-current to Colombian culture. In the political sphere, however, it is acknowledged that the trend is to maintain power inequalities, which go hand in hand with economic and social inequality. While the experts agree that managers are initially distrusting, the managers in the focus groups maintain that they enter the relationship with subordinates from a position of trust, until the subordinates prove otherwise. As one of the experts suggests, things are changing in Colombia. During the rise of the guerrilla movements during the 1990s, companies generated a series of internal intelligence mechanisms and procedures to prevent themselves from being infiltrated by members of terrorist groups who would use the information obtained to extort and kidnap. This dynamic brought greater distance in relations and distrust within the company and people placed more trust in the family circle and people who were known than in strangers. This has changed drastically as the security situation has improved. This putting aside of distrust is seen particularly among younger managers, who are more open and participative, and the power distance is narrowing.

Personal Factors in Hierarchical Trusting Relationships

Both the managers and the subordinates taking part in the focus groups agree that there are personal factors that influence trust building. Specifically, they said that a key factor for generating trust is knowing the boss or subordinate. This means not only knowing his professional resumé but knowing him as a person, his family, his personal motivations. This was one of the key issues highlighted both by managers and by subordinates when talking about trust building. Knowing working methods and transparency in processes and communication help create trusting relationships. All of the participants consider trust to be vitally important for a good work relationship. It is impossible to have a good work relationship without trust between the parties. In general, they consider that managers trust their people and that this is fundamental for getting results. They also say that, as a general rule, the managers start the professional relationship by trusting the subordinate. If this trust is betrayed, it is very difficult to rebuild. At the same time, they point out the need for open, respectful communication for trust to grow.

Subordinates do not see age as a significant factor in trust but managers do. They think that, if their subordinates are older than them, it is more difficult for them to gain trust. However, if their subordinates are younger than them, it is easier. Both groups agree that the time spent working together has a positive influence on the trust relationship and is more important than age and tenure in the company, although these factors too have a positive influence. Neither managers nor subordinates think that gender plays a very significant role in generating trust. Managers acknowledge that women are more dynamic and flexible and they prefer mixed gender teams. However, there is a consensus among managers and subordinates that the female boss–male subordinate relationship is more difficult and less desirable. But one female manager remarked: "I get on better with male subordinates than with female subordinates. I have had both male and female bosses and I always get on better with male bosses, communication is better with men than with women." However, taking precedence over the other personal factors is the need for open communication between both parties and a respectful attitude.

The experts agree that the duration of the relationship and tenure in the company are the two main factors that influence trust building. For them, mutual knowledge is key for generating trust because then people know what to expect from each other,

Table 10.1 Colombia: significant controls (correlations)

	Organizational tenure: subordinate	Academic level: subordinate
MTB		
OCB		
MTS	0.235*	0.292**
STM		

Notes
** Correlation significant at 0.01 level.
* Correlation significant at 0.05 level.
MTB = managerial trustworthy behavior, STM = subordinates' trust in managers, MTS = managers' trust in subordinates, OCB = organizational citizenship behavior.

and consistency is indispensable if the relationship is to evolve in a positive direction. Gender and company size occupy lower positions. However, the experts add an element that is very important for trust building: education, understood as the subordinate's and/or manager's academic level.

It is interesting to note that the experts' remarks account for the results obtained in the quantitative study on the importance of the different items that determine trust building (Table 10.1).

Regarding the subordinate's organizational tenure as a factor that has a positive effect on the manager's trust, one of the experts observed that "it gives a certain confidence that the person knows how to move around in the organization, understands what is happening, knows who the players are and provides good support to the other party if needed."

Likewise, when discussing the subordinate's academic level, one of the experts said:

When there are problems, a manager will ask: Who is in charge and what qualifications does he/she have and with this information, he will react calmly if the person who is dealing with the difficult situation has the right academic background.

There are two fundamental variables in building and maintaining trust: education and knowledge, which can be obtained by experience and academic training; fusion of these two variables in the same person gives the manager peace of mind.

Antecedents and Outcomes of Hierarchical Trusting Relationships

Neither managers nor subordinates doubt that trust is essential for a good professional relationship. The subordinates say that to have a good professional relationship and for the trust to grow, communication is fundamental, but this communication must be respectful and non-threatening. Communication must be frank and transparent; the expectations must be clear so that subordinates can fulfill them. There must be delegation, support, and feedback. For their part, managers agree that open communication is vital for building trust and, consequently, for ensuring a good professional relationship, but they underscore the need for it to be on both sides, even though they are aware that, in Colombia, it is much easier for managers to be open with subordinates than for subordinates to be open with managers. One manager indicated:

Sometimes the subordinate does not open up because he is thinking: What will my boss think? What could happen? What could he say to me? The manager takes it more in his stride; he is in a more comfortable position.

For that very reason, managers must take that extra step and create spaces for communication. Trust is generated when subordinates are able to express their opinions, even if they are contrary to their managers', provided that they are expressed respectfully and clearly. Both managers and subordinates emphasize that trust appears and grows when professional and personal expectations are met—that is, when clarity in communication enables the agreed objectives to be fulfilled.

Figure 10.1 summarizes the most important antecedents and outcomes of trust in the manager-subordinate relationship, as deduced from the qualitative study: experts and focus groups.

Certain behaviors help subordinates to trust their managers. From the subordinates' viewpoint, perhaps the most important is support. To know that they are delegated tasks in which they make the decisions but the manager is there to back them. One of the subordinates remarked: "I think she was very much in control [her boss], but she let me do it. I felt supported and I trusted that she was going to be there."

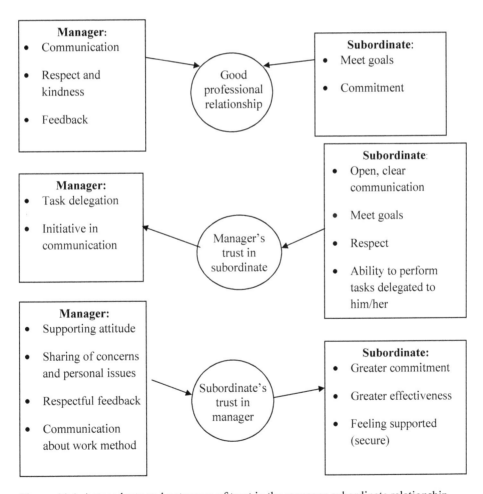

Figure 10.1 Antecedents and outcomes of trust in the manager-subordinate relationship

Communication about processes and results is also important. It is important to talk about work methods and compare advantages and disadvantages and then choose the one that suits both best:

> That is when a working relationship is built and effective teams are created. You find out how the other person likes things to be done and you can look at what you think is good and what you think is not so good and how you can fit in with that.

Subordinates also said that trust is created when supervisors share concerns with them and ask them about personal matters:

> When they share part of their life with you, when they ask you your opinion or your advice, or when they feel that I'm not OK or I'm uncomfortable or I'm going through a difficult time, and they have the courage to ask me about it. That generates a lot of trust for me.

The ability of managers to give respectful feedback is also a behavior that generates trust.

Both subordinates and supervisors suggest that trust also has a series of positive effects on professional relationships. The subordinates all agree that, when they are trusted to perform the tasks delegated to them, the supervisor can get on with his own job of managing instead of doing. Or, to put it another way, time spent on excessive control and monitoring "can slow down other processes that he may be checking." Indeed, lack of trust reduces productivity, since there are more controls to go through and less flexibility for decision-making. Furthermore, as one subordinate remarked, when there is no trust "you are continuously changing how you work because you think you're not doing it right or because your boss doesn't like it, and that can have a harmful effect on performance, work capacity and quality."

In some cases, the trust created can lead supervisors to delegate too many tasks, overwhelming the subordinate with work, and the latter's attempt to meet expectations can have negative effects. On the other side, when the subordinate feels that the supervisor trusts him/her, commitment is increased.

The Dynamics of Manager–Subordinate Trust

Both managers and subordinates and the experts participating in this study agree that trust grows over time. One cannot trust at the drop of a hat. And although it is true that work experience and academic background can initially inspire confidence, for the managers it is always a decision whose outcome is not certain: "You start from the idea that you want to trust"; "You have to be willing to trust." In this sense, managers agree that there is another element that helps people take that first step toward trust: humility. "There are people who think that nobody can do the job better than them. These people find it very hard to trust. They say: 'I have to check everything'." They also agree that this difficulty is found particularly in people who have recently become "boss," until "they realize that the manager's job is not to look at every detail, but to be at the helm and make sure that things keep moving forward."

That is why it is important for managers to give autonomy to subordinates so that they can give the best of themselves in their work. Trust, they say, is a relationship that is always in construction, dynamic, in which you must also receive:

> You start to delegate to a person, you start to empower him, that person starts to give results and you start to feel you have a good support, or rather, he is doing it better than I could do it, then you start to trust more, the person feels more empowered and his professional growth takes off.

The subordinates also stress the need for constant, timely communication. "As a subordinate, your duty is to keep your boss informed. Not informed about everything or you'll drive him crazy (…) but about the things he needs to know at that particular time." For this to happen, they agree that a minimum level of trust is necessary and "confidence within the subordinate himself to talk with his manager; to understand that not everything can go well."

Although it is true that both supervisors and subordinates highlight the subject of time as one of the keys in trust building, the two sides show differences when talking about how to start it. Managers stress two activities: listen to new subordinates to get to know them and talk with them; and explain to them clearly what the expectations are and how the work is done. Although the order in which they would do these two things varies, they agree that they should devote more time to both activities, and assure that they would always start by trusting: "You have to believe in people, believing is trusting. Your responsibility is to be close to them, because they are new, but you have to believe in people." This follow-up would initially be closer in work activities so that the manager is ready to give the necessary feedback or clear up any doubts that may arise. On a more personal level, informal spaces (traveling, breaks, etc.) would be used to get to know the subordinate as a person.

Subordinates agree with managers that knowing their supervisor, both as a person and how they work, is vital for starting a trusting relationship. Some would initially refrain from engaging in personal conversations: "I would not ask him 'How's the family?' or anything like that when I come to the office in the morning." They agree that they would have to start the process of getting to know them, which would require an open attitude from them, a willingness to find out who the person is, find out how he thinks, what his personality is. They all agree that it would be hard but it is necessary to adapt, to act in such a manner that trust can be given, knowing that it is possible that it may not be given.

The study's quantitative data confirm the statements made by the focus groups and shed new light on the dynamics of trust in Colombia. Compared with the results for the complete model (18 countries), it can be said that the same trend is followed. However, there are certain distinctive features. OCBs engender trust in managers in a similar direction but to a lesser extent than in the complete model. Trust in subordinates leads to specific behaviors by supervisors but to a lesser extent than in the other countries. In turn, the supervisors' behaviors encourage development of their subordinates' trust in a similar manner as in the model. And lastly, perhaps the most striking finding is the relationship between subordinates' trust and OCBs, which is quite a lot higher in Colombia than in the general model (Table 10.2).

The quantitative data show asymmetry in the responses to supervisors' and subordinates' behaviors. Managers' behaviors have a greater impact on trust generation

Table 10.2 Standardized regression weights for the trust model in Colombia and the overall sample

	OCB→MTS	MTS→MTB	MTB→STM	STM→OCB
Colombia only	0.33**	0.27*	0.72**	0.34*
Complete model	0.68**	0.34**	0.89**	0.08*

Notes
** Regression weight significant at 0.01 level.
* Regression weight significant at 0.05 level.

within subordinates (0.72**) than subordinates' behaviors have on supervisors' trust (0.33**). One possible explanation for this is given by the managers in the focus groups, when they say that they feel that they should take the first steps in trust and it is them who should show the way with their behaviors. The power distance existing in Colombia would mean that the subordinates' role is to respond to the signs that the manager is giving and that is the only way that the relationship can develop. This may explain the strong correlation between the subordinate's trust in the manager and his own organizational citizenship behavior (0.34* vs. 0.08* in the model). Once he has been given this trust, which is neither assumed nor expected given the prevailing culture, the subordinate strives to respond with behaviors that take the process further and have impact in different areas. The lower impact of subordinates' behaviors on trust in them may precisely be because supervisors naturally expect such behaviors from them. This would also account for the weaker correlation between managers trust in subordinates and managers' trustworthy behaviors (0.27* vs. 0.34**). Managers say they must trust until that trust is betrayed; there is no need for them to be trusted first before they can behave in a certain way: they delegate, trust, empower, without any reference to prior trust.

The panel experts also agreed that the model is universal and applicable to Colombia but they suggest that there are certain personal and cultural elements that could help enrich the model or explain better the dynamics of trust. One subject that the experts mention in particular is the situation of insecurity in Colombia, which, although improved, has marked a generation now in management posts and the weight of the various social imaginaries about what is owed to managers; how people behave in their professions; and the so-called "native malice": a way of behaving that would seek personal and family welfare before that of society or the community.

Discussion and Conclusions

The quantitative and qualitative results confirm a generalized model of trust that has been described in the existing literature. Trust is considered indispensable for starting and developing a good work relationship. However, it needs time and a dynamic that demands commitment from all the parties involved. Although tenure and professional and academic training are important, personal mutual knowledge has the greatest impact on the development of trust. This aspect is highlighted by managers and subordinates, who identify knowledge of personal and family circumstances as a key element in generating and developing trusting relationships. It is precisely the manager's and subordinate's ability to talk about these subjects with each other that determines how trust levels are experienced. Lack of trust, in the managers' and subordinates' opinion, has a negative effect on productivity, with duplicated processes, delivery delays, etc.; and it also affects the organization's talent development and retention because the subordinates are demotivated. Lack of trust does not develop human capital for the company.

Cultural variables also contribute to the model's explanatory framework. This study confirms for Colombia what was already said in the GLOBE study and then underscored by Salgado (2005): there is a marked individualism but a family collectivism. In other words, collectivism is very strong if the endogroup consists of family and close friends but, beyond that, individualism predominates. This also explains the strong role that personal knowledge and the establishment of bonds of friendship between managers and subordinates, already mentioned earlier, play in generating and developing trust.

The quantitative data for Colombia show a higher correlation than the complete model between subordinate trust in the manager and organizational citizen behaviors (OCB), which would confirm for Colombia what was originally pointed out by Salgado and Chaparro (2006): the role of trust in the manager as a predictor of these behaviors. This in turn points a way in which human talent management can design strategies that foster subordinates' trust in managers and, by this means, increase organizational citizenship behaviors.

Research on the role of human talent management in Colombia shows an evolution toward a more strategic role (Calderón et al., 2010). In order to fulfill this role, and taking into account the results of this study, certain behaviors can be encouraged, developing the skills that are required to establish trusting relationships and stimulate corporate cultures that allow development of these skills. In this sense, taking into account the impact of managers' behaviors in building trust, the challenge of management training mentioned by Calderón et al. (2010) becomes even more pressing, particularly in a culture such as Colombia's, where power distance seems to leave the initiative in the hands of those in hierarchically higher places. Likewise, a new and deeper look may help design internal communication strategies, taking into account how they affect trust generation and, therefore, labor relations. These are not confined to communication campaigns and policies, but also include awareness that it is the interpersonal communication skills which determine the quality of these relationships and the consequences for the organization's productivity.

Although we sought to obtain a sample of manager-subordinate relationships that was representative of Colombia, most of the participants live in Bogotá, the country's capital. If the sample were to be expanded to include other parts of the country, it might be possible to introduce microcultural variables that would enrich this study's results. One issue that is barely mentioned in this study is the role of gender in building trusting relationships between manager and subordinate. Although it is true that the focus group participants and the experts say that it does not play a decisive role, participants have also said that it is easier to develop trust with male managers. Given the growing number of women in management positions, it is necessary to determine the existence of these perceptions, their causes, and their consequences. It is also necessary to establish whether there are differences in the strategies used by men and women to generate and maintain trust in professional relationships.

References

Alta Consejería para la Reintegración (n.d.). *Proceso DDR en Colombia*. Retrieved on 9.8.11 from www.reintegracion.gov.co/Es/proceso_ddr/Paginas/balance.aspx.

Angulo, A.S.J., Zarama, V., Rozo, W. & Burgos, A. (2009). ¿En qué está la Paz? Cifras del conflicto armado, April 24. Retrieved on April 12, 2012 from http://cinep.pasosdejesus. org/node/673.

Banco de La República (2001). *Reporte del Emisor*, Mejía Margarita María (ed.), January, no. 20, Bogotá. www.banrep.gov.co/documentos/publicaciones/pdf/20.pdf.

Bernardi, R.A. & Guptill, S.T. (2008). Social desirability response bias, gender, and factors influencing organizational commitment: An international study. *Journal of Business Ethics*, 81:797–809.

Calderón, G. (2008). *Aproximación a un modelo de gestión humana que agregue valor a la empresa colombiana*. Manizales: Universidad Nacional de Colombia.

Calderón, G., Naranjo, J.C. & Álvarez, C.M. (2007). La gestión humana en Colombia: Características y tendencias de la práctica y de la investigación. *Estudios Gerenciales*, 23: 39–64.

Calderón, G., Naranjo, J.C. & Álvarez, C.M. (2008). *Estrategia empresarial y gestión humana en empresas colombianas*. Bogotá: Universidad Nacional de Colombia – Unibiblos.

Calderón, G., Naranjo, J.C. & Álvarez, C.M. (2010). Gestión humana en la empresa colombiana: sus características, retos y aportes. Una aproximación integral. *Cuadernos de Administración*, 23: 13–36.

Cuéllar, M.M. (2000). *Colombia: un proyecto inconcluso. Valores, instituciones y capital social* (vols. I and II). Bogotá: Universidad Externado de Colombia.

DANE (2010). Anuario Estadístico de la CEPAL. www.dane.gov.co/daneweb_V09/index. php?option=com_content&view=article&id=993%3Aanuario-estadistico-de-la-ccepal&catid=101%3Acuentas-ambientales&Itemid=1.

Encuesta Nacional Valores. (2006). *Nuestra identidad. Estudio Colombiano de Valores*. Bogotá: Raddar.

Guerrero, M. (2009). El liderazgo sale a relucir. *La Nota Económica*, April, p. 1.

Hofstede, G. (2001). *Dimensiones culturales*. Retrieved on 5.6.11 from www.geert-hofstede.com/ colombia.html.

IDMC, Internal Displacement Monitoring Centre (2009). *Colombia: Government Response Improves but Still Fails to Meet Needs of Growing IDP Population*. Retrieved on 9.8.11 from www.internal-displacement.org/8025708F004CE90B/(httpCountries)/CB6FF99A94F70AE D802570A7004CEC41?OpenDocument&expand=3&link=11.3&count=10000#11.3.

Konovsky, M.A., Villanueva, C. & O'Leary, B. (2001). *Further Developments of a Social Exchange Model of Organizational Citizenship Behavior*. Document presented at the 2001 Meetings of the Latin American Research Consortium, Monterrey, Mexico.

Latinobarómetro (2007). Informe Anual 2007. www.latinobarometro.org/latino/LATContenidos. jsp.

Latinobarómetro (2009). Informe Anual 2009. www.latinobarometro.org/latino/LATContenidos. jsp.

Ocampo, J. (1997). *Historia Básica de Colombia*, 7th ed.. Bogotá: Plaza & Janes Editores.

Ogliastri, E., McMillen, C., Altschul, C., Arias, M.E., Bustamante, C., Dávila, C., Dorfman, P., Ferreira dela Coletta, M., Fimmen, C., Ickis, J. & Martinez, S. (1999). Cultura y liderazgo organizacional en diez países de América Latina. El estudio GLOBE. *Academia Revista Latinoamericana de Administración*, 22: 29–57.

Ogliastri, E., Ruiz, J. & Martínez, I. (2005). Human resource management in Colombia. In M. Elvira & A. Dávila (eds), *Managing Human Resources in Latin America: An Agenda for International Leaders*. London and New York: Routledge, pp. 165–177.

Patti, J. & Cepeda, A. (2007). Citizenship competencies in Colombia: Learning from policy and practice. *Conflict Resolution Quarterly*, 25: 109–125.

Santos, E. (2009). *Colombia día a día: Una cronología de 15.000 años*. Bogotá: Editorial Planeta.

Salgado, E. (2005) *La confianza en Colombia. Un estudio sobre la relación entre confianza y participación en asociaciones voluntarias*. Bogotá: Ediciones Uniandes.

Salgado, E. & Chaparro, M.P. (2006) Antecedentes de los comportamientos ciudadanos en la organización. Un estudio desarrollado en Colombia. *Cuadernos de Administración*, 19: 57–79.

Sepúlveda, P., Vaca, P. & Fracica, G. (2009) Percepción del crecimiento y la diversificación en emprendimientos bogotanos: Para reflexionar. *Estudios Gerenciales*, 25: 77–105.

World Values Survey(1981–2008) Official Aggregate v.20090901, 2009. World Values Survey Association (www.worldvaluessurvey.org). Aggregate File Producer: ASEP/JDS, Madrid.

11 Manager–Subordinate Trust Relationships in China

CHUCK (WEI) HE

Introduction

> China is a sickly, sleeping giant. But when she awakens, the world will tremble.
>
> Napoleon Bonaparte (1803)

This quote from Napoleon Bonaparte reflects, to a certain degree, the worries of the Western world. In the past 30 years, China has undergone a remarkable change in business. The country has experienced a transformation from a planned economy to a market economy, from debt receiver to the largest debt owner, and from self-sufficiency to being one of the major players in the world market. This change also impacted on people's daily lives. China is a collectivist country, characterized by informal groups (Davies, 1995). Heavily influenced by Confucian philosophy, Chinese society emphasizes "wu lun," the five cardinal relationships in Chinese society: emperor–minister, father–son, husband–wife, elder brother–younger brother, and friend–friend. Except for friend–friend, the cardinal relationships are related to power distance in Western literature. People from upper levels have more power than people from lower levels. Individuals must conform and accept their role in society and behave appropriately. As a result, Chinese society can be likened to a large family, structured in different orders. People in this family trust and take care of each other. Thus, trust is one of the essences of this family, which implies an aspiration toward a conflict-free and group-oriented system of social relations (Buttery & Leung, 1998). With the evolution of Chinese society, some relationships are losing strength, while others have been deeply transformed. For example, the relationship between emperor and minister has become the relationship between manager and subordinate.

Although the evolution of relationships may impact on trust among the Chinese, it is less clear how much the role of trust in China will change. In this chapter, we start with a short account of historical developments in China, together with a description of the contemporary institutional environment, in particular, the educational, legal, and social systems, and an overview of the current economic and social context. We then present a summary of human resource management practices and developments and preferred leadership styles in the organizational context. Subsequently, we move to the substantive area of trust. Extant literature on multiple aspects of trust relationships in the workplace context in China are reviewed before presenting our empirical results. The chapter concludes with a discussion of some of the main results obtained in the context of the extant literature and highlights potential implications for management and leadership practice, along with potential avenues for future research.

Highlights of Manager–Subordinate Trust in China

- The Chinese do not have as much variation in antecedents and outcomes of trust relationships as those in the Western context.
- It is interesting that China is experiencing the transformation from planned economy to market economy, so the trust mechanism mixes the traditional Chinese style and Western one.
- Identified by collectivism, the Chinese participants in our study tend to trust within certain groups, which are guanxi networks.
- Relevant positions in guanxi networks determine whether subordinates can enjoy certain privileges and managers can easily gain trust.
- In the same way, relevant positions in guanxi networks may make managers or subordinates more willing to take risks and trust the counter party.

Historical Perspective

China is one of the world's oldest civilizations and is regarded as the oldest continuous civilization (Jervis, 2009). The term China originated from Cin, a Persian name for the Chinese pottery imported by Europe. The official names of China varied from dynasty to dynasty. China has been the official name since the Qing Dynasty. China has the longest continuous culture, surviving from ancient times: its history can be traced back 8000 years. China was among the few civilizations which invented writing. It has gone through the primitive, slavery, feudal, partial capitalist, and socialist stages. China was very influential until its last feudal dynasty, the Qing Dynasty, when it became weak and was defeated by many countries. Consequently, some of its land, such as Hong Kong and Macau, was acquired by other countries.

In 1912, the National Party (also called Kuomintang, KMT) overthrew the Qing Dynasty, marking the end of feudal society. However, there was no peace after that. China experienced massive chaos during that period: the two world wars and civil war. In 1949, the Communist Party defeated the National Party and established the People's Republic of China.

With an area of about 9.6 million square kilometers, it ranges from plateaus and mountains in the west to lower lands in the east. China has a population of 1.6 billion—that is, 22 percent of the world's population. China has adopted a one-child policy, in which each family can have only one child, so the real population may exceed 1.6 billion. Most Chinese live in the coastal area, reflecting the economic development in those areas. China has 56 ethnic groups, with more than 90 percent of the population being Han. Even after several wars, each group maintains its own unique culture and customs.

The dominating philosophy is that created between 551 and 479 BC by Confucius, the well-known Chinese thinker and social philosopher. It is deeply embedded in Chinese society and has established relatively stable values and principles which guide proper behavior and interpersonal relationships (Jia *et al.*, 2005).

However, China did not experience an industrial revolution and it weakened in the nineteenth century. In the late nineteenth century, China was invaded by several countries. After that, China experienced international chaos until the end of the Second World War in 1945. The Chinese economy was heavily damaged by its civil wars, which led to the overthrow of Imperial rule. As a result, amidst the aftermath of the civil war, the newly established Republic faced the arduous task of restoring normal life and reinvigorating industry. During the next 30 years, the Chinese government worked hard to bring the Chinese out of poverty. This effort was guided by actions from the former Soviet Union, the most powerful communist country at that time, and was successful in raising most peasants out of poverty to a level of subsistence. It was also aligned with Confucius' philosophy in terms of equality. However, this situation did not last for long. Afraid of class struggle, Mr. Mao Zedong, Chairman of China, launched the Cultural Revolution, aiming at giving opportunities to peasants to express themselves. During the Cultural Revolution, everyone could stand up to criticize others, with the result that many people suffered severe persecution. In the end, the Chinese were more preoccupied with fighting each other than with economic development.

The Cultural Revolution lasted for ten years and caused serious damage to China. For instance, from 1957 to 1976, the average wage in China remained almost unchanged. Many basic goods were under supplied or rationed. During that period, the Chinese did not trust each other and even amused themselves by putting others in jail.

In 1978, President Deng Xiaoping decided to adopt an open policy. Since then, China has maintained annual growth rates above 10 percent, ahead of all other countries in the world (China Statistics Bureau). By 2010, China had overtaken Japan as the world's second largest economy, surpassed only by the United States.

Institutional Context

Economic Context

In 2010, China overtook Japan as the world's second largest economy, with a GDP of over US$5800 billion. However, China's GNI per capita of only US$ 3735 puts it in ninety-seventh place (Table 11.1). The big gap reflects the mismatch between overall and individual wealth: China is still having problems in transferring national wealth to its people. Since 2000, a lot of Chinese companies have invested abroad, with an annual growth rate over 30 percent. Most mergers are state-owned enterprises (SOEs) and are concentrated in the energy sector, with over US$ 40 billion in 2009 and 2010. However, a number of private companies have stepped onto the world stage. For instance, in the last ten years, TCL acquired Thomson in France, Lenovo acquired IBM in the US, and Geely acquired Volvo in Sweden. There have also been some failures: Saic Group failed in its attempt to buy SsanYong, and PingAn was unable to acquire Fortis.

Table 11.1 Statistics of the Chinese economy

GDP (2010)	US$ 5800 billion
Growth	10.3%
Ranking	2
GDP per capita (2009)	US$ 3735
Ranking	97
Industry composition (2009)	Agriculture: 10.6%
	Industry: 46.8%
	Services: 42.6%
Exports (2010)	US$ 1578 billion
Imports (2010)	US$ 1395 billion
Foreign exchange reserves (2010)	US$ 2847 billion

Social Context

China has a one-child policy. Each couple can only have one child, except for families with disabled children and those living in rural areas. The total fertility rate fell from 36 percent in 1949 to 14 percent in 2008. However, due to its large size, China is still the world's most populated country. China promoted a social security system in the 1950s. However, until the late 1980s, it only covered urban residents, who accounted for less than 20 percent of the population. The current social security system covers pensions, unemployment benefits, basic medical insurance, sick leave, and maternity leave. But even now, the social security system covers less than 25 percent of population.

Political Landscape

China has never been a democratic country. During the period of dynasties in China's history, until 1912, all monarchs were either hereditary or took the throne by force, never by democratic elections. After the communist victory in the Chinese civil war, the People's Republic of China, modern China, was established on October 1, 1949, heralding a new era for China. The new China is a single-party socialist republic, with power under the leadership of the Communist Party. Although there are eight so-called "democratic parties" within the Communist Party of China, they seldom make any noise. There are no legal political opposition groups. According to the Chinese Constitution, the National People's Congress is the country's highest authority. However, the Constitution states that the National People's Congress is also under the leadership of the Communist Party.

Since the return of Hong Kong and Macau to China, those two regions have adopted special social systems which are different from those on mainland China. They follow their own legal systems and have a limited democracy.

Educational System

In mainland China, the Law on Nine-Year Compulsory Education, which took effect in 1986, states that all citizens must attend school for at least nine years, usually from the age of 6–7 until age 15. All compulsory public education is run and financed by the Ministry of Education. Besides these public schools, the government has allowed private schools since the early 1980s. However, these private schools were initially for foreigners, not for Chinese citizens. Education in China is structured in four levels: primary school (6–12 years, compulsory); junior school (12–15 years, compulsory); senior high school or vocational school (15–18 years, not compulsory); and university or college (18–22 years, not compulsory). All students must take the National Examinations in order to attend university or college. Males and females have equal rights in the compulsory education system.

HR Practice

In 1979, three years after Mao's death, Mr. Deng Xiaoping took power and decided to give priority to economic development. He proposed the "open policy" and implemented the transformation from a planned economy to a market economy. Because there were no existing models that could guide him, Mr. Deng innovatively put forward two principles: "Fly by the seat of one's pants" and "No matter if it is a white cat or a black cat, a cat that can catch rats is a good cat." These two principles encouraged some Chinese to leave their hometowns and go to coastal cities in search of opportunities. Their actions challenged the traditional belief that Chinese only trust those who have certain social and kindred relationships with them, such as "wu lun" because now they must do business with strangers with whom they have no previous connection. At the same time, a large number of multinational companies entered China and several private companies were established, which were not allowed before. The Chinese now had three options when looking for a job: State-owned enterprises (SOEs), foreign-owned enterprises (FOEs), and privately owned enterprises (POEs).

Generally speaking, FOEs offer higher status and better career prospects (Schmidt, 2011). For example, they offer employees global training, experience outside China, higher pay, and a clear career path. A fresh college graduate may reach the top executive level in China in their late thirties or early forties. In addition, a survey conducted by the Corporate Executive Board (2011) showed that employees of multinationals are much more satisfied with their work and prospects. Employees working in FOEs have a clear boundary between work and family. For instance, they seldom hold meetings out of office hours andthey do not know much about their colleagues' family members.

SOEs offer employees job security and a sense of belonging. For example, most SOEs provide various kinds of welfare facilities, such as kindergartens, daycare, and medical insurance. In addition, they also provide "Hu Kou," the system of residency permits, to non-local college students. Hu Kou is a household registration record which officially identifies a person as a resident in an area and includes information such as name, parents, spouse, and date of birth. People with Hu Kou will enjoy certain privileges, such as free schooling and medical benefits. People without Hu Kou cannot send their children to local schools or must pay premium tuition rates. Thus, the Hu Kou provided by SOEs is very attractive to young, non-local college graduates. But Hu Kou is also associated with tenure. It means that graduates must serve the company for a minimum number of years. The employees of SOEs are like a large family. Everyone knows each other's family members. They often organize family gatherings and visit each other on holidays.

POEs in China do not offer comfortable working environments like the FOEs, or stability like the SOEs. However, it offers employees more space to grow. For example, some employees have the dream of being listed on the second board in the stock market, which will make them millionaires.

Leadership Styles

Relationships in China have traditionally been characterized by having a high level of power distance and collectivism. The essence is to maintain harmony within the large family, including the authority of the upper class and reciprocity among group members. It is also reflected in hierarchical relationships. Chen *et al.* (2002) studied the commitment of Chinese employees and concluded that Chinese employees were more attached to individual leaders than to organizations. This aligns with other findings about Chinese relationships. The Chinese tend to focus on their own teams, rather than on the organization as a whole. Accentuated by the high power distance, everyone has their responsibilities in different social groups. Within an organization or a team, if everyone fulfills his/her obligation, the team will work well and harmony will be achieved. Another symbol of harmony is the high uncertainty avoidance. Respecting leaders and abiding by rules are very common in hierarchical relationships in China.

Leadership styles in China also reflect the country's economic development. Before economic reform, the leadership style was heavily influenced by Confucian philosophy, which was characterized by being kind, benevolent, and righteous. Managers were not directly responsible for the final financial outcome because everything was planned and determined by the government—for example, how many units would be produced each day and how much they would cost. So, at that time, it was very important to maintain harmonious relationships. This was also consistent with the Communist ideology, which included loyalty to the party and wholehearted service to the people. After the economic reforms of 1979, FOEs and POEs entered the market and competed with the SOEs. This not only changed market rules but also introduced modern management philosophies in China. Tsui *et al.* (2004) explored various leadership styles in China and identified the heterogeneity in leadership styles in contemporary China. They argued that the behavioral dimensions of leadership styles in China are quite similar to those in the Western context. The relationship-related dimensions show differences, due to the different cultural context. This means that the Chinese tend to use universal behaviors to achieve objectives, while they will use Chinese-specific behaviors to maintain relationships.

Previous literature findings also align with the results of the interviews and focus groups which form part of this study. The interviews show that the term "leader" is always related to trust. If people do not trust their "leaders," they will not perceive them as "leaders." According to the interviewees, they trust those who can illustrate a whole picture and give constant direction. They also admit that trust is a perception or feeling, which will give them confidence even in times of uncertainty. In terms of the characteristics of good leaders, interviewees mentioned two interesting features. On one hand, they want their managers to disclose sensitive and accurate information, even if this invades other people's privacy. On the other hand, they want their managers to show integrity and transparency. These two features seem to be in conflict. They attribute this phenomenon to a "not in my yard" strategy. Thus, leadership in China is expected to be demanding and controlling, which reflects its origin in the planned economy. However, at the same time, people expect their leaders to care for them.

Literature Review on Trust in China

After Doney *et al.*'s article (1998) in the special edition of the *Academy of Management Review*, a lot of studies were undertaken to understand the influence of culture on trust relationships. Studies on trust in interpersonal relationships have been very fruitful in China during the past two decades. For example, in the Chinese context, trust was studied in order to understand leadership, teamwork, innovation, and conflicts (e.g. Atuahene-Gima & Li, 2006; Hui *et al.*, 2005; Jin & Ling, 2005; Li *et al.*, 2006). These studies showed that, in the context of trust, subordinates tend to be more innovative, to be more willing to contribute and help others, and to have a higher level of commitment. These findings suggest that trust is closely related to positive outcomes, such as in-role performance, job attitude, low turnover rates, organizational commitment, and organizational citizenship behaviors (Chen & Francesco, 2003; Fey *et al.*, 2004; Hui *et al.*, 2005; Jin & Ling, 2005; Law *et al.*, 2001). Findings from these studies have enriched our knowledge of the trust development process and show no inconsistency with findings from studies performed in the Western context.

Scholars in Chinese studies agreed that trust exits in exchange relationships and is developed by people. Managers are initiators in trust relationships. If subordinates trust their managers, they will engage in extra or in-role performance.

Studies on trust in China have also analyzed trust development at different levels: the organizational level (e.g. Chao *et al.*, 2004; Huff & Kelley, 2003; Jin & Ling, 2005; Wong *et al.*, 2006) and the individual level (e.g. Atuahene-Gima & Li, 2002; Yuan, 2002). The study by Chao *et al.* (2004) found that the management system will impact employees' trust in organizations in China. Some studies in China showed that trust played an essential role in hierarchical relationships. Tsui *et al.* (2004) studied various leadership styles in China and concluded that the manager's leadership style will lead to subordinates' trust or distrust. A study by Hui *et al.* (2005) showed that trust, characterized by Leader Member Exchange (LMX), will mediate relationships between transformational leadership, task performance, and OCB. Other studies also show that trust is a crucial element of leadership effectiveness in China (e.g. Li *et al.*, 1999). They all proposed that trust can lead to leadership effectiveness. In other words, trust mechanism is similar both in the Chinese and in the Western context.

Although researchers have made great progress in research on trust in the Chinese context, there are few studies on the Chinese scale of trust. Most research on trust in China used a single-item direct measure of trust (Jung & Avolio, 2000; Yuan, 2002). To our knowledge, only Ding and Ng (2007) tested McAllister's (1995) scale of trust in the Chinese context and they concluded that the two-dimensional structure of McAllister's trust scale could be applied in that context. However, the question is whether trust means the same thing in China. In order to further explore what trust means in hierarchical relationships in China, we first interviewed 20 Chinese MBA graduates from a leading business school in China, either by telephone or in face-to-face meetings. During the interviews, we asked them to list three statements that best described trust in work relations. Because trust is a very popular concept in China, it was not necessary for us to explain the definition of trust. In order to limit participants' answers to the scope of our study, we asked them to limit their statements to work situations. We extracted 60 items from their statements. Then we categorized the 60 items into nine groups.

We then asked another group of 46 Chinese to rank these nine items from 1 to 9 (1 for the one that describes least the characteristics of trust and 9 for the one that describes them best). No repeated numbers were allowed in the ranking, meaning that each number could only be used once. Finally, we averaged the scores. Harmony appeared to have the highest score among the nine items, followed by transparency and happiness (Table 11.2). The harmony dimension also reflects the collectivistic character prevailing in China.

Personal Factors in Hierarchical Trusting Relationships

As illustrated by several studies, there are a number of factors that may influence trust during the initial stage of hierarchical trust relationships (e.g. Creed & Miles, 1996; Griffin, 1967; Larzelere & Huston, 1980; McAllister, 1995; Whitener *et al.*, 1998; Zucker, 1986). The results from our interviews showed the same findings. Similarity is among the top factors mentioned by the interviewees, although it could apply to several things, such as age, nature of previous companies, gender, etc. The Delphi panel experts mentioned that the young generation tends not to trust older generations (people in their fifties) because they think that they lack knowledge about how to manage modern organizations. As one participant mentioned, "I can hardly see the career development potential for young people in several organizations. Those so-called senior people are not so capable. The only reason for them to stay is their tenure. You know, they are not trustworthy." On the other hand, the older generation tends not to trust the young generation because they think that the young generation dreams of achievement without effort. As illustrated by one participant:

Table 11.2 Items of trust in work relations

	Items of trust in work relations	Average
1	Harmony	6.95
2	Transparency	6.16
3	Happiness	6.14
4	Mutual commitment	6.00
5	Identification	5.91
6	Believing attitude	4.19
7	Self-protection	3.42
8	Personal benefit	2.91
9	Power	2.30

Generation Y is not easy to be managed. I can see that they want to do things beyond their capability. However, they do not know that they cannot achieve that. They always dream to succeed in a short period. In other words, they lack patience for success. I do not trust that they will have things done.

People coming from the same kind of organization (SOE, FOE, POE) tend to have a higher level of trust. They think that the other person understands their situation and it is not difficult to communicate with them. For example, one interviewee stated, "I work in FOEs only. I never trust people from SOEs. They use different ways to make their work done. Some of them never write emails, but call you directly. I do not think that I trust them." Regarding gender difference, most participants agree with a Chinese saying: gender mix will increase productivity.

In addition to the Delphi panel, we conducted four focus groups (1.5 hours each). There were two pairs, each consisting of a manager and his/her direct subordinate. They came from the training, banking, IT, and textile industries. All participants had a university degree. All managers were male and there was only one female subordinate.

Most of our Chinese focus group participants believed that trust is setting one's heart at rest. As one participant mentioned, "Trust is confidence. If you ask one person to do something and you have confidence in him or her, then you trust him or her on this thing." They mentioned that time is absolutely crucial for trust relationships. The more time they have known each other or worked together, the more knowledge they have about the other party. Although people can pretend for a while, they will eventually reveal their true selves. Based on knowledge about others, which may include working style, ability, personality, and past record, they would even find justification for harm done by the other party. As mentioned by one participant, "As distance tests a horse's strength, so time reveals a person's heart. Even my long-time friends do something bad to me, I know that he or she has their own excuse and reasons." Besides the obvious effect of time, time can build affective bonds in trust relationships. China is ranked high in the collectivism dimension proposed by Hofstede (1983). Consequently, the Chinese tend to regard nurturing the relationship as a moral obligation. If you belong to a certain group in China, you do not need to establish trust, but only do things to reinforce the trust. As illustrated by one participant:

To be in the right group is very important. If you are in the wrong group, you will not expect promotion or increased salary. Your future in the organization is tightly associated with your group. Both you and your group are in the same boat.

In addition, respect is very important in China, which aligns with the higher level of power distance in China. Especially in hierarchical relationships in China, subordinates tend not to fight with their managers in public. The patriarchal management system is reflected in China's high level of power distance. Some participants stated that they used to call their direct report "teacher" or "mentor," rather than "manager" in the past.

Contextual Factors in Hierarchical Trusting Relationships

Our Delphi experts believe that trust in hierarchical relationships in China exists at different levels: individual and organizational. In China, managers are usually not regarded as representatives or agents of organizations, but as representatives of teams. This means that Chinese employees work for their managers, not for organizations. As some comments from experts illustrated: "It is quite common in China that a manager with the whole team jump to another company. It rarely happens in the Western world." "The horizontal communication among different teams never goes well in Chinese companies because most people only think of the benefit within their teams, not the organizations." Interestingly, if managers cannot give what subordinates want, this may impact on subordinates' trust toward organizations, not toward managers. Subordinates tend to think that the trustworthy managers have tried their best, but fail. These experts also argued that professional relationships in China often mix both work and personal situations. One expert mentioned:

> In China, managers often invite their subordinates to join family gatherings on holidays, which rarely happens in the Western world. Subordinates also regard it an honor if managers show up on important occasions and say something in front of their relatives.

Experts also mentioned several contextual factors that may impact on trust in hierarchical relationships in China: the nature of the company, company size and culture, and the national culture.

Nature of the Company

In SOEs, employees tend to trust their direct managers. In FOEs, employees tend to trust organizations because FOEs usually have a consolidated management system and the top regional managers tend to rotate every few years. In POEs, trust varies depending on the manager's leadership style. If top executives adopt a transactional leadership style, subordinates tend not to trust their managers. If top executives show care for their subordinates, subordinates tend to have a higher level of trust. As illustrated by one expert: "Since SOEs, FOEs, and POEs have different management systems, they have different trust mechanisms."

Company Size

In small companies, people tend to know each other. Sometimes, organization norms, such as gossip, will provide an important communication channel. People also tend to work together or closely and have more interaction. They tend to trust each other more if they have to work together. In large companies, there are several teams or business units, and it is the teams that are supposed to work together, not the individuals. Consequently, people in the same team have a higher level of trust, while people from different teams have a relatively lower level of trust.

Company Culture

Company culture was perceived as having an impact on employees' trust. If the company culture is dominated by hierarchy, and people have clear objectives and goals, employees tend to have a lower level of trust. They may think that they lack space to make full use of their capabilities and knowledge. However, if the company culture encourages sharing and teamwork, employees tend to have a higher level of trust. Employees may think that they are trusted and would like to recip-rocate by contributing to organizational effectiveness. As one expert explained: "If the organization gives people freedom to do things, employees tend to trust the organization. If the organization does not adopt a performance-based management system, employees tend to create their own groups and trust members from the same group."

National Culture

In terms of cultural dimensions, the experts in our panel discussion mentioned one dimension that may have a big impact on trust in hierarchical relationships in China: collectivism. The interpretation is mixed. There is a famous paradox expressed in a Chinese saying: one Chinese is a dragon; three Chinese are worms. This seems to contradict the high level of collectivism. Although Chinese society can be described as collectivistic, this kind of collectivism only exists within the group (guanxi networks).

Antecedents and Outcomes of Hierarchical Trusting Relationships

Both managers and subordinates view trust as an exchange relationship. During the interviews, subordinates view managers' ways of treating people and capability as essential to trust relationships. As one subordinate recalled:

I had an extremely trustworthy manager before. He is very visionary and sees things we can never imagine. He always leads the team to success. However, he is so humble at the same time, not only to people above him, within the team, but to everyone, even to the cleaning staff. In other words, he is not only a capable person, but a good person.

Another subordinate stated: "I only trust and follow a manager with integrity. Other-wise, he or she will lead you to nowhere." One manager stated:

Trust means getting things done. If my subordinates cannot get things done, I will not trust them. In addition, my subordinates must be loyal to me. Otherwise, I will kick them out of my team. You know, I must take all responsibilities if they blow it all.

All managers and subordinates agree that trust relationships can generate some good outcomes, such as good modes of work, motivation, higher involvement, and proactive behaviors. As one interviewee stated:

If I trust my managers, I will have more motivation to work for them. I would like to contribute more, even beyond my job description, if I trust my manager. If I trust my manager, I will enjoy working every day.

Figure 11.1 provides a diagrammatic summary of the major antecedents and conse-quences of trust in the manager–subordinate relationship arising from the qualita-tive data generated by our focus groups and expert panels in China.

One of the most unique non-Western concepts in the Chinese context is guanxi, which refers to informal relationships in China (Davies, 1995). Chinese people are connected through guanxi. For people in the same guanxi network, we use the term

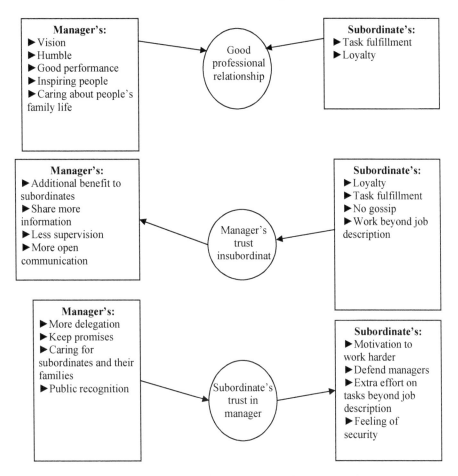

Figure 11.1 Antecedents and outcomes of trust in hierarchical relationships

in-guanxi members, and those who do not belong to the same guanxi network are called out-guanxi members. In-guanxi members are supposed to help, support, and take care of each other (Xin & Pearce, 1996). Only in-guanxi members can enjoy the advantages of the network. In work relationships, subordinates expect more benefits, such as bonus allocation, promotion opportunities, and resources, from in-guanxi managers (Law *et al.*, 2000). They also expect more protection from managers (Wong & Tam, 2000); in-guanxi subordinates have more positive expectations about the behavior of their in-guanxi managers. Consequently, the strength of guanxi networks should be positively related to subordinates' trust in managers. Following the same logic, if in-guanxi subordinates engage in organizational citizenship behaviors, in-guanxi managers may not regard them as extra-role behaviors, but as a kind of in-role behavior determined by guanxi networks. As a result, such behavior may not improve managers' impression of in-guanxi subordinates. However, if out-guanxi subordinates engage in organizational citizenship behaviors, this may improve managers' impression of them and may influence managers' decisions to increase their trust in those subordinates.

In our quantitative studies, we included guanxi as a variable in our trust model. We measured guanxi from two perspectives: the managers' and the subordinates'. We proposed direct and indirect effects of guanxi on both variables and relationships. The results show that guanxi from the managers' perspective is significantly higher than from the subordinates' perspective. It suggests that guanxi is not symmetric in dyadic relationships: the fact that I include you in my guanxi list does not necessarily guarantee that you will include me in your guanxi network. Second, guanxi contributes to each variable in the trust model by either enhancing or weakening its impact. In China, trust is also initiated by managerial trustworthy behaviors. However, those behaviors will interact with guanxi such that in-guanxi subordinates will perceive less managerial trustworthy behaviors than out-guanxi members, even if managers show the same amount of managerial trustworthy behaviors to both groups of subordinates. When subordinates make trust decisions, they take into consideration managerial trustworthy behaviors, the interaction between managerial trustworthy behaviors, and guanxi. Without the effects of guanxi, subordinates' trust in managers could lead them to engage in organizational citizenship behaviors. When guanxi is involved, subordinates will also consider guanxi as a criterion for engagement in extra-role activities, such as organizational citizenship behaviors, and do more to reciprocate trust relationships. When managers make decisions about whether to trust their subordinates or not, they will first observe their subordinates' behaviors.

In a similar way, managers will perceive subordinates' behaviors differently according to guanxi networks. They will perceive less organizational citizenship behaviors from in-guanxi members than from out-guanxi members. In addition to guanxi's interaction effect, it also contributes directly to managers' trust. Accordingly, managers' trust in subordinates is influenced by subordinates' organizational citizenship behaviors, the interaction between subordinates' organizational citizenship behaviors and guanxi, and guanxi itself. Finally, when managers show managerial trustworthy behaviors, they only consider the impact of guanxi, rather than their trust in their subordinates (Table 11.3).

Table 11.3 Non-standardized regression weights for the trust model in China

	STM	OCB	MTS	MTB
MTB	0.96***			
STM		0.31**		
OCB			0.99***	
MTS				0.24†
GS	0.15*	−0.13†		
GM			0.10*	0.22†
GSxMTB	−0.13*			
GMxOCB			−0.14*	

Notes
MTB = managerial trustworthy behavior, STM = subordinates' trust in managers, MTS = managers' trust in subordinates, OCB = organizational citizenship behavior.
GS refers to guanxi from the subordinates' perspective.
GM refers to guanxi from the managers' perspective.
GSxMTB refers to the interaction between GS and MTB.
GMxOCB refers to the interaction between GM and OCB.
*** refers to $p < 0.001$.
** refers to $p < 0.01$.
* refers to $p < 0.05$.
† refers to $p < 0.1$.

The Dynamics of Trust in Hierarchical Relationships

Trust relationships cannot be built in one day. It is always associated with time (Dirks & Ferrin, 2002). We got the same view from the interviews. The interviewees admitted that trust building is a function of time. If people have known each other for a long time, they tend to tolerate inappropriate behaviors by the other more than by people with whom they have less interaction. Even if the other party in a long-term relationship behaves in a manner contrary to trust, they try to find reasons for not breaking the relationship. However, people who have known each other for a short period tend to keep an eye on each other.

Specifically in hierarchical relationships in China, people's age, gender, education, past professional experience, and similarities play an important role in the initial contact because they are the only information that people have on each other. However, with time, people's decisions and behaviors are more important. With enough interaction, subordinates tend to have their own perception of managers. This means that, eventually, what managers say and do will determine the level of subordinates' trust. As one interviewee said:

> I do not believe one action from my manager, because even bad guys may have some moments of being good guys. It is true that everyone can do good things and bad things in their life. The question is how many good things he/she does and how many bad things he/she does and how much weight we give to those things. Only doing a small proportion of good things will not win my trust.

It is the same for managers. After a long time working with subordinates, managers will assess subordinates' aptitude, attitude, and performance. Of course, managers will pay attention to overall performance, not just one day's behavior. As one interviewee said:

> When I determine my level of trust toward my subordinate, I will consider several factors. I will obviously consider education and past experience. However, I will also give a lot of weight to my subordinates' performance and attitude. Performance is easy to measure; attitude is more difficult. I will look more at whether they are thinking proactively and helping others, taking into account a period of time, not just one day.

Even though managers and subordinates may have similar considerations for trust, the function is not the same. From interviews, we could see that, at the beginning of relationships, subordinates tend to be cautious about the relationship and have a minimum level of trust, or even no trust. On the other hand, managers tend to have a high level of trust toward subordinates and may reduce or increase the level depending on future interactions. Some interviewees attributed this phenomenon to their different positions in organizations. Managers are supposed to lead team members toward the desired performance. They must know how to delegate and allocate work to different people. Consequently, managers must take the risk and trust subordinates in the beginning. Subordinates are in a relatively passive position and wait for instructions from managers. As a result, it is not so necessary for them to initiate trust relationships with managers. This finding aligns with the proposals of Whitener *et al.* (1998).

Our quantitative data revealed some interesting insights about trust in hierarchical relationships in China. Comparing China with the overall results among the

18 countries, we find some similar patterns as well as some differences. Managerial trustworthy behaviors lead to a high level of subordinates' trust. This is similar to the situation of the overall model. However, subordinates' trust tends to lead to higher levels of subordinates' OCB, suggesting that Chinese subordinates tend to do more to reciprocate managers' behaviors. On observing subordinates' engagement in OCBs, Chinese managers tend to have a higher level of trust toward subordinates than in other countries. Our panel experts attributed this to the social network, more specifically referring to guanxi. As one expert stated: "If one person consistently does something good, either to me, the team, or the organization, I tend to think that he/she is my 'person'." As we mentioned before, people within the same guanxi network tend to trust each other. However, the trust comes not only from behaviors, but also from their belief in in-group members.

As the quantitative data showed, Chinese managers are more likely to trust their subordinates upon observing positive OCBs than the managers in the complete sample. Comparing with the complete model, the trust given by Chinese managers does not necessarily lead to more trustworthy behaviors. Data also revealed that Chinese subordinates are more willing to engage in OCBs if they trust their managers. But Chinese subordinates will not significantly increase their level of trust based purely on observation of managerial trustworthy behaviors. Lastly, in China, the effect of managers' trust toward their subordinates on their managerial trustworthy behaviors is not statistically significant (Table 11.4).

The Delphi panel experts agreed that the reciprocal model was applicable to China. However, they argued that other important factors might be missing from this model, which may have a bigger impact on trust relationships. One factor they mentioned is the managers' vision of the team. If he/she has the vision to lead the team to high performance, subordinates will be willing to put their future at risk and work for the manager. Another factor is context. If the overall culture within an organization is to encourage open communication and sharing, people tend to give honest feedback. Consequently, it is easier for people to establish trust in hierarchical relationships. Otherwise, people tend to distrust each other and always keep an eye on others. The Delphi panel experts further suggested that managers should take full responsibility for establishing a culture which will nurture trust relationships, reflecting arguments by scholars that managers are initiators of trust (Whitener *et al.*, 1998). Another aspect highlighted by the Delphi panel experts was the managers' and subordinates' personal factors. They argued that there were no universally accepted trustworthy behaviors or OCBs. The match between managers and subordinates was fundamental for establishing trust in hierarchical relationships. People have different criteria about what a good manager is and they will base their

Table 11.4 Standardized regression weights for the trust model in China and the overall sample

	OCB–>MTS	MTS–>MTB	MTB–>STM	STM–>OCB
China only	0.94**	0.26	0.91***	0.25**
Complete model	0.68**	0.34**	0.89**	0.08*

Notes
*** refers to $p < 0.001$.
** refers to $p < 0.01$.
* refers to $p < 0.05$.

perception of trust on such criteria. A manager perceived as trustworthy by one subordinate may not be perceived as trustworthy by another subordinate.

Another interesting point was brought to light by the Delphi panel experts. They argued that Chinese people tend to mix professional work and personal life. For example, Chinese subordinates will feel very proud if they manage to invite a high-ranking manager to attend their family gathering. If the manager speaks about them in public, they will feel that the manager keeps their "face," which refers to doing an action that you may think is not appropriate, but will earn or keep respect. As a result, they may have more emotional attachment to their managers. Partly due to the collectivism, Chinese subordinates may expect managers to protect their interests. In Western countries, the emotional attachment is not so strong. Employees tend to work for organizations, rather than individual managers. Consequently, Western subordinates may put more emphasis on watching managers' behaviors.

Discussion and Conclusions

The results of our study in China reflect some of the main findings in the extant literature. There is no doubt about the importance of trust. Specifically in China, trust is essential to harmonious relationships between a manager and a subordinate. Similar to the Western trust models, Chinese managers are also initiators in building trust relationships by showing managerial behaviors which are observed by subordinates. If subordinates view these behaviors as trustworthy, the likelihood that subordinates will trust their managers increases. If subordinates trust their managers, they may expect their efforts to be reciprocated in the future. This may lead subordinates to engage in more organizational citizenship behaviors. On observing organizational citizenship behaviors from their subordinates, managers may have a better impression of them and increase their trust in those subordinates. When managers trust their subordinates, they are willing to take more risks. As a result, they may show more managerial trustworthy behaviors to their subordinates. The distrusting relationship will follow the same logic. If managers do not show trustworthy behaviors, the level of subordinates' trust will decrease. Hence, subordinates will watch managers closely and be less willing to engage in OCBs. At the same time, managers may evaluate subordinates' aptitude and attitude by observing their engagement in OCBs. If they observe fewer OCBs from subordinates, they tend to decrease their level of trust in them and are not likely to show more managerial trustworthy behaviors. The trust development process in China is dynamic and reciprocal, but it is not symmetric. A manager trusting a subordinate does not mean that the subordinate will have the same level of trust in the manager at the same time.

Although the trust relationship in China follows the general trust model, certain cultural variables have a significant impact on the model. Both interviewees and Delphi panel experts highlight the existence of "guanxi" in hierarchical relationships. Their relative position in the guanxi network will influence people's perception of trust and their behaviors. Trust is also initiated by managerial trustworthy behaviors in China. However, those behaviors will interact with guanxi such that in-guanxi subordinates will perceive less managerial trustworthy behaviors than out-guanxi members, even if managers show the same amount of managerial trustworthy behaviors to both groups of subordinates. When subordinates make decisions to trust, they take into consideration managerial trustworthy behaviors, the interaction between managerial trustworthy behaviors, and guanxi. Without the effects of guanxi, subordinates' trust in managers could lead them to engage in organizational citizenship behaviors. When guanxi is involved, subordinates will also consider guanxi as a criterion for engaging in extra-role activities, such as organizational citizenship behaviors. When managers make decisions about whether or not to trust their subordinates, they will first observe their subordinates' behaviors. In a similar way to the previous case, managers will perceive subordinates' behaviors differently depending on the guanxi network. They will perceive less organizational citizenship behaviors from in-guanxi members than from out-guanxi members. Apart from the interaction effect of guanxi, guanxi also contributes directly to managers' trust. Therefore, managers' trust in subordinates is influenced by subordinates' organizational citizenship behaviors, the interaction between subordinates' organizational citizenship behaviors and guanxi, and guanxi itself. Finally, when managers show managerial trustworthy behaviors, they only consider the impact of guanxi, rather than their trust in their subordinates. The reciprocal model better illustrates the real situation of trust relationships in China.

Besides managerial trustworthy behaviors, several personal factors may also impact on trust relationships, such as similarities between a manager and a subordinate, gender, age, past experience, and reputation. However, with increasing time, these factors tend to have less influence on trust relationships. Contextual factors such as company size and company culture tend to impact on trust relationships. Different types of Chinese companies will foster different HR practices. HR practices in different companies can foster positive trust relationships or a negative atmosphere. Several studies have supported this view (e.g. Chao *et al.*, 2004; Yuan, 2002). Therefore, if an organization wants to promote trust relationships, it could start by analyzing its current culture and making action plans accordingly. It could start with a fair recruitment, selection, reward, and development system.

Our study provides several practical implications for expatriates who want to establish trust relationships with their Chinese subordinates. First, expatriates must become involved in Chinese subordinates' personal lives and join their guanxi networks. This is not easy for most expatriates, partly because of language and cultural differences. However, if expatriates become in-guanxi members, they will enjoy certain privileges even if they do not show a lot of trustworthy behaviors. Second, organizations could offer cultural training about guanxi to expatriates before sending them to China. This will increase expatriates' awareness of how Chinese interact with each other and how they are different from Western people. Our study also provides insights for Chinese who want to promote trust relationships within organizations. They must understand that their behaviors will be discounted by their positions in the guanxi network, so they must work harder to gain trust.

Although we attempt to capture a representative picture of trust in hierarchical relationships in China, several limitations may restrict the generalization of our study. The first limitation is the sample size. Most interviewees and the Delphi panel experts were college graduates. Thus, their view may not reflect the overall view from the majority of Chinese who do not have a college degree. Further studies could expand the scope to include more Chinese without college degrees. The second limitation is measurement. In our study, we used measurements from different sources—managers and subordinates—which may create confusion in causal relationships (Podsakoff *et al.*, 2003). Future research could study the ratings from the same source and compare results from managers and subordinates. Furthermore, trust relationships are dynamic, not static. Consequently, a longitudinal study should be conducted to explore the reciprocal nature of trust relationships.

References

Atuahene-Gima, K. & Li, H. (2002). When does trust matter? Antecedents and contingent effects of supervisee trust on performance in selling new products in China and the United States. *Journal of Marketing*, 66(3): 61–81.

Atuahene-Gima, K. & Li, H. (2006). The effects of formal controls on supervisee trust in the manager in new product selling: Evidence from young and inexperienced sales people in China. *Journal of Product Innovation Management*, 23(4): 342–358.

Buttery, E.A. & Leung, T.K. (1998). The difference between Chinese and Western negotiations. *European Journal of Marketing*, 32(3/4): 374–389.

Chao, C.C., Ya-Ru, C. & Xin, K. (2004). Guanxi practices and trust in management: A procedural justice perspective. *Organization Science*, 15(2): 200–209.

Chen, Z.X. & Francesco, A.M. (2003). The relationship between the three components of commitment and employee performance in China, *Journal of Vocational Behavior*, 62: 490.

Chen, Z.X., Tsui, A.S. & Farh, J.L. (2002). Loyalty to the supervisor versus organizational commitment: Relationships to employee performance in China. *Journal of Occupational and Organizational Psychology*, 75: 339–356.

Creed, W.D. & Miles, R.E. (1996). Trust in organizations: A conceptual framework linking organizational forms, managerial philosophies, and the opportunity costs of controls. In M.R. Kramer & R.T. Tyler (eds), *Trust in Organizations: Frontiers in Theory and Research*. Newbury Park, CA: Sage, pp. 16–38.

Davies, H. (1995). Interpreting guanxi: The role of personal connections in a high context transitional economy. In H. Davies (ed.), *China Business: Contexts and Issues*. Hong Kong: Longman.

Ding, Z.K. & Ng, F.F. (2007). Reliability and validity of the Chinese version of McAllister's Trust Scale. *Construction Management and Economics*, 25(11): 1107–1117.

Dirks, K.T. & Ferrin, D.L. (2002). Trust in leadership: Meta-analytic findings and implications for organizational research. *Journal of Applied Psychology*, 87: 611–628. Doney, P.M., Canon, J. P. & Mullen, M.R. (1998). Understanding the influence of national culture on the development of trust. *Academy of Management Review*, 23: 601–620.

Fey, C.E., Pavlovskaya, A. & Tang, N. (2004). A comparison of human resource management in Russia, China, and Finland. *Organizational Dynamics*, 33(1): 79–97.

Griffin, K. (1967). The contribution of studies of source credibility to a theory of interpersonal trust in the communication process. *Psychological Bulletin*, 68: 104–120.

Hofstede, G. (1983). The cultural relativity of organizational practices and theories. *Journal of International Business Studies*, 14: 75–90.

Huff, L. & Kelley, L. (2003). Levels of organizational trust in individualist versus collectivist societies: A seven-nation study. *Organization Science*, 14(1): 81–90.

Hui, W., Law, K.S., Hackett, R.D., Duanxu, W. & Zhen Xiong, C. (2005). Leader-member exchange as a mediator of the relationship between transformational leadership and followers' performance and organizational citizenship behavior. *Academy of Management Journal*, 48(3): 420–432.

Jia, W., Wang, G.G., Ruona, W.E. A. & Rojewski, J.W. (2005). Confucian values and the implications for international HRD. *Human Resource Development International*, 8(3): 311–326.

Jervis, N. (2009). What is a Culture? *World Communities*, the University of the State of New York, May.

Jin, X.H. & Ling, F.Y. Y. (2005). Model for fostering trust and building relationships in China's construction industry. *Journal of Construction Engineering & Management*, 131(11): 1224–1232.

Jung, D.I. & Avolio, B.J. (2000). Opening the black box: An experimental investigation of the mediating effects of trust and value congruence on transformational and transactional leadership. *Journal of Organizational Behavior*, 21: 949–964.

Larzelere, R. E. & Huston, T.L. (1980). The dyadic trust scale: Toward understanding interpersonal trust in close relationships. *Journal of Marriage and the Family*, 42: 595–604.

Law, K.S., Lee, C., Farh, L. & Pillutla, M. (2001). Organizational justice perceptions of employees in China: A grounded investigation. *2001 International Conference Global Business and Technology Association*, Istanbul, Turkey.

Law, K.S., Wong, C.-S., Wang, D. & Wang, L. (2000). Effect of supervisor-subordinate guanxi on supervisory decisions in China: An empirical investigation. *International Journal of Human Resource Management*, 11(4): 751–765.

Li, J., Xin, K.R., Tsui, A. & Hambrick, D.C. (1999). Building effective international joint-venture leadership teams in China. *Journal of World Business*, 34(1): 52–68.

Li, J.J., Zheng, Z., Lam, S.K. & Tse, D.K. (2006). Active trust development of local senior managers in international subsidiaries. *Journal of Business Research*, 59(1): 73–80.

McAllister, D.J. (1995). Affect- and cognition-base trust as foundations for interpersonal cooperation in organizations. *Academy of Management Journal*, 38: 24–59.

Podsakoff, P.M., Mackenzie, S.B., Lee, J.Y. & Podsakoff, N.P. (2003). Common method biases in behavioral research: A critical review of the literature and recommended remedies, *Journal of Applied Psychology*, 88: 879–903.

Schmidt, C. (2011). The battle for China's talent. *Harvard Business Review*, March: 25–27.

Tsui, A.S., Wang, H.U. I., Xin, K., Zhang, L. & Fu, P.P. (2004). "Let a thousand flowers bloom": Variation of leadership styles among Chinese CEOs. *Organizational Dynamics*, 33(1): 5–20.

Whitener, E.M., Brodt, S.E., Korsgaard, M.A. & Werner, J.M. (1998). Managers as initiators of trust: An exchange relationship framework for understanding managerial trustworthy behavior. *Academy of Management Review*, 23: 513–530.

Wong, Y.H. & Tam, J.L. M. (2000). Mapping relationships in China: Guanxi dynamic approach. *Journal of Business & Industrial Marketing*, 15(1): 57–70.

Wong, Y.T., Ng, H.Y. & Wong, C.S. (2006). Perceived organizational justice, trust, and OCB: A study of Chinese workers in joint ventures and State-owned enterprises. *Journal of World Business*, 41(4): 344–355.

Xin, K.R. & Pearce, J.L. (1996). Guanxi: Connection as substitutes for formal institutional support. *Academy of Management Journal*, 39: 1641–1658.

Yuan, W. (2002). Which managers trust employees? Ownership variation in China's transnational economy. *Asia Pacific Business Review*, 9(2): 138–157.

Zucker, L.G. (1986). Production of trust. Institutional sources of economic structure, *1840–1920*. In A. Cummings & B.M. Staw (eds), *Research in Organizational Behavior*. Greenwich, CT: JAI Press, pp. 53–111.

12 Manager–Subordinate Trust Relationships in Thailand

ASTRID KAINZBAUER[1]

Introduction

The Kingdom of Thailand is located in Southeast Asia and its land area is roughly the size of France. The country shares borders with Myanmar (Burma), Laos, Cambodia, and Malaysia. Formerly called the Kingdom of Siam, it was renamed Thailand in 1939. Thailand is a constitutional monarchy with a parliamentary form of government. The king is Head of State. The Thai king, who has been on the throne since 1946, is currently the longest-serving Head of State in the world and the longest reigning monarch in the history of Thailand.

The official language is Thai, and English is the most widely spoken foreign language, particularly among the younger generation and the business community.

The population of Thailand is relatively homogeneous and free of racial tension. The Chinese are the main minority (around 14 percent, concentrated mostly in the Bangkok area). In contrast to other Southeast Asian countries, the Chinese minority in Thailand is thoroughly assimilated and cannot easily be isolated as a distinct group—they have Thai names, speak the Thai language, and have often married into ethnic Thai families. As in other Southeast Asian countries, the small Chinese minority plays a dominant role in business in Thailand (Atmiyanandana & Lawler, 2003).

As the main religion, Buddhism has had an important influence in shaping Thai culture and beliefs, such as the belief in merit making, karma, and reincarnation. The concept of merit making (the idea of giving as a way to reduce selfishness and improve karma) is prevalent in many aspects of Thai life.

Thai business culture is typically characterized by a strong respect for hierarchy. Power and status differences are expected and reinforced in Thailand. Junior people show respect to senior people. Seniority is based on age, years with the company, and rank, among other aspects (Andrews & Siengthai, 2009).

Thailand is often called the "Land of Smiles" and Thais are said to have a smile for every emotion (Mulder, 2000). Thais have a strong sense of national pride and their

1 The author would like to thank Dr. Brian Hunt for his valuable comments.

national character, also referred to as "Thainess" (kwam pen thai), is shaped by the duality of Buddhism and the monarchy, which are considered constitutive elements of Thai culture and society.

This chapter will give a short overview of historical developments in Thailand and describe the current economic, social, and political context. We then provide an outline of HR practices and preferred leadership styles in the Thai business context. The remainder of the chapter is devoted to our study of trust. A literature review on various aspects of trust in Thailand provides the introduction for an extensive discussion of the findings of our empirical research in Thailand. We finally present potential implications for management practice in Thailand and suggestions for future research.

Highlights of Manager–Subordinate Trust in Thailand

- Our respondents believed that managers are initially not trusted in Thailand, but that trust can be earned through building personal relationships based on kindness and empathy.
- Thai participants pointed out that respect for a manager does not necessarily imply trust. Whereas respect *has* to be given based on the position, trust would only develop if the respected person proved to be trustworthy by being generous and putting other people's interests as well as the organization's interest before his/her own interest.
- Thai subordinates expected an attitude of respect and care from their boss as a basis for developing trust. The aspect of care included not only work-related matters but also personal matters of the employee and even his family members.
- Among the personal factors which influence trust building in Thailand, length of the relationship was regarded as the most important aspect. Tenure in the company was seen as another important factor, as this was linked to perceived experience, which would also instill trust.
- Thai focus group participants and experts unanimously agreed that gender does not affect trust in the workplace.
- Finally, our participants agreed that trust between managers and employees would lead to more open communication and less face-saving behavior, and therefore higher efficiency in the workplace.

Historical Perspective

Historically, the Tai people came from China and migrated south over several centuries. The kingdom of Sukothai was established in the thirteenth century. Later, the capital was moved to Ayutthaya. During the Ayutthaya period, a unified entity emerged for the first time. Ayutthaya was sacked by Burmese forces in 1767 and the capital was subsequently moved to Bangkok with the establishment of the Chakri dynasty. Modern Siam began its development under King Mongkut (Rama IV of the Chakri dynasty), who opened the country to international influence (James, 1931), and foreign trade became the government's focus. With the influx of Chinese and European merchants, Bangkok became one of the most important trading centers in East Asia.

Thailand was formerly called Siam. It is the only country in Southeast Asia that has never been subject to colonization. In 1896, the two major colonial powers in the region, Great Britain and France, signed an agreement which guaranteed Thailand's independence.

A coup d'état in 1932 ended the absolute monarchy and a constitutional monarchy was established. In 1939, the country was renamed Thailand, in order to reaffirm that the people of this country are "Thai" (Keyes, 2003).

Over the past 80 years, the country has experienced a number of military coups and overturns of government; the most recent one in 2006. Democratization has gained force in Thailand, through economic development and the creation of a middle class. But even though the mechanisms of democracy are in place, these are often undermined by powerful elites (Atmiyanandana & Lawler, 2003).

Thailand has a population of 66 million people and comprises a territory of 513,000 square kilometers. The country is divided into 76 provinces. The official language is Thai. About 34 percent of the population lives in urban areas. The most important ethnic groups are Thais (75 percent) and Chinese (14 percent). Other clearly defined minority groups are the Muslims in the four southern most provinces, Hindu and Sikh communities in Bangkok, and hill tribes in the north. The main religion in Thailand is Buddhism which is practiced by 95 percent of the population; a small minority is Muslim or Christian.

Thailand is a founding member of ASEAN (Association of Southeast Asian Nations), which was established in 1967 to promote economic growth and social progress in the region. Thailand has the second largest economy in Southeast Asia after Indonesia. The United States and Japan are Thailand's most important trading partners and sources of direct investment.

Today, Thailand is considered a newly industrialized country (NIC), with tourism and exports as major sources of income. Despite prolonged political unrest in 2010, Thailand's economy grew by 7.6 percent, its highest growth rate since the Asian economic crisis of 1997, and the highest growth rate at the time in Southeast Asia.

Institutional Context

Economic Context

Traditionally an agricultural country with rice as the most important crop, Thailand transformed itself into an agro-industrial country from the mid-1980s. Driven by an export-oriented industrialization strategy, the Thai economy experienced an unprecedented economic boom in the late 1980s and well into the 1990s. With almost a decade of spectacular GDP growth rates, which were among the highest worldwide, the euphoric business climate increasingly led to high risk-taking and property market speculation, which finally resulted in the bubble's collapse. The 1997 Asian economic crisis and the baht devaluation doubled Thai companies' debt burden and many of them went bankrupt due to lack of working capital and high interest rates. Unemployment increased dramatically and millions of people fell below the poverty line. The subsequent reforms and restructuring programs have made the Thai economy more competitive and more professional.

In July 2011, the World Bank upgraded Thailand's income categorization from a lower-middle income economy to an upper-middle income economy, based on a GNI per capita of US$ 4210 (World Bank, 2011).

Social Context

Life expectancy in Thailand is 73.6 years. The total fertility rate is 1.66 children per woman in 2011, which is lower than the global average of 2.7 (CIA World Factbook, 2011).

The provision of social security has increased in recent years. People employed in the formal economic sector enjoy benefits such as health insurance, maternity leave, child support, old-age pension, and unemployment benefits. However, a large number of people working in the informal economic sector have no access to social security except for the universal healthcare scheme (United Nations Development Programme, 2007). Despite continuous economic growth, there is still high inequality in access to education, health, and social services. Due to a big gap between urban and rural areas, the employment and social security situation is better in Bangkok than in the rest of the country.

Political and Legal Systems

Thailand has been a constitutional monarchy since 1932, when a revolution ended the system of absolute monarchy. The Thai king is Head of State. The current king, His Majesty King Bhumibol Adulyadej, was officially crowned in 1946 and is currently the world's longest reigning monarch.

The government of Thailand consists of three branches: the executive, the legislative, and the judiciary. Head of the executive branch of government is the Prime Minister, usually the leader of the largest party in the lower house of Parliament. According to the Constitution, the Prime Minister is selected by the House of Representatives and then appointed by the king. The Prime Minister selects ministers and deputy ministers, and together they form the Cabinet (also called the Council of Ministers).

The legislative branch of government is called the National Assembly and consists of the House of Representatives (the lower house of Parliament) and the Senate (the upper house of Parliament).

The judiciary branch is composed of three systems, namely, the Court of Justice, the Administrative Court, and the Constitutional Court.

Educational System

The Thai education system provides 12 years of free basic education, as guaranteed by the Constitution. A minimum of nine years of school attendance (age 6–15) is mandatory. However, access to education is still variable across Thailand. Among low-income households, only 80 percent of students complete nine years of education. The literacy rate in Thailand is 92.6 percent. Education is structured in four stages: Prathom 1–3 for age 6–8, Prathom 4 6 for age 9–11, Matthayom 1–3 for age 12–14 and Matthayom 4–6 for age 15–17. Pre-school (age 3–5) attendance is optional. On completion of Matthayom 6, students take a national test in order to receive the Certificate of Secondary Education. With a Certificate in Lower Secondary Education (after Matthayom 3), students can opt for vocational education. For entrance to universities, students have to pass the Central University Admission System (CUAS).

HR Practices

Thailand's labor market shows some distinct characteristics which make it different from other Asian countries.

Thailand has a relatively low percentage of salaried workers in the labor force, even compared with other Asian countries such as Malaysia, the Philippines, Taiwan, and Korea. In 2010, fewer than 45 percent of the total workforce of 38 million people were salaried. Of those 17 million salaried people, only 9 million received a monthly salary, the rest were paid daily, hourly, or piece-rate wages. As a potential negative implication of such a low percentage of formal workers, firms may be less likely to invest in HR measures such as training and development. In the private sector, 45 percent of all employees work in small businesses with fewer than ten employees, and only 26 percent work in big companies with more than 100 employees (SCB, 2011).

A second distinct characteristic of the Thai labor market is the important role of women in the Thai workforce. In 2010, women accounted for 46 percent of the total labor force and they are increasingly found in professional jobs. According to ILO data, 66 percent of all Thai women over 15 are working. This is one of the highest female labor force participation rates in Asia, right behind China with 67 percent and considerably higher than other Asian countries such as Japan, where only 48 percent of women over the age of 15 have a job.

The role of HR in Thailand has changed considerably over time. Traditionally, Thai companies perceived HR management as the payroll function. With increasing foreign direct investment, modern management practices were imported into Thailand by foreign companies. In practice, this meant hiring professional HR managers with formal HRM training. Their practices were in contrast to the majority of the business community where companies were mostly family-owned and followed a more traditional HR policy by hiring people who were close to the family network.

With the collapse of the Asian financial markets, many companies were forced to lay off a considerable number of people and streamline their business operations in order to survive. These dramatic events encouraged the adoption of professional management concepts to improve transparency and efficiency. Worker participation, welfare benefits, and increased job security became part of the HRM role and companies started to invest more in human resources. Large organizations attempted to endorse the notion of empowerment and encouraged flatter organization structures (Siengthai & Bechter, 2005).

Studies of the characteristics of HRM systems in Thailand have revealed differences in HRM practices depending on company ownership and size. Thai firms can be differentiated into three groups according to their HR policies: small family businesses, large companies which are still run as family businesses, and state-owned enterprises. Foreign-controlled companies (e.g. from Europe or the US) tend to emphasize employee involvement in decision-making and Western-style management, whereas Japanese companies, the largest group among foreign investors in Thailand, typically follow Japanese principles of organizational commitment and compliance with home-country practices (Atmiyanandana & Lawler, 2003).

A study among large Thai organizations (more than 200 employees) revealed that, even though the top management considered HRM to be an important component of an innovation strategy, the majority did not view the HRM department as a strategic partner in formulating business strategies. The study concluded that the majority of large Thai firms still view the role of the HR department from a compensation perspective rather than from a strategic asset perspective (Siengthai & Bechter, 2004).

Leadership Style

In Thailand, organizational structure and leadership are typically influenced by a strong respect for hierarchy and seniority. Paternalistic management with reliance on family members in key positions is typical for Thai and Thai–Chinese family-owned companies, which range in size from small businesses to large conglomerates.

One historical view suggests that the hierarchical structure in Thai society can be traced back to the fifteenth century, when all citizens were ranked by numbers (slaves received the lowest numbers and the royal family received the highest numbers). Even though this system was abolished 400 years later, the fundamental belief in social ranks endures. This belief is reinforced in Thai society through a strong respect for monarchy and the central role of Buddhism. In fact, the highest authority in the Thai social order is the sangha (Buddhist clergy) and even the Thai king must pay respect to monks (Atmiyanandana & Lawler, 2003). Hierarchy and status are also expressed symbolically in Thai language, which, like many other Asian languages, requires the speaker to acknowledge relative differences in status. The Thai greeting with the palms of the hands held together ("Wai") involves various degrees of bowing to symbolize respect for status and age.

Based on this hierarchical worldview, a boss in Thailand traditionally holds a great deal of authority and responsibility. Subordinates expect their boss to be an expert in conducting business, negotiating, and decision-making, and to give advice to subordinates (Sriussadaporn, 2006). Subordinates may be consulted for their opinions, but the final decision lies with the boss. This tendency may be even more evident in family-owned businesses. This is less evident in international companies with an international mix of people and backgrounds.

However, power in the Thai context is not interpreted with the negative connotation of coercion but rather it is associated with benevolence and kindness, which are important values in Thai society (Joiner et al., 2009). A caring relationship between leaders and followers is essential in a Thai workplace. The typical role description of a Thai leader can be characterized as a "benevolent father/mother." In this role, two key concepts come into play—phradet and phrakhun. The leader should possess knowledge, experience, and wisdom and be a decision-maker (phradet) but should also play the role of head of the family and protect his employees (*phrakhun*). When the right balance is attained between these two roles, the leader acquires "*baramee*" (power derived from respect, charisma). The role of the subordinates is to respect their leader and show loyalty and commitment (Komin, 1999; Holmes & Tangtongtavy, 1995). This emphasis was also reflected in the GLOBE study, where Thailand (as part of the South Asian cluster) showed a preference for "humane leaders," characterized as compassionate, generous, patient, and modest. The South Asian cluster ranked this dimension highest, surpassing all the other regional clusters (Gupta *et al.*, 2002).

In their study on leadership in Thai community organizations, Kemavuthanon and Duberley (2009) highlighted the significant impact of Buddhism on leadership in Thailand. Four Buddhist attitudes were identified as part of the personal qualities expected of a leader: goodwill (*Metta*), compassion (*Karuna*), appreciative gladness (*Mudita*), and equanimity (*Upekkha*). According to these authors, leadership in Thailand entails a holistic perspective as it concerns life both inside and outside of the organization and extends to employees' families and the local community.

Recent studies reported a tendency for Thai employees to prefer (and also perceive their leader to exhibit) a consultative leadership style, in which the leader consults with subordinates but retains the right to make the final decision (Yukongdi, 2010), and have identified empowerment as a factor which increases the work motivation of Thai subordinates (Kantabutra & Saratun, 2011).

Joiner *et al.* (2009) propose quality leader–employee relationships which encourage joint application of abilities as the link between traditional paternalistic leadership values and employee job satisfaction in the Thai context. Thai employees report job satisfaction when they are given an opportunity to apply their skills while working together with their leader.

Foreign managers in Thailand report that spending time on building personal relationships is crucial for business success. Awareness and understanding by foreigners of local cultural values such as *nam jai* (kindness) and *jai yen* (calm, relaxed attitude) are essential for winning the trust of their Thai subordinates. On the other hand, Thai subordinates who have adapted to working in an international work environment in foreign companies, which is perceived as more aggressive, competitive, and faster-paced, indicate that they might find it difficult to go back and work in the Thai organizational system (Sriussadaporn, 2006).

Literature Review on Trust

Trust is recognized as an essential element of conducting business in Asian cultures (Chatterjee & Pearson, 2002). In Thailand, building trusting relationships based on reciprocal loyalty often takes precedence over legal or contractual obligations. The importance of trust is based on the cultural dimension of collectivism (Hofstede & Hofstede, 2005), which predicts a strong sense of identity with members of the "in-group." Relationships in Thailand are structured in concentric circles, with very close family relationships in the inner circle. Indeed, the extended family is the most important social network in Thailand. The outer circles of social relationships consist of people one knows from attending the same school, through membership of the same club, or from interacting at work. The level of trust, sense of dependence, and obligation increase as one moves toward the inner circles. Thais refer to members of their "in-group" as *puak* (group) and these are people one can count on for support.

In the international business context, this means that spending time on building personal relationships and creating trust is an indispensable investment for foreigners who would like to do business in Thailand. This was confirmed in a study on international technology transfer in construction projects in Thailand (Waroonkun & Stewart, 2008). Building relationships (i.e. trust, understanding, and communication) between the transferor and transferee was determined to be the key predictor of value creation. In this study, 162 design and construction professionals in Thailand attested that the willingness to create strong bonds with local workers which are based on trust, communication, and understanding was one of the prerequisites for successful cooperation with foreign technology providers.

In collectivistic countries, cultural similarity generally supports the development of trust, as people tend to find it easier to interact with similar people. Golesorkhi's (2006) study on judgments of co-worker trustworthiness revealed that Southeast Asian respondents placed relatively high importance on co-workers' similarity to themselves, which was not the case with respondents from Europe and North America. This insight is also confirmed by other authors, such as Nisbett (2003), who claims that group embeddedness and perceived similarity of in-group members lead to trusting behavior. Koojaroenpaisan and Peterson (1997) had found the same effect when they identified a positive relationship between ethnic similarity and trust in the selection of suppliers among ethnic Chinese in Thailand. These studies underline the importance of perceived similarity for trust building in Asian cultures.

Being a trustworthy colleague in Asia implies personal attention and special care for peers. Cooperative behavior and mutual support is generally expected of co-workers. Golesorkhi's (2006) study on judgments of co-worker trustworthiness revealed considerable differences between Southeast Asian and European respondents. Southeast Asian respondents placed significantly more importance on co-workers' benevolence, evidenced by demonstrations of kindness, helpfulness, warmth, and caring. While these behaviors are viewed as essential in the Southeast Asian context, they may not be regarded as necessary or appropriate in a European workplace. The author suggests that, in multicultural workplaces, shared perceptions of trustworthiness cannot be assumed. Managers need to clarify expectations of care and concern in order to avoid misunderstandings and feelings of neglect or rejection, especially among Southeast Asian employees who expect higher levels of personal consideration in the workplace.

In the societal context, Thai citizens have been found to be on average less trusting toward their peers than the citizens of other Asian countries. In a 2003 study of "values and lifestyles in urban Asia" (Inoguchi *et al.*, 2005), Thai responses on the extent to which people trust each other were mostly below the average of the ten countries investigated (Japan, South Korea, China, Vietnam, Malaysia, Myanmar, India, Uzbekistan, Sri Lanka). In particular, Thais showed relatively little trust in Thai police officials and trust in the media was below average. On the other hand, trust in government institutions was at or above average for these ten countries, but Bangkok respondents showed less trust than respondents from the rest of the country and university graduates also showed less trust. Thais' level of trust in religious institutions was also slightly above average across the countries studied, and older respondents generally showed greater trust than younger respondents (Kamchoo & Stern, 2005).

Contextual Factors in Hierarchical Trusting Relationships

In the following sections, we outline the results of our empirical research in Thailand consisting of dyad-level focus groups with managers and employees and Delphi panel expert feedback.

We asked both the Thai focus group participants and the Delphi panel experts to assess whether Thai managers in general trust their subordinates and whether Thai subordinates in general trust their managers.

Our Thai focus group participants believed that Thai subordinates in general would not trust their manager very much. However, they related trust in the manager with several factors. Trust was seen as closely linked to the manager's attitude toward the subordinates. An attitude of respect and care for the employees was regarded as a basis for developing trust.

Time was also seen as a very important aspect in developing trust. At the beginning, subordinates would be very cautious and reluctant to trust their manager, but from observing consistency and integrity in his/her behavior over time, subordinates would eventually build trust.

The company's size was considered important only if it influenced the quality of personal relationships—for example, it might be easier to build personal relationships and trust in a family business than in a large company. Respondents recognized that the number of subordinates working for one manager might be higher in larger companies and trust might therefore be more difficult to develop due to lack of personal contact. However, family businesses in Thailand are often characterized by a top-down approach to management and, under these circumstances, Thai employees would give credit to the manager because of his/her position as the owner/boss, which may or may not be based on a genuine feeling of trust.

Thai managers, on the other hand, were perceived as more trusting by the focus group participants. This was linked to the fact that managers had the choice of hiring subordinates who they saw as capable and trustworthy. In the case of people whom the manager has not selected personally, building trust may take longer.

Our Delphi experts were more reserved in their evaluation of trust between managers and subordinates. They believed that Thai managers and subordinates in general do not necessarily trust each other and this was considered even more evident in the case of (small) businesses outside of Bangkok engaging in labor-intensive work and where workers tend to have low levels of education. In these businesses, managers would have to exercise a certain amount of control in order to signal to employees that they are being monitored (on attendance, punctuality, results). Our experts' view was that, if employees felt that they were not closely monitored, their performance might drop. The following statements from our experts confirm this opinion: "Trust is important, but control is necessary"; "With the majority of employees, bosses have to follow up very often to make sure things get done."

National *cultural dimensions* were also perceived to have an influence on trust building in Thailand. Our respondents were asked to evaluate Thai culture in terms of cultural dimensions such as power distance and collectivism (Hofstede & Hofstede, 2005). The focus group participants and Delphi experts evaluated Thailand as a *collectivistic* society with a strong family orientation and a high level of consideration for others in the group. Thais like to work in groups, eat lunch in groups, take group responsibility, and share success within the group. Thais feel responsible for each other and show empathy for the wellbeing of other group members. Group harmony is often perceived as more important than individual interests. Group orientation is also linked to perceived trust for the boss. If a subordinate loses trust in the boss based on a bad experience, he/she might influence other group members to share his/her perception. Peer influence on individual perceptions was reported as strong in Thailand. Our expert respondents shared the perception that Thailand is a collectivistic society based on strong family ties.

Among other factors, our focus group linked the relatively high level of collectivism in Thailand with economic development. Because Thailand lacks an efficient social security system, Thai family members have to care for and support each other. Focus group members, however, perceived a tendency toward less collectivistic behavior in Thai society compared to the past. Higher financial security on an individual level and increased international competition on the corporate level were seen as fostering a trend toward more individualistic behavior among Thais.

In terms of *power distance*, both the focus group and the expert respondents noted a high respect for seniority in Thai society. Thais are taught from an early age to respect their seniors. Seniority is linked to both age and perceived experience. If younger people are promoted to senior positions, they have to prove themselves and show achievements first, whereas older people are often trusted based on their age and perceived experience.

The high respect for hierarchy was attributed to the hierarchical structure of the social pyramid in Thailand, with the Thai Royal family at the top, followed by an elite of military, civil servants, and business people, followed by the rest of the population, mostly farmers and workers.

However, our experts noted that respect for authority does not necessarily imply trust. Whereas respect has to be given based on position, trust would only develop if the respected person proved to be trustworthy by being generous and putting other people's interests as well as the organization's interest before his/her own interest.

Personal Factors in Hierarchical Trusting Relationships

We asked our focus group participants and Delphi experts about the relevance of the following personal factors for building trust in Thailand: age, gender, length of relationship, and tenure in the company.

The focus group participants and the experts both felt that the length of the relationship was important for building trust in Thailand. Longer relationships between manager and subordinates provide a better basis for judging trustworthiness. Observations of trustworthy behavior over a certain period of time consequently lead to the development of trust.

Age was considered fairly important because Thai society is based on a strong respect for hierarchy and Thais tend to give more respect to older people. In the workplace, it is easier for older managers to gain the trust of their subordinates because age is often equated with expertise and experience. It is interesting to note that the age factor was considered more important by the subordinates and young managers in our focus group. More senior managers in our focus group considered that age was not an important factor and mentioned that achievement would have more impact on trust than the subordinate's age.

Tenure in the company was also considered fairly important because longer employment may lead to higher perceived knowledge and experience and therefore more trust.

Our experts, on the other hand, considered length of the relationship and tenure in the company as the most important factors. Tenure in the company was linked to building personal networks and managers with good networks may be considered more trustworthy by their subordinates. Age was considered important only if it influenced the perception of expertise and, therefore, contributed to the building of subordinates' professional trust in their manager.

Gender was seen as having no impact at all on trust in the workplace. All managers, subordinates, and experts in our study unanimously agreed that gender is not a significant factor for building trust in Thailand.

The focus group participants were asked to comment on the findings of the quantitative study on the significance of personal factors that explain variations in trust (see Table 12.1).

The results of the quantitative study show that managers' trust is linked to the subordinates' age, the time they have been working together, and how long the subordinate has been working in the company. Our focus group participants agreed with these findings and explained that, in Thailand, age is often seen as related to experience. Younger people may be perceived as less trustworthy because they lack experience and may make more mistakes. Similarly, people who have been with the company longer are seen as more experienced, and therefore more trustworthy.

The results of our quantitative study also indicate that female subordinates perceive less trustworthy behavior in their managers and that female managers have less trust in their subordinates. Our focus group participants did not agree with these interpretations because they saw no significant differences between men and women in the workplace in Thailand. One possible explanation offered was that women in general tend to be more cautious and more detail-oriented, but this seemed to be speculation rather than an interpretation based on personal experience in Thailand.

Antecedents and Outcomes of Manager–Subordinate Trust

We asked our focus group participants how they define a good professional relationship. From the subordinates' perspective, a good professional relationship was characterized as respect in each direction, sharing ideas, and supporting each other. Their expectations toward the manager were to be considerate, to care about the subordinates, and to protect them from harm. The perceived role of the

Table 12.1 Thailand: significant controls (correlations)

	Gender: manager (1→ man, 2→ woman)	Gender: subordinate (1→ man, 2→ woman)	Age: subordinate	Time manager and subordinate worked together	Organizational tenure: subordinate
MTB					
OCB		−0.304**			
MTS	0.226*		0.255*	0.342**	0.281**
STM					0.252**

Notes
** Correlation significant at 0.01 level.
* Correlation significant at 0.05 level.
MTB = managerial trustworthy behavior, STM = subordinates' trust in managers, MTS = managers' trust in subordinates, OCB = organizational citizenship behavior.

manager also included being a teacher and a coach, and supporting decisions made by subordinates.

Moreover, a good professional relationship meant separating personal and professional aspects: "… if you have done something wrong, the manager should not have a personal grudge against you."

For the managers, a good professional relationship meant open communication. "If there is a problem, we can speak about it right away and discuss it openly." This observation is linked to the tendency toward an indirect communication style in Thailand where opinions are often not expressed openly due to a strong respect for hierarchy. Our managers felt that a straightforward communication style and the courage to ask questions or ask for help are a clear sign of subordinates' trust.

> Thai subordinates are not quite open, they do not say what they really think. We have to figure it out based on their behavior. If my subordinate trusts me, she would bring up problems; if she didn't trust me, she would not share her problems with me.

Or as one subordinate put it: "If I did not trust my boss, I would be very careful with my opinion—what things I should or should not say."

Other behaviors that generated subordinates' trust in their managers were mentioned as follows:

For the subordinates, respect and protection by the manager were seen as important. The manager should also have the necessary qualifications and support the subordinates by teaching and coaching them. Our respondents mentioned that it is important for the manager to find the right balance between looking after the subordinates but not micromanaging them (which could be a signal of mistrust). In Thailand, the manager's behavior, including body language, facial expressions, and language tone, is carefully observed by subordinates and even subtle nuances are subject to interpretation. "If the boss does not follow up, we feel neglected. If the boss follows up too much, we feel not trusted. If the boss says 'I will do it,' it could be interpreted as 'you are not capable'."

Very important characteristics for a trustworthy Thai manager are kindness and empathy (the Thai expression *hen jai* means literally "to see into the heart"). Because of the high power distance between Thai managers and subordinates, which discourages two-way communication, it is even more important for Thai managers to intuitively interpret their subordinates' needs and expectations. Often, subordinates would not openly ask for help but would expect the boss to know when help is needed: "A good manager needs to be like a pineapple—have eyes everywhere."

The office atmosphere should be happy, open, and not too stressful. The manager should walk around and listen to everybody. Our respondents pointed out that, in the event of conflict, a trustworthy manager would listen to all sides and not have favorites. A good manager should also not get upset easily and not be very emotional (the Thai term is *jai ron*— "hot hearted" —and refers to losing your temper, which is considered grossly unsophisticated in Thai culture). Our respondents also mentioned that the manager should be a role model and walk the talk.

From the managers' perspective, in order to trust their subordinates, they expected open communication, honesty, a can-do attitude, and the ability to fulfill tasks and achieve consistent results. "When you trust people, you do not worry that they will behave/perform in an unexpected way."

Both managers and subordinates suggested several positive *outcomes of trust* for their professional relationship. The manager's trust in the subordinates leads to a more open communication style (less face-saving necessary) and more delegation and empowerment (with fewer sleepless nights for the boss).

Higher subordinate trust in the managers leads to higher subordinate confidence, higher efficiency (a consequence of open communication), more commitment to the job, happiness, higher motivation, and a feeling of security (which often leads to lower staff turnover).

One of the managers in our focus group emphasized that a trusting work relationship with employees is crucial for business performance and productivity as trust accelerates the organization's potential for growth.

Figure 12.1 provides a summary of the major antecedents and consequences of trust in the manager–subordinate relationship as evidenced by the qualitative data from the focus group and the expert panel in Thailand.

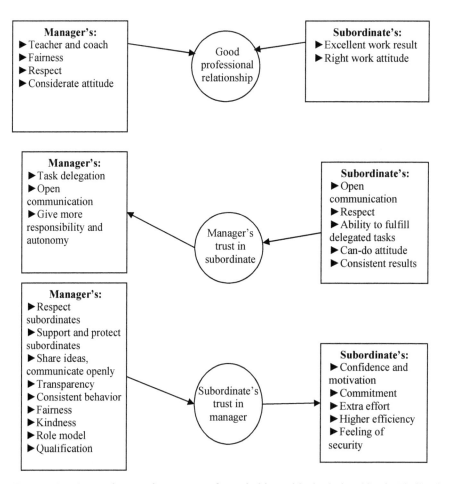

Figure 12.1 Antecedents and outcomes of trust in hierarchical relationships in Thailand

The Dynamics of Trust in Hierarchical Relationships

In our focus group interviews, both managers and subordinates agreed that trust can only be established over time.

From the managers' perspective, a number of behaviors were mentioned which would instill trust in their subordinates: for example, keeping promises, meeting deadlines, showing honesty, discreetness in delicate business matters, and open communication. Managers also pointed out that subordinates' achievements and results would provide a basis on which to develop deeper trust over time.

From the subordinates' perspective, support from the boss, fairness, and a caring attitude were regarded as crucial for gaining their trust. Caring about employees in Thailand was not only linked to work-related aspects but even included private concerns related to the employee's family. A trustworthy boss in Thailand would apply a holistic view. Employees would not be perceived strictly as subordinates, but may be seen as family members (especially in small companies). A manager who is genuinely concerned about the wellbeing of his employees and their families and is perceived as generous would earn trust more easily.

When asked how they would behave with a supervisor with whom they had not yet built trust, subordinates said that they would observe the supervisor's behavior and work style carefully over time and would try to adapt themselves to the supervisor's expectations. They also pointed out that they would be more careful and hold back on their opinions first. They might also be more reluctant to ask for help from the supervisor because they would be afraid of losing face. Our respondents linked this to the Thai value of *kreng jai*. Loosely translated as "consideration," this value makes Thais restrain their individual interest for the sake of a senior person. *Kreng jai* behavior can be based on respect for seniority or even fear. With increasing trust between manager and subordinate, the intensity of *kreng jai* and the need to protect one's face will slowly decrease. "If I trust my boss, I can be open to her, I do not have to protect my face. It makes my work easier."

The subordinates in our focus group emphasized that trust can only be built through working "together" with the boss. Overcoming difficulties together can be regarded as a test which develops confidence and trust. "The boss also needs to show his support so we can work together as a team."

One very common way of building trust within a company in Thailand was described by one of the respondents:

> We initiate social events (e.g. an informal breakfast meeting at 6.30, we share food, or we go for dinner). We basically have a good time together, it is a tool for building trust, it makes people feel closer and we can build a corporate culture where people can trust.

Most companies in Thailand organize events like sports days, etc. This supports the Thai value of *sanuk* (fun), which is crucial for employee commitment. Having fun together as a team also helps build trust and lower hierarchical barriers.

The quantitative analysis of the circular model of trust provides noteworthy insights into the dynamics of trust in Thailand as compared to the overall sample from 18 countries (see Table 12.2). In both samples, we find a high correlation between a subordinate's organizational citizenship behavior and a manager's trust

Table 12.2 Standardized regression weights for the trust model in Thailand and the overall sample

	OCB->MTS	MTS->MTB	MTB->STM	STM->OCB
Thailand only	0.79**	0.09**	0.81**	0.11
Complete model	0.68**	0.34**	0.89**	0.08*

Notes
** Regression weight significant at 0.01 level.
* Regression weight significant at 0.05 level.
No asterisk – Regression weight not significant.

in subordinates, as well as a high correlation between managers' trustworthy behaviors and subordinates' trust in the manager. However, in the Thai sample, our data indicate that there is no significant relationship between trust and behavior. In other words, the subordinates' trust in the manager and the managers' trust in the subordinates do not have a statistically significant effect on their organizational citizenship behaviors and managerial trustworthy behaviors, respectively.

The Thai data set shows symmetry in the dynamics of trust between managers and subordinates. According to the Thai data, trustworthy behavior leads to trust. However, existing trust does not seem to inspire trustworthy behavior. These conclusions are true for both managers and subordinates.

Our experts provided some additional insights into the model and commented on the dynamics of trust in Thailand. They agreed that the model is applicable to Thailand. However, they were convinced that the trust circle would first have to start from the manager. The underlying reason for this statement was the strong respect for hierarchy in Thailand, which would prevent employees from taking the first step toward a trusting relationship. Rather, subordinates would be careful, keep a distance, and observe their manager's behavior over time. The manager, on the other hand, was seen as being in a position to show trustworthy behavior first (even without receiving trust in return for some time). One example of trustworthy behavior that might instill trust was concern for employees "like family members." Our experts pointed out that Thais typically expect their boss to protect them in the workplace from harshness or too difficult work, thus taking on the role of a father/mother.

The lack of correlation between the subordinates' trust in their managers and their organizational citizenship behavior was attributed to a Thai characteristic mentioned by our experts. In our model, the components of organizational citizenship behavior were targeted toward the organization (e.g. sincere help offered to co-workers, loyalty toward the organization, initiative in improving the organization). However, our Thai experts mentioned that subordinates' trust in their manager may lead to trustworthy behavior toward this particular manager, but may not necessarily lead to trustworthy behavior toward the organization as a whole. Trust was considered to be a very personal feeling between two people and did not automatically extend to the whole organization. Our experts mentioned several known cases in Thailand where loyal staff left the organization together with their manager when he/she resigned. Evidently, their loyalty was more focused on their boss than on their company.

Our focus group participants added that a lot depends on the manager's attitude toward his subordinates and how he/she represents the company. Managers who emphasize the personal relationship too much ("you are working for me") could create personal loyalty which would lead to the above-mentioned effect. Managers who are loyal to their organizations and represent them well are more likely to create loyalty toward the company in their subordinates. Corporate culture and career prospects were also mentioned as important factors. If the subordinates saw their career success linked to personal support from their manager, they would tend to follow their manager. On the other hand, if they perceived career opportunities within their company (or a lack of opportunities in the job market), they might place their personal interest before their loyalty to the manager.

Discussion and Conclusions

In this last section, we would like to link the findings of our study on trust in the Thai workplace to relevant literature.

Both managers and subordinates in Thailand agreed that trust is important for a company's efficiency, productivity, and overall performance. While Thais were generally perceived as not overly trusting, our respondents were in agreement on the positive influence of trust on organizational culture and performance. Trust was regarded as time-bound, where both managers and subordinates would contribute to the development of trust through consistency in their behavior, competence and results achieved, and mutual respect and a caring attitude.

Our study confirms the notion of trust as a context-specific concept informed by cultural values. In Asian cultures, building trust is recognized as an essential element in business interactions. However, the perception of what is considered trustworthy behavior and the ways in which trust can be built depend on local cultural expectations (Schumann *et al.*, 2010, Chatterjee & Pearson, 2002).

Our research shows that, even though Thailand is characterized as a high power distance environment with high respect for the boss, this respect does not automatically translate into trust from the subordinates toward their boss. Instead, trust needs to be earned through demonstration of competence, fairness, and a caring attitude. Managers who are dedicated to their job and act as a role model, who show an altruistic attitude and care about helping their team and their organization earn trust more easily. Also, support from the manager does not only extend to professional matters; it can even include employees' personal and family matters. Trustworthy behavior from the manager will subsequently reduce the perceived power distance between boss and employees.

The subordinates in our focus group emphasized that trust can only be built through working "together" with the boss. Overcoming difficulties "together" can be regarded as a test which develops confidence and trust. These insights support the findings of the GLOBE study (Gupta *et al.*, 2002) that Thailand showed a preference for "humane" leaders who show compassion and generosity. It also supports the findings of Yukongdi's (2010) study that Thais prefer a consultative leadership style where the leader retains the right to make the final decision.

Our focus group and Delphi experts (both male and female) agreed that gender has no impact on trust in the workplace. This is not surprising, given that Thailand is ranked as one of the Asian countries with the highest equality in the workplace

(Hausmann *et al.*, 2010). Thailand is also ranked among the countries with the highest female labor participation rate in Asia (66 percent, according to ILO data).

In terms of practical implications for organizations in Thailand, our study offers several suggestions to managers. First, the results of our quantitative study suggest that employees who show organizational citizenship behavior (OCB)—that is, positive extra-role behavior—create a feeling of trust in their managers and thereby support the development of a trusting organizational culture. Possibly as a direct result, there may be long-term positive effects on organizational performance. Consequently, it is suggested that managers and organizations in Thailand focus more on positive extra-role behavior—for example, by including this as an explicit component of selection and appraisal systems.

Furthermore, managers in Thailand should be encouraged by their organizations to actively link their subordinates' loyalty to the organization (rather than to themselves) and act as representatives of the organization (in order to avoid the risk of losing a whole team when one manager leaves).

And finally, managers in Thailand need to focus on overcoming the barriers of strong hierarchy orientation and build personal relationships in order to win their subordinates' trust. A caring attitude toward employees (and even their families), kindness, and empathy, as well as a corporate culture which incorporates *sanuk* (fun), are likely to create a working environment based on mutual trust.

Our empirical study on trust in the Thai workplace has been limited to Bangkok and the surrounding areas. While Bangkok is, without doubt, the most important business location in Thailand, we recognize the limitations of our results. One potential direction for future research might be a more comprehensive study including other regions of Thailand. Moreover, it is likely that trust building is influenced by the level of education and the type of occupation. These factors would warrant a more detailed investigation in order to gain comprehensive insights into the nature and development of trust in organizations in Thailand.

References

Andrews, T. & Siengthai, S. (eds) (2009). *The Changing Face of Management in Thailand*. London: Routledge.

Atmiyanandana, V. & Lawler, J. (2003). Culture and management in Thailand. In M. Warner (ed.), *Culture and Management in Asia*. London: Routledge Curzon, pp. 228–248.

Chatterjee, S.R. & Pearson, C.A.L. (2002). Trust and managerial transition: Evidence from three small Asian countries. *Cross Cultural Management*, 9(4): 19–28.

CIA World Factbook (2011). Thailand. Retrieved on August 28, 2011 from www.cia.gov/library/publications/the-world-factbook/geos/th.html.

Golesorkhi, B. (2006). Gender differences and similarities in judgments of trust worthiness. *Women in Management Review*, 21(3): 195–210.

Gupta, V., Surie, G., Javidan, M. & Chhokar, J. (2002). Southern Asia Cluster: Where the old meets the new. *Journal of World Business*, 37: 16–27.

Hausmann, R., Tyson, L.D. & Zahidi, S. (2010). *The Global Gender Gap Report 2010*, Geneva: World Economic Forum.

Hofstede, G. & Hofstede, G.J. (2005). *Cultures and Organizations: Software of the Mind*, 2nd ed. New York: McGraw-Hill.

Holmes, H. & Tangtongtavy, S. (1995). *Working with the Thais: A Guide to Managing in Thailand*. Bangkok: White Lotus.

Inoguchi, T., Basáñez, M., Tanaka, A. & Dadabaev, T. (eds) (2005). *Values and Life Styles in Urban Asia: A Cross-Cultural Analysis and Source book Based on the Asia Barometer Survey of 2003*, Mexico City: Siglo XXI Editores.

James, R.E. (1931). Siam in the modern world. *Foreign Affairs*, 9(4): 657–664.

Joiner, T.A., Bakalis, S. & Rattanapitan, G. (2009). Traditional leadership in Thailand: The role of applying abilities for mutual benefit. *International Journal of Business and Economics*, 9(1): 85–95.

Kamchoo, C. & Stern, A. (2005). Thailand: The primacy of prosperity in democracy. In T. Inoguchi, M. Basáñez, A. Tanaka & T. Dadabaev (eds) (2005). *Values and Life Styles in Urban Asia: A Cross-Cultural Analysis and Source book Based on the Asia Barometer Survey of 2003*, Mexico City: Siglo XXI Editores.

Kantabutra, S. & Saratun, M. (2011). Identifying vision realization factors at a Thai state enterprise. *Management Research Review*, 34(9): 996–1017.

Kemavuthanon, S. & Duberley, J. (2009). A Buddhist view of leadership: the case of the OTOP project. *Leadership & Organization Development Journal*, 30(8): 737–758.

Keyes, C. (2003) The politics of language in Thailand and Laos. In M. E. Brown & S. Ganguly (eds), *Fighting Words: Language Policy and Ethnic Relations in Asia*. Cambridge, MA: The MIT Press, pp. 177–210.

Komin, S. (1999). The Thai concept of effective leadership. In H. S. R. Kao, D. Sinha & B. Wilpert (eds), *Management and Cultural Values: The Indigenization of Organizations in Asia*. New Delhi, Thousand Oaks, London: Sage, pp. 265–286.

Koojaroenpaisan, P. & Peterson, R.T. (1997). Chinese/American comparison of the universality of trust as an applied conceptual tool in wholesaler selection decisions. *Journal of Marketing Channels*, 6(1): 55–75.

Mulder, N. (2000). *Inside Thai Society: Religion, Everyday Life, Change*. Chiang Mai: Silkworm Books.

Nisbett, R. (2003). *The Geography of Thought: How Asians and Westerners Think Differently ... and Why*. New York: The Free Press.

SCB Economic Intelligence Center (2011). How businesses will need to adapt to the changing workforce, April 2011. Retrieved on September 1, 2011 from www.scb.co.th/eic/en/scb_eic_home.shtml.

Schumann, J.H., Wangenheim, F.V., Stringfellow, A., Zhilin, Y., Praxmarer, S., Jiménez, F.R., Blazevic, V., Shannon, R.M., Shainesh, G. & Komor, M. (2010). Drivers of trust in relational service exchange: Understanding the importance of cross-cultural differences. *Journal of Service Research*, 13(4): 453–468.

Siengthai, S. & Bechter, C. (2004). Human resource management in Thailand. In P. Budhwar (ed.), *HRM in Southeast Asia and the Pacific Rim*, London: Routledge, pp. 141–172.

Siengthai, S. & Bechter, C. (2005). Human resource management in Thailand: A strategic transition for firm competitiveness. *Research and Practice in Human Resource Management*, 13(1): 18–29.

Sriussadaporn, R. (2006). Managing international business communication problems at work: A pilot study in foreign companies in Thailand. *Cross-Cultural Management: An International Journal*, 13(4): 330–344.

United Nations Development Programme (2007) *Thailand Human Development Report 2007*. Bangkok: UNDP.

Waroonkun, T. & Stewart, R.A. (2008). Modeling the international technology transfer process in construction projects: evidence from Thailand. *The Journal of Technology Transfer*, 33:667–687.

World Bank (2011) Thailand now an upper middle income economy. Retrieved on August 18, 2011 from www.worldbank.org/en/news/2011/08/02/thailand-now-upper-middle-income-economy.

Yukongdi, V. (2010). A study of Thai employees' preferred leadership style. *Asia Pacific Business Review*, 16(1/2):161.

13 Manager–Subordinate Trust Relationships in Pakistan

SADIA NADEEM

Introduction

Pakistan is a country of 170 million people which was established as a separate political entity approximately 64 years ago. Topographically, it is a beautiful land of five rivers, with high mountain ranges spanning the north, and plateaus, plains, and deserts covering a large part of the central and southern region. Covering an area of 796,095 square kilometers, it is divided into four provinces or states, each with its own history and culture. The history of civilization in this area dates back to 8000 BC at Mehrgarh, and to the fourth and third millennia BC for the Indus Valley civilizations, currently a part of the Sindh and the Punjab province. The world heritage site of the city of Mohenjo-Daro is in the province of Sindh, and Harappa and Taxila are parts of the Punjab province. The Silk Route, followed by Alexander the Great around 330 BC, and before that by traders traveling from Europe and the Middle East to China, passes through the northern province of Khyber-Pakhtoonkwa. The Mughal Empire, from the eleventh to the eighteenth century, was another era of glory for this land, as culture, art, and architecture blossomed, leaving behind grand monuments, such as the Lahore Fort and Badshi Mosque.

Over the recent years, the Pakistani society has evolved significantly. Like most countries, globalization and the information age have had their impact on the values and culture of Pakistan. Media, such as television and the internet, has affected living preferences and the value system in rural and urban areas. Simultaneously, the greater influence of English-speaking countries, particularly the US and the UK, can be seen in the text books, compounded by the return of Western educated individuals. Further, multinationals have brought with them their own culture and values, which have gradually infiltrated the existing values, particularly in urban areas where they have had greater presence.

Overall, Pakistan is a collectivist society where power distance is high and assertiveness is low (Hofstede, 1980; Nadeem, 2010b). Because of high power distance, autocratic behavior is more readily accepted in the society and in organizations. Being a non-assertiveness society, there is greater acceptability of face-saving behavior among individuals, subordinates, and leaders—that is, face-saving gestures are not associated with negativity but are accepted as a norm. However, while Pakistan scored high on collectivism in the Hofstede study (1980) and extremely high for in-group collectivism in the GLOBE study in Pakistan (Nadeem, 2010b), the institutional collectivism scores in the latter study were medium-high.

It is in the above context that this chapter sets the scene by providing a brief account of the history of the region which now comprises Pakistan, along with an overview of the economic, social, and cultural context. This is followed by a concise summary of the existing management practices and preferred leadership competencies in Pakistan. We then move on to the topic of trust, which presents empirical findings from a survey of 141 managers and subordinates and interviews with 20 managers and subordinates. The chapter concludes with a summary of key findings and recommendations for practitioners and researchers.

Highlights of Manager–Subordinate Trust in Pakistan

- All Pakistani participants agreed that trust was an essential ingredient of a good professional relationship, though, surprisingly, it was never talked about directly in organizations.
- Trust between managers and subordinates was found to be a cyclical, but not a balanced, relationship. Overall, managers trusted their subordinates more than vice versa, probably because managers had a higher viewpoint, more information, and more authority.
- It was repeatedly pointed out that, in Pakistan, trust needed to be built from point zero in most relationships, as it was not common to assume that a degree of professional trust would exist. Once real trust was built, it was perceived to be stronger and more long-lasting than other societies.
- The respondents highlighted that trust had segments and levels—that is, one may completely trust a subordinate to deliver day-to-day objectives while trust another subordinate with confidential information, of a professional nature in some situations, and also of a personal nature when the level of trust increases.
- The terms of "pretend trust," "artificial trust," and "superficial trust" were used by several participants, which were elaborated as face-saving gestures on the part of employees because of an expectation on the part of the managers, reflecting low assertiveness in the society.
- Among the personal factors, age, education, and gender all influenced trust building between managers and subordinates. Subordinates found it easier to trust older and more educated managers, with an age gap of 10–15 years considered ideal. Males were trusted more as managers, reflecting low gender egalitarianism.
- People found it easier to trust people from their own family, tribe, region, or even the same university; this is a reflection of high in-group collectivism in the society.

Historical Perspective

Pakistan, meaning "the land of the pure" is a word of Urdu and of Persian language. Pakistan was created on August 14, 1947, when the British left the subcontinent after 90 years of rule. Prior to this, various Muslim dynasties had ruled the subcontinent since the arrival of Mohammad bin Qasim in the eighthcentury. The strongest among these were the Mughal, where powerful kings like Babar, Humayun, Akbar, Jehangir, Shah Jehan, and Aurangzeb ruled what constitutes modern-day Pakistan, Southern Afghanistan, India, and Bangladesh. As a main gateway of trade for China and the Far East, as well as being rich in art, culture, spices, and precious stones, the subcontinent attracted the attention of Portuguese, Spanish, French, and British traders in the seventeenth and eighteenth centuries. Over time, the East India Company gradually penetrated the subcontinent, making it a British colony in 1857. In the decades to follow, the Indian National Congress and the Muslim League started political movements to gain independence from British rule, both focusing on their own religious/national identity, dividing the subcontinent into the Islamic Republic of Pakistan and the Republic of India in August 1947.

Pakistan's brief history and its socio-economic development have been strongly influenced by its neighbors and global politics. To the north lies Afghanistan; the Soviet occupation of Afghanistan, which started in 1979, resulted in Pakistan becoming a part of this war, initially because of US interest in the war against the Soviets, and a few decades later, as a friend and a foe in the war against terrorism after 9/11. On the eastern side of Pakistan lies India; the relationship between the two countries has been tense since independence from the British because of initial disagreements about the way land was divided, resulting in, for example, the on-going Kashmir dispute. Iran and China lie on the east and north, respectively. Both Pakistan and Iran opposed the Soviet occupation and the war in Afghanistan throughout the 1980s, and prior to that, during the times of Raza Shah Pahliv, the two countries enjoyed cordial relationships. However, since the 1990s, with US interest in Iran, including recent sanctions against Iran, external pressures have had a detrimental effect on these bilateral relations. The last key neighbor, China, has been a key supporter of Pakistan, with both countries enjoying close brotherly relations.

Politically, Pakistan is a parliamentary democracy. However, over the last 60 years, Pakistan has been repeatedly ruled by military or military-supported rulers, adversely affecting the functioning of civil society. The military rulers include General Ayub Khan (1958–1969), General Yahya Khan (1969–1971), General Zia-ul-Haq (1977–1988), and General Pervez Musharaf (1999–2008). The two key political parties are the Muslim League and the Pakistan People's Party. The Muslim League was formed under the leadership of Nawaz Sharif in 1988 and is a separate party from the original Muslim League (Pakistan), which was the main political party at the time of independence. Sharif was the elected Prime Minister of Pakistan from 1990 to 1993 and again from 1997 to 1999, from the Muslim League platform, which has now been divided into two main parties, Muslim League (N) and Muslim League (Q). The Pakistan People's Party was founded by Zulfiqar Ali Bhutto, who served as the Prime Minister of Pakistan from 1971–1977, and his daughter, Benazir Bhutto, also served twice as the Prime Minister in the 1990s. A third upcoming party is the Pakistan Tehreeq-i-Insaaf, which has been founded by the cricketer-turned-politician Imran Khan. Though Khan has been a critic of the ruling governments and is popular among the youth and the educated, his political party has not achieved any political victory.

Institutional Context

Economic Context

The geographical region which now constitutes Pakistan has been an agrarian econ-omy, where the fertile land of the Indus valley brought settlers to create the Indus valley civilization before the fourth millennia BC. At the time of independence in 1947, agriculture was the major sector of the economy, with limited industry. Paki-stan is now a semi-industrial economy which includes textile, leather, chemicals, food processing, and other industries, in addition to a rapidly developing services sector. Currently, the GDP stands at $202.83 billion, with agriculture, industry, and services contributing 21 percent, 18 percent and 53 percent, respectively. How-ever, agriculture provides employment to 45 percent of the population, followed by wholesale, and retail and manufacturing, which provide employment to 16.3 percent and 13.2 percent of the labor force, respectively. The per capita income was $1254 in 2010–2011 (Economic Survey, 2011).

With an estimated labor force of 54.9 million (LFS, 2010), the official unemploy-ment figures stand at 5.6 percent. However, approximately 30 percent of those who are counted as employed are unpaid family workers, which include a large propor-tion of women, but also a significant number of men (LFS, 2010).

Social Context

The role of family, tribes, and relations is embedded in the societal values of Paki-stan. The estimated population was 177 million in 2011 as opposed to 32.5 million in 1947, and the current total fertility rate is 3.5 (LFS, 2011). This rapid increase in population and the existing total fertility rate is a partial reflection of the importance of a (large) family for social security. Most families live together as extended fami-lies and, in the absence of a formal social security system, such as unemployment benefits and public pensions, for a large proportion of individuals, support is pro-vided by the (extended) family.

Currently, 37 percent of the population resides in urban areas, a proportion which has grown rapidly over the last few decades (Economic Survey, 2011). The key motivation behind the migration to urban areas is better employment opportunities and living standards.

Political and Legal System

Pakistan is a democracy with a parliamentary system of government, where the President is the ceremonial Head of State and the Prime Minister is the Head of Government. The National Assembly is the lower house of the Parliament and is a democratically elected body consisting of 342 members (in 2012), who are elected for a time period of five years by universal adult suffrage. The Senate is the upper house of Parliament, where elections are held for half the seats every three years. It has equal representation from all four provinces and each Senate member is elected by its respective provincial assembly members for a period of six years. However, as discussed, Pakistan's political history over the last six decades is laden by multi-ple shifts between democracy and military rule.

Education System

The literacy rate in Pakistan is 57.7 percent, which varies significantly between the urban and rural areas, where this rate is 73.2 and 49.2 percent, respectively (Economic Survey, 2011). Education is structured at multiple levels: primary (5–10 years old), secondary (11–15 years old; ten years of education in total) and higher secondary (15–17 years old; 12 years of education in total), which is followed by Bachelors and Masters degree programs at colleges and universities. In the urban areas, the above described traditional system of secondary and higher secondary education co-exists with the British system of O-levels (13–15 years old) and A-levels (16–18 years old). Thus, students completing either their Higher Secondary School Certification program or their A-level education join colleges and universities for further education. Further, both English and Urdu (the national language) are used for education at primary and secondary level, whereas all teaching at higher secondary school level and in colleges and universities is done in English, mostly using a syllabus developed by and books written by Western authors.

HR Practices

HR practices have evolved in Pakistan over the last two to three decades, primarily because of increasing globalization and establishment of multinational corporations in larger cities. Multinationals such as the Pakistan Tobacco Company (subsidiary of British American Tobacco) and Unilever have been known to use international personnel management practices in Pakistan since they started operating in 1947 and 1948, respectively. In the financial services sector, international banks such as Citibank and Deutsche, both established in Pakistan in 1961, have provided competition for labor and services to the national banks, many of whom have continuously modernized their HR practices, particularly over the last 20 years. The telecom sector, which has been the recipient of the largest proportions of foreign direct investments over the last few years, is also known for its use of sophisticated HR practices, with organizations such as Telenor and Mobilink inviting local and foreign consultants to implement the latest management practices.

These organizations have established well-designed HR systems, including: extensive practices for recruitment and selection; psychometric tests and assessment centers for hiring of graduates and middle-level managers; systematic evaluation of performance through performance management systems; performance related pay; employee empowerment initiatives; use of self-managed teams; talent management; and quality-of-life initiatives. Managers in these organizations discuss and debate advantages of the use of sophisticated HR systems to improve the motivation and performance of employees and hence to gain competitive advantage.

However, there is no regional or national survey which can provide an overview of the HR practices used by organizations across the country. Operations of local and international forums, such as the Islamabad Human Resource Forum, the Lahore Human Resource Forum, and the Pakistan Chapter of the Society of Human Resource Management (SHRM), are attempts to share knowledge of leading-edge HR practices among organizations and improve the overall practice of human resource management in the country.

While many large national and multinational organizations, and small and medium-sized organizations operating in technologically advanced sectors, such as software houses, are adopting world-class HR practices, these cover only a limited proportion of the 57.7 million labor force of Pakistan. Overall, 45 percent of the labor force is employed in the agriculture sector, where a large majority of employment is informal in nature. Moreover, the informal sector also accounts for more than 73 percent of employment outside rural areas (Economic Survey, 2011). Together these figures imply that, while modern HR practices cover a significant minority of employees, a large majority of the workforce is managed under the traditional personnel management principle or through informal contracts. It is also noteworthy that, when individuals move from rural to urban areas seeking employment opportunities, they bring old values and informal work practices with them.

Leadership Style

The most desirable leadership competencies in Pakistan are the universally accepted ones, including the expectation that the leaders will have high integrity and be inspirational. These competencies are highlighted by three independent studies, each designed to identify behaviors that managers expect those whom they perceive as leaders in their organizations to exhibit. The first of these studies is the GLOBE study, for which data were collected in Pakistan in 2009, with the results indicating that integrity, being inspirational, being a visionary, and having the ability to build and lead a team are the highest rated competencies (Nadeem, 2010a). The second is the trust, leadership, and organizational citizenship behavior study (this book chapter is based on selected parts from the same study) in which 141 managers from Pakistan rated desirable leadership competencies. Integrity, charisma, optimism, and coaching received the highest scores, respectively (Ehsan *et al.*, 2011). The third is a Delphi study, conducted over a period of three months, in which data were collected from 30 managers in three rounds. The finalized list of competencies had integrity, fairness, decisiveness, and ability to inspire others as the highest scoring competencies, respectively (Zaheer, 2010).

While some competencies are universally accepted, the culturally contingent behaviors highlight uniqueness across regions or countries (House *et al.*, 2004). Comparing opinions of Pakistani managers versus those of the US and the UK in the GLOBE study, there is more acceptability of autocratic behavior and less expectation of participative behavior, and managers expect leaders to be more procedural and exhibit face-saving behaviors (Nadeem, 2010a). The cultural dimensions of Hofstede and GLOBE (Hofstede, 1980; House *et al.*, 2004; Nadeem, 2010b) clearly explain this variation. The greater acceptability of autocratic behavior and lesser expectation of participative behavior are clearly because of high power distance in the society, while a more procedural approach links to average scores in uncertainty avoidance. Greater acceptability of face-saving behavior is linked to low assertiveness in society. The desire for a more procedural approach in management can also be partially explained by the key challenges faced by Pakistani business leaders, which include energy crisis, lack of infrastructure, and the law and order situation in the country (Zaheer, 2010). Comparing opinions of Pakistani managers with those of the Chinese and Indian counterparts, the differences become less marked than comparisons with the US and the UK, the most noteworthy being that face-saving behavior is equally acceptable in all three countries (Nadeem, 2010a).

Background of Trust

Trust translates to the word "*bharosa*" or "*aitimaad*" in Urdu. However, a third word, "*yaqeen*," is stronger, but must be used as "*yaqeen*" in somebody and not "*yaqeen*" on somebody in order for it to reflect the true meaning of trust. Trust was described by the fieldwork participants as a "feeling" which develops over time. This feeling develops primarily because of a legacy or history of repetition of certain actions—unprompted, unsolicited, and impromptu. These actions go beyond the normal ask of a person. It is also described as faith that the other person will keep your expectations in mind and be sincere and truthful toward you. As it is a feeling, one cannot define a starting point—that is, one cannot say that "now" this person can be trusted because they have done "this."

All participants in the fieldwork used the words "reliability" and "consistency" as those most commonly associated with trust. To have the confidence that a person will deliver what s/he has promised, under almost all circumstances, with or without any formal accountability, is the basis of trust. Other words associated with trust include integrity, loyalty, commitment, credibility, and reciprocity by those who were interviewed, specifically to identify antecedents of trust. However, focus group participants and managers also used the term "comfort level" as a substitute, an antecedent, or a consequence of trust. Also, reliability, dependability, and consistency were linked with trust in such a way that, in the absence of these, credibility, loyalty, commitment, or comfort level did not have a relationship with trust.

Trust is a new topic for research in Pakistan, and hence no information was available from past research projects. Some insight can be obtained from the global Edelman Trust Barometer, which indicates that there has been a decline in trust around the world, particularly in governments (Edelman, 2012). Governments are trusted less than businesses, media, and NGOs, and business leaders are clearly trusted more than political leaders. Government officials are the least trusted spokespersons around the world. Moreover, neither businesses nor government are meeting the expectations of individuals. Some of the key areas where businesses are not meeting expectations are treating employees well, responsible actions by organizations, transparent practices, honest and frequent communication, and putting customers ahead of profits. While Pakistan is not included in the Edelman study, these general trends appear to be in line with observations in Pakistan. Further, trust in institutions can also be linked to perceptions of corruption in institutions. The World Corruption Index (Transparency International, 2011) data show that people in Pakistan perceive that corruption has increased over the last three years and that the level of corruption is higher in police and political parties as compared to businesses.

The World Values Survey (World Values Survey, 1995, 2005) asks questions about general trust in people—that is, whether people, in general, can be trusted or does one need to be careful in trusting people. In the 1995 wave, the average score of the 727 respondents from Pakistan was 1.81, as opposed to 1.75 for the global average. Thus, there was a lower level of interpersonal trust in Pakistan compared to other countries. The question on trust was not available in the 2000 wave, but was included in the 2005 wave. Unfortunately, the 2005 data for Pakistan are not available. However, the global mean value of 1.74 in 2005 as opposed to 1.75 in 1995 indicates that the value of trust does not fluctuate significantly over time.

We move on to the next section with these generalized ideas of trust in Pakistan as there was no Pakistani research available on trust in the field of psychology, sociology, or management sciences.

Contextual Factors in Hierarchical Trusting Relationships

Trust in a manager–subordinate relationship was considered to be an essential part of a good professional relationship. All participants either themselves mentioned that trust was cyclical in nature or, when this cyclical nature of trust was mentioned, they all agreed; trust of a manager in the subordinate leads to greater trust of the subordinate in the manager, which further enhances the trust of the manager in the subordinate, resulting in a cyclical positive relationship. However, participants in the fieldwork had diverse views about whether, generally speaking, people in Pakistan trusted their bosses. Terms of "pretend trust," "artificial trust," or "superficial trust" were used by a few participants. While such terms are oxymorons, it was elaborated as a face-saving gesture (there is a high tolerance of face-saving behavior in Pakistani society) on the part of an employee because of an expectation on the part of the managers. Others highlighted their positive relationships with their bosses, where their trust was genuine; nevertheless, even these participants were not confident in the generalization that bosses were trusted by subordinates. The primary reason given for this lack of genuine trust was an infiltration of the lack of trust in the political system and leadership into organizational culture.

Participants also felt that managers had greater trust in subordinates than vice versa. The managers' trust had its origins in positions of power or authority and a respect which was given to elders and seniors in Pakistani culture. To elaborate, this means that subordinates were more likely to deliver, be consistent, and be dependable because of the formal authority held by managers. It was highlighted that trust has levels and there are segments of trust in almost all relationships. One may completely trust a subordinate to deliver their day-to-day objectives, while trust another subordinate with confidential information. Trust was also something which took time to develop. However, it is not directly proportional to the length of time for which one had known a person—that is, while trust cannot be established instantaneously, bosses may have more trust in employees they have known for a shorter time period than in those they have known over a longer time period.

The size of the company clearly played a part in the level of trust between managers and subordinates, in both directions. There was consensus that trust was higher and easier to build in smaller organizations than in larger ones. Individuals working at multiple levels in a small organization know each other better. They are like a family, as a manager commented:

> There are only a few people in smaller companies, and a culture develops in the small company on the basis of the practices of these people. And if there aren't many personal variations and angles, then in such a company it is an ideal family-like atmosphere.

When hiring new employees, additions are carefully made to this family, so that the new recruits fit in well. Almost everybody works together and knows each other—hence a higher level of trust, like a family. One the other hand, some large organizations can have an open culture and standard procedures, which are likely to result in transparent relationships. However, quite often it is beyond the control of managers to deliver what they promised to employees because of procedures in large organizations—hence resulting in decreased trust. Some participants even pointed out how managers in large organizations may hide behind organizational policies and procedures, indicating a deeper lack of trust (of intentions).

In terms of cultural dimensions, participants were asked to evaluate Pakistan's standing along the individualism–collectivism and power distance dimensions. All experts and participants in focus group discussions labeled Pakistan as a highly collectivist society. While there is a small change toward individualism in professional life, overall, the society is collectivist. This directly impacts trust. At a very basic level, the subordinates expect that their managers are going to support and favor them as they are like a family, an expectation which does not necessarily exist in an individualistic society. Also, there is a bond beyond the professional life—that is, a link in personal life as well.

Taking this discussion to the next level, one manager commented: "Unfortunately, people associate or favor people from their own tribe, region, even the same university. This happens in even good companies, so it happens far more in other organizations. Ideally it should not happen." Managers and co-workers belonging to one's province, region, tribe, or extended family (depending on different levels of "in-groups") are trusted more or can gain trust more easily. Another participant commented about the general relationship of trust in organizations and collectivism by saying:

> (Generally speaking) … it is very easy to trust someone who belongs to your tribe, and if this person is also older in age and has more experience, they are often given the status of a "pir" or a "guru" with blind faith in them.

Collectivism within the organization is strongly reinforced by social collectivism, where extended family supports individuals in the absence of a national social security system, and where a large part of the labor force is employed in the informal sector—employment in the informal sector is on the basis of whom you know: usually referrals from extended family or the individual's tribe. While all participants in our discussions were employed in urban areas and none in the informal sector, it was emphasized that many employees who move from the informal to the formal sector (or rural to urban areas), or whose family members and relatives are working in the informal sector, bring with them stronger in-group and out-group values. Overall, in an unfamiliar work environment, many, particularly blue–collar, workers have blind trust in seniors or the more educated people from their tribe or region.

Pakistan is a high power distance society. Generally speaking, those in positions of authority are given respect because of their position. A participant commented: "There is an assumption that if this person has been appointed in a particular position, he must have the right credentials and can deliver. Hence he can be trusted." In a meeting, the chair is expected to be the wisest person. People do not tend to challenge what he will say because they trust him. However, this trust is in the ability to perform a professional responsibility. Subordinates pointed out that some managers and leaders are manipulative in the use of their positions. Even under these circumstances, most of the subordinates commented that, as long as the managers were delivering a basic minimum level of performance, they had no choice but to somewhat (professionally) trust their managers because most communication and work was cascaded down through the managers.

Personal Factors in Hierarchical Trusting Relationships

All participants agreed that personal factors affected the relationship of trust between managers and subordinates. The key factors discussed included age of the manager, age of the collaborator, the age difference between the manager and the collaborator, gender of the manager, gender differences between both parties, length of the relationship between the manager and the subordinate, and education level of the manager.

All participants agreed that age affected trust, but there were multiple facets to this relationship. A large majority of the subordinates agreed that it was easier to trust older managers, as one commented: "Age results in maturity and a sense of responsibility; hence it is easier to trust older people." In comparison, younger people can be careless and work may not be a priority for them. However, a wide age gap— say, of 20 years or more—was said to have a detrimental effect on the relationship of trust (most people were thinking of their line managers at this point in time, and not of senior executives in the company). A wide age gap meant that open communication was not possible, there were no similar interests, and a reasonable level of comfort could not be developed, which meant that trust could not be developed.

Managers felt that age of the manager should not affect trust, particularly where the manager is clearly professional competent, but this was not the case in reality, as a respondent commented: "Age (automatically) earns you trust; white hair earns you trust; [smiling] a white beard earns you trust." The younger managers had to work hard to earn the subordinates' trust and repeatedly prove themselves professionally, after which trust could then be earned. This is a partial reflection of the social and religious values, where elders are deeply respected, and in joint family systems, where decision-making is left to the elders.

Managers also commented on how it was easier to build a relationship of trust with the younger collaborators, particularly because of their enthusiasm to learn more, to contribute to the organization, and hence to deliver. In comparison, the older workers can become manipulative: "As you get older, you know all the loopholes on how you cannot perform and pretend to perform, and manipulate the system to make it appear as if you are performing." Another factor which can be included in this discussion on age is the nature of the job; it is comparatively easier to accept a younger person as a manager in jobs which require higher technical competencies, such as an engineer, doctor, or geologist, as opposed to those requiring soft skills. Overall, there was a general positive cycle of trust between older managers and younger collaborators (with an ideal age gap of 10–15 years), and a negative cycle of trust between younger managers and older collaborators.

Regarding gender, a significant majority of the respondents agreed that it was easier for males to earn the trust of their team members than it was for females. Overall, there are a small number of females in managerial positions in Pakistan and these are in specific sectors, such as financial services and telecommunication. Even within these sectors, and particularly beyond these sectors, men were trusted more as managers. A male manager commented:

> I have to say it is a male-centric society. I will not say a male-dominated society but certainly a male-centric society. Women managers need to prove themselves more before they can be trusted; it shouldn't be like this, but it is.

Another participant commented, "I have to admit, unfortunately it is like this—females are accepted in many roles in our society but not trusted to do a job beyond a certain level." A third participant added:

> It is our typical culture (of our general masses) that when we see a female sitting on top of us as a boss, our inner complex is irritated. Thus they become biased, and hence trust is not what it should be. It has nothing to do with whether the female manager is actually trustworthy or not.

Some female subordinates commented that gender did not make any difference in a trust relationship with managers. Overall, this strong reaction against trusting female managers is a reflection of low gender egalitarian in Pakistani society.

Length of the relationship was considered to be an important but, by some, a secondary factor. All participants agreed that trust certainly took time to establish. Some suggested that, in most professional relationships, a few months could result in a strong trusting relationship (provided there was regular interaction), while others suggested the time period of a year or two. However, time can also harm the bond of trust, which in many cases, once broken, is hard to reestablish. Others agreed with this but added that, over time, pure professional trust became personal trust, and in ideal relationships this trust grew stronger with each passing year, "like a plant which is given water and food, and in years becomes a strong tree, providing shade and shelter." Once "true" trust was found, and it was real, it went beyond incidents or events. Most participants believed that in Pakistan, (real) trust took a longer time to establish, but once established, was likely to be stronger and longer-lasting than other societies.

Managers and subordinates were asked to comment on the findings of the survey and on the personal factors that explained variation in trust (Table 13.1).

The positive correlation of the age of the manager, organizational tenure of the collaborator, and age of the collaborator with managerial trustworthy behavior were all discussed in detail by the interviewees as personal factors affecting trust relationships, as discussed in detail in the preceding paragraphs. Regarding significant relationships with academic level of the manager, the logic and discussion were similar to that of managerial age—that is, highly educated managers were usually perceived to be more mature and developed, thus exhibiting trustworthy behavior. Adding further to this discussion, a manager commented: "We are moving toward a knowledge-centered economy. The more educated managers can give more guidance and coaching and deliver better." A subordinate commented: "I have two managers and … once I found out that one of them had greater knowledge, I always go directly to him for guidance—I trust his advice more." It was accepted by all that academic level of manager would influence trust, except when certain highly educated individuals brag or flaunt themselves or their qualification (which was not a common

Table 13.1 Pakistan: significant controls (correlations)

	Age: manager	Organizational tenure: collaborator	Academic level: manager	Academic level: collaborator	Gender: manager (1-> man, 2-> woman)	Age: collaborator
MTB	0.291**	0.202	0.268**	0.222**		0.207*
OCB	0.168**	0.218**	0.217**		−0.167*	0.183*
MTS			0.225**	0.198*		
STM	0.184*		0.216**			

Notes
** Correlation significant at 0.01 level.
* Correlation significant at 0.05level.
MTB = managerial trustworthy behavior, STM = subordinates' trust in managers, MTS = managers' trust in subordinates, OCB = organizational citizenship behavior.

practice). A similar positive relationship existed for managers' trust in subordinates and academic level of collaborators, since educated subordinates were also more likely to exhibit greater maturity, reliability, and responsibility.

Antecedents and Outcomes of Manager–Subordinate Trust

Trust is an essential ingredient of a good professional relationship—this view was shared by all participants in interviews and focus group discussions. It is an element which is never directly talked about in organizations, but no organization can function without it. It is a feeling which most managers subconsciously think about while making many of their decisions, yet hardly ever discuss.

From the subordinate's perspective, trust meant that the manager would do what they say they would do. It also meant that they would be fair, transparent, and consistent in their actions. Perhaps the most important factor was that, in positions of conflict, the manager would take a stand for the employee and protect the (interest of the) employee. The latter was considered to contribute toward a deep, trusting relationship, as a subordinate expressed: "The subordinates expect that a manager will protect them, if there is trust between them." Another subordinate commented: "There is a certain degree of expectation that he will take a stand for you, support you, and favor you." A group of subordinates said that they had recently faced an issue in their workplace where the fault was partly theirs, perhaps because of an abrupt reaction to a situation which could have been handled otherwise. Their manager took a stand for them, defending the reason behind their actions. One subordinate commented: "(when he took that stand for us) I felt like I could do anything for this organization and my manager." Another said: "I walked out of his office and I could not stop smiling—I trust him with anything now and I know I can do so much."

There was also an expectation that managers demonstrate their trust though recognition: "Supervisor's trust is shown by how much your supervisor recognizes your efforts as an employee, particularly in public," or through how much a manager confides in you.

Managers trusted subordinates who were consistent in their behavior and repeatedly delivered the targets or tasks assigned to them. A manager commented: "An employee is trusted in his deliverability and this trust is also verified on deliverability." Trusted subordinates also exercised discretion: "We have access to some very important documents about our business. If we are talking about sensitive information which is business related, you have to understand if people can be trusted with that information or not."

Overall, it was discussed that, in general, subordinates do not trust managers; managers trust subordinates more. This is because of uncertainty. There is limited visibility of the manager to the subordinates, which makes them skeptical, hence resulting in a lack of trust. The antecedents and outcomes of trust are summarized in Figure 13.1.

The list of benefits identified by respondents includes benefits at the organizational, team, and individual level. Participants commented that trust resulted in improved organizational performance through increased productivity, as a manager commented: "If there is no trust, then the productivity suffers. There is a direct

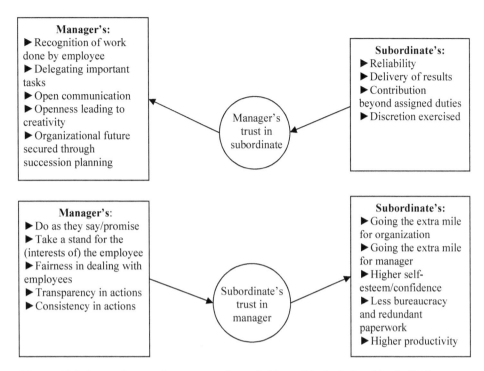

Figure 13.1 Antecedents and outcomes of trust in hierarchical relationships in Pakistan

relationship." Another manager said: "If you don't trust either your seniors or your juniors, you will not be able to deliver." Without trust, managers spent more time trying to align people's objectives and goals to the corporate goals or mission. With trust, these goals were openly shared and owned by all employees, which could take the organization further. In a trusting environment, it was easier to go after difficult targets, as people could openly discuss the challenges.

Trust and its benefits were perceived to have a long-term horizon. For example, a positive outcome of trust was open communication and information flow, which also encouraged creativity. Similarly, the people who were trusted in the organization became a part of succession planning. If the managers trusted a subordinate, they usually did not keep such a subordinate to themselves, but wanted them to be better placed, hence: "S/he who can be trusted is the future prospect of the organization."

Lack of trust makes it difficult to operate in a workplace. It requires redundant systems to be put in place for checks and counter checks, and even then employees may spend productive energy trying to find ways to get around these systems. Further, in a low trust environment, ownership and belongingness decreased, and people did not want to contribute, sometimes just decreasing their efforts, as a manager commented: "In an organizational setting, there are so many ways of not contributing. Administratively, you cannot say anything in many of these circumstances, and you cannot even make them work." Thus absence or deficit of trust resulted in decreased output because of multiple simultaneous negative cycles.

For teams, similar benefits of improved output, information flow, and performance existed. A manager commented:

> Trust is the fuel for growth. If there is no trust, you can pass time, but the most important factor for team cohesiveness is trust. If you have trust in the people around you, then the sky is the limit. It is a superficial relationship without trust, a relationship without depth.

At the individual level, respondents felt that they would be unable to deliver their best, or to carry out their job properly, if they did not trust their seniors and juniors.

The Dynamics of Trust in Hierarchical Relationships

Trust (*aitimaad, yaqeen, or bharosa*) is a "feeling" which may exist in a relationship between a manager and a subordinate. All participants in the fieldwork pointed out that it was a feeling they had not talked about before taking part in the study, and it was a word that was hardly ever used in the organization. All participants also agreed that trust existed in most of their professional relationships, varying from a weak professional trust to a strong trust which had developed over time, and in certain cases moved beyond professional life into their personal relationships with professional colleagues, subordinates, and bosses.

Trust was a feeling which evolved over time. It was an emotion which existed in a one-to-one relationship and was not a dimension of or linked to the organizational culture and practices. Some managers expressed the view that, in many countries, a certain degree of trust existed in all professional relationships at the onset because of professionalism, which then needed to be reassured. In Pakistan, trust needed to be built from point zero in most relationships, as it was common not to assume that a degree of professional trust would exist. However, having a common friend or association (e.g. with the same university, family, or tribe) provided a certain degree of initial trust.

Most managers and subordinates commented on how trust grew over time in a good relationship; it grew in strength and in the segments covered by trust. When you met someone, you were more likely to start trusting them at a basic level—then events built it up. A manager commented: "If someone joined you six months ago, you would trust him to do certain things, but you would not (completely) trust him. To give someone a blank check of trust requires time." Another summarized his point of view:

> It is essentially time, the period I have known this person for. Basically you cannot trust anybody that you have not known for long. Anybody can appear trustworthy for certain things but the only test, the real test, is time.

A manager explained that the best way to build trust was to start interacting professionally with newcomers, to focus on one's responsibilities, and to act as a role model: "I start trusting people (with their job), and they start trusting me, and then I trust them more and then the degree of trust is higher." Another explained the cyclical nature of trust as:

> When you start having faith, when you trust people … for example, I have always trusted my subordinates, more than double the faith that they had in me. I simply

did not just have this trust, but I also displayed this trust … this encouraged people, and gave them more confidence. This confidence was then reflected in me and our work, and then they had blind faith in me, and even if I would give them an out-of-the-way task, they would deliver.

Reciprocity was a very important part of trust or a trusting relationship. It was considered "natural" that if you trust someone, in return you expect that the other person would somewhat trust you. This message was summarized well by a manager who commented: "Trust doesn't look like a one-way street." A subordinate expressed it in different words: "If a leader is showing that I don't trust you, how is the person who is following him or her supposed to trust them?"

The quantitative data on the cyclical model of trust offers interesting insights into how trust and the dynamics of trust converge or diverge, comparing Pakistan and other countries (Table 13.2). When the theoretical model of trust was discussed with experts or with managers, they all agreed that the cyclical nature of trust made complete sense (Note: This was after exploratory discussions on the topic.)

Comparing Pakistan with the overall findings from 18 other countries, the strength of the relationship between organizational citizenship behavior leading to managers' trust in the subordinate is the same. Similarly, the regression weights of managerial trustworthy behavior affecting subordinates' trust in managers are comparable. Both the above-mentioned links of the model have strong regression weights (0.68** and 0.81**, respectively). Thus there is a strong dynamic of trust between managers' and subordinates' trust—however, this is not symmetrical. A manager's trustworthy behavior leads to greater trust by the subordinates in the manager.

At the remaining two points of the cyclical model, the model based on Pakistani data differs from the complete model. Overall, in the complete model, subordinates' trust in the manager is found to have an extremely weak though significant link with the citizenship behavior of the employees. This relationship is much stronger for Pakistan (regression weights of 0.08* versus 0.38**, respectively). Even prior to sharing the quantitative data, the experts, managers, and subordinates had commented on how subordinates would go the extra mile for the trusted manager. A subordinate had commented about a trusted manager, "… I felt like I could do anything for this organization and my manager."

Other reasons for this stronger link include the existence of weak systems in organizations, which results in increasing the significance of the manager in the day-to-day life of the subordinate. For many individuals, the manager is the organization. Hence if they trust the manager, they would exhibit greater citizenship behavior. Further, being a collectivist society, subordinates who feel like a part of the trusted

Table 13.2 Standardized regression weights for the trust model in Pakistan and the overall sample

	OCB–>MTS	MTS–>MTB	MTB–>STM	STM–>OCB
Pakistan only	0.68**	0.05	0.81**	0.38**
Complete model	0.68**	0.34**	0.89**	0.08

Notes
** Regression weight significant at 0.01 level.
* Regression weight significant at 0.05 level.

group with the manager feel a greater sense of belonging and ownership, and hence exhibit citizenship behavior.

The second point at which the model based on Pakistani data differs from the complete model is the relationship between manager's trust in subordinate and manager's trustworthy behavior. This was a moderate and significant relationship for the complete model, but this link did not exist for the model based on Pakistani data. The experts provided different explanations. To start with, the weak link in the cycle could be because, in many Pakistani companies, merit is not the basis of recognition. As discussed, one of the ways a subordinate knows that the supervisor trusts him or her is recognition. If, in a significant majority of companies, recognition is given not on merit but on another basis (e.g. being a member of your in-group), then managerial trustworthy behavior will not improve even if the employee is exhibiting trustworthy behavior.

A second explanation is that the manager does not improve his or her behavior because s/he is in a comfort zone, as trust was repeatedly associated with comfort. A manager commented: "A sense of complacency prevails and the manager starts thinking that things are progressing satisfactorily. You perhaps develop over-confidence in your people and yourself. Yes, this happens. You see that things are quite settled and things derail." This was further supported by stronger comments from another expert:

> You know, if you think of self-actualization in Maslow's hierarchy, many managers don't reach this stage. Most managers, when they reach a certain level, think of themselves as not needing further improvement. S/he cashes on the once-established repo only—they start using their clout.

It was agreed that the lack of continuous self-improvement is a part of Pakistani culture, particularly at higher hierarchical levels, and is probably an unintentional or subconscious reaction. This general attitude is also reflected in improving one's trustworthy behavior on the basis of the reaction of the subordinates, and partly reflects lack of maturity of managers.

Discussion and Conclusions

The results of our study in Pakistan replicate some of the ideas in the international literature and at the same time provide unique insights into how trust in Pakistan is different from other societies. As a first study of its kind on trust in Pakistan, we are unable to relate the findings to the Pakistani literature. Hence, links with the international literature, supplemented by studies on the culture of Pakistan, form the basis of our discussion.

Trust in Pakistan is seen as a dynamic, cyclical process, which takes time to build, and often develops in stages—that is, it is initially low and in selected segments and, in a positive relationship, it gets stronger and covers multiple segments or increases in bandwidth over time. This process of trust building, and its evolution over time, is suggested by the literature on trust, which itself evolved from the 1995 publication of Mayer, Davis, and Schoorman (Mayer *et al.*, 1995; Schoorman *et al.*, 2007). Trust in the early stages is seen as a calculative trust, in limited areas/bandwidths, and, with the passage of time, becomes relational trust with a possible increase in bandwidth (Rousseau *et al.*, 1998). The same idea is expressed as trust being multifaceted and multiplex by Lewicki *et al.* (1998), resulting in the common practice of trusting individuals in one segment but not others, particularly in the initial stages.

However, the time required to build trust and key anchors in this process of building trust may vary across cultures. In their discussion on cross-cultural implications of trust, Schoorman *et al.* (2007) suggested that task-oriented cultures had higher initial trust of strangers, while relationship-oriented cultures needed time to develop this initial trust. Yamagishi *et al.* (1998) showed that the Japanese trust strangers less than the Americans, while in China (Child & Möllering, 2003), it is significantly easier to trust (extended) family members than strangers. Our findings were similar, with managers suggesting that professional trust was usually not assumed in relationships and, if the other person in the relationship was a stranger, trust had to be built from pointzero. As a collectivist and relationship-oriented society, our findings also suggested that initial trust could be assumed on the basis of belonging to the same (extended) family, tribe, or caste.

Reciprocity of trust was strongly supported in our findings. The social exchange theory (e.g. Blau, 1964), and the literature on trust which is based on this theory, suggests the same—that is, one person's trust in another influences the other's trust in that person (Brower *et al.*, 2000; Butler, 1991). Subordinates care whether a manager trusts them and reciprocate his trust (Dirks & Ferrin, 2002). This feature of mutuality of trust is also based on the leader–member exchange theory (LMX), where the work of Schriesheim *et al.* (1999) highlights the critical nature of the quality of the exchange relationship.

However, this relationship is not necessarily "balanced" (Brower *et al.*, 2000). It is possible for a manager to trust a subordinate more or vice versa (e.g. Brower *et al.*, 2000; Mayer *et al.*, 1995). Schoorman *et al.* (2007) suggest that there is likely to be a predefined asymmetry of trust between the managers and subordinates, as managers have a higher viewpoint and hence are able to gather more information about the subordinates. Further, they have greater power and hence less risk is involved in their actions which require trusting the employee. Hurley (2006) also highlights how relative power affects trust—if the trust or is in a position of authority, s/he is more likely to trust because of lesser vulnerability. In our data, both quantitative and qualitative, we found it to be an asymmetrical relationship, with managers' trust in subordinates being higher that subordinates' trust in managers.

Overall, the general trustworthy behaviors pointed out in the literature, such as in the extensive review by Whitener *et al.* (1998), are found to exist in Pakistan. They suggested that the five factors of behavioral consistency, behavioral integrity, sharing and delegation of control, communication, and demonstration for concern capture the variety of factors that influence employees' perceptions of managerial trustworthiness. The point of difference in our empirical findings is taking a stand for the employee, which was emphasized repeatedly in our fieldwork, and is different from demonstration of concern, where the focus is on benevolence, sensitivity, and refraining from exploiting employees.

The cultural dimensions of high collectivism and power distance (Hofstede, 1980; Nadeem, 2010b) also provide a deeper understanding of the observed behaviors. Greater trust in the in-group and being easier to develop trust in the in-group were two expected outcomes of a collectivist culture. However, a stronger relationship between subordinate's trust in the manager and organizational citizenship behavior in Pakistan than other countries was also partly explained on the basis of a collectivist culture—that is, the subordinate feeling a part of the in-group and reciprocating. High power distance explained lack of modification of managerial behavior on the basis of employee behavior. It also provided an explanation for age and education as personal factors affecting trust. Low gender egalitarianism in the society resulted in gender being one of the key factors affecting trust; low assertiveness resulted in the use of terms such as "artificial," "pretend," or "superficial" trust, as face-saving gestures.

The social and political system of Pakistan also had an impact on trust in our findings. Zaheer and Zaheer (2006), discussing the institutional basis of trust—trust which comprises of the legal, political, and social systems that support the monitoring and sanctioning of social behavior—reviewed the work of eminent scholars who have studied the context of trust (Fukuyama, 1995; Lane, 1997; Lane & Bachmann, 1996; Yamagishi *et al.*, 1998) and suggested that greater stability and consistency in institutional conditions that govern business and social relationships results in greater or quicker building of trust between parties. In Pakistani society, where multiple shifts between democracy and military rule have resulted in a lack of established systems in civil society and a lack of trust in whatever systems and structures are established, trust was found to be a purely person-to-person relationship and additionally requiring the "in-group" element or a longer time period to develop. However, once developed, it was perceived to be more long-lasting and stronger than other societies, a perception which needs to be tested in further research.

For practitioners, authors such as Hurley (2006) suggest ways of improving trust with subordinates; for Pakistani managers, the suggestion is to continue to improve their trustworthy behavior by staying away from complacency and by working continuously on trust in professional relationships.

Overall, we would also like to mention that the quantitative data were collected from the federal capital and the provinces of Punjab and Khyber-Pakhtoonkhuwa. The interviews and focus group discussions were carried out with individuals working in the federal capital and Punjab. Trust may vary between provinces and between people belonging to urban or rural areas. The issues of occupational groups and gender, as discussed in other chapters of this book, can also provide greater insight into the topic. While more research needs to be done to understand trust in Pakistan, the comments of one participant would be the best ending to this chapter: "Trust is such a powerful word, like love. However, most people in our society take it negatively. We should use it more positively."

References

Blau, P.M. (1964). *Exchange and Power in Social Life*. New York: John Wiley and Sons, Inc.
Brower, H.H., Schoorman, F.D. & Tan, H.H. (2000). A model of relational leadership: The integration of trust and leader-member exchange. *Leadership Quarterly*, 11: 227–250.
Butler, J.K., Jr. (1991). Toward understanding and measuring conditions of trust. *Journal of Management*, 17: 643–663.
Child, J. & Möllering, G. (2003). Contextual confidence and active trust development in the Chinese business environment. *Organization Science*, 14: 69–80.

Dirks, K.T. & Ferrin, D.L. (2002). Trust in leadership: Meta-analytic findings and implications for research and practice. *Journal of Applied Psychology*, 87(4):611–628.

Economic Survey (2011). *Economic Survey 2010–11*, Islamabad: Ministry of Finance.

Edelman (2012). Edelman Trust Barometer 2012. Retrieved on 20.4.12 from http://trust.edelman.com.

Ehsan, A., Nadeem, S. & Cardona, P. (2011). *Trust, OCB and Leadership (TOL): Comparisons across Cultures*. Paper presented at the 4th International Applied Business Research Conference (IABRC), November 28–29, Islamabad, Pakistan.

Fukuyama, F. (1995). *Trust: The Social Virtues and the Creation of Prosperity*, New York: The Free Press.

Hofstede, G. (1980). *Culture's Consequences: International Differences in Work-Related Values*, Thousand Oaks, CA: Sage Publications.

House, R.J., Hanges, P.J., Javidan, M., Dorfman, P.W. & Gupta, V. (2004). *Culture, Leadership and Organizations: The GLOBE Study of 62 Societies*, Thousand Oaks, CA: Sage Publications.

Hurley, R.F. (2006). The decision to trust. *Harvard Business Review*, 84: 55–62.

Lane, C. (1997). The social regulation of inter-firm relations in Britain and Germany: Market rules, legal norms and technical standards. *Cambridge Journal of Economics*, 21(2): 197–215.

Lane, C. & Bachmann, R. (1996). The social constitution of trust: Supplier relations in Britain and Germany. *Organization Studies*, 17: 365–395.

Lewicki, R.J., McAllister, D.J. & Bies, R.J. (1998). Trust and distrust: New relationships and realities. *Academy of Management Review*, 23: 438–458.

LFS (2010). *Labour Force Survey 2009–10*, Islamabad: Federal Bureau of Statistics.

LFS (2011). *Labour Force Survey 2010–11*, Islamabad: Federal Bureau of Statistics.

Mayer, R.C., Davis, J.H. & Schoorman, F.D. (1995). An integrative model of organizational trust. *Academy of Management Review*, 20: 709–734.

Nadeem, S. (2010a). *Doing Business Under Adverse Conditions in Developing Countries*. Symposium presentation at the Academy of Management Conference, August 6–10, Montreal, Canada.

Nadeem, S. (2010b). *Using GLOBE to Understand HR in Pakistan*. Paper presented at the Academy of Management Conference, August 6–10, Montreal, Canada.

Rousseau, D.M., Sitkin, S.B., Burt R.S. & Camerer, C. (1998). Not so different after all: A cross-discipline view of trust. *Academy of Management Review*, 23: 393–404.

Schoorman, F.D., Mayer, R.C.& Davis, J.H. (2007). An integrative model of organizational trust: Past, present and future. *Academy of Management Review*, 32(2): 344–354.

Schriesheim, C.A., Castro, S.L.& Cogliser, C.C. (1999). Leader-member exchange (LMX) research: A comprehensive review of theory, measurement, and data-analytic practices. *Leadership Quarterly*, 10: 63–113.

Transparency International (2011). Global Corruption Barometer 2010. Retrieved from http://archive.transparency.org/policy_research/surveys_indices/gcb/2010/results.

Whitener, E.M., Brodt, S.E., Korsgaard, M.A. & Werner, J.M. (1998). Managers as initiators of trust: An exchange relationship framework for understanding managerial trustworthy behavior. *Academy of Management Review*, 23: 513–530.

World Values Survey (1995). World Values Survey Official Data file v.3. World Values Survey Association (www.worldvaluessurvey.org). Aggregate File Producer: ASEP/JDS, Madrid.

World Values Survey (2005). World Values Survey *Official Data file v.20090901, 2009. World Values Survey Association (www.worldvaluessurvey.org). Aggregate File Producer: ASEP/JDS, Madrid.*

Yamagishi, T., Cook, K.S. & Watabe, M. (1998). Uncertainty, trust and commitment formation in United States and Japan. *American Journal of Sociology*, 104: 165–194.

Zaheer, S. (2010). *Leadership Competencies for Doing Business in Pakistan*, MBA thesis, FAST School of Business, Islamabad, Pakistan.

Zaheer, S. & Zaheer, A. (2006). Trust across borders. *Journal of International Business Studies*, 37: 21–29.

14 Manager–Subordinate Trust Relationships in the Philippines

MARIA VICTORIA CAPARAS[1]

Introduction

The Philippines is an archipelago of 7107 islands and 88.5 million people (2007 census). Most of the population is concentrated in the 20 largest islands, with a little over half of the country's total population living on the biggest island, called Luzon. An estimated 55 percent of the population lives in urban areas.

Ranked eighty-fifth among 139 economies in the 2010–2011 Global Competitiveness Report by the World Economic Forum, the Philippines lags behind most of its Southeast Asian neighbors. Nevertheless, its economy has shown resilience to the global financial crisis, rising oil and food prices, and even natural disasters, thanks in large part to the dollar remittances from overseas Filipino workers, and the high global demand for English-speaking Filipino professionals. However, minimizing the effects of corruption in social services delivery and the business climate remains a formidable challenge.

The Philippines is home to more than 100 ethnic groups. Although the Philippine society is heterogeneous, the Filipinos have a strong sense of regionalism. Ethnocentrism can also be a manifestation of the high in-group collectivism. Filipinos tend to group themselves with fellow natives from the same region or ethnic group, whether at university, in corporations, or in a foreign land as migrants. Geography may also help account for the closeness between Filipinos of similar origins. For example, two main island groups of the Philippines are home to nine major ethnic groups. The *Tagalog*, *Ilocanos*, *Pampanguenos*, *Pangasinans*, and *Bicolanos* are all concentrated in Luzon. The *Cebuanos*, *Boholanos*, *Ilongos*, and *Waray-Waray* are in the Visayan islands. In addition, several Muslim ethnic groups are in the southern islands of Mindanao. Variants of this spirit of regionalism are found in the instant friendships between Filipinos who are alumni of the same school or university, or are connected by mutual acquaintances or relatives. They also tend to cluster on the basis of shared political views. The value of regionalism undeniably influences

1 The author would like to thank the members of the Delphi panel for their valuable insights: Prof Nanette Dungo, Dr Victor Abola, Mr Jesus Zulueta, and Mrs Rosario Ventura.

business practices, such as recruitment, selection, development, promotion, or appointments. For example, Chinese–Filipino firms tend to recruit those who are conversant in Mandarin, Cantonese, and Min Nan (its most dominant variant in the Philippines being Hokkien or Fokkien). The challenge to leadership is to maximize homogeneity or build a business case for diversity.

The Philippines has a collectivistic, family-centered culture. The family orientation is carried over into the workplace with its strengths and weaknesses. Filipino managers maintain very close personal relationships with their peers and subordinates. As organizational leaders, managers feel responsible for the personal and family welfare of their workers. In return, their employees look to them with respect, obedience, and gratitude. Jocano (1999) argues that the Filipinos' leadership style possesses three essential attributes: personalism, paternalism, and familism. Personalism emphasizes interpersonal relations and face-to-face encounters in contrast to a cold, impersonal treatment. It is manifested in expectations of personalized service, assistance in times of needs, and avoidance of public confrontations that can make one lose face. Paternalism is compassionate leadership that does not rule out consultative decision-making. Familism is group orientation that encourages a strong sense of belonging to the organization as one big family and is built on collective concern and sentiment.

This chapter will examine the cultural and organizational values underpinning the results of an empirical research of trust in Filipino manager–subordinate dyads. It will also explore how a variety of institutional factors provides a context for trust within organizations. The insights from this chapter are intended to be particularly relevant to global firms that would like to start or expand business in the Philippines, providing a clearer and more complete picture of the factors needed to successfully carry out business in the country.

Highlights of Manager–Subordinate Trust in the Philippines

- The study participants agree that managers and subordinates generally trust each other. Managers trust the people they have hired on the basis of their selection criteria. Subordinates, who do not get to select their managers, initially trust them by virtue of the power vested in their position and their trust will increase over time if they see that their managers are competent and the quality of the interpersonal relationships with their subordinates is good.
- Paternalism is a salient cultural context of trust between managers and subordinates. There is a higher level of trust when subordinates see their employers as parents and the workplace as their second home. As a gesture of reciprocity for the personal, caring treatment, employees show greater diligence at work, initiative, loyalty, and obedience.
- The Filipinos' strong sense of regionalism influences their trusting behavior. A subordinate will easily trust his manager if they come from the same region, and vice-versa.
- The manager's age significantly influences the subordinate's trust in him, as age reflects knowledge and experience. On the other hand, managers can trust any subordinate who is competent and shows the right work attitudes, regardless of age.

- Historically, Filipino women have had equal rights with men in inheritance, property, education opportunities, etc. Gender did not appear as a significant factor that influences the development of trust in our survey, focus group discussions, and Delphi panel.
- Our study of manager–subordinate trust in the Philippines revealed the significant role played by job competence in creating trust. A trusted subordinate is one who gets the job done. A trusted manager is skilled in his job. Hence, a good professional relationship basically implies a smooth workflow, and essentially a mutual trust in each other's capabilities and work attitudes.

Historical Perspective

The first people in the Philippines were believed to have come to the islands about 25,000 to 30,000 years ago as part of the migration from Central to Southeastern Asia. Characteristic of these aboriginal inhabitants is "his diminutive size, his frizzy hair, his black skin color, and his meager culture" (Krieger, 1942). Subsequent migratory waves from about 5000 years ago brought the Indonesians and the Malayans—"two varieties of the Oceanic Mongolic subrace"—who were typically brown-skinned, straight-haired, and of average height (Kroeber, 1919). But a far greater variation in physical features indicates a higher degree of migration to the islands than has been generally accepted (Virchow, 1899). Furthermore, the natives speak many different dialects, albeit showing a certain linguistic unity with the Malayo-Polynesian speech family that extends to Indo-China and the Asian mainland (Krieger, 1942). Hindu influence, seen in many Sanskrit words and script, also indicates maritime trade and travel from the neighboring islands of Borneo and Java—more deeply and directly permeated by the Indian culture—about 2000 years ago. Extensive trade with China and Vietnam was recorded by the tenth century. In 1380, Arab traders introduced the Islamic religion and culture in Sulu in Southwest Philippines.

A Portuguese explorer in the service of King Charles I of Spain, Ferdinand Magellan, discovered the island of Cebu in 1521 en route to the Moluccas or the Spice Islands. Narratives of the Spanish conquest revealed an amalgam of islands that had not only international commercial trade but also a high level of literacy among both men and women: "These islanders are so given to reading and writing that there is hardly a man and much less a woman, who does not read and write in the letters of the island of Manila" (Chirino, 1890: 58). In 1565, the islands took the official name of Philippines (*Las Islas Filipinas*) in honor of the Spanish King Philip II. Three centuries of Spanish rule left a legacy of the Catholic religion and substantial Hispanic influences in Philippine education, culture, science, and industry. In addition, the oppressive aspects of colonial rule awakened patriotic desires for self-rule. In 1898, soon after the Spanish fleet was destroyed in Manila Bay, Spain ceded the Philippines to the United States. Half a century of American control brought about a democratic system of government, the extensive teaching of the English language, and a liberal capitalist way of doing business.

The Philippines gained independence from the United States on July 4, 1946. The post-independence period was beset by the challenges of postwar reconstruction, containment of pro-communist forces, and economic reforms. In 1972, President Ferdinand Marcos justified the imposition of martial law on the basis of growing lawlessness and the communist rebellion. His 20-year rule curtailed civil liberties, suppressed democratic institutions, encouraged corruption, and stunted economic development. A joint civilian and military uprising more popularly known as "people power" forced Marcos into exile and installed his political opponent's widow, Corazon Aquino, as President. Aquino confronted the major challenge of revitalizing democratic institutions and reviving the economy, but her presidency was hampered by several military coup attempts. The administration of Fidel Ramos, elected President in 1992, was marked by greater political and economic stability. His political platform of national reunification laid the foundation for talks with communist insurgents, Muslim separatists, and military rebels. In 1998, a popular movie actor, Joseph Estrada, was elected by a large following from the poor masses to whom he promised poverty alleviation and crime reduction. Within three years in power, Estrada faced charges of corruption and impeachment. His Vice-President, Gloria Macapagal-Arroyo, assumed the presidency in 2001 and was elected for a six-year term as President in 2004. Trained as an economist and with a strong background in politics as the daughter of former President Diosdado Macapagal, Arroyo was able to achieve a satisfactory economic record, although her leadership was besieged with charges of electoral fraud and corruption. She was replaced after her term ended in 2010 by Benigno Aquino III. Benefitting from the wave of public sympathy when his mother and former President Corazon Aquino died of cancer in 2009, the current Head of State ran for elections and won on the platforms of job creation, health care, and judicial reform.

Institutional Context

Economic Context

The country's GDP relies significantly on the services sector (50 percent), followed by industry (33 percent) and agriculture (17 percent). Growth in services is fueled by business process outsourcing, information technology, and tourism. Electronics have dominated export revenues (60 percent), while export growth is seen in petroleum and minerals, machinery and transport equipment, and coconut products. The highest investment is in electricity, gas and water supply, manufacturing, and real estate, with Japan, the United States, and the Netherlands as the major sources of direct foreign investment. GDP growth in 2011 is forecast at 5 percent, after an unprecedented 7.6 percent growth in 2010—its highest recorded growth in 34 years (Board of Investments, 2010). The country was not severely affected by the Asian financial crisis of 1997 or the economic crisis in US and Europe of the late 2000s. Its current economic resilience is attributed to gross international reserves and balance of payments positions (Agcaoili, 2011). Another significant buffer to the global economic downturn, dollar remittances from over 8.5 million Filipinos overseas expanded by 8.2 percent in 2010 (IRO, 2011). As of August 2011, their remittances for the year have amounted to $13 billion, 78 percent of which came from land-based workers and 22 percent or $2.8 billion was sent by sea-based workers (BSP, 2011). The unemployment rate is 7.2 percent as of April 2011, down from 8 percent in 2010.

Social Context

Life expectancy at birth is 72 years for women and 67 years for men as of 2005 (NSCB, 2011). The average fertility rate is 3.2 children per woman as of 2004. All private sector employees are covered by social security managed by the Social Security System (SSS). The government runs an equivalent program for workers in the public sector. Social security programs include old-age benefits and replacement income for workers in cases of sickness, disability, maternity, and death. Dependents' pensions, funeral benefits, and miscellaneous loans are also covered. A national health insurance program provides medical and health benefits to workers in the private and public sector. The Social Security Act of 1997 extends compulsory coverage to self-employed workers, but this sector makes up only 19 percent of the total SSS members (Verceles & Ofreneo, 2009). People can start receiving a pension at 60. Late retirement is allowed at 65 for both men and women. The Philippines has a relatively high gross replacement rate for low-income earners (95 percent), compared to global standards in pensions. This means that full-career workers with permanently low earnings have almost the same income when they retire as when they were working (OECD, 2009).

Political and Legal Systems

The Philippines is a democratic Republic. The national government's executive branch consists of the President, and 33 department secretaries and equivalent ranks in specialized agencies. The President is both the Head of State and Commander-in-Chief of the Armed Forces. Legislative power is vested in a bicameral congress consisting of the Senate (24 seats) and the House of Representatives, which had a total of 285 members in 2011. Judicial power is vested in a 15-member Supreme Court and the lower courts. An integral part of the judicial system of the country, the Shari'ah Court for Islamic law, has jurisdiction over domestic and contractual relations among Muslims and operates in some Mindanao provinces. The territorial and political subdivisions of the Philippines consist of provinces, cities, municipalities (towns), and *barangays*. The *barangay* (Malay term for boat) is the smallest local government unit, equivalent to a barrio or a village. The oldest political party is the *Nationalista Party*, founded in 1907. However, the Philippines is a multi-party system where no political party has espoused a consistent platform and enforced discipline to prevent turncoats.

Educational System

Education is offered through formal and non-formal systems. English is the official language used in both public and private schools, but Filipino (mainly based on *Tagalog*) is widely spoken. The literacy rate is 94.9 percent (UNESCO, 2011). Formal education has the 6–4–4 structure—that is, six years of primary or elementary education, four years of secondary or high-school education, and another four years to gain a bachelor's degree. Public school education (primary and secondary) is free and compulsory. The academic year starts in June and ends in March, covering a period of 40 weeks. By 2012–2013, the Department of Education is projecting to launch the K+12 program. Aimed at putting the Philippine basic education on a par with global standards, the K+12 refers to kindergarten (five years old) and 12 years of elementary and secondary education before a high-school diploma is granted.

Spending only 2.2 percent of the GDP on education, the government promises to provide K+12 free in all public schools (DepEd, 2010).

HR Practices

The Philippines has a labor force population of 39.2 million and a labor force participation rate of 63.7 percent. About 53 percent of employed people work in the services sector, 33 percent in agriculture, and 14 percent in industry. There are more workers in full-time (62 percent) than in part-time employment (36 percent). In terms of employment status, 55 percent are wage and salary workers, 30 percent are self-employed, 4 percent are employers, and 11 percent are unpaid family workers (Bureau of Labor and Employment Statistics, 2011).

Given a vast and expansive labor force, it can be expected that companies are faced with the challenge of selecting, hiring, training, and retaining the best employees. Indeed, in a survey of 400 large enterprises (Bureau of Labor and Employment Statistics, 2008), the top two HR issues are "recruitment/shortage of qualified applicants" (39.3 percent) and "high labor turnover rate" (30.5 percent). As regards the type of HR programs, the most common are staff training (93.2 percent), employee welfare (78.9 percent), and performance management (68.3 percent). In particular, the training provided by the companies is primarily designed to upgrade the workforce's competencies and competitiveness (94.5 percent). Use of more sophisticated technologies by firms is associated with a more strategic approach to human resources management practices, especially in training and development (Audea et al., 2005).

Conclusions about strategic HR practices have been drawn mostly from empirical studies of large companies who have the resources to invest in them. However, large companies make up only 0.4 percent (3080) of the 780,437 business enterprises operating in the Philippines. Micro-enterprises, which have one to nine workers, make up 91 percent, and small and medium-sized companies, with 10 to 199 employees, constitute 8.6 percent of the total number of firms (Department of Trade and Industry, 2011). In large companies, training programs may consist of formal and structured training in numerous competencies to achieve functional flexibility, job rotation, provision of an in-house training center, sending out selected employees for external training, and conducting "echo sessions" upon their return (Skene, 2003). By contrast, the limited budget for training in smaller companies leads to a more informal apprenticeship, on-the-job learning, conservation of tacit knowledge, and building a culture of trust to minimize turnover (Beerepoot, 2008).

In their study of strategic human resources management in multinationals located in the Philippines, Selmer and de Leon (2001) observed that these programs effectively integrated some Filipino values, such as concern for others and family spirit. They argued that a distinctively Filipino (*Pinoy*) HRM management style can go hand in hand with highly Westernized practices. Based on Jocano's (1999) framework of the Filipino core value system, the *Pinoy*-style HRM consists of three core elements: *kapwa* (relational), *damdamin* (emotional), and *dangal* (moral). The relational standard *kapwa* is manifested in *pakikisama*, or getting along with people, being concerned and supportive, and *pakikiramay*, which is the ability to sympathize and share with other people's suffering. The premium placed on the emotional standard *damdamin* is observed when Filipinos try to avoid conflicts and confrontations, observe proper and refined behavior (*delicadeza*), and preserve self-esteem (*amor propio*). The moral standard *dangal* refers to the pride in and commitment to revered ideals and is manifested in reciprocity (*utang na loob*) or the feeling of indebtedness to return a favor granted, even if the grantor does not expect a reciprocal action. In this regard, the level of understanding of the cultures underlying the behavior and attitudes of managers and subordinates will significantly influence the successful implementation of strategic human resources programs in the local context, regardless of firm size.

Leadership Style

Filipino managers' leadership style is generally person- and team-oriented. Effective leaders rarely use their formal power to impose authority. They rely on smooth interpersonal relationships (*pakikisama*) whose results may vary from simple reciprocal behavior to a high level of cooperation or loyalty. Business leaders promote the value of the organization as a family where concern for employees often extends to their personal lives and their family members.

In the GLOBE study of 62 societies, the Philippines scored high in performance orientation, which pertains to the degree to which the organization or society encourages and rewards group members for performance improvement and excellence (House *et al.*, 2004). The Filipinos put a high premium on performance. This value is deeply rooted in their sense of justice (*katarungan*), in that a person should receive due reward for the effort he has put into his work and his educational preparation for it. A similar conclusion was found by Neelankavil (2000). Studying the determinants of managerial performance in four diverse cultures, he found that Filipino middle-level managers rated academic achievements and past experience very highly. In this regard, the Filipino leader motivates by inspiring followers to deliver according to high performance standards.

In the same GLOBE study, people's aspirations are not strongly related to their current practices, but the Philippines is included among the societies with a high practices score in performance orientation (House *et al.*, 2004). This can be explained by the Filipino concept of fatalism (*bahala na*). On the one hand, fatalism reflects an over-reliance on God or fate. But it has also implicit in it the confidence to move on. Thus, in work situations, Filipinos may interpret current injustices or lack of rewards as "not meant to be mine yet," and will continue to aspire that perseverance, hard work, and diligence will be rewarded in due time. Jocano (1999) observes that *bahala na* generates three modes of response: *tiwala* (confidence), *sigla* (enthusiasm), and *kaya* (capability).

The emphasis on performance partly explains the high gender egalitarianism in Philippine society. Women can work wherever they have the professional preparation and the wish. Most employees can work equally well with a male or female manager. Gender matters less than a track record of quality work performance. The Philippines has a history of gender equality. Back in the pre-colonial era, women were not considered second-class citizens as descent was traced equally through both male and female lineages. They had equal rights with men in inheritance, property, and education opportunities. Women held pre-eminent roles such as priestesses, presiding over religious affairs, or as rulers of provinces, such as Queen Sima of Cotabato in the seventh century and Princess Urduja of Pangasinan in the fourteenth century. Faced with double standards during the colonial era, women either vigorously petitioned for the recognition of their rights or openly joined and led revolutionary battles, such as Gabriela Silang and Trinidad Tecson. Roffey (2000) described Filipino women as able to effectively combine business success and power with virtuous conduct and aesthetics in physical grooming. The woman manager can retain her femininity in a masculine executive role. Unlikely to manifest aggressive behavior, she will be persistent and independent, while seeking to maintain trust and social cohesion in her environment through hospitality and personalized concern, with a leadership style that stands out for being collaborative and supportive, rather than individualistic and competitive.

Philippine society places strong emphasis on visionary leadership. In the GLOBE study, the Philippines held one of the top places in this leadership characteristic, along with the US and Canada. This means that the effective Filipino leader knows how to connect with his workers' deep sense of spirituality and humanity, which makes them aspire for what works in the longer term—spiritual well-being, integral dignity, and harmonious relationships, even amidst lack of material wealth.

Other important contexts of leadership in the Philippines are the high level of power distance and in-group collectivism. Academic titles or business ranks are important to the Filipinos, not only because of the investment expended into achieving them but also for their usefulness in gaining immediate respect and esteem in a new environment. Nevertheless, once the introductions are done with, titled people may quickly request to be addressed by their family or first name. This implies that relationships still matter more than structure in a hierarchical Philippine society. Also, Filipinos are open to role changes as they are assumed to be not fixed or given. For example, through belief in the "wheel of life," it is accepted that a person may be in a superior role today but in a subordinate role tomorrow. But for as long as he is the manager, he makes the decisions, he is in charge, and he has to be obeyed.

High in-group collectivism is manifested in the time and effort spent on building smooth relationships. Individual dignity is highly dependent on how one is viewed or regarded by the other members of the group. There is a strong need for group members to be involved or consulted in a group decision, or to feel that one has been part of group decision-making. The personal relationships built by managers with their subordinates can make a decisive contribution to work motivation, loyalty, and cohesiveness with the organization, especially in times of crisis. Preferential treatment for one member of the group can undermine a leader's authority and the group's unity.

Lastly, Philippine society is low in assertiveness and uncertainty avoidance. Communication is indirect and less confrontational. When a speaker says "we," it may just mean "I" to avoid being too direct or aggressive in speech. Aggressive behaviors are not culturally desirable in Filipino leaders. Filipinos likewise tend to avoid making plans to the last details. This somehow reflects their fatalistic attitude—risks and uncertainties are part of life and cannot be avoided. Thus, leaders are faced frequently with challenging situations caused by loose schedules, time-bound commitments are evaded, and timetables are juggled constantly. Also, timeliness is not a virtue for Filipinos, but punctuality may be stressed in corporate cultures that depend heavily on client satisfaction.

Literature Review on Trust

The Philippines has been described as a low-level society in terms of trust. For example, Labonne *et al.* (2007) found that trust among individual members is lower in Philippine communities with inequalities in assets, and the poorer people in a given community tend to trust less. Quah (2010) compared the Philippines and Singapore using various governance and corruption perception indices and argued that the former has a lower level of trust due to its relative lack of political stability and ineffectiveness to combat corruption. Li and Wu (2010) observed that, although both China and the Philippines thrive in corruption, the Philippines has a relatively low level of trust, influencing a more inefficient and predatory corruption.

Some studies analyzed the contexts and factors that increase the level of societal trust. Using an impact assessment method, Capuno and Garcia (2010) proved that a more effective public dissemination of local governance performance can bring about greater trust in local leaders and induce a higher level of civic participation. Specifically, exposure to the performance assessment scores of their own local governments could increase the probability of joining community organizations or projects by 20 to 60 percentage points. In contrast, the authors noted that the results of other performance indicator systems announced in national or regional media matter less to constituents. In a study of civilian review boards, which handle citizens' complaints about the police, De Guzman (2007) used a cross-sectional survey of complainants and police officers and found that citizens trust a review board that is impartial and competent. The venue for filing or hearing cases is less relevant to citizens; thus, a civilian review board may hold its hearings either within the physical confines of a police department or at the local government. What is more important to public trust is the board's image for integrity in handling cases, where integrity is measured on the basis of its membership and balanced representation.

San Antonio (2008) looked into the impact of advisory school councils in public secondary schools and argued that stakeholders vested more trust in school authorities that had implemented a school council due to the greater opportunities for open communication and involvement in collegiate or collaborative processes. Moreover, within the council, the factors that influenced their level of trust include the members' readiness to share ideas, cooperation, dedication, and genuine concern for the school's welfare. On the contrary, the members were not inspired to participate actively when the other members were either indifferent or hesitant about expressing their ideas, voiced destructive criticisms or manifested domineering behavior, or did not devote time or dedication to the council's activities. Trust became a lubricant for school reforms. San Antonio (2008) also investigated the effect on trust of stakeholders' characteristics and found that trust levels did not significantly differ on the basis of age, gender, and constituency.

Little has been written about the high level of interpersonal trust, how it is formed, and what factors lead trust to be given or withheld. One interesting piece of literature comes from the nursing profession. Pasco *et al.* (2004) studied how trust develops in a cross-cultural relationship. Using a focused ethnography of Filipino–Canadian patients' experience of nursing care, the authors concluded that a patient's willingness to trust the nurse will depend on the latter's qualities, such as kindness, courteousness, approachability, and respectfulness, regardless of race. Moreover, as an outcome of that trust, the level of interaction with the nurse will develop from being *ibang tao* (not one of us) to *hindi ibang tao* (one of us), characterized by *paki-kipagpalagayan-loob* (mutual comfort) and *pakikiisa* (oneness). The authors clarified that this model of relationship is not linear, as trust is continually tested during hospitalization. Trust may fail if the nurse fails to respond appropriately, communicate adequately, or work proactively toward being *hindi ibang tao*.

In Roffey's (2000) Filipino research of businesswomen and entrepreneurs, she discovered that building trust is an essential strategic management approach. For example, women executives empower their subordinates by showing trust in their capabilities to perform their duties and make decisions. Women leaders also reinforce the family spirit and social cohesion within the business organization through their trusting relationship with and personalized concern for its members.

Restubog and Bordia (2006) operationalized the concepts of workplace familism and erosion of trust by psychological contract breach and conducted a survey of 267 employees enrolled in part-time MBA courses in the Philippines. The authors found a stronger negative relationship between breach and civic virtue when workplace supervisor familism was high. When the workplace provides socio-emotional support functions like in a family, there is a greater likelihood for employees to engage in positive behaviors and to view their managers as meeting their personal expectations. In this regard, trust is preceded by an employee's expectation that he or she would be taken care of and nurtured by the organization and his or her immediate supervisor. A cultural context is the emphasis on keeping one's word (*palabra de honor*) as a form of commitment or loyalty.

Contextual Factors in Hierarchical Trusting Relationships

Data gathered from focus group discussions (FGD) and the Delphi panel give us rich qualitative information about trust in hierarchical relationships in the Philippines. First, managers and subordinates generally trust each other. Managers trust the people they hire on the basis of their selection criteria, which include competence and shared values with the organization. Subordinates trust their boss, first on the basis of his leadership position, which then builds over time, when they have proven his job knowledge and experienced a good quality relationship with him. A lack of trust will produce conflicts. The Delphi panel experts also agree that managers generally trust their subordinates, and vice-versa, until proven otherwise with behaviors that betray trust.

However, the degree of trust may vary depending on several factors, such as company size, and organizational and national culture. According to subordinates, "a smaller organization has less walls between superiors and subordinates" and "it is easier to approach the higher-ups." For managers, a small company means less risk when a subordinate betrays management's trust, closer interaction with people, or greater flexibility when people are relatively less specialized, unlike larger organizations. On the other hand, a large company can generate more trust if the volume of work persuades senior management to push decision-making down the line. A big firm may also send a strong message about the firm's financial ability to take care of its employees' welfare. Nevertheless, there is general consensus among the FGD participants that size matters less than the way that managers and subordinates get along with each other (*pakikisama*)—this camaraderie being fostered by the manager's leadership and communication style.

The FGD participants likewise agreed that the Filipinos' friendly culture—knowing how to adjust to and relate with others—makes them more trusting and trustworthy. But a Delphi panel expert noted certain acquiescence in the Philippine culture that underlies a tendency to doubt, originating "in an authoritarian home where older members of the family require strict compliance with their words without question." With this kind of conditioning, people tend not to question, and instead manifest trusting behavior externally. "I believe, however, that open communication lines can overcome this issue." In this regard, we can say that the national culture determines the level of trust that managers and subordinates start to work in, but they can facilitate or hinder trust development by the choices they make as leaders and followers.

A salient dimension of Philippine culture that facilitates trust is the treatment of the employer as a parent, and the workplace as a second home. One of our experts said that a good indicator of a high level of trust is the invitation extended by a worker to his manager to be the godfather in his children's baptism. The workers look up "to their bosses as people who will take care not only of them but also of their offspring." Any help is valued as a debt of honor ("*utang na loob*") and, as a norm of reciprocity, the favor is returned by the employees in greater diligence at work, loyalty, obedience, etc.

Still on the topic of culture, the FGD participants who worked in Filipino–Chinese companies observed that trust formation is more difficult in mixed organizational cultures. As mentioned in the historical notes earlier, the Philippines have been trading with the Chinese since the ninth or tenth centuries. At present, among the ethnic groups, the Chinese make up 1.5 percent of the entire population. A participant noted: "it is a different culture with the Chinese, they are choosy about who they trust." One study observed that, in Chinese business relationships, *guanxi* (connection) opens the door but *xinren* (deep trust) keeps you inside. *Guanxi* provides the connection to opportunities and *xinren* determines the level of emotional commitment in the business relationship (Kriz & Keating, 2010). A Delphi panel expert mentioned that Chinese managers' practice of hiring Chinese subordinates is one way for them to ensure a trusting work relationship on the basis of shared values. However, the author of this chapter did not pursue the topic more fully as it was considered that this collection would have another chapter on trust in China. In addition, she believes that the trust in hierarchical relationships in Filipino–Chinese or Chinese–Filipino employees has a lot more historical background and cultural nuances than can be explained in the limited pages available for this chapter. Neither is it easy to decide whether the Chinese learned from the Filipinos to be more trusting or the Filipinos learned from the Chinese to be less trusting, relying on the passing of time to either earn or bestow trust.

The industry also provides a context for the level of trust. A manager from an audit/accountancy firm said that the training in the profession by itself makes people exert effort to prove themselves trustworthy.

> The work of an accountant always has its own checks and balances. He double checks everything. For example, even if a job applicant says that he comes from a prestigious college, he still has to earn my trust. I give the same treatment to

everyone. And I observe all the actions of my subordinates to verify that they are worthy of my trust. And especially if this is their first job, I keep a close watch on their tasks and outputs.

Similarly, a Delphi panel expert qualifies trust in the service industry. He argued that:

> trust is not necessarily important any more when service standards, controls, and procedures have been established. However, the underlying assumption is that trust is largely important because even the lowest subordinate in the service industry carries the company's brand name. In manufacturing, there is a lot of distance between managers and subordinates because of the existence of procedures—subordinates can function well as long as the rules of the game are quite specific. In agriculture, landowners do not necessarily trust their tenants, but it depends on how sophisticated the farm is.

Personal Factors in Hierarchical Trusting Relationships

The managers who participated in the FGD agree that they can trust any subordinate, young or old. What matters more than age is the ability to perform, sense of responsibility, or flexibility to make adjustments. One manager specified:

> A 30-year-old employee might not be flexible and active at work as he might have many burdens already. But a person who is 18 or 19 years old might be lackadaisical, although it is possible that someone will be responsible even at that age. If he is older, he might be more capable and responsible. But the downside is that it might be more difficult to instruct him if he has a firmly set mind about how things should be done.

On the other hand, subordinates will invariably place more trust in a manager who is older than them. Age becomes synonymous with experience and knowledge. They may trust a younger manager eventually, but at the beginning of the relationship, they would doubt the manager: "Is he capable of doing the work/managing a department?" Another subordinate admitted that he would not be comfortable with a younger manager and the solutions he might be proposing at work, although he would "respect his authority as the boss." Two Delphi panel experts agreed with them. For one, "age is important, because workers assume that the older you get, the more wisdom you have." Another argued that age generally does not matter, except in the case of "a distinctly younger boss and his older subordinate. The latter would have less trust in the younger boss, because he thinks he knows more, has more experience, even if the former has high academic achievement (e.g. MBA, etc.)."

As to tenure, both managers and subordinates coincide in the view that a longer tenure builds greater trust because tenure is a signal of good performance in the job. It may also be more meritorious to have tenure in the company after having worked in different departments because it implies that the person has learned to adjust with different groups of people. For the managers, subordinates with tenure also means a greater familiarity with the company's culture and with other members of the organization ("they know the rules and expected behavior"), which is advantageous to job performance. In a similar vein, the subordinates likened the manager's tenure to greater knowledge of one's job and effectiveness as a manager. Having more employees with tenure also signifies that the company has generated devotion, and consequently there is more trust.

Gender is not an important consideration for either group. Managers emphasize job performance more than gender, although they noted the advantages of having women in work requiring attention to details or assigning men to off-site tasks. Subordinates generally do not consider gender as a factor influencing trust, two of them citing the principle of equality of the sexes: "Both are equal, even in work." A male expert affirmed, "People are not as discriminating on the gender side. Filipino men are very comfortable working with women, and having women as their bosses. I have seen that in all situations. Gender is not really an issue."

It is not disputed either that the length of the relationship between manager and subordinate makes both parties more confident with each other inasmuch as trust is earned over time. Subordinates see the advantage of longer relationships in "a better appreciation of my boss's management style," "more ease in dealing with one another," "more openness in the relationship," and "a stronger bonding." Similarly, a Delphi panel expert assumed "that the longer this relationship has existed, the more personal knowledge of each other's character, and personality traits, that enables each one to 'understand' the other." Another expert specified:

> There's a time factor in the development of trust during which one assesses the other in terms of stability, reliability, sincerity, honesty. Once a relationship has lasted some time, it means trust has grown, to break out of it hurts, and it may not happen very often, which makes this variable relatively stable as a determinant of trust.

Similarity in terms of place of origin or race appeared as a personal factor that helps in forming trust in hierarchical relationships. One female subordinate ascribed the trust in her female manager to the fact that both of them are from the same province: "In my case, my manager earned my trust immediately because we are both from Davao." A Delphi panel expert included it among the demographic characteristics which are important for trust, and ranked it number three, after length of relationship and tenure, and before gender. He observed that "Chinese-owned or managed companies tend to have more trust in their Chinese employees, and the same may be said of people coming from one particular region (e.g. Cebuanos to Cebuanos; Ilocanos to Ilocanos)."

The results of our quantitative study correspond with the opinions expressed by the FGD participants and the Delphi panel experts. First, a manager's age is negatively correlated with subordinate's trust in the manager. The younger the manager, the less tendency there is for subordinates to trust him. Second, the subordinate's age correlates with organizational citizenship behavior (OCB), which involves pro-active behaviors or going the extra mile at work. We have seen earlier that an older subordinate implies someone who is more responsible, as well as being more capable of doing the job. A Delphi panel expert associated age with maturity, which brings with it a proactive attitude to "seek clear explanations and take relatively sure steps to resolve any ambiguity encountered." Third, the subordinate's academic level correlates with OCB (see Table 14.1). The cultural emphasis on education and the organizations' preference for college graduates, even for entry-level positions, imply the belief that higher education produces workers who possess not only greater competencies to meet work standards, but also enhanced attitudes as a

Table 14.1 The Philippines: significant controls (correlations)

	Age: manager	Age: subordinate	Academic level: subordinate
MTB			
OCB		0.233**	0.335**
MTS			
STM	−0.180*		

Notes
** Correlation significant at 0.01 level.
* Correlation significant at 0.05 level.
MTB = managerial trustworthy behavior, STM = subordinates' trust in managers, MTS = managers' trust in subordinates, OCB = organizational citizenship behavior.

mature professional in the workplace. There is a greater expectation that a college degree holder will be more diligent, resourceful, dependable, and cooperative than a high-school graduate.

Antecedents and Outcomes of Manager–Subordinate Trust

When one works closely and regularly with another person in a hierarchy, it is important to have a good professional relationship. This means above all that the basic work requirements and all other expectations are met. One manager specified the existence of "teamwork to get the job done." Another manager understood it as achieving "good results in terms of production quotas." For the professional relationship to be a good one, the bosses tend to put the responsibility on the subordinates to "know their job descriptions," "meet expectations," "deliver quality work," "be willing to work according to their job descriptions," "not need to be reminded about what they should do," or "be responsible and do their tasks well."

When the work is being done as expected, managers appreciate that their subordinates are "straightforward with the problems they meet at work," do not wait until "things get out of hand," "are humble enough to admit their mistakes or do not hide their mistakes," and "openly ask for assistance when needed." In the spirit of mutual respect, managers "do not dictate but rather give value to their subordinates' inputs, to what they think is right, and what they have learned on the job." In return, the subordinates value their managers' judgments.

For the subordinates, a good professional relationship implies "that there is teamwork, good output and easier work," "working harmoniously to achieve a common goal," "that the manager listens to employees' feedback and suggestions," and "seeing each other eye to eye." It is based on trust and it also generates trust as well. The subordinates in the FGD specified that a good professional relationship leads to a smooth workflow, warm camaraderie, and "mutual trust in each other's strengths and weaknesses."

What behaviors precede the manager's trust in the subordinates? Job performance tops the list. For example, "the job must be done correctly and efficiently," there must be "consistency of quality and timeliness of work delivery," and "they have a good record of past performance in the company or outside it." The trustworthy subordinate not only gets the job done but "he also exceeds performance standards." A subordinate who is trusted is independent: "can work with minimum supervision", has self-reliance, and takes initiative. Nevertheless, he or she is also honest, sincere, and transparent in informing the manager of problems that crop up in work. Lastly, it can be seen from the behavior of trusted subordinates that they have "a certain kind of love for their work" or "*may malasakit*".

When the managers trust their subordinates, they believe that the outcomes will be evident in their own feelings of assurance and satisfaction that the work will be done well, if not faster, and they can devote their time and attention to other concerns. One manager said that the volume of work demands her to be "willing to entrust more work and to have confidence that subordinates can deliver the job." A manager intentionally gives "more challenge to the subordinates to test their potential" for harder work or a bigger responsibility. The effects of trust can also be seen in a more harmonious workplace. One manager likened it to "harmony that exists within a family where each member fulfills his/her obligations without forgetting the concerns of the other members."

What behaviors precede the subordinates' trust in the manager? Competence is top priority. The manager "knows what he is doing" and has "working knowledge" or "experience in the industry or company." The manager "delegates tasks and makes sure that these are accomplished," "communicates his expectations clearly," "empowers us to make decisions," and "gives feedback on performance." The manager who earns the subordinate's trust motivates and leads by inspiring his employees "to make themselves more useful at work" or "to give their best," gives them challenging assignments, gives credit where it is due, lends support and encouragement when needed, and treats everyone fairly. A trustworthy manager shows genuine concern for his subordinate as a worker and as a person. One subordinate could not forget that his manager even offered to buy them food after seeing how tired they were at work. A manager is also trusted when he looks after their professional development by coaching them in their work, like the manager who "teaches his staff the promotion strategies that work best in marketing." He is "approachable," starts friendly conversations about non-work topics, such as the family, and extends the relationship beyond the confines of the office. For example, a manager has the sensitivity "to ask how we are doing," or "to chat with us about current topics that don't have anything to do with work."

When the subordinates learn to trust their managers who behave in the aforementioned manner, they will be "more effective at work," "more motivated and persistent" in their jobs, "willing to work extra hours and do whatever the boss will ask from them," or "take initiative to do needed tasks without being asked." They will also be "willing to learn new skills" and "appreciate that what the boss asks from them is good not only for the company but also for their own development." Feeling greater security at work, they will value the company as their second home and care for it. At the very least, "they would not do anything to destroy it" ("*hindi ka gagawa ng anumang makakasira sa kumpanya*").

Figure 14.1 summarizes the connotations of good professional relationships, as well as the antecedents and outcomes of trust in hierarchical relationships as gathered from focus group discussions.

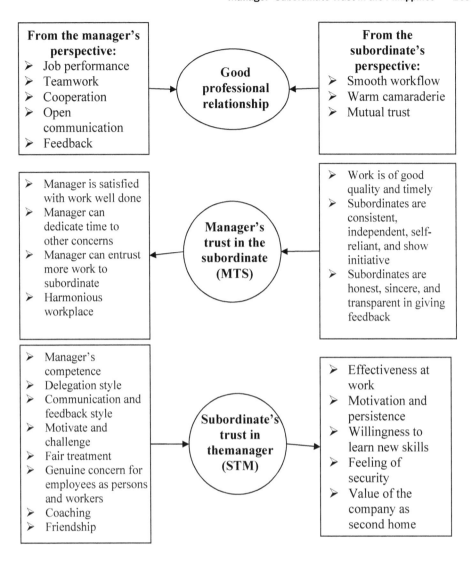

Figure 14.1 Antecedents and outcomes of trust in hierarchical relationships

The Dynamics of Trust in Hierarchical Relationships

For a hierarchical relationship to work on a daily basis, trust is an important element. But trust can vary in depth and strength. For example, a relationship that has been tested by many difficulties and crises over the course of time will develop a deeper trust. On the other hand, trust between manager and subordinate in a payroll department may become very strong in a short period because the task's accountability requires it. If trust does not exist, either the manager or the subordinate loses the job.

The managers were in agreement that they already trusted their subordinates even before the latter trusted them. This is because the managers get to know them and their capabilities before they are hired. "Their credentials become the basis for giving trust to the subordinate." When doubt arises within the hiring process, the manager will investigate the accuracy of the credentials presented and will not hire applicants who do not deserve his trust. However, once the doubts are clarified in favor of the applicant, then more trust is generated. Once the person is hired, the quantity of trust may differ depending on the work. One manager in the FGD group said that "trust is given right away." He works in a bank with a huge volume of work for a manager, and hence many decisions are delegated to the subordinates. For him, trust in the lower-rank employees is essential. "Before you delegate anything to them, for them to make decisions, you should trust your people and you must have confidence in them." If there is little trust, then the manager will have an excessive amount of work that can render him ineffective. Another manager stated that trust develops in stages. Upon entry into the manager's organization, the subordinate undergoes training and "a lot of coaching. As you review their work, you build confidence in your people."

The subordinates in the FGD argued that trust is important from the very beginning of their professional relationships. "If you don't trust your manager, how will you obey what he is asking you to do?" However, trust may co-exist with a certain level of hesitation, as in the case of the subordinate who has more tenure in the company than his manager. "Anything can happen. You will have a problem if he does not meet your expectations." The hesitation is founded on the fear that a current level of good performance may be hampered by the arrival of a new boss who might not fully know the work demands. But trust is earned once the new manager proves to be an additional help, instead of a hindrance, for the department.

Table 14.2 shows our quantitative data on the dynamics of trust in hierarchical relationships in the Philippines. The country results are compared with the consolidated results from 18 countries. First, the data show that the subordinates' organizational citizenship behavior serves as a source of or contributing factor to managers' trust in subordinates that is very similar to the complete model. We have discussed the descriptions of these relationships earlier in the section on the antecedents and outcomes of trust. Second, the manager's trust in his subordinates will positively relate to managerial trustworthy behavior, although to a lesser degree than in the complete model. This can be explained by the fact that, in the Philippines, managers are expected to meet the standards of their position (competence and integrity) and to achieve the organization's goals, whether or not they have developed trust in their subordinates. Third, managerial trustworthy behavior will positively relate to the subordinate's trust in the managers, again to a lesser degree than in the complete model. This can be explained by the fact that the managers in the Philippines are initially trusted by virtue of their position, their title, and their achievement in becoming a manager (high power distance). Lastly, there is a higher correlation

Table 14.2 Standardized regression weights for the trust model in the Philippines and the overall sample

	OCB–>MTS	MTS–>MTB	MTB–>STM	STM–>OCB
Philippines	0.66**	0.29*	0.71**	0.20*
Complete model	0.68**	0.34**	0.89**	0.08*

Notes
* Regression weight significant at 0.01 level.
** Regression weight significant at 0.05 level.
No asterisk – Regression weight not significant.

between the subordinates' trust in their managers and their organizational citizenship behavior. This may be explained by the norm of reciprocity (*utang na loob*) when the subordinate feels indebted to a trusted manager and manifests his gratitude through extra-role behaviors.

Two of our four Delphi panel experts concur that the arrows can point in opposite directions. One of them observed that the model portrays a certain linearity that does not reflect the possible discursive effects of underlying factors, such as, for example, certain personal characteristics of individuals or cultural sensitivities which can create tension in the development of trust.

> I would suggest a more interactive flow, sensitive to the recognition of internal and external factors noted, which may be both positive and negative, provoked by the uncertainties of culture, time, space and speed of change that may affect the trust-building process. A reconfigured model will feature a two-way arrow connection to recognize both the linearity and the contradictory nature of the flow.

For this expert, the contradictory flow represents the fact that negative factors may disturb the development of trust in the manager–subordinate relationship.

Discussion and Conclusions

This chapter has provided descriptions of the construct of trust in manager–subordinate dyads in the Philippines. Focus group discussions and a Delphi panel were employed to interpret the results of the quantitative study conducted in the Philippines in 2007. Aware of the need to place a study of manager–subordinate trust in a wider cultural context to gain a better understanding, this chapter also explored the historical background and institutional environment of trust. It has examined what has been reported about trust both in the societal and in the business setting.

Our study reveals that there is a very high level of trust between two people who work closely together. Subordinates already have an initial trust in their managers by virtue of the latter's leadership position. Managers already have an initial trust in future subordinates because they have the advantage of knowing the latter's competencies during the hiring and selection process. This initial trust escalates as the manager proves his subordinates' capabilities in action, while the subordinates are more empowered to prove through their work performance that they are worthy of the trust (Roffey, 2000). We have also confirmed the positive effect of in-group orientation or "familism" in the subordinates' good work attitudes or the prevention of any behavior that might erode trust (Restubog & Bordia, 2006). Such familism is reinforced by the manager's personalized concern for the employee's personal and family welfare, and consequently the latter's high need to reciprocate with loyalty and dedication to his tasks. Moreover, similar to the findings of De Guzman (2007), competence is key to a constituent's trust in people or groups in governing positions. Lastly, the answers of our FGD support the view of San Antonio (2008) that open communication, cooperation, and mutual trust facilitate professional relationships.

Various dimensions of the Philippine and Asian cultures elucidated in the GLOBE study (House *et al.*, 2004) provide a deeper understanding of the manager–subordinate trust dynamics. The high performance orientation influences the subordinates to trust their managers. The fact that a person is a manager suggests that he can be trusted for the huge effort he has expended to reach that position (academic background, job experience, and performance). In the same manner, a subordinate who exceeds performance expectations easily earns his manager's trust. Considering the high gender egalitarianism in Philippine society, it is noteworthy that gender does not influence a trust relationship. A female manager or subordinate may not be a recipient of trust not because of gender but most probably because she is not performing in her job. A visionary leadership style connects well with the followers, who trust that they are in good hands in both the professional and the personal spheres. Ethnocentrism facilitates trust among members of the in-group regardless of their level in the hierarchy.

In this regard, our quantitative data showed that a manager's trustworthy behavior positively relates to the subordinate's trust in the manager, although to a lesser degree than in the global model. We explained this by the fact that managers in the Philippines are initially trusted by virtue of their position, their title, and their achievement in becoming a manager (high power distance). We also found a high correlation between the subordinates' trust in their managers and their organizational citizenship behavior. We found an explanation in the cultural norm of reciprocity (*utang na loob*). The subordinate normally feels indebted to a trusted manager and manifests his gratitude through extra-role behaviors.

This chapter makes an important contribution to the study of trust in a particular context. The Western influence in the Philippines (through American and Spanish colonization) could take for granted that Western management practices can find easy acceptance in the local context. However, our study showed that much of what transpires in a trusting relationship has roots in strong cultural traits. It is important both for foreigners setting up businesses in the Philippines and for locals who are educated in Western practices to understand these cultural nuances for developing trust. For instance, we have found that, although competence generates trust, a competent manager's young age could negatively influence the subordinates' trust in him.

There are inherent limitations in our research design. Our sample involved only the employees of companies located in Metro Manila. It may not reflect the trust dynamics of less heterogeneous populations. Bias may have come from respondents educated in Western management theory and practice, and hence the study may not have captured the truly emic nature of trust. Bias could have also come in through the author, who, while being a native, has followed postgraduate studies in management abroad. Future research needs to test our framework of a hierarchical trusting relationship and could explore the differences in trust dynamics in different industries. The ethnocentric Philippine society could also provide an interesting study of trust according to the different regional or ethnic groups. Such a study could be relevant for businesses (e.g. call centers and business process out sourcing) extending their operations outside of Luzon (where Metro Manila is located) to the other major islands.

References

Agcaoili, L. (2011, November 8). *PH Can Survive Global Economic Crisis: IMF.* Retrieved November 2011 from www.abs-cbnnews.com/business/11/07/11/ph-can-survive-global-economic-crisis-imf.

Audea, T., Teo, S. & Crawford, J. (2005). HRM professionals and their perceptions of HRM and firm performance in the Philippines. *International Journal of Human Resource Management*, 16(4): 532–552.

Beerepoot, N. (2008). Diffusion of knowledge and skills through labour markets: Evidence from the furniture cluster in Metro Cebu (the Philippines). *Entrepreneurship & Regional Development*, 20(1): 67–88.

Board of Investments (2010). *Rising Business Confidence.* Annual Report, Makati.

BSP (2011). *Overseas Filipinos' Remittances.* Retrieved November 2011 from Bangko Sentral ng Pilipinas: www.bsp.gov.ph/statistics/keystat/ofw.htm.

Bureau of Labor and Employment Statistics (2008). Survey on human resource management practices. *Labstat Updates*, 12.

Bureau of Labor and Employment Statistics (2011). Highlights of the January 2011 Labor Force Survey. *Labstat Updates*, 15(4).

Capuno, J. & Garcia, M. (2010). Can information about local government performance induce civic participation? Evidence from the Philippines. *Journal of Development Studies*, 46(4): 624–643.

Chirino, P. (1890). *Relacion de las Islas Filipinas*, 2nd ed. Manila: Esteban Balbas.

De Guzman, M. (2007). Integrity of civilian review: A contemporary analysis of complainants' and police officers' views in the Philippines. *Police Practice and Research*, 8(1): 31–45.

Department of Trade and Industry (2011). *Micro, Small and Medium Enterprises (MSMEs): Statistics*. Retrieved November 2011 from www.dti.gov.ph/dti/index.php?p=321.

DepEd (2010). *Discussion Paper on the Enhanced K+12 Basic Education Program.* Retrieved November 2011 from www.deped.gov.ph/cpanel/uploads/issuanceImg/K12new.pdf.

House, R.J., Hanges, P.J., Javidan, M., Dorfman, P.W. & Gupta, V. (2004). *Culture, Leadership and Organizations: The GLOBE Study of 62 Societies.* California: Sage.

IRO (2011, September 30). *The Philippines: A Fortified Economic Story.* Retrieved November 2011 from Investor Relations Office, Government of the Philippines: www.iro.ph/article_doc/2663226a_ROP_Presentation.pdf.

Jocano, F.L. (1999). *Towards Developing a Filipino Corporate Culture: Uses of Filipino Traditional Structures and Values in Modern Management.* Quezon City: Punlad.

Krieger, H.W. (1942). *Peoples of the Philippines.* Washington DC: Smithsonian Institution.

Kriz, A. & Keating, B. (2010). Business relationships in China: Lessons about deep trust. *Asia Pacific Business Review*, 16(3): 299–318.

Kroeber, A. (1919). *Peoples of the Philippines.* New York: American Museum of National History.

Labonne, J., Biller, D. & Chase, R. (2007). *Inequality and Relative Wealth: Do they Matter for Trust? Evidence from Poor Communities in the Philippines.* Social Development Department, Washington DC: World Bank.

Li, S. & Wu, J. (2010). Why some countries thrive despite corruption: The role of trust in the corruption-efficiency relationship. *Review of International Political Economy*, 17(1): 129–154.

Neelankavil, J.P. (2000). Determinants of managerial performance: A cross-cultural comparison of the perceptions of middle-level managers of four countries. *Journal of International Business Studies*, 31(1): 121–140.

NSCB (2011). *Philippine Minimum National Data Set.* Retrieved November 2011 from National Statistical Coordination Board: www.nscb.gov.ph/stats/mnsds/default.asp.

OECD (2009). *Pensions at a Glance Special Edition: Asia/Pacific.* OECD and World Bank.

Pasco, A.C., Morse, J. & Olson, J. (2004). Cross-cultural relationships between nurses and Filipino Canadian patients. *Journal of Nursing Scholarship*, 36(3): 239–246.

Quah, J. (2010). Trust and governance in the Philippines and Singapore: A comparative analysis. *International Public Management Review*, 11(2): 4–37.

Restubog, S.L. & Bordia, P. (2006). Workplace familism and psychological contract breach in the Philippines. *Applied Psychology: An International Review*, 55(4): 563–585.

Roffey, B.H. (2000). Strategic leadership and management in the Philippines: Dynamics of gender and culture. *Labour and Management in Development*, 1(10): 1–31.

San Antonio, D.M. (2008). Creating better schools through democratic school leadership. *International Journal of Leadership in Education*, 11(1): 43–62.

Selmer, J. & de Leon, C. (2001). Pinoy-Style HRM: Human resource management in the Philippines. *Asia Pacific Business Review*, 8(1): 127–144.

Skene, C. (2003). Change and continuity: Recent developments in HRM in the Philippines. *Asia Pacific Business Review*, 9(4): 106–128.

UNESCO (2011). Retrieved November 2011 from UNESCO Office in Bangkok: www.unescobkk.org.

Verceles, N. & Ofreneo, R. (2009). *Policy Brief on Social Security: Philippines.* May. Retrieved November 2011 from www.homenetseasia.org/SSS%20BRIEF%20FINALApril22.pdf.

Virchow, R. (1899). *The Peopling of the Philippines.* Washington: Smithsonian Institution.

15

Manager–Subordinate Trust Relationships in West Africa[1]

FRANCA OVADJE

Introduction

There is a growing interest among researchers in trust and its antecedents and consequences. Several studies have been carried out on the phenomenon (Mayer & Davis, 1999). This is perhaps due to the fact that "[i]t is becoming increasingly recognized that trust in the workplace is a critical factor leading to enhanced organizational performance" (Gould-Williams, 2003:29).

In their meta-analysis of trust research, Dirks and Ferrin (2002) found that trust is positively associated with workplace attitudes such as organizational commitment and job satisfaction, as well as organizational variables such as performance and organizational citizenship behavior. Trust was negatively related to turnover intention. They conclude that trust is a powerful concept in the study of workplace attitudes and organizational variables such as performance.

Trust in hierarchical relationships is perhaps even more important in collectivist societies such as African countries. It is therefore important to understand how Africans define trust and what the outcomes of trust are for individuals and organizations. Such studies are likely to have huge practical implications for the management of people in the continent, while contributing to the trust literature.

In this chapter, I present the findings of the study on trust in West Africa. First, I will introduce the reader to the historical and institutional context, after which I will briefly review what we know about human resource practices and leadership in Africa. Before presenting the research results, I will review the literature on trust in Africa. The chapter ends with a discussion of the findings and their implications.

1 I am grateful to Esther Akinnukawe and Charlemagne Dallied Kien for collecting some of the data used in this study.

Highlights of Manager–Subordinate Trust in West Africa

- The West African sample described trust as reliability, dependability, credibility, loyalty, honesty, and respect. Consistency, consideration, and relationship were other descriptors of trust.
- Trust involves putting the person before the results. Bosses who are trusted see subordinates as persons and not as instruments for attaining organizational objectives.
- The size of the organization did not matter for trust building in the boss–subordinate relationship. However, in small organizations, the impact of a trusted managing director may be exaggerated. In large organizations, the structures and the direct boss may moderate this influence.
- Contextual factors such as family characteristics were said to be important for trust. Respondents felt that people who are born into polygamous homes are generally less trusting that others.
- Respondents considered organizational culture an important context for trust building. Trust thrives in organizational cultures where political behavior is reduced to a minimum and organizational systems exist which limit the power of managers.
- The experts emphasized that ethnicity and religiosity were prima facie cases for trust, especially at the beginning of the boss–subordinate relationship. Gender was also important for trust; mature, married women were considered more trustworthy.
- While reliability and dependability were important for trust, managers would rather delegate tasks to and groom subordinates they trust, even if they are not the best performers.
- Respondents also highlighted some of the negative effects of trust. Subordinates who do not enjoy a trust relationship with the boss may be jealous of colleagues who do. This may have negative consequences for team cohesion and performance.
- In summary, we found that behaviors lead to trust but trust does not lead to behaviors.

Historical Perspective

The region of Africa which is called West Africa extends from Senegal in the west to Cameroun in the east. It is made up of 18 countries. The population of West Africa was estimated at 315 million in 2007. It is a very young population: 60 percent of the people are under 25 years old.

One hundred and fifty years ago, these countries did not exist. Instead, there were various kingdoms. Each kingdom had its governance structures, its customs, etc. Through territorial wars, some kingdoms grew and became pre-eminent, embracing several tribes.

The earliest kingdom in the north of West Africa was the Ghana Empire. It extended through most of the north of the sub-region. The empire was already in existence in 773 AD. The people traded with the Berbers from the Sahara. With the Arab conquest of North Africa in the eighth century, many of the Berber traders accepted Islam. The Soninke (the Ghana people) sold gold and ivory to the northerners. The kingdom of Ghana retained its pre-eminence until it fell in the thirteenth century.

The Mali Empire soon replaced Ghana as the most powerful state in the Sahel region. The trans-Saharan trade in gold, ivory, salt, kola nuts, and slaves continued to thrive. The Mali Empire gained prominence during the reign of Mansa Musa in the fourteenth century. By the fifteenth century, Mali had become weak and was replaced by the Songhai Empire. The latter reached its zenith under the leadership of the Askia dynasty.

South of Sahelian West Africa, Arab influence was hardly felt. From Senegal to Cameroun, there were many kingdoms, including the Jolof and Waalo of Senegal; the Asante of Ghana; and Owo and Benin in Nigeria. Some of these states engaged in trade with the kingdoms in the north, which in turn participated in trans-Saharan trade. Not much has been written about the early history of these kingdoms. The people were mainly subsistence farmers, hunters, craftsmen, and metal workers. Inter-tribal wars were rife. Some kingdoms became important: the Ashante in present-day Ghana and the Oyo Empire, which extended in the nineteenth century from western Nigeria to as far as present-day Togo. This was the situation when the Portuguese arrived at the coast of West Africa in the fifteenth century.

Between the fifteenth and sixteenth centuries, Portuguese merchants traded with the peoples along the coast of West Africa. The trade was in gold, spices, and slaves. They introduced cash crops such as tobacco, cocoa, rubber, palm oil, and coffee. Between the seventeenth and nineteenth centuries, other European countries joined the trade in ivory, slaves, salt, and firearms. European explorers penetrated the rainforest all the way to the Sahel region.

Trade with the Berbers in the north and the Europeans on the coast brought Arab and European influence to West Africa. The Europeans brought Christianity and many of the people of the coastal regions were converted. They also brought Western education, setting up missionary schools in several villages and towns. Islam and Arabic education came through the north. In the early nineteenth century, Usman dan Fodio, a Fulani, ascended to the Sokoto Caliphate. He organized a jihad and succeeded in uniting most of present-day Northern Nigeria. Islam became the religion of most of the north.

By the beginning of the twentieth century, most of West Africa had been colonized. The colonialists drew the maps of what would later become independent states. These territories encompassed several tribes. Nigeria, for example, includes 250 ethnic groups. People who hitherto belonged to kingdoms defined along tribal lines became part of one country.

The colonial governments set up governance structures in the colonies. Locals were employed in the civil service. A large majority of the people continued to work in their farms, workshops, etc. If a farmer wanted to till his land, he invited his peer group to assist him. Mutual support was common in traditional society.

Colonial rule lasted several decades. Ghana was the first country to gain independence in 1957. The colonial structures—the civil service, the army, courts, etc.—were maintained by the new governments and run by locals, most of whom had a Western education.

To summarize thus far: West Africa has been influenced by both Arabs and Europeans. They brought Islam and Christianity to the West African people. They also introduced Arabic and Western education. The colonial government was probably the first manager–subordinate relationship in the region.

Institutional Context

Economic Context

West African economies are agrarian economies. In Ivory Coast, for example, agriculture provides employment for 63 percent of the labor force. Exports are mainly agricultural products and minerals (oil, gold, etc.). Nigeria has the largest economy, with a GDP of US$ 369.8 billion in 2010 and a real GDP growth of 5.6 percent in 2009 and 6.8 percent in 2010. Seventy percent of the labor force works in agriculture, most of which is for subsistence.

Ivory Coast recorded impressive growth rates in the 1970s and 1980s (7.5 percent between 1960 and 1980). However, since its civil war in 2002 and the ensuing political instability, real GDP growth rates have dropped: 4.2 percent in 2009 and 3.6 percent in 2010 (Central Intelligence Agency, 2008).

Following independence, many African nations expanded the public sector. There was a need to gain economic independence and accelerate economic growth in the absence of a vibrant private sector. In the last decade, however, many countries have privatized state-owned and run enterprises to increase efficiency. This led to massive job cuts in the public sector.

The Economic Community of West African States (ECOWAS) was founded in 1975 to promote economic development in the region. All the countries in West Africa except Cameroun, Chad, and Mauritania are members. The average GDP growth rate for the region since 2000 has been about 4.5 percent (www.oecd.org). In spite of this, poverty levels remain very high.

Foreign direct investment (FDI) in Africa has increased in recent years. Even though total inflows were only 3 percent of global FDI, the percentage has increased to 5 percent (United Nations, 2010a). According to the World Investment Report (United Nations, 2010b), Africa is witnessing new sources of FDI. China alone is investing US$1 billion in Africa every year (Kamoche, 2011). Ghana is beginning to exploit its newly found oil deposits.

Infrastructure remains a challenge in the sub-region. To reduce costs and become competitive, companies are becoming more performance-focused (Jackson, 2004).

To summarize thus far: In spite of the recent global economic crisis, the region has recorded impressive economic growth figures in the last few years. There is an increasing focus on performance in both public and private enterprises. However, the benefits of economic growth have yet to trickle down to the ordinary man.

Social Context

West Africa is culturally diverse: there are five major tribes (60 dialects) in Ivory Coast and 250 tribes in Nigeria. The tribe is a very important institution in the

African context. One is born into the tribe irrespective of the particular place of birth. The tribe is a group of people with common ancestry and who are rooted in a particular geographical area. Tribes also have their customs, mode of dress, etc. Even today, the tribal chiefs or kings wield a lot of influence in the community, even though they are not part of the government. It is not surprising among the Yorubas for the governor of a state to visit his Oba (or chief) and prostrate himself before him.

In spite of the increasing urbanization (about 50 percent of the population lives in urban areas, and the rate of urbanization is about 3.4 percent per annum), the African is not cut off from his tribe. It is common practice for those living in cities or far from home (the tribal home) to travel to their village to celebrate the village festival, funerals, Christmas, or Sallah with the family.

Past research has found some common cultural values among Africans. One is collectivism. In a collectivist society, people expect leaders to care for the community, sacrificing their personal goals and objectives, if necessary. Both West and East Africa scored very low on individualism in Hofstede's (1994) study.

According to Mangaliso (2001:31), African values (Ubuntu) include: humaneness, dignity, empathy, and compassion. In the GLOBE study (House *et al.*, 2004), Nigeria (the only West African country studied) had a very high humane orientation, very high power distance, and a high uncertainty avoidance.

Work was an important part of life in traditional African society. Every man worked for himself or for a master who taught him the trade and then set him up to practice on his own. Loyalty was to oneself or another "living, breathing entity" (Olugbile, 1997:48). Communal work was carried out whenever it was needed.

Traditional society had a welfare system in which "people contributed according to their abilities but [were] guaranteed the satisfaction of basic needs" (Olugbile, 1997; Ovadje & Ankomah, 2001). Today, there is no formal social welfare system. The poor, the unemployed, etc., rely on their extended family members for survival. Life expectancy at birth in 2009 was 58 years in Ivory Coast and 48 years in Nigeria (World Bank).

In summary: Africans are very rooted in their tribe and community. They value humaneness, collectivism, and respect. The greatest social security is the extended family. The African worker brings these values and attitudes to the workplace.

Political and Legal Systems

Since independence, West African nations have introduced some democratic structures and processes. However, there were several military coups in the three decades between 1970 and the 1990s. Today, it seems that democracy is slowly taking root in the region.

West Africa has suffered from several wars, the most recent being the conflict in Ivory Coast, which led to the displacement of about a million people. Ivory Coast was stable during the presidency of Houphouet-Boigny, who ruled for over three decades. Nigeria was politically unstable for several years until the return to democracy in 1999. The level of political stability varies among West African countries.

The legal system in Ivory Coast is based on French civil and customary law, while that of Nigeria is based on British common law. The Judiciary is made up of the Supreme Court, the Federal Court of Appeal, and the magistrate courts. Some of the northern states in Nigeria have introduced the Sharia law. The results of the World Values Survey (2005–2008) show that the people have very little confidence in the justice system (only 25 percent in Ghana and 15 percent in Burkina Faso had confidence in the justice system in their countries). It is pertinent to note that the legal system in these countries exists alongside the traditional system—the customary courts, where disputes may be settled, marriages contracted, etc.

Educational System

Literacy levels are generally low in the region, except in Nigeria, Ghana, and Liberia. The literacy rate in Nigeria is 68 percent (60.6 percent for females) and in Ivory Coast is 48.7 percent (38.6 percent for females). Literacy levels are higher among young people.

In Nigeria, the Universal Basic Education program provides free and compulsory primary education (ages 6–11). In 2008, the Ivorian government spent 4.6 percent of GDP on education. The Nigerian government will spend 8.03 percent of its 2011 budget on education and 5.58 percent on health. In spite of the large number of tertiary institutions in Nigeria, human resource managers say that one of their key challenges is the absence of skilled personnel (Anakwe, 2002).

In this section, we have tried to situate our study in the socio-cultural, political, economic, and historical context of Africa. According to Blunt and Jones (1992:16), contextual factors "constitute crucial environmental influences on the practice of management, and organisational behaviour generally." From the foregoing, it is clear that the history, culture, etc. of West Africa is very different from that of Western Europe or North America. It is plausible, therefore, that these differences would have an impact on the trust relationship in boss–subordinate dyads across these contexts.

In the next sections, we review some of the literature on human resource practices and leadership in the region.

HR Practices

Human resource strategies and practices create the organizational context within which employees and managers carry out their roles. According to Tzafrir *et al.* (2004: 633), "HRM policies and practices have a widespread influence and impact throughout the organisation and on employees' attitudes and behaviours."

Human resource management (HRM) in West Africa (in the formal sector) has become less of an administrative function and assumed a more strategic role. According to Kamoche (2011:1):

> In every economy we can find firms that have successfully cultivated an enviable reputation as the employer of choice due to their progressive HRM practices. Technological advancement, particularly in mobile telephony, has enabled firms to design rewarding jobs that target the upwardly mobile, technically competent

section of the labour force, in addition to revolutionizing the way customers access information, financial resources and so forth.

Arthur *et al.* (1995), in their study of HRM in West Africa, found that the most important HRM practices were performance management, selection, training, and development. Senior managers rated these practices higher than the HR managers did. They found a considerable similarity in practices in the US, Ghana, and Nigeria.

Ovadje and Ankomah (2001), Debrah (2001), and others have argued that HRM practices exist within a socio-political and economic environment. While HRM practices may be present in an environment, they may be implemented differently due to contextual factors. The local culture, for example, can be expected to have a pervasive influence on HRM practices and policies.

The HRM practices of large firms are different from those of SMEs (Ovadje & Ankomah, 2001:177). A large proportion of the SMEs in West Africa operate in the informal sector. HRM practices in small firms can be expected to be administrative, concerned with recruitment, payroll, and some record-keeping. As Debrah (2001: 196) put it: "Any meaningful HRM in Ghana will be limited, essentially, to the large and medium-sized companies in the manufacturing and service sectors."

Anakwe (2002) found that HRM practices in Nigeria are a blend of Western and local practices. Thus, the cross-vergence perspective best explains HR practices in Nigeria. HR managers responded to the challenges in their particular context. Some of these challenges were: skill shortages, government regulation, legislation, rapid change, and organizational culture (Anakwe, 2002:1051).

The interest in HRM is due (at least in part) to its relationship with organizational performance. Past research shows that HRM practices are positively related to organizational performance (Huselid, 1995; MacDuffie, 1995). HR practices create the context within which bosses and subordinates carry out their assigned responsibilities. Tzafrir *et al.* (2004:631) argued that "HRM practices create a climate which may or may not engender trust in managers." Through practices such as training and development, selection, etc., HR managers can impact the boss–subordinate relationship.

Leadership Style

"The need for management and leadership styles, and motivation theories that are consistent with the social–cultural realities [of Africa] has been an enduring theme in the literature" (Kamoche, 2011:1). Yet few mainstream studies on leadership have been conducted with African samples.

In the GLOBE study (House *et al.*, 2004), Nigeria had the highest score on humane orientation as a value; practice was also relatively high. The study notes that humaneness is a distinctive characteristic of Sub-Saharan Africa (p. 187). According to Mangaliso (2001:24), "Ubuntu [humaneness] is the foundation for the basic values that manifest themselves in the ways Sub-Saharan African people believe and behave toward each other and everyone else they encounter." Humaneness is about caring for others. Ovadje (2010) found in her study of Nigerian managers that turnover intention was negatively related to perceived organizational support and the boss's management style. She concluded that caring was the most important factor in the decision to stay or to leave.

Power distance was found to be very high in Nigeria (the only West African country included in the GLOBE study). In high power distance cultures, followers expect an autocratic or paternalistic decision-making style. West African societies are hierarchical and male-dominated (House *et al.*, 2004).

These results resonate with the findings of Ituma *et al.* (2011), which indicate that the second most important definition of career success by Nigerian managers was the achievement of social standing; the attainment of prestige and recognition in society. The hierarchical nature of this society is also evidenced in the third most common definition of career success: career advancement through climbing the corporate ladder to the apex of the organization. This makes sense in societies were power is concentrated in very few positions at the apex of the organization (Blunt & Jones, 1992:82).

Nigeria had the second highest score on the assertiveness scale in the GLOBE study; performance orientation was low and uncertainty avoidance was high. Both West and East Africa scored very low on individualism, indicating that they are collectivist societies. Leaders are expected to care for the community, sacrificing their personal goals and objectives, if necessary; the interest of the community comes before that of the individual.

Epie (2002) found a relational orientation in her study of negotiation styles among Nigerian managers. They are likely to adopt a win-win negotiation style in negotiations on behalf of their organizations. She also found that women are more risk-averse than men.

Literature Review on Trust

Trust is an important factor in the African context where people and relationships matter more than results, and where institutions are relatively weak (Utomi, 1998). A meta-analytical study by Dirks and Ferrin (2002:621) shows that trust in leadership is related to work attitudes, citizenship behaviors, and job performance. Most past studies on trust were carried out in Western societies.

The World Values Survey includes five West African countries: Benin, Burkina Faso, Ghana, Nigeria, and Senegal. Findings of this survey suggest that the level of interpersonal trust in the region is very low (the highest was Benin with a 56.2 trust index and the lowest was Ghana with a 17.4 index in the 2007 survey). West Africans feel that most people cannot be trusted. However, in the same study, it was found that 20 percent of them trust people they know personally and 40 percent trust people they meet for the first time. These results suggest that interaction is important for trust in this context.

The survey also indicates that a majority of West Africans have confidence in churches (over 70 percent have a great deal of trust in churches) but they have very little confidence in other institutions (armed forces, press, police, government, and the justice system). Trust in major companies was also very low, with only

10 percent having a great deal of confidence in large companies. This result is not surprising, given the weak institutions that exist in these countries (see Utomi, 1998). Family and religion were the most important institutions in their lives.

The only study on the boss–subordinate relationship in West Africa is that by Adebayo and Udegbe (2004). They studied the role of gender in the quality of the boss–subordinate relationship in Nigeria. They argue that, where there is a good-quality relationship, there is high trust. The findings of their study indicate that gender has no significant effect on the relationship but "opposite dyads perceived better quality of boss–subordinate relationship than those in the same-sex dyad" (Adebayo & Udegbe, 2004:522). The lowest quality of relationship was the female boss–female subordinate dyad. Interestingly, the best quality of relationship was in the male boss–female subordinate dyad. It appears that men trust women and vice-versa.

Trust in traditional African society was placed in the person. According to Olugbile (1997:48), "in traditional society when a person worked, his loyalty was either to himself as a self-employed person or to his Oba, clan leader or Emir, or some other highly placed person for whom he laboured." Relationships are central in the African context. These relationships are not conceived of as economic exchanges; people simply cared for others. The African believes he is a person through others (Mangaliso, 2001). There is a commitment to helping one another (Jackson, 2004: 28). In the Igbo tradition (a Nigerian tribe), the clan supports its members. If a member of the clan is not doing well, the clan comes together to support him; to help him find his feet. There is a high level of trust within the in-group (clan, village).

The nature of the relationship is important for trust. As Olugbile (1997:60) put it: "where the boss uses only particular individuals because they are his own [boys] (that is from his ethnic area or owing him personal loyalty), the other workers are left out and they are obliged to fend for themselves." Those who are trusted by the manager are likely to feel empowered: the manager is willing to take risks with them so he delegates important tasks to them. This empowerment enriches their experiences and motivates prosocial behavior (Brower *et al.*, 2009).

Trust in West African organizations is likely to be greater in boss–subordinate dyads of the same tribe, clan, or other similar ties. These family or tribal ties are strong bases for interpersonal trust. Key positions in the organization may be given to people of the same tribe (Olugbile, 1997:134). These individuals are motivated to perform out of a sense of loyalty to the boss (their brother) and ethnic pride (ibid.). The out-group, those outside the inner circle, is not likely to trust the manager since his actions do not elicit trust. Evidence of this phenomenon was found in the GLOBE study (House *et al.*, 2004): the only West African country in the study, Nigeria, had a very high score for in-group collectivism but institutional collectivism was low.

Trust in hierarchical relationships has been found to be related to individual and organizational performance (Tzafrir *et al.*, 2004; Dirks & Ferrin, 2002). The results of the study by Gould-Williams (2003) suggest that bundles of HR practices and interpersonal trust are associated with organizational performance. In their study, Tzafrir *et al.* (2004) found that some HR practices—empowerment, organizational communication, and procedural justice—were significantly related to employees' trust in their managers.

Contextual Factors in Hierarchical Trusting Relationships

In this section, we present the results of our study on the boss–subordinate relationship in West Africa. From our interviews with managers, subordinates and Delphi experts, the main descriptors of trust in this study are: reliability, dependability, credibility, loyalty, honesty, and respect. Stating the facts, even if this would mean being sanctioned, was considered important for trust from both the boss's and the subordinate's perspective. There must be no disguises, no attempts to hide the facts. According to the respondents, trust demands a high level of transparency.

Trust was associated with respect in this study. There is a degree of self-esteem in the trust relationship which the boss must protect. Playing to the subordinates' strengths, for example, assures the subordinates that the boss is not going to embarrass them. While one subordinate may be stellar in one area, she may be weak in another. Respondents were of the opinion that playing to the subordinate's strengths in the distribution of tasks helps build trust.

The managers and subordinates we interviewed also highlighted the importance of loyalty in trust building. Loyalty was defined as covering the other's back. As one of the experts put it:

> We are all prone to mistakes. The first basis for trusting someone is that, in the event of a slip by me, the other person will protect my interest: he will define it and take action to protect it even when I am not available.

Another respondent put it this way: "The people I trust believe in me, they can vouch for me. They watch my back and stand for me."

Somewhat linked to loyalty is honesty and openness to feedback from the boss. One of the Delphi experts we spoke with defined trust as:

> the assurance that things will work out as they ought. It is openness in communication and feedback. The person you trust tells you the truth, which is sometimes something you don't want to hear. You trust that the feedback you receive is correct. There are no surprises; the boss is not secretly marking down the subordinate.

Subordinates who feel trusted find it easy to discuss their weaknesses and flaws; they are confident that they will not be taken advantage of. The boss does not keep a list of the subordinates' mistakes and flaws. From the boss's perspective, the possibility of mischief is important for a trust relationship. A loyal subordinate does not engage in sabotage or mischief.

At a secondary level, trust was described as consistency, consideration, and relationship. One respondent explained: "L'amitié et la fraternité jouent un rôle important pour l'établissement d'une confiance durable [friendship and fraternity play an important role in the establishment of trust]." According to the Delphi experts, if the subordinate feels the boss is mainly concerned about results, they are not likely to trust him. The extent to which the boss is able to look beyond the individual's contribution to the person himself is critical for a trusting relationship.

We investigated the impact of organizational size on the trust relationship. Respondents felt that size did not matter but the impact of trust or lack of it is magnified in large organizations. As one of our Delphi experts put it:

In large organizations, the potential impact of a trusted CEO is larger, and clearer. However, if the CEO is not trusted, the impact is exaggerated in small organizations as subordinates are in direct contact with him or her. There are no intervening variables to moderate his excesses. In large organizations, the negative impact may be moderated by structures, the direct boss, etc.

Respondents identified other contextual factors which affect the trust relationship. According to some of our respondents, the environment into which one was born is an important factor. People born into polygamous homes are generally less trusting. These homes are very political environments. Each wife and her children vie for the master's attention, resources, etc. There is mutual distrust and suspicion among the children of the different wives. Children born into this environment are likely to grow up to be less trusting of others.

The organizational culture also plays a role in trust building. Some organizations were said to be very political, full of intrigues. In some of them, social climbers make it to the top, not achievers. In this environment, a decent person may begin to adjust to the unwritten rules and lose his decency and trustworthiness. Organizational systems are also important in building an atmosphere that facilitates trust. According to the Delphi experts, people want to get what is due to them. This is difficult to achieve in organizations in which managers are very powerful, where the manager decides who goes for training abroad, who gets a bonus, who is fired, etc., and the criteria are not clear. The result is a perception of injustice, which leads to distrust.

Personal Factors in Hierarchical Trusting Relationships

Both the managers and subordinates interviewed agreed that several personal factors affect the trust relationship. According to our Delphi experts, both ethnicity and religion are prima facie cases for trust between the boss and the subordinate. The fact that both the manager and the subordinate belong to the same ethnic group creates an initial bond between them. The manager naturally relies on the subordinate for some information and to carry out some tasks, including personal ones, such as buying lunch for the boss. The subordinate may even speak to the boss in the native tongue. This further cements the relationship. The impact of ethnicity on trust is more pronounced in a non-diverse workforce. In these organizations, people of the same tribe tend to stick together and support one another. Trust relationships are therefore likely to develop along tribal lines.

Religion was also considered very important for trust in hierarchical relationships. Both the boss and the subordinate become aware of each other's dispositions and character as they interact. If the subordinate is very religious, this immediately creates a level of trust in the manager. One manager elaborated: "If he [the subordinate] is religious, I am confident that he will not deliberately sabotage to get at me. I can rule out mischief because he is a Christian."

Respondents said that gender was important for trust in the boss–subordinate relationship, with women being considered more trustworthy than men. Among women, married and mature women were considered more trustworthy. As one expert put it: "A mature, settled woman will not do certain things." Typically, a new male boss looks for a mature female subordinate to teach him the ropes.

Reliability, which was associated with trust in this study, is based on the subordinate's ability to perform certain tasks. Respondents opined that the boss must be confident that the subordinate will carry out the job assignment satisfactorily, that delegation will not put him in danger. In some cultures, competence is particularly important for trust. For the Bete tribe of Ivory Coast, a leader must be able to carry out his functions. It is difficult for a Bete to trust a boss who lacks skills and competencies.

Respondents distinguished between trust in intentions and trust in the subordinate's abilities. They noted that a boss may not delegate tasks to a subordinate, even if he is competent, because of lack of trust.

The experts commented on the results of the quantitative survey of the relationship between personal factors and trust (see Table 15.1).

The results show that *gender difference is positively associated with managerial trusting behavior (MTB)*. The experts agreed that females would rather trust males and vice-versa. One of them said: "If I wanted to travel and did not want my boss to know, I would tell a female subordinate. I knew she would protect me. I trusted my male subordinates too, but I trusted the females more."

According to one of the interviewees, mature women are more trusted by bosses and subordinates than younger women. One expert commented that a few cases of fraud in his organization involved females, and they were young girls.

The survey results suggest that *the age of the manager is negatively related to managerial trusting behavior*—that is, older managers are less trusting. According to the experts, this depends on the subordinates' age. If the manager is in the same age bracket as the subordinates, he may not trust them. If subordinates are much younger, the manager does not see them as threats. The young subordinates also see the need to be groomed by the older manager, so they protect and support him.

The subordinate's age was found to be negatively related to subordinates' trust in managers (STM). Young subordinates lack experience; they tend to be relatively new employees. They have no other reference points and no mindset. They more

Table 15.1 West Africa: significant controls (correlations)

	Organizational tenure: manager	Gender difference (0–> difference, 1–> equality)	Age: manager	Time manager and subordinate worked together	Age: subordinate
MTB		0.258*	−0.242*		
OCB	0.286*			0.298*	
MTS	0.261*				
STM		0.266*			−0.261

Notes
** Correlation significant at 0.01 level.
* Correlation significant at 0.05 level.
MTB = managerial trustworthy behavior, STM = subordinates' trust in managers, MTS = managers' trust in subordinates, OCB = organizational citizenship behavior.

easily accept the boss and try to please him. Thus, younger employees are likely to trust the manager more than older employees.

Our survey results also indicate that *the manager's tenure is positively associated with both organizational citizenship behavior (OCB) and managers' trust in subordinates (MTS)*. The Delphi experts did not agree on this finding. One of them stated that trust or distrust is built within six months of the relationship. It is later consolidated. The manager's personality and his empathy, demonstrated in his actions, are what count for trust, not tenure.

Another expert agreed with the finding but with a caveat: the manager must have had a very successful career in the organization. That is, the longer the manager's tenure and the more successful he is, the more subordinates will trust him and engage in extra-role behaviors. The length of service must be commensurate with position, a position that is attained on merit.

Finally, the statistical results suggest that the length of time that the manager and subordinate have spent working together is positively related to OCB. Once again, there was a caveat: the manager must have been successful.

Antecedents and Outcomes of Manager–Subordinate Trust

Antecedents of Manager–Subordinate Trust

The qualitative study carried out in Nigeria and Ivory Coast shows that managers and subordinates considered trust to be vital to the boss–subordinate relationship. From the boss's perspective, professional competence was considered important for trust building but trust goes beyond reliability in terms of skills and competence. Admitting one's flaws helps cement the professional relationship between the boss and the subordinate.

Bosses trust subordinates who do not take advantage of their (boss's) flaws. The subordinate who respects the boss and does not sabotage his efforts in the team is likely to be trusted. Telling the truth—giving honest feedback—was also considered important for trust. As one respondent put it: "Trust is describing the facts as they happened even if such information may lead to sanctions." Loyalty was also considered an antecedent of trust. One respondent spoke about a loyal subordinate who visited an important client on the boss's behalf. The latter was very happy to receive a call from the client telling him "that boy is your boy."

Bosses who trust their subordinates tend to delegate important tasks to them, share confidential information with them, and take time to groom the subordinate for higher responsibilities.

From the subordinate's perspective, trust in the relationship was considered enriching. As one subordinate put it: "Trust is critical. The worst thing about the lack of trust is in your heart; it kills you." Fairness was said to be very important for building trust. If decision criteria are clear to all and consistently followed, subordinates are likely to trust the boss. Keeping commitments was also said to be important for trust building. Commitments relating to the welfare of subordinates were considered essential. The boss must be consistent, predictable, and reliable.

According to the Delphi experts:

> People need to have a sense that you care. If you have a problem, the boss must at least listen, even if he cannot solve the problem. In this way, the subordinate's mind is freed to concentrate on what has to be done.

Another way of showing care is to avoid embarrassing the subordinate in public. The boss must also be loyal and respectful; he should praise subordinates in public and scold privately.

Finally, communication was considered essential for a trust relationship. As one subordinate put it: "95 percent of trust building has to do with communication: letting subordinates know what has to be done." It also includes giving honest and timely feedback. Once the feedback has been given, especially negative feedback, the boss is expected to forget the past and not keep a dossier of negatives on the subordinate.

Outcomes of Manager–Subordinate Trust

The managers and subordinates we interviewed associated trust with productivity, fluid communication, and personal growth. A lot of time and effort is saved as the boss does not have to confirm from other sources what the subordinate has said. Trust was also said to be a source of motivation. As one respondent put it: "He lets me do my work and he sees the results. He listens to advice and lets me do it my way sometimes. When there is no trust, your boss is on your neck all the time."

According to one respondent:

> The greatest outcome is the atmosphere that is created. It is not tangible but everyone feels it. People are relaxed at meetings, the truth is told—what we did well and what we did not do so well. Some tell you, "Oga, we cannot do it that way."

An interesting outcome mentioned in the interviews is the effect of a trust relationship between the boss and one subordinate on other colleagues. Those subordinates who do not enjoy the trust relationship with the boss may be jealous of their colleagues who do. One manager put it succinctly, "When you enjoy trust from one person, it can promote jealousy in another." This jealousy may have negative consequences for team cohesion and performance.

Respondents talked at length about the consequences of lack of trust. They agreed that, when there is no trust, the boss finds it very hard to operate. One of the experts told the story of an expatriate CEO who was not trusted by the local directors. The latter suspected he wanted to sell one of the product lines, which would lead to job losses. The directors frustrated most of the CEO's plans; he did not achieve much during his stay in the country.

A lack of trust has consequences for both the boss and the subordinate. The boss spends more time monitoring and controlling. He delegates less, even if subordinates are competent. There is miscommunication and withholding of information by subordinates, which could affect the quality of decisions taken by the boss. The boss spends time and effort validating information given by subordinates. Ultimately, productivity is adversely affected and the boss is overworked.

From the subordinates' perspective, there are more conflicts when there is mistrust. The subordinate who is not trusted is de-motivated, sometimes frustrated. The tense atmosphere may increase stress levels in subordinates who may become ill. If the situation persists, they may consider leaving the organization.

Figure 15.1 provides a summary of the antecedents and consequences of trust in the manager–subordinate relationship obtained from our interviews.

The Dynamics of Trust in Hierarchical Relationships

At the beginning of this section, we present the results of the qualitative study on the dynamics of trust. At the end of the section, the statistical results are presented and analyzed. First, the results of the interviews.

There was no general agreement from the interviews as to the process through which trust develops. For some respondents, it is important to trust subordinates at the beginning of the relationship. Over time, the subordinate's behavior and actions reinforce that trust or trust is withdrawn.

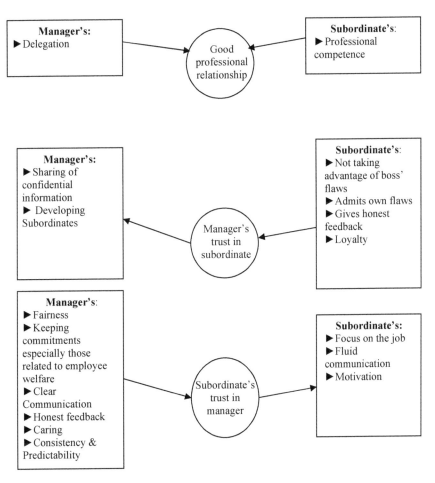

Figure 15.1 Antecedents and outcomes of trust in hierarchical relationships

Both personal and cultural factors were said to influence the dynamics of trust. Ethnicity and religion were said to be important factors. If the manager and subordinate belong to the same tribe, trust is more likely to exist at the very beginning of the relationship. If one of them is perceived by the other to be very religious, the other is likely to trust the religious person. Gender also plays a role in the trust relationship. A new male boss taking charge of a department is likely to search for a mature woman and place a lot of trust in her. This is because of the general belief that women are more trustworthy than men.

According to the respondents, family background and tribal values may also dispose certain individuals to trust at the beginning of the relationship. For example, the Senoufo tribe in Ivory Coast is likely to trust the leader ab initio. Even when his actions prove he cannot be trusted, the Senoufo are likely to look for the causes of the mistrust and take action to establish trust. The Bete tribe expects employees to behave in a way that will elicit the boss's trust. People who grew up in polygamous homes are less likely to be trusting; they are more likely to wait till the other party shows he or she can be trusted. One manager commented: "Ab initio, you do not trust. Subordinates have to show they deserve trust."

A strong recommendation from a trusted colleague facilitates the boss's trust in the subordinate at the beginning of the working relationship. One manager told the story of her boss who, from the very beginning of the relationship, exhibited trusting behaviors: delegated responsibilities, shared confidential information, etc. She later heard that her former boss had strongly recommended her to the new boss.

A Delphi expert commented: "Trust develops over time. You can be disappointed by first impressions. You get to know one another, know the styles, what the others like, what they don't like, etc." In the absence of a prima facie case for trust, a relationship must first be developed. During the getting-to-know-you period, both parties read the signals from the others' behavior and actions. They also get to know each other's style, personality, etc. Within a period of time (six months according to one manager), a decision is taken to trust or not to trust. This decision may be changed with time as trust can be withdrawn and vice-versa. Our study suggests that there is no linear relationship between the length of time the boss and subordinate have worked together and trust between them. This result corroborates meta-analytical findings by Dirks and Ferrin (2002).

The findings of the quantitative study (see Table 15.2) confirm the qualitative results. We found, as expected, that subordinates' organizational citizenship behavior (OCB) was associated with managers' trust in subordinates (MTS). We also found that managerial trustworthy behaviors (MTB) led to subordinates' trust in

Table 15.2 Standardized regression weights for the trust model in West Africa and the overall sample

	OCB->MTS	MTS->MTB	MTB->STM	STM->OCB
West Africa only	0.65**	0.04	0.69**	0.08
Complete model	0.68**	0.34**	0.89**	0.08*

Notes
** Regression weight significant at 0.01 level.
* Regression weight significant at 0.05 level.

managers (STM). It seems that the trust dynamic is hinged on actions, behaviors. Subordinates trust managers when managers have shown that they can be trusted. Managers do the same: they trust their subordinates when the latter have performed actions which indicate they are ready to go beyond their job assignments. As one expert put it: "If [the manager] exhibits trusting behaviors, it is likely that subordinates will reciprocate. Leadership influence is strong."

Surprisingly, there was no relationship between STM and OCB. It seemed reasonable to expect that subordinates who trust their managers would engage in prosocial behaviors but a relationship was not found in this study. Our results suggest that other factors explain OCB in subordinates.

We did not find a relationship between MTS and MTB. Our qualitative study suggests that contextual factors, as well as personal and cultural factors such as gender, ethnicity, and religion, are more important determinants of trust in the African context.

Discussion and Conclusions

The findings of this study suggest that behaviors lead to trust, but trust does not lead to behaviors. This result is unexpected. According to social exchange theory, reciprocity is at the heart of exchanges between people. This theory, which was developed in the West, "assumes that trust emerges through the repeated exchange of benefits between individuals" (Whitener et al., 1998). A manager performs benevolent acts (managerial trustworthy behaviors) with the expectation that the subordinate will reciprocate. Our findings do not support this theory.

In this study, there was no relationship between MTS and MTB, and between STM and OCB, suggesting that subordinates' trust in the manager does not lead to extra-role behaviors. It could be that these behaviors are "viewed as normative, that is, something that one is generally expected to do as part and parcel of loyalty to and identification with a larger group" (Paine & Organ, 2000, cited in Poon, 2006:527). Poon (2006) concluded that "trust may have less influence on helping behaviours in collectivist cultures."

The results of this investigation suggest that social exchange theory may be an inadequate explanation of the boss–subordinate relationship in Africa. In Africa, relationships are not based on exchanges but on a network of obligations. African society is collectivist. People are not seen as instruments for gain; rather, Africans recognize that people have a value in themselves as people. The needs of the collective—the family, clan, village, etc.—come before one's personal needs. According to Mangaliso (2001:24), "human interactions in the African context are pervaded by a spirit of caring, community, harmony, hospitality…" One is expected to treat others as one's brothers and sisters. Jackson (2004:62) found "high levels of humanism, collective responsibility, community self-help and mutual assistance in many African societies."

It is clear that African cultural values are altruistic, other-centered. Thus, African managers and subordinates are likely to engage in extra-role behaviors independently of the level of trust in the particular boss–subordinate dyad. In fact, Whitener et al. (1998:523) argued that "the values held by managers are likely to provide the primary internal compass that promotes several dimensions of trustworthy behaviours." It is not surprising therefore that trust does not lead to extra-role behaviors in the African cultural context.

If behaviors lead to trust but trust does not lead to behaviors, what then are the antecedents of behaviors (MTBs and subordinates' OCBs)? Our qualitative study helped us identify possible factors. Ethnic affiliation, religiosity, and the organizational context facilitate trusting behaviors. Managers and subordinates are likely to display trusting behaviors to those who are similar to them by the fact of belonging to the same tribe, clan, and/or extended family.

Our study also shows that managers are likely to display trusting behaviors toward subordinates whom they consider to be practicing Christians (to be religious). This result provides support for the findings of the World Values Survey (2005–2008). Almost 70 percent of respondents in the West African countries surveyed indicated that they had a great deal of trust in churches, compared to 20 percent in the police, and less than 30 percent in government and in the justice system. Less than 10 percent had a great deal of confidence in major companies. Religion is very important in the lives of West Africans. It is not surprising that religiosity plays an important role in the trust relationship between managers and subordinates. In their experiments with dyads of strangers, Tan and Vogel (2008) also found that religiosity is positively associated with trust.

The organizational context, in terms of its political climate and whether or not organizational systems and processes are implemented in a fair and transparent manner, may affect the behavior of managers and subordinates. If systems and processes are perceived to be fair and the organizational culture is not highly politicized, managers and subordinates are likely to exhibit more trustworthy behaviors.

A major finding of this research is that trusting behaviors on the part of both supervisors and subordinates were associated with trust by the other party. According to Dirks and Ferrin (2002: 614), "the boss's decisions and actions are likely to be seen by subordinates as signals of the nature of the relationship and/or the character of the boss." The subordinate's behavior is also interpreted by the boss as an indication of the value that the subordinate attaches to the relationship.

In conclusion, both subordinates and managers agreed that trust is vital for a good relationship. They highlighted the many benefits for the organization and themselves of a trust relationship. The organizational context was found to be important for a trust relationship. Trust was defined as loyalty, covering for me if necessary, giving honest feedback, and the absence of fear. Friendship and fraternity were also crucial; the manager must see subordinates above all as people and not as means for achieving organizational objectives. Fairness was also considered salient for a trust relationship between the boss and the subordinate. Finally, both managers and subordinates expect the other to show he can be trusted before making themselves vulnerable.

This study has practical implications for organizations and human resource managers. A big challenge facing HR managers in Nigeria is the shortage of skills (Anakwe, 2002). One consequence is the need to retain top talent once identified. Our study suggests that trust in the boss–subordinate relationship can improve motivation and retention. HR managers can create the right environment for interpersonal trust in the organization. They should ensure that performance management systems are merit-based and that appraisals are perceived to be fair. Decisions regarding bonuses, salary increases, promotion, etc., must be fair and perceived as such. This requires good communication with managers and subordinates and between them.

Voice mechanisms give employees the opportunity to seek redress if they consider a process or an outcome to be unfair. These mechanisms may include grievance committees, suggestion boxes, etc. HR managers should ensure not only that these mechanisms exist but that they are in use.

HR managers should pay more attention to creating and sustaining an organizational culture that is characterized by what Barney and Hansen (1994) called trustworthy values and beliefs. In the African context, these values include: caring, honesty, fairness, loyalty, and open communication. Without this environment, little subordinate development through mentoring, coaching, and delegation is likely to happen.

The study also highlights the negative effects of a non-diverse team. Actions to ensure that teams are diverse would mitigate the negative effects of trust based on tribal and religious affiliation on other team members.

Our results provide support for the divergence thesis (McGaughey & De Cieri, 1999). Trust should be understood within a cultural and institutional context. What trust means and how it develops may be embedded within cultural values and attitudes.

This work also has implications for HR managers and international management. HR policies and practices which build trust in one context may not work in another. It is important to develop people management strategies and policies that are context-specific. The application of Western theories to the West African context could have negative consequences for the boss–subordinate relationship and the organization.

Our study also has implications for managers of global teams and, specifically, Western managers of teams in Africa. We found that similarity is important for initiating a trust relationship. Since ethnic and religious affiliation may not be possible, international managers should look to other similarities, such as a common friend, a recommendation from a former boss, etc., if they want to build trust with their subordinates.

While professional competence is good, it was not very important for a trust relationship in the boss–subordinate dyad. Rather, caring and loyalty were found to be very important for trust building. Africans want to know that the boss cares about their wellbeing, listens to their problems (sometimes non-work-related problems), and avoids embarrassing them in public. The person comes before the job, and the job gets done. Relationships in Africa are not motivated by economic or social exchange; rather, they are conceived as interactions between people who have a value in themselves. Put simply: do not attribute someone's trust in you to his behavior.

This study has a number of limitations. The sample was drawn from two countries in West Africa. It can be argued that both countries are representative of the sub-region. However, we acknowledge the fact that differences exist across the various cultures in the region. More research is required in other countries and among other groups. Another limitation of this study is that our sample was drawn from the formal sector. Given the size and importance of the informal economy in these countries, further research on the phenomenon in the informal sector is needed. To recap the major finding, subordinates and bosses are saying: If you trust me, show me; demonstrate it with your actions and behavior.

References

Adebayo, D.O. & Udegbe, I.B. (2004). Gender in the boss-subordinate relationship: A Nigerian study. *Journal of Organizational Behavior*, 25(4): 515–525.

Anakwe, U. (2002). Human resource management practices in Nigeria: Challenges and insights. *International Journal of Human Resource Management*, 13: 1042–1059.

Arthur, W., Woehr, D., Akande, A. & Strong, M. (1995). Human resource management in West Africa: Practices and perceptions. *International Journal of Human Resource Management*, 6: 347–367.

Barney, J.B. & Hansen, M.H. (1994). Trustworthiness as a source of competitive advantage. *Strategic Management Journal*, 15: 175–190.

Blunt, P. & Jones, M.L. (1992). *Managing Organizations in Africa*. New York: Walter de Gruyter.

Brower, H.H., Lester, S.W., Korsgaard, M.A. & Dineen, B.R. (2009). A closer look at trust between managers and subordinates: Understanding theeffects of both trusting and being trusted on subordinate outcomes. *Journal of Management*, 35: 327–347.

Central Intelligence Agency (2008). The World Factbook. www.cia.gov/library/publications/the-world factbook/geos/ni.html.

Debrah, Y. (ed.). (2001). *Human Resource Management in Ghana*. London: Routledge.

Dirks, K.T. & Ferrin, D.L. (2002). Trust in leadership: Meta-analytical findings and implications for research and practice. *Journal of Applied Psychology*, 87(4): 611–628.

Epie, C. (2002). Nigerian business negotiators: Cultural characteristics. *Journal of African Business*, 3(2): 105–126.

Gould-Williams, J. (2003). The importance of HR practices and workplace trust in achieving superior performance: A study of public-sector organizations. *International Journal of Human Resource Management*, 14(1): 28–54.

Hofstede, G. (1994). *Cultures and Organizations.* London: HarperCollins.

House, R.J., Hanges, P.J., Javidan, M., Dorfman, P.W. & Gupta, V. (2004). *Culture, Leadership and Organizations: The GLOBE Study of 62 Societies*. Newbury Park, CA: Sage Publications.

Huselid, M.A. (1995). The impact of human resource management practices on turnover, productivity and corporate financial performance. *Academy of Management Journal*, 38(3): 635–672.

Ituma, A., Simpson, R., Ovadje, F., Cornelius, N. & Mordi, C. (2011). Four 'domains' of career success: How managers in Nigeria evaluate career outcomes. *The International Journal of Human Resource Management*, 22: 3638–3660.

Jackson, T. (2004). *Management of Change in Africa*. London: Routledge.

Kamoche, K. (2011). Contemporary developments in the management of human resources in Africa. *Journal of World Business*, 46: 1–4.

MacDuffie, J.P. (1995). Human resource bundles and manufacturing performance: Organisational logic and flexible production systems in the world auto industry. *Industrial and Labor Relations Review*, 48(2): 197–221.

McGaughey, S. & De Cieri, H. (1999) Reassessment of convergence and divergence dynamics: Implications for international HRM. *International Journal of Human Resource Management*, 10(2): 235–250.

Mangaliso, M.P. (2001). Building competitive advantage from ubuntu: Management lessons from South Africa. *Academy of Management Executive*, 15(3): 23–33.

Mayer, R.C. & Davis, J.H. (1999). The effect of the performance appraisal system on trust for management: A field quasi-experiment. *Journal of Applied Psychology*, 84: 123–136.

Olugbile, F. (1997). *Nigeria at Work*. Lagos: Malthouse Press.

Ovadje, F. (2010). Exploring turnover among middle managers in a non-Western context. *International Journal of Business Research*, 10(2): 64–80.

Ovadje, F. & Ankomah, A. (eds). (2001). *Human Resource Management in Nigeria.* London: Routledge.

Poon, J.M. L. (2006). Trust-in-supervisor and helping coworkers: Moderating effect of perceived politics. *Journal of Managerial Psychology*, 21(6): 518–532.

Tan, J.H. W. & Vogel, C. (2008). Religion and trust: An experimental study. *Journal of Economic Psychology*, 29: 832–848.

Tzafrir, S.S., Harel, G., Baruch, Y. & Dolan, L.S. (2004). The consequences of emerging HRM practices for employees' trust in their managers. *Personnel Review*, 33(6): 628–647.

United Nations (2010a). South-South cooperation: Africa and the new forms of development partnership. *Economic Development in Africa Report*. Geneva: UNCTAD.

United Nations (2010b). Investing in a low-carbon economy. *World Investment Report*. Geneva: UNCTAD.

Utomi, P.O. (1998). *Managing Uncertainty: Competition and Strategy in Emerging Economies*. Nigeria: Ibadan Spectrum Books Limited.

Whitener, E.M., Brodt, S.E., Korsgaard, M.A. & Werner, J.M. (1998). Managers as initiators of trust: An exchange relationship framework for understanding managerial trustworthy behaviour. *Academy of Management Review*, 23(3): 513–530.

World Values Survey Association (2005–2008). World Values Survey (www.worldvaluessurvey.org). Aggregate File Producer: ASEP/JDS, Madrid.

16

The Role of Culture in
Hierarchical Relationships

PABLO CARDONA, MICHAEL J. MORLEY,
AND B. SEBASTIAN REICHE

Through the different chapters in this volume, we have observed how different socio-political and cultural factors affect the process of trust development between manager and subordinate. However, in spite of important differences in the strengths of some parameters and in the significance of certain control variables, we can conclude that our main model, presented initially in Chapter 1, remains valid across countries and holds explanatory power in explaining manager-subordinate trust dynamics in the variety of contexts explored in this research. Specifically, managerial fairness was found to influence subordinates' trust in managers, which in turn leads subordinates to engage in organizational citizenship behavior. Based on this behavior, managers judge subordinates' trustworthiness and then reciprocate with fairness.

However, before drawing our final conclusions, an important question arises in the context of our overall research effort across countries: Can we measure in more general terms how culture affects the trust model? In order to answer this question, in this final chapter, we seek to analyze the moderating role of collectivism in our model. Collectivism has been the most widely used cultural dimension in existing research (e.g. Oyserman *et al.*, 2002) and evidence suggests that the level of collectivism may influence the formation of trust (Huff & Kelley, 2003). It has been commonly assumed that those with a collectivist orientation form higher trust relationships than individualists since they have a more interdependent world view that leads them to place a stronger importance on nurturing relationships with others (Chen *et al.*, 1998; Triandis, 1995). Given the focus on the transition between behaviors and affective states in manager-subordinate trust formation in our model presented earlier, in this chapter we are not so much interested in the direct and distinct effect of collectivism, but rather in how this cultural dimension may influence the relationships among the four variables in our model.

Collectivism and the Relationship between Trust and Managerial Fairness

We first contend that collectivism will moderate the relationships between trust and managerial fairness. Research suggests that fairness may play a more important role in influencing behavioral outcomes in individualist societies. For example, Farh *et al.* (1997) found a significant synergistic moderating effect of organizational justice and modernity, a variable that captures the level of individuality and self-reliance and is conceptually similar to individualism, on OCB. In addition, the literature on leader–member exchange has also revealed a weaker relationship between perceived fairness and leader–member exchange, which entails notions of manager-subordinate trust (Brower *et al.*, 2009), in collectivist environments (Erdogan & Liden, 2006). In another study, Bond *et al.* (1985) showed that, when treated unfairly (e.g. receiving verbal insult from a superior), Chinese people (high on collectivism) tend to be less critical of their supervisors than American people (high on individualism). In collectivist societies, fairness perceptions may thus have a weaker impact on subordinates' level of trust in managers.

Similarly, we expect that the relationship between manager trust in subordinates and managerial fairness may be weaker in collectivist societies. Research has demonstrated a positive relationship between collectivism, adherence to group norms, and degree of conformity (Bond & Smith, 1996; Earley & Gibson, 1998). We may therefore expect that managers in collectivist societies adhere to a greater extent to a specific style or level of fairness that represents the prevailing norms in the workplace context. Thus, their level of trust in subordinates will have a weaker impact on their fair behavior.

Collectivism and the Relationship between Trust and OCB

We expect that collectivism will also weaken the relationship between trust and OCB. First, collectivists will perceive certain behaviors as a form of reciprocal obligation rather than as a result of a specific interaction experience or with the aim of impressing other actors. In collectivist societies, helping behaviors tend to be considered as moral obligations rather than voluntary actions (Triandis, 1995). In other words, collectivists are more likely to give priority to interpersonal responsibility in helping than to justice assessments regarding reciprocation (Miller, 1994). Because OCB is conceptualized as a type of helping behavior, individuals are more likely to demonstrate OCB in collectivist societies. Second, there is evidence that collectivism may moderate the relationship between affective states and behaviors. For example, Francesco and Chen (2004) found a weaker relationship between affective commitment and extra-role behavior in collectivist settings. Third, research evidence shows that the level of OCB is generally higher in collectivist societies compared to individualist contexts (Farh *et al.*, 1997). Furthermore, these authors argue that equity-based justice has a stronger influence on OCB in individualist than collectivist societies. As a result, in collectivist cultures the effect of subordinates' trust in managers may not be as significant as in individualist ones in predicting subordinates' OCB.

Although research on the outcomes of OCB and its effect on trust in collectivist and individualist settings is more limited, we suggest that a similar logic may apply. Specifically, if OCB is viewed as a form of obligation rather than a particular interaction response in collectivist contexts (Francesco & Chen, 2004), its presence is less likely to influence a manager's assessment of whether or not to trust a particular subordinate. Taken together, we expect that collectivism weakens the relationships between trust and OCB.

Testing the Moderating Role of Collectivism

We operationalized *collectivism* through the respective country-level scores provided by Hofstede and Hofstede (2005), as these cover all countries in our study. We analyzed the interaction effects of collectivism separately for each of the four relationships in our model. Accordingly, we ran a series of four random-effect maximum likelihood regression analyses with STATA 10.0 (Rabe-Hesketh & Skrondal, 2008). While STATA generally allows for testing multiple levels of analysis at the same time, our group size at the country level is not sufficiently large to produce converging results for a three-level analysis of our data. Since our main interest was to examine the moderating effect of collectivism, we decided to focus on two levels only, the manager level and the country level, with the latter being accounted for by our collectivism variable. After estimating the intercept-only model, we entered the controls and main effects in Step 2 and the interaction terms in Step 3. Table 16.1 reports all regression results.

As shown in Models 3, 6, 9 and 12, collectivism significantly negatively moderates two of the four relationships considered in our trust model. Specifically, Model 6 shows that collectivism has a significant negative interaction effect with subordinate trust in manager on OCB ($b = -0.07$, $p<0.05$). To understand the nature of the cross-level interaction, we employed the procedure outlined by Aiken and West (1991). Specifically, we substituted the high and low values of the moderator (one standard deviation above and below mean) into the regression equation and plotted the interaction effect on a graph (see Figure 16.1). Post-hoc analyses (Aiken & West, 1991) revealed that subordinate trust in manager is positively related to OCB when collectivism is both low ($b = 0.38$, $p <0.01$) and high ($b = 0.24$, $p <0.01$) and that the relationship is weaker when collectivism is high.

In addition, Model 9 demonstrates that collectivism has a significant negative interaction effect with OCB on manager trust in subordinate ($b = -0.07$, $p<0.01$). Figure 16.2 plots this interaction effect at high and low levels of collectivism.

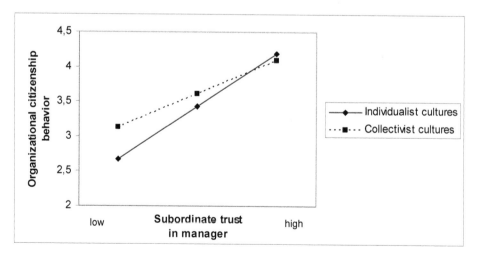

Figure 16.1 The relationship between subordinate trust in manager and organizational citizenship behavior in individualist and collectivist cultures

Table 16.1 Multi-level moderated regression results for collectivism[a]

Variables	STM			OCB				MTS			MF		
	Model 1	Model 2	Model 3	Model 4	Model 5	Model 6	Model 7	Model 8	Model 9	Model 10	Model 11	Model 12
Intercept	3.96**	0.54**	0.54**	3.92**	2.58**	2.59**	4.00**	1.82**	1.84**	4.17**	2.71**	2.68**
Relationship duration		0.01*	0.01*		0.02**	0.02**		0.01**	0.01**		0.00	0.00
Age differences		−0.00	−0.00		0.01*	0.01*		−0.00	−0.00		0.00	0.00
MF		0.82**	0.83**									
STM					0.31**	0.31**						
OCB								0.55**	0.54**			
MTS											0.36**	0.37**
Collectivism		−0.03	−0.02		0.04	0.30*		0.07	0.34**		0.01	−0.12
MF × collectivism			−0.00									
STM × collectivism						−0.07*						
OCB × collectivism									−0.07**			
MTS × collectivism												0.03
Log likelihood	2569.7	1898.5	1898.5	2449.3	2002.3	1999.9	2355.5	1771.8	1768.2	2363.0	1971.0	1970.6
Δχ²		1342.3**	0.00		893.9**	4.8*		1167.3**	7.3*		784.0**	0.88

[a] $n = 741$. Unstandardized regression coefficients are shown here.
MF = managerial fairness; STM = subordinate trust in manager; MTS = manager trust in subordinate; OCB = organizational citizenship behavior.
* $p<0.05$.
** $p<0.01$.

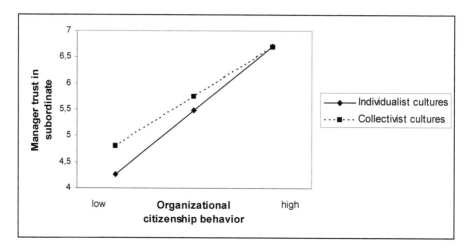

Figure 16.2 The relationship between organizational citizenship behavior and manager trust in subordinate in individualist and collectivist cultures

Post-hoc analyses showed that OCB is positively related to manager trust in subordinate when collectivism is both low ($b = 0.61$, $p < 0.01$) and high ($b = 0.47$, $p < 0.01$) and that the relationship is weaker when collectivism is high. At the same time, we found no evidence that collectivism moderates the relationship between managerial fairness and subordinate trust in manager ($b = -0.00$, $p > 0.05$) or that it moderates the relationship between manager trust in subordinate and managerial fairness ($b = 0.03$, $p > 0.05$).

Final Conclusions

The results suggest that our model of manager-subordinate trust building holds across a number of different cultures. Specifically, we found that managerial fairness positively relates to subordinate trust in manager and that the latter positively relates to subordinates' OCB. Also, OCB was shown to positively relate to manager trust in subordinate, which in turn positively relates to managerial fairness. In other words, by consistently demonstrating fairness in their behavior, managers will be able to foster trust among their subordinates, who will then show a greater willingness to go the extra mile for the organization. Similarly, once subordinates demonstrate extra-role behaviors beneficial to the organization, their managers will develop more trust in them and reciprocate with higher levels of trustworthy behavior.

In this regard, the degree of collectivism at the societal level helps to explain some of the between-culture variance of our trust model. Specifically, we discovered that subordinates' trust in their manager has a weaker influence on their OCB in collectivist cultures while, at the same time, subordinates' OCB was lower in individualist than collectivist cultures when subordinates' trust in their manager is low. This is in line with our earlier reasoning that collectivists may view extra-role behaviors as a form of obligation rather than as a result of a specific interpersonal exchange. In addition, we found subordinates' display of OCB to have a weaker influence on managers' trust in subordinates in collectivist cultures, although, at low levels of OCB, a manager's trust in subordinates appeared to be higher in collectivist cultures. Managers in collectivist cultures are thus more likely to trust their subordinates even if subordinates do not engage in extra-role behaviors, suggesting that behavioral cues are less important in collectivist societies for building interpersonal trust. Our finding that the moderating effect of collectivism is particularly prominent with regard to those relationships involving OCB indicates that this construct is relatively more culturally sensitive, a notion that is consistent with existing research (e.g. Farh *et al.*, 1997).

Theoretical Implications

In the study reported in this volume, we conceptualized the dynamics through which trust between managers and subordinates can be established and tested the validity of the proposed relationships across a wide range of different cultures. In doing so, we have sought to contribute to the trust literature in at least three ways. First, our study addresses the call for investigating the reciprocal nature of interpersonal trust dynamics (Schoorman *et al.*, 2007). In particular, our model highlights that manager-subordinate trust stems from different behaviors on the part of the manager and the subordinate and that the transition between trust as an affective state and its behavioral drivers and responses is mutually reinforcing. At the same time, our results indicate that trust building differs across cultures. This has important implications for culturally diverse manager-subordinate dyads. Specifically, when managers and subordinates come from environments that vary in their levels of collectivism, differences in the interpretation and enactment of behavioral cues may lead to potential asymmetries and could potentially slow down trust formation. We encourage future research to test this assumption in a cross-cultural context.

Second, our research provides organizational members with clear behavioral cues through which mutual trust can be developed and strengthened. More specifically, our study echoes existing research findings suggesting that fairness is a critical antecedent of trust (Cohen-Charash & Spector, 2001). Similarly, subordinates' display of OCB may trigger more trust on the part of the manager. However, our model is not limited to positive, reinforcing cycles of trust formation, but also lends itself to the study of damaged trust. Indeed, if managers fail to treat their subordinates in a fair manner, subordinates' trust in their managers may decrease, resulting in a reduction of extra-role behaviors and decreasing managers' trust in subordinates. In this vein, our results suggest that behaviors such as citizenship and fairness can potentially serve as mechanisms to initiate a bilateral process of trust repair (Kim *et al.*, 2009).

Third, empirically our research demonstrates the universality of dyadic trust formation across a wide range of cultures, pointing to important cross-cultural commonalities in trust dynamics. However, whereas the structure of our trust model and the direction of the relationships examined did hold across the cultures under study, our findings suggest that the level of collectivism prevalent in a society moderates some of the hypothesized relationships. This indicates that interpersonal trust dynamics entail both emic and etic characteristics. In this vein, relationships that hold across different cultures but whose magnitudes differ across these contexts have been referred to in the literature as variform functional universal (Bass, 1997). We also address the call for more research on the potential impact of culture on OCB (Podsakoff *et al.*, 2000). Whereas initial evidence points to a direct effect of collectivism on extra-role behaviors (e.g. Van Dyne *et al.*, 2000), our findings suggest that collectivism weakens the relationship between trust and OCB.

Limitations and Future Research

While this study contributes to our understanding of the dynamics of trust formation in various cultures, real-world research of this nature inevitably has limitations. One of our study's strengths, the multi-source nature of our dyadic data, reduces common source bias (Podsakoff *et al.*, 2003). However, although a certain time lag existed in the data collection process (i.e. the managers answered the questionnaires first before distributing the employee survey to their subordinates), our data remain cross-sectional in nature. Future research may use longitudinal research designs to explore the reciprocal nature of our trust model in more detail (see Serva *et al.*, 2005).

Additionally, although our study explicitly adopted multi-level techniques to capture the different levels of analysis (see Tsui *et al.*, 2007), we only used national cultural value scores as part of our cultural analysis, implicitly assuming that contextual values are more important than individual values in moderating interpersonal relationships. We encourage future research to also measure individual cultural values to further understand how they may affect the relationships in the model. Furthermore, our model of interpersonal trust dynamics is limited to one manager and one subordinate behavior (fairness and OCB). Future research would benefit from a more comprehensive investigation of other potential behaviors that may influence hierarchical trust dynamics. Also, other contexts such as work teams (Serva *et al.*, 2005) are likely to affect trust formation. The fact that the length of the hierarchical relationship played an important role in our study further leads to the question of whether there is an optimal time span for trust building or whether there is a threshold after which trust degenerates. Existing research suggests that relationship length may have a non-linear interaction effect with trustworthy behaviors on trust building (Levin *et al.*, 2006).

Finally, we acknowledge that our measurement model did not achieve perfect equivalence across the cultures included in our study, leading us to drop a few items of our original scales. Although this practice is justifiable (see Cheung & Rensvold, 1999), future research should explore in more detail the underlying emic nature of trust dynamics in hierarchical relationships.

Implications for Managerial Practice

Our study offers several potential lessons to both managers and employees for enhancing interpersonal trust in hierarchical settings and for the character and quality of the preferred management style in different contexts. Acknowledging the importance of trust in the workplace, managers may consciously demonstrate trustworthy behaviors in the form of fairness in order to promote trust of their subordinates in them, which may in turn trigger higher levels of subordinates' OCB. On the other hand, subordinates may engage in OCB to foster trust of their managers in them, leading to greater trustworthy behavior by the managers. As this process is reciprocal in nature, both managers and subordinates may benefit from the reinforcing effect of trust formation in enhancing their workplace encounter.

At the same time, these dynamics also entail potential drawbacks since they shape certain behavioral expectations that lead to the creation of an implicit psychological contract on both sides. Once positive dynamics are established, if managers fail to maintain their previous level of trustworthy behavior, subordinates may perceive a breach of their psychological contract in the social exchange, which may result in negative outcomes, including the loss of trust (Dulac *et al.*, 2008). This is particularly important in the context of cross-cultural work encounters. Finding and nurturing the human resources required to implement an international strategy is of critical importance to business, something which is attested to by a stream of research highlighting inter alia: the importance of effective staffing strategies for the successful implementation of international business strategies, especially strategic alliances and cross-border mergers in informal, emerging, and culturally distant markets; the decision points relating to different approaches to international staffing; the problem of shortages of international managers, particularly in emerging markets, where there is often fierce competition between MNCs and local organizations; the requisite supports necessary in order to ensure a satisfactory outcome from the organizational and individual perspective; and the management and utilization of knowledge flows which may accrue (Collings *et al.*, 2007). Operating across national boundaries has always brought with it a bewildering variety of cultural and institutional specificities that make managing in this context especially complex, with the result that, as Torbiorn (1982) put it, many thousands of words have been devoted to the subject of the ideal candidate for overseas assignments and their associated complexity. As a potential response to this complexity, the notion of developing a cross-cultural fluency and an appreciation and acceptance of difference has a long pedigree in several streams of literature and much has been claimed for it in terms of enhancing one's personal and professional armory (Morley & Cerdin, 2010). If managers and subordinates alike lack the cultural awareness to appropriately enact and interpret behavioral cues, the potentially reinforcing process of trust formation may quickly degenerate into a negative spiral of damage of trust. An organization's capacity to harness, develop, and effectively utilize intellectual capital and nurture the human resources required to implement an international strategy are of critical importance to MNCs (Dowling & Welch, 2004). The development of a competent global workforce is increasingly being recognized as a major determinant of success or failure in international business (Briscoe & Schuler, 2004), and cross-cultural training, designed to meet individual and organizational needs, is increasingly emerging as an important element of the landscape of international business (Caligiuri *et al.*, 2005). However, despite the growing recognition of the advantages of effective cross-cultural training, the effort undertaken so far is often relatively modest (Parkinson & Morley, 2006). We hope this study reinforces the conviction that it is important for organizations to provide cross-cultural training, not only to those individuals that regularly travel and work internationally but also to those employees that remain in their domestic units but are likely to interact with individuals from foreign cultures—for example, in the case of foreign subsidiary employees in a multinational company who are supervised by parent-country expatriate managers.

References

Aiken, L.S. & West, S.G. (1991). *Multiple Regression: Testing and Interpreting Interactions.* Thousand Oaks, CA: Sage.

Bass, B.M. (1997). Does the transactional-transformational leadership paradigm transcend organizational and national boundaries? *American Psychologist*, 52: 130–139.

Bond, M.H., Wan, K.-C., Leung, K. & Giacalone, R.A. (1985). How are responses to verbal insult related to cultural collectivism and power distance? *Journal of Cross-Cultural Psychology*, 16: 111–127.

Bond, R. & Smith, P.B. (1996). Culture and conformity: A meta-analysis of studies using Asch's (1952b, 1956) line judgment task. *Psychological Bulletin*, 119: 111–137.

Briscoe, D.R. & Schuler, R.S. (2004). *International Human Resource Management*, London: Routledge.

Brower, H.H., Lester, S.W., Korsgaard, M.A. & Dineen, B.R. (2009). A closer look at trust between managers and subordinates: Understanding the effects of both trusting and being trusted on subordinate outcomes. *Journal of Management*, 35: 327–347.

Caligiuri, P., Lazarova, M. & Tarique, I. (2005). Training, learning and development in multi-national organisations. In H. Scullion & M. Linehan (eds), *International Human Resource Management: A Critical Text*, Houndmills, Basingstoke: Palgrave Macmillan, pp. 71–90.

Chen, C.C., Chen, X.-P. & Meindl, J.R. (1998). How can cooperation be fostered? The cultural effects of individualism-collectivism. *Academy of Management Review*, 23: 285–304.

Cheung, G.W. & Rensvold, R.B. (1999). Testing factorial invariance across groups: A reconceptualization and proposed new method. *Journal of Management*, 25: 1–27.

Cohen-Charash, Y. & Spector, P.E. (2001). The role of justice in organizations: A meta-analysis. *Organizational Behavior and Human Decision Processes*, 86: 278–321.

Collings, D., Scullion, H. & Morley, M. (2007). Changing patterns of global staffing in the multinational enterprise: Challenges to the conventional expatriate assignment and emerging alternatives. *Journal of World Business*, 42(2): 198–213.

Dowling, P. & Welch, D. (2004). *International Human Resource Management: Managing People in a Multinational Context*, 4th ed., London: Thomson Learning.

Dulac, T., Coyle-Shapiro, J.A.-M., Henderson, D.J. & Wayne, S.J. (2008). Not all responses to breach are the same: The interconnection of social exchange and psychological contract processes in organizations. *Academy of Management Journal*, 51: 1079–1098.

Earley, P.C. & Gibson, C.B. (1998). Taking stock in our progress on individualism-collectivism: 100 years of solidarity and community. *Journal of Management*, 24: 265–304.

Erdogan, B. & Liden, R.C. (2006). Collectivism as a moderator of responses to organizational justice: Implications for leader-member exchange and ingratiation. *Journal of Organizational Behavior*, 27: 1–17.

Farh, J.-L., Early, P.C. & Lin, S.-C. (1997). Impetus for action: A cultural analysis of justice and organizational citizenship behaviour in Chinese society. *Administrative Science Quarterly*,42: 421–440.

Francesco, A.M. & Chen, Z.X. (2004). Collectivism in action: Its moderating effects on the relationship between organizational commitment and employee performance in China. *Group & Organization Management*, 29: 425–441.

Hofstede, G. & Hofstede, G.J. (2005). *Cultures and Organizations: Software of the Mind*, 2nd ed. New York: McGraw-Hill.

Huff, L. & Kelley, L. (2003). Levels of organizational trust in individualist versus collectivist societies: A seven-nation study. *Organization Science*, 14: 81–90.

Kim, P.H., Dirks, K.T. & Cooper, C.D. (2009). The repair of trust: A dynamic bilateral perspective and multilevel conceptualization. *Academy of Management Review*, 34: 401–422.

Levin, D.Z., Whitener, E.M. & Cross, R. (2006). Perceived trustworthiness of knowledge sources: The moderating impact of relationship length. *Journal of Applied Psychology*, 91: 1163–1171.

Miller, J.G. (1994). Cultural diversity in the morality of caring: Individually-oriented versus duty-oriented interpersonal code. *Cross-Cultural Research*, 28: 3–39.

Morley, M. & Cerdin, J. (2010). Intercultural competence in the international business arena. *Journal of Managerial Psychology*, 25(8):805–809.

Oyserman, D., Coon, H.M. & Kemmelmeier, M. (2002). Rethinking individualism and collectivism: Evaluation of theoretical assumptions and meta-analyses. *Psychological Bulletin*, 128: 3–72.

Parkinson, E. & Morley, M. (2006). Cross-cultural training. In H. Scullion & D. Collings (eds), *Global Staffing*, Oxford: Routledge, pp. 117–138.

Podsakoff, P.M., MacKenzie, S.B., Paine, J.B. & Bachrach, D.G. (2000). Organizational citizenship behaviors: A critical review of the theoretical and empirical literature and suggestions for future research. *Journal of Management*, 26: 513–563.

Podsakoff, P.M., MacKenzie, S.B., Lee, J.-Y. & Podsakoff, N.P. (2003). Common method biases in behavioral research: A critical review of the literature and recommended remedies. *Journal of Applied Psychology*, 88: 879–903.

Rabe-Hesketh, S. & Skrondal, A. (2008). *Multilevel and Longitudinal Modeling Using Stata*, 2nd ed. College Station, TX: Stata Press.

Schoorman, F.D., Mayer, R.C. & Davis, J.H. (2007). An integrative model of organizational trust: Past, present, and future. *Academy of Management Review*, 32: 344–354.

Serva, M.A., Fuller, M.A. & Mayer, R.C. (2005). The reciprocal nature of trust: A longitudinal study of interacting teams. *Journal of Organizational Behavior*, 26: 625–648.

Torbiorn, I. (1982). *Living Abroad: Personal Adjustment and Personnel Policy in the Overseas Setting*. New York: John Wiley and Sons.

Triandis, H.C. (1995). *Individualism and Collectivism*. Boulder, CO: Westview.

Tsui, A.S., Nifadkar S.S. & Ou A.Y. (2007). Cross-national, cross-cultural organizational behavior research: Advances, gaps, and recommendations. *Journal of Management*, 33: 426–478.

Van Dyne, L., Vandewalle, D., Kostova, T., Latham, M.E. & Cummings, L.L. (2000). Collectivism, propensity to trust and self-esteem as predictors or organizational citizenship in a nonwork setting. *Journal of Organizational Behavior*, 21: 3–23.

Author Biographies

Editors

Pablo Cardona Soriano is Full Professor at IESE Business School in Spain and a Visiting Professor at CEIBS in China. He has been the Head of the People Management in Organizations department at IESE. He earned his Ph.D. from the University of California, Los Angeles (UCLA) and an MBA from IESE Business School. His research focuses on OCB, trust, motivation, and cross-cultural management. He has published in journals including Strategic Management Journal, International Journal of Manpower, Leadership & Organization Development, Group & Organization Management, and Motivation & Emotion. He has taught in the US and in different countries in Europe, Latin America, Africa, the Middle East, and Asia. He has developed executive programs for multinationals such as Danone, Colgate, Philips, and Sony. He has written business cases on companies including Sony, Victorinox, and SAP, and several books on topics such as Leadership Competencies and Management by Missions.

Michael J. Morley is Professor of Management at the Kemmy Business School, University of Limerick, Ireland, where he teaches international and cross-cultural management. He has served as Head of the Department of Personnel & Employment Relations, Head of the Department of Management & Marketing, and Assistant Dean for Research at the Kemmy School. He has published 20 books, along with numerous papers in scholarly journals and edited volumes. He is currently serving on the Editorial Boards of 12 international journals. He has been awarded the University of Limerick Distinguished Performance Medal for his research contributions on three separate occasions. In 2010/2011, he was a Visiting Professor at IESE Business School in Barcelona.

Quantitative Study Coordinator

B. Sebastian Reiche is Assistant Professor in the Department of Managing People in Organizations at IESE Business School, Spain. He earned his Ph.D. from the University of Melbourne, Australia. His research focuses on international assignments and global work, cross-cultural management, knowledge transfer, social capital, and employee retention, and has appeared in a number of scholarly outlets, including the Journal of International Business Studies, Journal of Management Studies, Human Resource Management, and Journal of World Business. He regularly blogs on the topic of expatriation (www.blog.iese. edu/expatriatus).

Country Chapters

USA

Carlos Rodríguez-Lluesma is Assistant Professor of Organizational Behavior at IESE Business School. His research focuses on the interactions among work, technology, and the organization. Carlos holds a Ph.D. in Organizations, Technology, and Entrepreneurship from Stanford University, an MBA from IESE Business School, and a Ph.D. and BA in Philosophy from the University of Navarra. Prior to IESE, Carlos taught philosophy at the University of Navarra.

Yosem E. Companys is a Ph.D. student at Stanford University. His research is on how social media affects people's patterns of collective action and entrepreneurship. Yosem holds an MA in Sociology from Stanford University, an MPA. from Harvard University, and a BA in Economics from Yale University. Prior to Stanford, Yosem worked for Goldman Sachs, Procter & Gamble, and Merrill Lynch.

Pablo Garcia Ruiz is Associate Professor of sociology at the University of Zaragoza (Spain) and Visiting Professor at IESE Business School. His research focuses on power and identity in and around organizations. He holds a Ph.D. in Philosophy from the University of Navarra and an Executive MBA from IESE Business School.

Greece

Barbara Myloni is a Lecturer of Management at the University of Patras, Greece. Her research has been focused on various issues of human resources management and organizational behavior. Her Ph.D. looked at the transferability of HRM practices within multinational companies in the Greek context. She has contributed to several international projects representing Greece, as well as collaborated with UNCTAD (Geneva) regarding multinationals and foreign direct investments. Her research interests include strategic and international HRM, leadership, motivation, and organizational culture.

Norway

Tor Grenness is Associate Professor at the Department of Communication, Culture and Languages at BI Norwegian Business School. He has a doctorate in Business Administration (DBA) from Henley Business School/Brunel University

(2000). His main research interests lie within the area of cross-cultural/comparative management. Among his recent publications are: "The impact of national culture on CEO compensation and salary gaps between CEOs and Manufacturing Workers," *Compensation and Benefits Review*, 2011, 43(2); "Will the Scandinavian leadership model survive the forces of globalization? A SWOT analysis," *International Journal of Business and Globalisation*, 2011, 7(3); and "Hofstede revisited: is making the ecological fallacy when using Hofstede' sinstrument on individual behavior really unavoidable?" *International Journal of Business and Management*, 2012, 7(7).

Spain

Olena Stepanova holds a Master in Psychology of Intercultural Actions (University of Nancy 2, France) and a postgraduate degree in Systemic Coaching, and is a Ph.D. candidate in Social/Organizational Psychology at the Autonomous University of Barcelona. She graduated in psychology after studying in the Ukraine and the US. She has worked in a personnel consulting company and collaborated with various academic and social institutions, particularly with IESE Business School, working in research at the Department of Managing People in Organizations. Her research focuses on work–life integration, work–family issues, family-friendly policies, cultural change, and coaching. She has co-authored various book chapters, published by Cambridge University Press, Elsevier and Edward Elgar.

Poland

Konrad Jamro is a doctoral student at the University of California, Irvine. His research interests include trust, organizational citizenship behaviors, and effective leadership, all in a cross-cultural context. He has presented papers at various conferences, including the Academy of Management, International Academy of Management and Business, and International Association for Cross-Cultural Psychology. As a Research Fellow at IESE Business School, he has co-authored a couple of cases. Prior to joining academia, he worked as an engineer and consultant in Poland, USA, China, and South Korea. He holds an MBA degree from IESE Business School.

Romania

Dan V. Caprar (Ph.D., University of Iowa) is a Lecturer at the Australian School of Business, University of New South Wales. His research focuses on the interaction between business and its socio-cultural context, with a particular interest in the impact of foreign business on local cultures. He is a member of the Editorial Board for the *Journal of International Business Studies* and a member of the Research Committee for the *Academy of Management's International Division*. Dan was born in Romania, spent several years in the US, and lives now in Sydney, Australia.

Andrea Budean (Ph.D., Babes-Bolyai University, Romania) is a consultant with Danis Consulting, a company offering organizational development services in Romania. Previously she lectured at the Faculty of Psychology, Babes-Bolyai

University, and was involved in research related to human resources management. Andrea is currently conducting research and consulting projects related to international acquisitions, focusing mainly on consequences at the individual level.

Russia

Alexey Svishchev is the Dean of Practice-oriented Economics and Commerce Faculty at MGIMO University, Moscow, Russia. At the same time, he works as a full-time Professor in the Management and Marketing Department at MGIMO University, part-time Professor at the Academy of National Economy under the Government of Russia, and at the State University of Management, Moscow, Russia. His Ph.D. thesis in World Economy was focused on logistics issues and competitive advantages of the Russian aircraft industry on the international market (2006). He is the author of HRM courses designed for the mentioned universities and several articles on different aspects of HRM. He also works as a Revising Editor of "Vestnik MGIMO" Journal. His main interests are in the field of HRM, especially cross-cultural differences, Eastern European and Russian specific features of HRM, and leadership.

Brazil

Diogo R. P. Zanata is a Ph.D. student in Business Management at IESE Business School, University of Navarra in Barcelona (Spain) and the current coordinator of the Cross-Cultural Management Network (CCMN). His research interests liein cross-cultural research, person–environment fit, leadership competencies, and international HRM. He has a B.Sc. and an M.Sc. in Engineering from the Polytechnic School of the University of São Paulo (Brazil). As a Research Fellow at ISE-Instituto Superior da Empresa (São Paulo, Brazil), he wrote some cases and teaching notes.

Cesar F. C. Bullara is a Lecturer of Managing People in Organizations at IESE Business School, a Professor at ISE-Instituto Superior da Empresa in São Paulo (Brazil), and a Visiting Professor at IEEM in Uruguay. He has also been involved as coordinator in a number of research projects on social responsibility and work–family balance. He holds a Master and Ph.D. in Philosophy from Pontifica Universita Della Santa Croce, Roma, and his areas of interest are motivation and self-knowledge, team-building and development of competencies, leadership, ethics, and anthropology.

Colombia

Sandra Idrovo Carlier is Professor of Managing People in Organizations at INALDE Business School, Universidad de La Sabana, in Colombia, where she is the Research Director and leads that same area. Her research interests and publications deal with harmonizing work and personal life, women in management, and employee motivation. She has published in Colombian and international peer-reviewed journals on work–family balance and management education. She contributes often with analysis on organizational culture for Colombian newspapers.

Alejandro Moreno Salamanca is Professor of Managing People in Organizations at INALDE Business School in Colombia. He is Visiting Scholar of universities in Austria and Spain. His research interests are focused on leadership and virtue ethics. He has contributed to some managerial magazines and newspapers in Colombia. In 2005, his managerial experience earned him a Chairman´s Award from Liberty Mutual Group, one of the Fortune 500 Companies.

Pámela Leyva Townsend is Research Assistant in the Managing People in Organizations area at INALDE Business School in Colombia. She is involved with different research projects dealing with harmonizing work–family life and women in organizations.

China

Chuck (Wei) He is the Director of Executive Education and the Associate Director of EMBA (Chinese) at the Chinese University of Hong Kong. He received his Ph.D. from IESE Business School and MBA from CEIBS. His research and teaching is centered on the areas of leadership, trust, coaching, and culture. He has taught and consulted with a number of companies and designed in-company training programs, both in China and in Europe. He is also a certified executive coach.

Thailand

Astrid Kainzbauer currently holds the position of Assistant Dean of International Relations at the College of Management, Mahidol University, Thailand. She specializes in the area of intercultural management and organizational behavior. With many years of teaching experience in this field, she has been a Visiting Lecturer at business schools in Western and Eastern Europe, Australia, Asia, and South America. Dr Kainzbauer regularly conducts executive training/coaching for companies such as GlaxoSmithKline, General Motors, Hutchison, Merck, and Procter & Gamble. Her research interests include intercultural management and intercultural training, as well as cultural influence on teaching/learning styles.

Pakistan

Sadia Nadeem is an Associate Professor and Head of FAST School of Management, NUCES, Islamabad, Pakistan. She began her professional career as an electronic engineer, and holds an MBA and a Ph.D. in Management from Cass Business School, City University, London. Her research interests are in leadership, organizational justice, high performance work systems, HR metrics, and work–life balance policies. She has presented her work at a large number of international conferences, including the Academy of Management and the British Academy of Management. She is also a Chartered Member of the Chartered Institute of Personnel and Development (CIPD), UK, a member of the Governing Council of HR Forum, Islamabad, and an active member of SHRM Forum/Pakistan.

Philippines

Maria Victoria Caparas is an Associate Professor at the University of Asia and the Pacific in Manila, Philippines. She teaches Human Behavior and Managing People in Organizations. She earned her Ph.D. in Management from the IESE Business School of the University of Navarra (Spain) and her MBA. from the Imperial College Business School, London (United Kingdom). Dr Caparas' research interests include work–family balance, women's advancement, people management, cross-cultural leadership, diversity, and inclusion.

West Africa

Franca Ovadje has a Ph.D. in Business Administration from IESE Business School, Spain. She leads sessions in Human Resource Management, Leadership and Change at the Lagos Business School. She is also a Visiting Professor of the Strathmore Business School in Kenya. Her current research interests include identifying and developing leaders, intercultural research, and leading change. She was a recipient of the African Management Scholar Award in 2005. She is a pioneer member of the faculty of the Lagos Business School. Dr Ovadje is the founding director of the Centre for Leadership and Ethics at the Lagos Business School.

Index

Hofstede, G. 298; Brazil 159, 164, 165;
China 204; Greece 43; Norway 64;
Pakistan 235, 239; Romania 117–18;
United States 24, 35; West Africa 279
homophily 16, 26–7
honesty: Brazil 166, 173; Greece 51, 53, 54;
Philippines 266, 268, 269; Poland 110;
Romania 125–6, 129, 130; Spain 88;
Thailand 227, 229; West Africa 276, 284,
293
Hui, W. 202
human resource (HR) practices: Brazil 163–4,
174; China 200–1, 212; Colombia 178,
181–3; Greece 44–5; Norway 64, 74–5;
Pakistan 238–9; Philippines 259–60;
Poland 100–1; Romania 121–2;
Russia 138, 139, 142–3, 156–7; Spain 77,
81, 93; Thailand 219–20; United States
20–1, 35; West Africa 280–1, 292–3
humane orientation: Greece 44; Nigeria 279;
Norway 60; Russia 144; Spain 82;
Thailand 221, 231; West Africa 281
Hurley, R.F. 251, 252

immigrants: Brazil 163; Greece 47; United
States 16
impartiality 53
"incubating period" 17, 32
individualism: Brazil 159, 167;
Colombia 186, 193; fairness 296–7;
Greece 38, 43, 44, 46, 47, 48–9, 55;
Norway 64, 67; organizational citizenship
behavior 300; Pakistan 242; Poland 104,
105; Russia 143, 144, 147, 156; Spain 82,
85, 92; Thailand 224; United States 20, 21,
24, 35, 67; West Africa 279, 282
industry sector: Brazil 167; Philippines 265;
Russia 146–7; Spain 85
inequality: Brazil 164, 167; Colombia 177;
Greece 38, 47, 55; Russia 143;
Thailand 218; United States 15–16
inferiority complex 48
informal economy: Colombia 182;
Pakistan 239, 242; Thailand 218; West
Africa 281, 294
informality 59, 65, 67, 72
Inglehart, Ronald 165
institutions, trust in: Brazil 165; Colombia 184,
185; Greece 42, 46, 55; Norway 65–6;
Pakistan 240, 252; Poland 102, 113;
Romania 123, 133; Russia 144–5; Spain 83;
Thailand 222–3; United States 16, 23; West
Africa 282–3, 292
integrity: Brazil 160, 170, 171, 173;
China 202, 206; cognitive trust 2;
Greece 53; Latin America 184;
Norway 69, 70, 71; Pakistan 239, 240,
251; Philippines 262, 270; Poland 97,
107, 108, 109, 112; Russia 151; Spain 77;
Thailand 223

Ireland 4
Ispas, D. 121
Italy 43
Ituma, A. 282
Ivory Coast 278, 279–80, 286, 287, 290

Jackson, T. 291
Jamro, Konrad 96–116
Japan 219, 220, 251
job satisfaction 275; Norway 70, 71, 74;
Poland 109; Spain 90, 92; Thailand 221
Jocano, F.L. 255, 259, 260
Joiner, T.A. 221
Jones, M.L. 280

Kainzbauer, Astrid 215–33
Kamoche, K. 280–1
Kemavuthanon, S. 221
kindness: Colombia 189; Greece 51, 52;
Thailand 216, 220, 221, 222, 227, 228, 232
knowledge: Brazil 169; Colombia 192;
Greece 51; knowledge-intensive
industries 25; Spain 84, 93
knowledge workers 65
Koojaroenpaisan, P. 222
Kovaleva, Tatiana 146
Kreps, D. 31

Labonne, J. 262
labor relations: Greece 48; Norway 60;
Russia 144; United States 16, 20–1, 35
Latin America 164, 183, 185; business
culture 159; collectivism 24, 165; GLOBE
study 184; leadership 177–8
"Latino style" 82
Latinobarómetro 165, 175, 184
leader-member exchange (LMX) theory 2, 3;
China 202; fairness 297; Pakistan 251
leadership: Brazil 159, 164–5; China 201–2,
205; Colombia 177–8, 183–4; Greece 39,
42–5, 48; Latin America 177–8;
Norway 64–5; Pakistan 239–40;
Philippines 255, 260–1, 272;
Romania 122–3; Russia 143–4; Spain 77,
78, 81–2, 85; teams 84; Thailand 220–
1, 231; United States 21–2; West
Africa 281–2
Lee, K. 6
legal systems: Brazil 162, 166; Colombia 181;
Norway 63; Pakistan 237; Philippines 258;
Romania 120; Russia 141–2; Spain 80;
Thailand 218; United States 20; West
Africa 280
length of relationship *see* relationship duration
Letki, N. 123
Lewicki, R.J. 251
Li, S. 262
Lindell, - 65
Littrell, R.F. 122
LMX *see* leader-member exchange theory

Pakistan 246, 247, 250; Russia 152;
Spain 89
recruitment: Brazil 163; China 212;
Colombia 182; Greece 44, 45;
Pakistan 238, 242; Philippines 259,
270, 271; Romania 122; Spain 77, 81;
Thailand 219
regionalism: Philippines 254–5, 266;
Romania 117–18
regulation 60
Reiche, Sebastian 1–14, 296–305
relationship duration 6, 8; Brazil 160, 168,
169; China 204, 209; Colombia 187–8;
Greece 38, 50–1, 55; Pakistan 241,
244; Philippines 266; Poland 105;
Romania 127, 128; Russia 148, 149, 153;
Spain 86, 89; Thailand 216, 224, 226;
trust building 302; United States 26; West
Africa 286, 287, 290
relationship-oriented cultures 251
reliability: cognitive trust 2; Greece 53;
Norway 60, 66; Pakistan 240, 246, 247;
Philippines 266; Poland 97, 107, 109, 110,
112; Romania 130; Russia 151; social
context 218; West Africa 276, 284, 286,
287
religion: Colombia 179, 185; Pakistan 243;
Philippines 256; Poland 102; Spain 79;
Thailand 215, 217, 220, 222; West
Africa 276, 277, 278, 283, 285, 290, 291,
292, 293
research & development (R&D) 84
respect: Brazil 160, 170, 171; China 204;
Colombia 189; Greece 51, 52, 53, 54;
Philippines 267; Poland 110; Russia 152;
Spain 87, 89, 90; Thailand 216, 221, 223,
224, 225, 227, 228, 231; United States 31;
West Africa 276, 279, 284
responsibility: Brazil 170, 171; collectivist
societies 297; Norway 67–8, 70, 71, 72;
Poland 107, 108, 109; Romania 130;
Russia 150; Spain 88, 92; Thailand 228;
United States 24, 29–30, 32
Restubog, S.L. 263
Richelieu, A. 124
rights 96, 98
risk: China 211; Spain 82; United States 29–
30, 31, 34–5
Rodríguez-Lluesma, Carlos 15–37
Roffey, B.H. 261, 263
role modelling: Russia 152; Spain 89;
Thailand 227, 228, 231
Romania 4, 117–36; antecedents and outcomes
of trust 129–31; contextual factors in
hierarchical trusting relationships 124–6;
dynamics of trust 131–3; economic
context 117, 120; educational system
120–1; historical perspective 119; human
resource practices 121–2; leadership
style 122–3; literature review on

trust 123–4; personal factors in hierarchical
trusting relationships 126–9; Poland
comparison 111; political context 119, 120;
social context 120
Roumeliotou, M. 45
rural areas: Pakistan 239; Thailand 218;
United States 24, 36
Rus, C. 124
Russia 4, 137–58; antecedents and outcomes
of trust 150–2; contextual factors in
hierarchical trusting relationships 146–7;
dynamics of trust 153–5; economic
context 137–8, 140–1; educational
system 142; generalized trust 45;
historical perspective 139–40; human
resource practices 138, 139, 142–3, 156–7;
leadership style 143–4; literature review on
trust 144–6; personal factors in hierarchical
trusting relationships 148–50; Poland
comparison 111; political context 140,
141–2; social context 141

Salamanca, Alejandro Moreno 177–95
salaries see compensation
Salgado, E. 185, 193
San Antonio, D.M. 262, 271
Scandinavia: business culture 59;
collectivism 48; cultural dimensions 44;
egalitarianism 65; generalized trust 45, 46;
labor relations 35; leadership 65
Schoorman, F.D. 250, 251
Schramm-Nielsen, J. 65, 74
Schriesheim, C.A. 251
selection practices: Brazil 163; China 212;
Greece 45; Pakistan 238; Philippines 255,
271; Poland 101; Romania 121, 122;
Spain 93; Thailand 232; West Africa 281
self-esteem: Greece 43; Pakistan 247;
Philippines 260; United States 30, 31, 34;
West Africa 284
Selmer, J. 259
Senegal 276, 277, 282
seniority: Brazil 160, 164, 167; China 203;
Russia 148; Spain 78, 86, 87;
Thailand 215, 220, 224; see also tenure
Shockley-Zaback, P. 124
similarity: Brazil 172; China 203, 212;
Norway 66; Spain 86; Thailand 222;
United States 16, 26–7; West Africa 293
skills: Brazil 170, 171; Colombia 182;
Greece 51; Philippines 269; Russia 148,
152; Spain 86, 89, 90, 93; West Africa 292
small companies: Brazil 167; China 205;
Colombia 183, 186; Greece 42, 49,
55; Norway 66; Pakistan 239, 241;
Philippines 259, 263; Poland 100, 101,
105; Romania 121, 131; Russia 147;
Spain 81, 84, 85; Thailand 219; West
Africa 276, 281
Smith, C.A. 6

United States 4, 15–37; antecedents and outcomes of trust 27–30; contextual factors in hierarchical trusting relationships 24–5; dynamics of trust 30–4; economic context 18–19; educational system 20; generalized trust 45; historical perspective 17–18; human resource practices 20–1, 35; leadership style 21–2; literature review on trust 23; personal factors in hierarchical trusting relationships 26–7; political context 19–20; social context 19
urban areas: Pakistan 234, 237, 239, 242; Thailand 218; United States 24; West Africa 279
Uslaner, E. 47

Valentin, L.N. 122
Valle, J. 83
values: African 279, 291–2, 293; Brazil 159, 160, 164–5, 166, 169, 172, 174, 175; European Values Survey 45; Greece 44; Norway 60, 74; Pakistan 234, 237, 239, 242, 243; Philippines 259–60; Poland 100, 112; research limitations 302; Russia 138, 144; Spain 82; Thailand 220, 221, 231; United States 22; *see also* World Values Survey
Venezuela 184
Viegas Bennett, C. 134
violence 179–80, 183
vision 74, 91, 92, 184
Vogel, C. 292

welfare state: Norway 60, 62–3; Russia 141; Spain 80
West, S.G. 298
West Africa 4, 275–95; antecedents and outcomes of trust 287–9; contextual factors in hierarchical trusting relationships 276, 284–5, 291; dynamics of trust 289–91; economic context 278; educational system 280; historical perspective 276–8; human resource practices 280–1, 292–3; leadership style 281–2; literature review on trust 282–3; personal factors in hierarchical trusting relationships 285–7; political context 279–80; social context 278–9
Whitener, E.M. 71, 209, 251, 291–2
women *see* gender
World Values Survey (WVS): Brazil 165, 166, 175; Colombia 185; Norway 60, 65; Pakistan 240–1; Spain 83; United States 23; West Africa 280, 282, 292
Wu, J. 262

xenophobia 47

Yahontova, E.S. 145
Yamagishi, T. 251
Yukongdi, V. 231

Zaheer, S. and A. 252
Zanata, Diogo 159–76
Zander, L. 65